P9-ARY-035

APTITUDES
AND
APTITUDE TESTING

By Walter V. Bingham

APTITUDES AND APTITUDE TESTING. New York and London, Harper & Brothers.

HOW TO INTERVIEW. By Walter V. Bingham and Bruce V. Moore. Third edition, revised. New York and London, Harper & Brothers.

PROCEDURES IN EMPLOYMENT PSYCHOLOGY. By Walter V. Bingham and Max Freyd. Chicago and New York, A. W. Shaw Company (now McGraw-Hill Book Company).

PSYCHOLOGY TODAY. Edited by Walter V. Bingham. Chicago, University of Chicago Press.

STUDIES IN MELODY. Princeton, Psychological Review Company.

APTITUDES

AND

APTITUDE TESTING

by

WALTER VAN DYKE BINGHAM

PUBLISHED FOR THE
NATIONAL OCCUPATIONAL CONFERENCE
BY
HARPER & BROTHERS PUBLISHERS
NEW YORK AND LONDON

APTITUDES AND APTITUDE TESTING

FOURTEENTH EDITION
A-U

To

Millicent Bingham

PREFACE

To forge ahead in a field of activity presupposes aptitude for it. Capacity to become proficient in the work to be done, and to find in it a certain zest, is vital to happiness and health of mind, whether in school and college, in business and government, in a trade or a profession. Misdirection of effort is costly. Loss is incurred by society as well as by the individual himself when ambitions are ill-advised. If a man is misplaced in his work, he is likely to find that adjustments are increasingly troublesome in his personal and family relations also. No wonder, then, that a clear understanding of the nature of aptitudes and of means for disclosing them should be sought by adults groping for a firmer occupational foothold in a swiftly changing world no less than by younger persons who have begun to think, eagerly and seriously, about their careers. On behalf of these myriad questioners this book has been prepared. But it is addressed primarily to others, namely, to those in or out of educational institutions whose concern it is to help inquirers intelligently to plan their training and their later occupational advancement.

The counseling function, vast and varied in its possibilities, has emerged as a strikingly significant phase of twentieth-century life. Ours is a complex as well as a fast-moving civilization. It is not always easy to find one's way unaided. And so, special provision for personal conference with those who are making their plans has increasingly been recognized as an obligation of educational institutions, of social and governmental agencies, and of employers. Communities, large and small, are experimenting with guidance services. Great universities have their personnel bureaus to which students may come for information about opportunities and requirements in different areas of occupation. In industries, too, employment managers are not content to aim merely at selecting and developing the applicants who show the most promise; for these interviewers can and do offer valuable suggestions to many whom they cannot hire. There is widespread acceptance of responsibility for counseling.

Those who counsel are rightly of the opinion that their task is one to which the science of differential psychology is relevant. Who of them would not welcome help from such a quarter if its procedures really made possible the measurement of significant symptoms of aptitude for various pursuits? Buttressed by reinforcements of his own judgment, a consultant would feel himself on firmer ground when offering suggestions or raising questions in the mind of the one with whom he confers. But there prevails a wholesome uncertainty—not to say skepticism—with reference to the extent to which the use of standardized tests of aptitude is advisable today.

Can tests now available be depended upon to bring to light anything of importance about a person which a shrewd, sympathetic listener cannot learn in interview, after looking at records of past accomplishments while at school and at work? Has the analysis and identification of factors conditioning subsequent progress been sufficiently thorough and detailed? Are test scores reliable enough to warrant reference to them when making individual diagnoses, as well as when comparing groups? In any event, is not the giving of tests, and, more especially, the interpretation of results, so complicated and technical that only the few who have long specialized in aptitude measurement should venture to give any consideration to test data when counseling? Of what value can records of test performance be to educators, employers, placement officers, and others who consult with individuals about their plans? Pointed questions, these. They cannot be dismissed with a word; for the replies presuppose a background of understanding with regard to the nature of aptitudes, the fields of occupation, and the theory of mental measurement.

The author has not dogmatically answered the questions raised. His purpose has been to supply the needed background. This volume treats first, therefore, of what aptitudes are, and how a puzzled inquirer may be helped to recognize his own possibilities. In relation to this problem, much is said about the theory and practice of testing, so that when a reader has thought through the substance of the successive chapters, he should be in a position to make up his own mind about the value of these techniques. Aptitude-testing will be seen in its proper setting within the whole process of guidance, where it fills a useful, if subordinate, place.

W. V. B.

New York
December 7, 1936

PREFACE

1942 PRINTING

THIS book about people's aptitudes and their measurement was due for a revision when clouds of impending war began to darken the horizon. To help the armed services to appraise and conserve the nation's manpower then took precedence over other demands, and the task of rewriting this volume was laid aside.

The publishers have nevertheless granted an opportunity of drawing attention to books which have appeared since 1937 in which may be found additions to knowledge about the nature of aptitudes, and ways of estimating a person's potentialities.

W. V. B.

Washington.
June 25, 1942.

RECENT PUBLICATIONS

1. Bennett, George K. and Cruikshank, Ruth M., *A Summary of Manual and Mechanical Ability Tests* (Preliminary Form). New York: The Psychological Corporation, 1942.
2. Buros, O. K. (Ed.) *The 1940 Mental Measurements Yearbook*. Highland Park, N. J.: The Mental Measurements Yearbook, 1941.
3. Cleeton, G. U.: *Studies in the Psychology of Vocational Adjustment*. Pittsburgh: Carnegie Institute of Technology, 1940.
4. Darley, John G., *Clinical Aspects and Interpretation of the Strong Vocational Interest Blank*. New York: The Psychological Corporation, 1941.
5. Farago, L. (Ed.) *German Psychological Warfare. Survey and Bibliography*. Second Edition. New York: Committee for National Morale, 1941.
6. Garrett, H. E., *Statistics in Psychology and Education* (Revised Edition). New York: Longmans, Green, 1941.
7. Hildreth, G. H., *A Bibliography of Mental Tests and Rating Scales*. New York: The Psychological Corporation, 1939.
8. Horst, P., *The Prediction of Personal Adjustment*. New York: Social Science Research Council, Bull. No. 48, 1941.
9. Kelley, T. L., *Talents and Tasks*. Harvard Education Papers, No. 1, 1940.

10. McKinney, Fred, *Psychology of Personal Adjustment*. New York; London: Wiley, Chapman & Hall, 1941.
11. Mosher, W. E. and Kingsley, J. D., *Public Personnel Administration* (Second Edition). New York: Harper & Brothers, 1941.
12. Lindquist, E. F., *Statistical Analysis in Educational Research*. Boston: Houghton Mifflin, 1940.
13. Paterson, D. G., Schneidler, G., & Williamson, E. G., *Student Guidance Techniques*. New York: McGraw-Hill, 1938.
14. Roethlisberger, F. J. and Dickson, W. J., *Management and the Worker*. Cambridge: Harvard University Press, 1940.
15. Scott, W. D., Clothier, R. C., Mathewson, S. B., and Spriegel, W. R., *Personnel Management*. New York: McGraw-Hill, 1941.
16. Stagner, R., *Psychology of Personality*. New York: McGraw-Hill, 1940.
17. Stead, W. R., Shartle, C. L. and associates. *Occupational Counseling Techniques*. New York: American Book Company, 1940.
18. Thurstone, L. L., *The Reliability and Validity of Tests*. Ann Arbor, Michigan: Edwards Bros., 1939.
19. Trelvar, Alan E., *Elements of Statistical Reasoning*. New York: John Wiley & Sons, Inc., 1939.
20. U. S. Employment Service, *Dictionary of Occupational Titles*. 2 vols. Washington, D. C.: U. S. Government Printing Office, 1939.
21. Wechsler, D., *The Measurement of Adult Intelligence* (Second Edition). Baltimore: Williams & Wilkins, 1941.
22. Williamson, E. G., *How to Counsel Students*. New York: McGraw-Hill, 1939.
23. Young, K., *Personality and Problems of Adjustment*. New York: Crofts, 1940.

CONTENTS

PART ONE

APTITUDES AND GUIDANCE

Basic Concepts—The Place of Tests in Counseling

Chapter I

INTRODUCTION

1. The setting. 2. Considerations in choosing an occupation. Questions asked of counselors. 3. Questions asked by counselors. 4. Hazards of aptitude testing. 5. Compensations for the tentative character of inferences from test performance. 6. Recapitulation: the rôle of tests in counseling.

1

"WHAT am I best fitted for? Which trade shall I learn, or which profession shall I follow? In what occupation can I earn a living by doing work that I like to do and can do well? What are my aptitudes and how shall I go about capitalizing them in school and afterwards?"

Insistent questions! They are asked by young people with years of preparation ahead, and by mature workers groping for a secure foothold in an unstable economic society. They are asked not only of teachers and deans in school or college, but of placement officers and employment managers, of pastors and social workers. These, as well as professional vocational counselors and consulting psychologists, are often called upon to confer with some one in doubt regarding his aptitudes and their relation to his future plans.

The help which any one of these counselors can render when a question of aptitude is brought to him is proportional to his personal insight and wisdom—his understanding not only of the intricacies of human nature, but also of the world of occupations and of the pathways through education and experience which lead to vocational goals. The value of this assistance bears a direct relationship to the length of time he can devote to the question and to the amount and correctness of the information available regarding the inquirer. Snap judgments are worse than useless. Suggestions offered without searching scrutiny of the total situation are not infrequently misleading and sometimes ludicrous.

For these reasons an experienced vocational and educational counselor, in helping a person to find the best solution of his particular problem, first brings into focus all the relevant information obtainable, from personal acquaintance and interviews, from records of school progress and working experience, from available test scores and interest questionnaires. Knowing something about the opportunities offered by the different fields of occupation and the abilities required in order to follow them to a satisfying level of success, he then encourages his client systematically to explore the possibilities, to decide on immediate steps, and to select, at least tentatively, a more remote goal.

Increasingly the query is raised among educators and personnel counselors as to the place and function of aptitude-testing within this process of orientation and vocational planning. Under what circumstances, they ask, may tests be of real assistance? How dependable are the measures they provide? How closely does a person's performance in one of these standardized situations correspond to what he might do another day or a few years hence? Do the yardsticks against which aptitudes are measured remain the same or are they like the rubber dollar? And do the people measured stay essentially as they are, or change with the passing of time so greatly that it is futile to infer from a person's past and present test performances what he will be able to do at some future date?

These are pertinent questions. Counselors appreciate the need of accurate information about the capacities of those who confer with them. They want to know whether test scores furnish an answer which is more dependable than unaided common sense. Their inquiries may be even more pointed. What credence should be given to the test scores of previous years, now often found on students' cumulative record cards? What newer tests might with advantage be given now? Can they be satisfactorily administered and the results appraised by anyone not a doctor in psychology with a broad background of occupational and clinical experience? Is the information so secured worth what it costs?

The chapters which follow deal with just such problems; but before approaching them directly it is necessary to have clearly in mind the setting within which tests of aptitudes are designed to be of use. This situation warrants inspection from two angles: first, from the point of view of the person who is engaged in plotting his future course; and then, from that of the counselor who is helping to orient him. Surely any just appraisal of the merits or the inadequacies of tests as aids in counseling should be made with due appreciation of an individual's total problem and also of the entire process of guidance within which the discovery of that individual's aptitudes is, after all, but a single phase.

2

A person planning his future in the light of his fitness for a certain occupation faces a variety of problems. He may appropriately ask:

1. What level of general education is expected of people who enter this occupation? Have I the necessary schooling or can I acquire it?

2. In addition to the general schooling, how long a period of specialized education or training is ordinarily necessary? Where can I secure it, and what will it cost?

3. What level of intelligence has been found to characterize the people who enter upon and make progress in the occupation? Do my general mental abilities resemble those of persons in this field?

4. Are any special talents or aptitudes necessary? If so, are they a part of my endowment?

5. Specifically, what kinds of activity are most characteristic of this occupation? Do I like to do these kinds of things? Should I find the work and the surroundings congenial?

6. What are the average annual earnings of people in this occupation? At what rate should I start, and what income might I eventually expect? Are there exceptional rewards at the top?

7. Is employment relatively secure and steady, or intermittent, seasonal, hazardous?

8. What are the opportunities for advancement? Is this a blind alley, or does it open doors to other occupations?

9. What is the ratio of employment opportunities to the supply of competent applicants? How keen is the competition I should face?

10. Where does this occupation rank in social prestige? If I were to succeed in it, would my friends applaud, or would they look down on me for following it?

These ten questions do not by any means exhaust the list of inquiries a person may wish to make before tentatively deciding as to the suitability for him of any single occupation. He may shrewdly ask whether the occupation is growing, or on the wane, and whether the opportunities for employment are widely distributed geographically, or are localized in a few centers. He may be concerned to know something about the characteristics of the fellow workers with whom he would be in daily contact, and about the working conditions. What of the labor policies, the hours, the vacations, the opportunities for recreation and travel? Is the work essentially social, or solitary? Exclusively mental, or partly manual? Heavy, or light? Does it offer the variety, or the uniformity, which he likes? Will he set the pace, or take his tempo from a machine? Is the occupation so specialized that if conditions alter and he has to shift his employment, he will have to begin all over again, or will his experience and training stand him in good stead when changing to some related field? Will he be closely supervised? Will he have to supervise or persuade others? What are the social, personal, and temperamental requirements for satisfactory adjustment to the occupation?

Of all these questions, perhaps only one or two have taken definite shape in this person's mind before the first interview. One of the counselor's functions is then to make more of these questions explicit—to insure that at least the most vital aspects of the problem are faced before a tentative decision is made as to the suitability of the proposed occupation. Or the inquirer may not even have arrived at the stage of giving serious consideration to any one occupational field, but instead be groping in search of some calling or other that might appeal to him and offer an opportunity. In that event the counselor encourages him to undertake a systematic exploration in books about occupations and in places where people work. But before going very far in suggesting readings, plant visits or other excursions into the maze of occupations, the counselor is certain to want a clear picture of his client's situation.

3

A counselor is fortunate if he has been able to bring together and to summarize, in advance of the first interview, the recorded facts about his client's school progress, outside activities and employment; and also such information as is obtainable from teachers, employers, companions, and possibly parents, regarding his social behavior, his health, his temperament and traits of character, and his outstanding accomplishments. In the interview such data are reviewed and amplified. The counselor inquires about the home and the family, the occupations and achievements of relatives, their financial circumstances and prospects. He asks searching questions. "What have you done particularly well?" . . . "What do you like to do?" . . . "Tell me what callings your friends have suggested, and why you do not think seriously of following them." . . . "Of what kinds of careers have you daydreamed?" . . . "What sort of position do you aim to fill ten years from now?" Satisfactions as well as achievements in several branches of study and in different kinds of work are compared. Vocational activities within the probable range of his talents are brought up for review and for possible trial. Resourceful in discovering clues to aptitudes, a counselor helps his client to notice where these clues lead. Together they explore his personal resources and compare them with the opportunities ahead.

The balance sheet of vocational assets and liabilities assembled in this way is only a trial balance. Any estimate of a person's aptitudes, of his educational and vocational potentialities, reached during the course of a single interview, however penetrating, is at best a shrewd guess. It is a first rough approximation, subject to correction from time to time as fresh facts are brought into focus. The search is then continued for evidences of unusual ability in whatever direction. Specific disabilities and distastes are brought to light and frankly faced in order to decide whether they are really serious and whether they can be side-stepped, compensated for, or corrected. If a tentative choice of a field of occupation has not been reached, two or three of the most likely fields may be selected for intensive examination and comparison, and, if feasible, for tryout. Subsequent interviews serve to clarify the client's judgment as to the nature and the future of these occupations, and as to his probable fitness for entering upon and advancing in them.

It is in situations of this sort that the need is acutely felt for aids in estimating aptitudes. Has this unplaced school-teacher the interests, capacities, and talents to become a trained nurse, a librarian, a salesgirl, an oral hygienist? Does this lad with an uncanny knowledge of birds have it in him to become a taxidermist or an ornithologist? Does this well-trained but idle young architect have the keenness for statistics, the business sagacity, the forcefulness, and the social vision to warrant him in abandoning architecture for a possible career in the new profession of housing technologist? Counselors are asking whether there are any tests of aptitude which might have a bearing on such specific and very real issues as these. Are there tests which would be useful to a young man in arriving at a choice between two trades, such as toolmaker and draftsman, or to a girl entering senior high school and hesitating between home economics and training for office employment? What of this vigorous lad, determined to study engineering? Can he make the grade or has he, after all, only an uninformed ambition and a consuming interest in tinkering with machines? Instruments designed to measure certain of these aptitudes have been forged in the laboratories of psychology and sharpened by experimentation in schools and industries. Counselors should have a broad background of acquaintance with these instruments, for two reasons: first, in order to decide which tests, if any, are appropriate in specific instances; and second, in order correctly to interpret the results when obtained.

The frequency with which counselors are called upon to make well-informed inferences from test data has increased rapidly during the past twelve years, as the highly desirable practice of maintaining cumulative records has spread from school to school. Wherever this practice prevails, it is customary to note on each student's card, term after term, his marks in each course pursued, his rank in class, his attendance, deportment, and health, and his scores in standard tests of achievement in various academic subjects such as arithmetic, handwriting, English usage, physics, and so on. His participation in organized activities outside of the classroom is also recorded, together with any unusual accomplishments or incidents that might throw light on his talents and interests. Finally, his card contains his standing in psychological examinations specifically designed to measure his aptitudes, both scholastic and vocational. The data at hand may include some such items as the student's vocabulary score on entering and on leaving high school; his achievement test scores in several academic subjects; his Stanford-Binet mental age when twelve years old; the marks he attained in two or three standard tests of scholastic aptitude; and measures of his performance in tests labeled "musical talent," "mechanical ability," "manual skill," "social intelligence," "vocational interests," "spatial relations," "clerical aptitude," "chemistry aptitude," "aptitude for teaching," and the like. A thorough understanding of how these data were secured and of what they really signify is required when estimating the likelihood of a student's future success if one course of study is pursued rather than another, or if preparation for a certain calling is contemplated.

The value of the cumulative record becomes obvious in those instances in which several test scores and other items—no one of which by itself could furnish a dependable indication of future accomplishment—nevertheless tend to confirm one another. Just as the reliability of a test can be somewhat increased by doubling its length or by administering two equivalent forms and averaging the results, so the reliability of a counselor's estimate of a client's aptitudes is enhanced by basing it, not on his score in a single test, but on an accumulation of measures. The records of what the client has done in several standardized examinations, considered together, may then tip the scales of decision.

4

To make judicious inferences from all the items which creep onto a cumulative record is at once an absorbing and a hazardous undertaking. The significance attributed to the test scores will vary with the counselor's theory of the nature of aptitude and of aptitude-testing, as well as with his knowledge of the particular tests, the way they were administered and scored, and the relationships which have been found to hold between scores on these tests and the probabilities of subsequent achievement. Some scores have meaning only when they are relatively very high or very low. Certain tests have been christened with names implying that they measure abilities other than those they actually sample. A few, curiously, have been found to be truly significant in ways which their inventors did not suspect. MacQuarrie's Test for *Mechanical* Ability (so-called—whatever may be the combination of perceptual and manipulative processes which it samples), has been found by at least one investigator to correlate with subsequent progress in office work better than do certain tests designed to measure *clerical* aptitude. Similarly, the number-checking and word-checking test, known as the Minnesota Vocational Test for Clerical Workers, has been found to correlate better than the MacQuarrie with measures of progress of toolmaker apprentices! What's in a name? Danger and confusion, if the label misleads anyone into using a test without first assuring himself as to two things: first, the nature of the specific abilities exercised by an individual when taking the test; and second, the need for the same abilities when learning to do the work of the occupation in question. Without a background of familiarity with the actual meaning of scores on tests like these which the schools have administered, counselors and vocational psychologists are at a loss. They may infer abilities not actually implied by the record, or, on the other hand, may overlook items suggestive of exceptional talents. When bringing into proper perspective the data either from past performances or from freshly administered examinations, there is reason for exercising the same degree of wisdom and scientific knowledge that a physician is expected to use in making a diagnosis. Seasoned judgment is required in order to gauge the true meaning of the items on a person's test record.

If scientific evidence is required in order to emphasize the need of precaution in interpreting test performance, it is abundantly supplied in E. L. Thorndike's important study, *Prediction of Vocational Suc-*

cess.[1] In the investigation here described, 2,225 children, either in the eighth grade of school or not far from fourteen years of age, were examined by means of a battery of tests of intelligence, of clerical skills and aptitudes, and of what Thorndike calls mechanical adroitness. The educational and occupational progress of these boys and girls was then followed for about eight years. Contact was maintained with a very large percentage of the group. For those who left school and went to work, records were secured covering time employed, kind and level of employment, earnings, and degree of interest in the job. These measures of vocational success were then correlated with the data that had been available at age fourteen, in order to ascertain the extent to which it would have been possible at that time to predict from these data the vocational differentiation and progress which later occurred. It was found that certain of the data had a significant relation to subsequent progress in school and to success in employments of a clerical nature. Even the so-called mechanical tests showed a low but nevertheless positive correlation with the criteria of clerical success. Not so with the attempt to predict success in the very broad field which was designated, for lack of a better term, as "mechanical," and for reasons which will shortly appear. This "mechanical" category was made to include such diverse types of work as unskilled manual labor, factory work, and the trades. How disparate these three classes of employment are, we shall see in Chapters X and XI. And yet into this same hopper were put also such jobs as operating an automobile, professional dancing, prize-fighting, and indeed any work which involved chiefly either bodily strength *or* skill. Just why occupations obviously requiring such different aptitudes were grouped together, is not clear from the report; nor why trouble was taken to compute statistical correlations between measures of success in a field so heterogeneous and scores on a mechanical assembly test known to have a rather low reliability. But this was done. The correlations came out zero, or nearly zero. Such results, if not examined closely, might raise serious doubt of the possibility of making judicious use of any tests at all when counseling with reference to this vast area of work—tests of strength, of dexterity, of manual versatility, or of mechanical intelligence, for example, to aid in ascertaining whether a boy's bent runs more toward a trade requiring a good deal of mechanical aptitude, or toward some factory machine-operating job which requires no mechanical aptitude whatever, but which does call for manual aptitude—a very different matter. Thorn-

[1] E. L. Thorndike and others. *Prediction of Vocational Success.* New York: The Commonwealth Fund, 1934.

dike's investigation will make any student of it properly cautious about attempting to estimate vocational aptitudes from meagre test data. As he says (page 72), "Better predictions than ours can come only from fuller or more suitable data than ours." To point toward these fuller and more suitable data, is one of the purposes of this book.

To choose from among the many tests offered by laboratory investigators and publishers those most suitable for different purposes, also calls for more than a passing acquaintance with the field of aptitude-testing. In order to supplement the information at hand about a person's traits and past achievements, his vocational counselor may want to ascertain his abilities and interests as measured by some special tests of artistic talent, or of scientific bent, or of fitness to learn stenography, or of aptitude for mathematics. Such tests have been devised and circulated. The examiner wants to know how dependable are the data they furnish. Will they add to his insight and increase his grasp of the probabilities? Will their use repay the investment in time and money? If reliable tests of demonstrated worth are not to be had, he wants to know it. The chapters which follow should help in deciding as to which tests are most likely to prove illuminating in particular situations, and also in attaching to the test data such significance, and only such significance, as is really inherent in them.

This double purpose of aiding both in the choice of tests to be given and in the evaluation of data from tests administered by various examiners in previous years, makes it necessary to consider in this volume not only well-standardized tests of known validity which would at the present time be approved as the best available for use in connection with vocational and educational counseling; some tests recently popular, but now superseded, also come within the scope of this review, while others, still widely used but of questionable value, must at least be mentioned if only to draw attention to their limitations. For a counselor faces the necessity of weighing whatever data the psychological examiners may have placed on a student's record.

Aptitudes indicate potentialities. Aptitude tests measure abilities and interests. They ascertain what an individual actually does in certain standardized situations, and from these measurements the estimate of capacity for future accomplishment is an inference—a statistical probability, not a certainty. Moreover, tests cannot sample all the important aspects of behavior, nor plumb the depths of vocational purpose. Even with full data at hand, an inquirer's questions regarding his aptitudes can rarely be answered precisely and with positive assurance. No known scheme of interview or examination can grind out an exact solution to an equation which contains so many variables and unknowns.

Scientists have, to be sure, looked forward to a time when a laboratory would be equipped to measure each of the many significant factors in a person's mental constitution and physique, for comparison with the patterns and proportions of those components of human nature known to be needed for success in each typical occupation. In such a Utopia, it would be necessary only to administer a somewhat extensive battery of tests, punch the scores on suitable cards, feed these cards into Professor Hull's computing machine, and out would come the answer. But the researches preliminary to such a procedure have been estimated to require perhaps ten years and to cost upwards of a million dollars—too much of an undertaking for university laboratories in times like these, even though the ultimate benefits from such an inquiry might well be worth many thousand millions to society. Today, with the best resources available, student and counselor can reach only tentative conclusions.

5

Fortunately, there are compensations for this lack. It is not wholly to be regretted that no forecaster is capable of predicting with entire precision the sort of career a person might most appropriately undertake; for such a counselor would be tempted to rob his client of the privilege of self-discovery. The wise consultant asks more questions than he answers. He raises considerations that challenge thought, stimulate self-appraisal, develop an objective attitude toward self-analysis, and encourage explorations into unfamiliar areas of experience.

Self-knowledge is a gradual growth. To gain a clear understanding of one's aptitudes is an achievement of years rather than of hours. Not often does a person choose his ultimate goal early and work directly toward it from childhood to maturity. More frequently the forks and turns in the path become obvious only as they are approached. Each year may bring a deeper insight into desires and talents, and a sharper knowledge of the occupations within which abilities may function best. During this period of self-discovery it is a counselor's privilege not to do a person's thinking for him or to tell him what to do; but rather to facilitate his growth in understanding of himself and of the working world. Then his informed decisions are his own. Moreover, in the very process of arriving at these decisions he learns how best to approach the important problems that are bound to arise from time to time in the future.

As aids to self-understanding, scientifically constructed tests of aptitudes are not a substitute for insight and common sense. They may, however, serve to supplement or modify the considered judgment of a counselor who combines and weighs all the facts, from the personal history and the personal interview as well as from the test record.

A county agricultural agent, talking with a shrewd old Iowa farmer about his soil, suggested that he send a sample to the agricultural college for analysis. "Them professors?" said the farmer, picking up a lump of black loam and crushing it in his gnarled fingers. "I kin tell more about what will grow best in this soil just by a-feelin' of it than they kin with all their test tubes and contraptions." And he certainly could tell a good deal. What he overlooked was the fact that the soil analysts could find out "just by a-feelin' of it" quite as much about the sample as he could; and that, in addition, they could resort to chemical and bacteriological tests to confirm or correct their judgments.

Like the professor of soil chemistry, the vocational counselor appraises the fertility of the human sample. He learns to judge what it can produce to best advantage and what it will probably need in the way of enrichment. But, again like the analyst of soils, he knows that his opinions are fallible and seeks such checks upon them as scientific tests can furnish.

The day has gone by when a counselor's responsibilities could be fully met without any reference whatever to the records of a person's behavior in the carefully standardized situations called tests. Measures of individual differences which may be compared with educational and occupational norms repose side by side with school marks in the files of information kept by many educational institutions about their present and former students. Knowledge has been steadily accumulating with respect to the subsequent achievements of persons whose excellence and speed of performance in test situations had been ascertained. By all odds the most dependable indicators of what anyone will be able to do in the future are found in the measurements of what he has done and what he can do now. Surely, then, it is a flagrant waste for an adviser to overlook the indications of a person's aptitudes and ineptitudes furnished by the measures of his behavior while being tested.

And yet, the process of inferring from test results the probabilities of future achievement is not alone a matter of shrewd common sense. A counselor unfamiliar with differential psychology and but vaguely aware of the meaning and limitations of commonly available test scores is quite as liable to error as is a scientific psychologist who happens to have only an amateur's acquaintance with the vast field of occupations. Psychologist and counselor ought to work together. They should at least learn to understand each other's language; or better still, unite in one person the scientifically buttressed human insight of the clinical psychologist, and the vocational counselor's intimate knowledge of educational opportunities and occupational requirements.

6

To recapitulate: The obvious main function of standardized tests of aptitudes is to help in estimating the probabilities that a person would be able to follow successfully an occupation he is considering. Related uses are to discover unsuspected talents; to suggest possible alternative fields; to bring to attention endowments which might well be capitalized, and disabilities which should be recognized and removed or compensated for; and in general, to provide the inquirer, whether youthful or mature, with food for objective thinking about himself and his future relations to the world of work.

When helping a person to size up his chances of achieving a particular goal or to estimate the probabilities that he can prepare for a certain calling and follow it with satisfaction, his records of performance on certain standardized tests may have considerable weight. Surely, counselors ought to be well informed as to the significance, be it large or small, attaching to scores in standard tests, and as to the uses to which these scores may safely be put. The counselor—or the psychologist who assists him—needs also a basis of sound judgment in choosing tests for general use and for specific purposes and should know the details of test administration well enough to give them skillfully himself, or at least to judge whether the scores supplied to him by other examiners have been obtained by rigid adherence to standard procedure, without which the resulting measurements are misleading. To vocational and educational counselors, as well as to consulting psychologists, more than a cursory acquaintance with aptitude tests and their interpretation has become indispensable.

This chapter has suggested in a preliminary way the place of tests within the whole process of guidance. It will be seen in clearer perspective as the nature of aptitudes and the means of ascertaining them are reviewed in greater detail. In the two chapters which immediately follow, the meaning of the term "aptitude" is made precise and brought into relation to the facts about individual differences. The nature of intelligence and of interest, together with the part played by these important factors in determining educational and vocational aptitudes, is set forth in Chapters IV-VII. A chapter devoted to the significance of measures of past achievements as indicators of subsequent potentialities brings to a close Part One of this volume. Part Two, "Orientation within the World of Work," begins by surveying and classifying the fields of occupation, as a preface to chapters about aptitudes and aptitude tests in special fields, manual, clerical, and professional. Then in Part Three, "The Practice of Testing," principles which guide in choosing tests, administering them and interpreting the data they yield, are summarized and illustrated; after which a number of representative tests are described, with directions for giving them and tables of norms with which an individual's performance may be compared. It is earnestly hoped that no reader not already versed in aptitude-testing will follow an impulse to turn at once to these final sections and put them to immediate use. They presuppose what comes before. Essential precautions in test administration and interpretation should first be grasped, and seen against a background of knowledge with regard to the nature of aptitude, the fundamental subject to which our attention now turns.

Chapter II

THEORY OF APTITUDE

BASIC CONCEPTS

1. Meaning of aptitude. 2. Definition of terms: ability, proficiency, capacity, capability, skill, talent, genius. 3. Aptitudes as aspects of personality—i.e., *of the system of dynamic tendencies which differentiates a person from others. 4. Aptitudes as symptoms. Prognosis from observed behavior, past and present.*

1

Precisely what is meant by "aptitude"? The term is in constant use. It is not likely to be misconstrued. But writers have used it with different emphases, some stressing inherited capacity, others, present ability, or ease of acquisition, or dominant interest, or some other aspect of aptitude. So, to avoid any possible ambiguities, consideration of the theory of aptitude and of aptitude testing appropriately begins with definitions. We shall compare the meaning of the term with the meanings of related but not identical concepts: ability, capacity, capability, proficiency, skill, talent, genius. Taking our point of departure from usages recommended in Warren's *Dictionary of Psychology*, we shall explore the assumptions lying back of them and review certain facts of differential psychology which furnish warrant for these assumptions. Here we shall find the scientific foundation for the theory and the practice of aptitude testing.

"Aptitude" is defined in Warren's *Dictionary* as "a condition or set of characteristics regarded as symptomatic of an individual's ability to acquire with training some (usually specified) knowledge, skill, or set of responses such as the ability to speak a language, to produce music, etc." In referring to a person's aptitude for mathematics, or art, or carpentry, or law, we are looking to the future. His aptitude is, however, a present condition, a pattern of traits, deemed to be indicative of his potentialities.

Note that nothing is said in this definition as to whether the "condition or set of characteristics" is acquired or inborn. And quite properly so. Too often it has been implied that the term "aptitude" has reference to a person's native endowments only. Tests of aptitude, according to this mistaken view, should undertake to disclose the natural bent, the strength of the different dispositions, tendencies, and capacities inherent in the individual's original constitution, without regard to the modifications in these capacities which have occurred in the course of experience. But this cannot be done. At least it is not possible with means at our disposal today. Even if it were, the resulting information would not be what is needed in individual counseling. We want the facts about a person's aptitudes *as they are at present*: characteristics now indicative of his future potentialities. Whether he was born that way, or acquired certain enduring dispositions in his earliest infancy, or matured under circumstances which have radically altered his original capacities is, to be sure, a question not only of great theoretical interest but of profound importance to society at large; for the answer has a bearing on public policy in regard to universal education, the functions of the school, and eugenic legislation. But it is of little practical moment to the individual himself at a time when he has already reached the stage of educational and occupational planning. His potentialities at that period of his development are quite certainly the products of interaction between conditions both innate and environmental. His capacity for gaining manual skills, his intelligence, his emotional make-up, his moral character, indeed all the aspects of his personality, are in varying degrees subject to limitations that have been imposed by opportunities for growth and exercise, as well as by his original nature. No matter what his constitution may at first have been, it has unfolded, taken shape, been encouraged here and thwarted there, during the impact of favorable or unfavorable stimulation from the environments in which he has developed. And so, when appraising his aptitude, whether for leadership, for selling, for research, or for artistic design, we must take him as he is—not as he might have been.

Aptitude, moreover, connotes more than potential ability in performance; it implies fitness, suitability for the activities in question. How could one say that a young woman had an aptitude for nursing without first knowing not only her capacity to acquire the necessary proficiencies, but also the relative degree of satisfaction which the exercise of these proficiencies would yield? One does not deem oneself suited for a kind of work which would be strongly distasteful, nor even for an occupation so simple that it offers no challenge to one's interest. When appraising aptitudes, we are on the alert for symptoms of "ability to acquire" a genuine absorption in the work, as well as a satisfactory level of competence. Indeed, a person who cannot develop a liking for an occupation along with proficiency in it, cannot properly be said to have an aptitude for it because he lacks the necessary drive.

Aptitude, then, is a condition symptomatic of a person's relative fitness, of which one essential aspect is his readiness to acquire proficiency—his potential ability—and another is his readiness to develop an interest in exercising that ability. Anyone who has come to a clear realization of his capacities, his informed interests, and the nature of the occupations he is considering, has achieved some basis for appraising the relative strength of his aptitudes.

Returning to Warren's definition, it is necessary to qualify his emphasis on ability to acquire "with training" some specified knowledge, skill, or set of responses, by mentioning that the training need not necessarily be formal or overt; it may be self-imposed practice or even undirected experience. Also, the "responses" to be acquired include affective reactions of satisfaction and volitional acts of persistence in the activities in question, as well as the necessary knowledge and skill.

With these interpretations, the definiton of aptitude as given above corresponds to both technical and general usage. It might be said of General Grant that he exhibited superb talent in military strategy, but little aptitude for public speaking or for business affairs; that Socrates, supreme in his ability to provoke young men to think clearly about the issues of life, was a good but undistinguished soldier, and unlike his intellectual grandson, Aristotle, apparently had no aptitude whatever for becoming a perfectly groomed gentleman; that Isaac Newton evinced no aptitude for his father's occupation, farming, but more than average aptitude for politics, government and public affairs, a strong bent for theological research, and an unequaled aptitude amounting to genius of the highest order in the field of theoretical mechanics; also, that although his interest in theology was deep and more enduring than in mathematical and physical investigation, he showed no such superlative capacity for that field of research.

2

The meaning of "ability" which occurs in the definition of aptitude, itself calls for comment. *Ability* means power to perform responsive acts. These acts may be complex coordinated movements, solutions of intellectual problems, discriminating judgments of appreciation, or other sorts of behavior—as, for instance, the maintenance of coolness and self-restraint under conditions of provocation or emergency. The amount of a person's ability in a given direction is ordinarily expressed in terms of the difficulty or complexity of the tasks he can perform, the number he can perform at specified levels of difficulty, or the speed and precision of his performance.

A distinction should be made between ability, proficiency, capability, and capacity. We shall use the term "ability" in its broadest sense as meaning power to perform designated responsive acts, without implication as to whether this power is potential or actual, native or acquired. A person with literary ability can—is able to, has it in him to—write well, either at the present time or after he has had the requisite training and experience. If such a person is now a ready writer, his ability may be called *proficiency*. Proficiency refers to the degree of ability already acquired, in contrast to *capacity*, which is potential ability. A person's literary capacity is the upper limit of the power he may eventually develop under the most favorable conditions. His *capability*, like his capacity, is his maximum ability with further training, but applies more particularly to his potentialities for the near future, in view of his present stage of development. An individual's capacity to acquire the knowledge and skill necessary for successful achievement in a specified industrial employment or job is called "competency" by no less an authority than Viteles;[1] but this usage is not common.

Special abilities peculiar to certain types of performance are distinguished from *general ability*, construed by some writers as the sum of one's specific abilities, and by others as a common factor operative in all or many types of performance and manifest in different degrees in different individuals. We shall adopt the first of these meanings, without prejudice to the theoretical possibility of a general common factor, or factors.

Skill is ease and precision in performing complex motor acts. Following Pear, also Viteles, skill may be more precisely described as

[1] M. S. Viteles, *Industrial Psychology*, p. 120. New York: W. W. Norton, 1932.

"a pattern of well-adjusted performances characterized by complexity, integration, and adaptability to changing situations."

Talent is a relatively high order of aptitude. More specifically, a talented person is one who is susceptible to an unusually high degree of training. *Genius* is not so readily characterized. It is recognizable in its fruits—achievements leading to exceptional eminence, whether in art, religion, drama, government, philosophy, science, invention, military strategy, poetry, musical composition, exploration, diagnosis of disease, or other valued field of activity. To describe the extraordinary pattern of capacities and motive powers which makes possible such accomplishments is a task which has challenged thinkers throughout the centuries. They have asked what combination of originality and industry, of intelligence and the desire to excel, of peculiar abilities innate and acquired, are essential to genius. The answers have been most varied and contradictory. The primitive belief that the man of genius was of supernatural parentage, of different clay from other mortals, and hence inexplicable, has persisted in the more recent but now discredited hypothesis that he is a biological mutant, product of a uniquely novel combination of trait determiners carried in the genes of the chromosomes that have predestined the structure of his organism. Equally untenable is Lombroso's doctrine that the genius is a degenerate biological "type"; for while some geniuses, to be sure, have been unbalanced, madness is not the rule. Measurement of the abilities and traits of people representative of the entire range of human talent has now made it necessary to abandon once and for all any theory of types which sets the genius apart from others as essentially different in kind. His capacities and concentration of interests differ from ours in amount. He starts with endowments not unique in character, but maximal of their sort, and develops in an environment which, prejudicial though it may sometimes appear, nevertheless brings them to their fullest fruition. Genius, then, is superlative ability, either to invent or originate, or to execute. It is found in the topmost range of the distribution of human aptitudes, but is not in a class or type by itself.

3

There is a temptation to think of a person's aptitude as though it were a substance, a possession, a thing which belongs to him. Aptitude is of course not the name of an object. It is an abstract noun. It points to a quality—a quality or characteristic of a person.

Aptitude, as we have seen, refers to those qualities characterizing a person's ways of behavior which serve to indicate how well he can learn to meet and solve certain specified kinds of problems. To say that Paderewski had an aptitude for statesmanship means that he was able in a great emergency to master the art of government quickly and to meet like a veteran the crises of political control. As indicative of *how* an individual may be expected to perform in certain vocational situations, the term aptitude assumes, in a sense, the nature of an adverb while retaining the grammatical form of a noun. A test to measure a person's aptitude for the work of counseling—if there were such a test—would disclose *how* he would be likely to behave in the counseling situation; it would measure those aspects of him as a person which are indicative of his probable manner of response to the problems brought to him in the course of his counseling. His aptitude for counseling is not an existential object, extraneous to him, possessed by him; it is an integral aspect of him as a person. This distinction may seem like a philosophical nicety; but it must be remembered that only in a rhetorical sense do we speak of a person's "aptitude for teaching" or "aptitude for art" as some *thing* which he has, rather than as an attribute of what he *is*.

Similarly, a person's "intelligence," "interests," "social effectiveness," "character," and indeed all his psychological traits, are not objects belonging to him, but attributes of him as an individual—a living, behaving organism.

The tendency to objectify traits as though they were somehow external to the self, possessed by it, is particularly obvious in the popular use of the word "personality." We say that Jeritza *has* personality, that a glamorous cinema star has "it," meaning, when we stop to think about the matter, that they are persons whose physical appearance and emotional behavior strongly attract or impress others. In technical usage, the term *personality* is much broader; indeed, it is one of the most comprehensive of psychological concepts, embracing as it does *the whole system of dynamic tendencies which differentiates one person from another*. Inclusive of physique, temperament, intellect, and character, it is more than the sum of an individual's traits, physical and mental, emotional and intellectual, social and temperamental, passive and active; for "personality" refers also to the way in which all these traits are organized and integrated, the pattern according to which they function together. Personality is what a person is. Aptitudes are, then, aspects of personality.

4

Aptitude, as we have seen, is a condition indicative of a person's power to acquire specified behavioral patterns of interest, knowledge and skill. Any brief formulation, however, fails to do full justice to the meaning carried by such a term. It must be still more closely scrutinized.

Aptitude is a present condition, yes, but with a forward reference. It is a condition or set of characteristics regarded as *symptomatic*, indicative of potentialities. It should nevertheless be apparent that in measuring a person's aptitudes we are not undertaking to place a yardstick against some mysterious intangibles. Neither do we attempt the legerdemain of measuring something which does not yet exist, namely, future accomplishments. A test of aptitude samples certain abilities and characteristics of the individual as he is today. It helps to find out what he can do now and how well he can do it. The responses he makes under specified conditions are ascertained—specimens of his performance when motivated in prescribed ways. By such means, data are secured as to what the person actually does under the circumstances imposed by the test. His behavior is measured. From these symptoms, any estimate of his future possibilities of accomplishment is an inference.

This is the gist of the theory of aptitude-testing. Measure selected samples of a person's behavior, and then, by reference to the facts as to what others who have been tested have done subsequently, compute the probabilities that he, too, will behave in a certain manner.

To repeat: aptitude tests do not directly measure future accomplishment. They make no such pretense. They measure present performance. Then, *in so far as behavior, past and present, is known to be symptomatic* of future potentialities, the test data supply a means of estimating those potentialities. *The estimate is necessarily in terms of probabilities only.*

The tests widely used to measure scholastic aptitude furnish a familiar illustration. The chances that an applicant for admission to a college will be able to complete his course are computed by comparing his score in a good test of scholastic aptitude with scores made by his predecessors who have eventually turned out to be successful or unsuccessful in college. A test of this sort differs from an ordinary examination in English, mathematics, history, or foreign language, in that the answers can be graded objectively, without recourse to the opinions of the reader; the problems cannot so often be answered from memory; the separate tasks are much more numerous; and each one has been chosen for inclusion in the test because it is of a sort which is known, from statistical studies of items in tests previously tried, to be symptomatic of capacity to do college work. Other data, such as school marks and rank in class during the preparatory years, and marks obtained in a comprehensive examination or in examinations covering the subject-matter of the separate courses offered for entrance, are also used to estimate fitness to undertake collegiate study. The most accurate predictions—and even these are, unfortunately, subject to error in many individual instances—have been based upon a carefully weighted combination of preparatory-school marks, rank in class, rating of the school attended in terms of the proportion of its graduates who have done well in college, entrance-examination marks, and aptitude test scores. The scholastic aptitude examinations, like those in subject-matter, ascertain what the applicant does in the examination-room. What he can do in the college classrooms and laboratories is then estimated by comparing his test performance with that of his predecessors who have already made good or failed.

This same principle is basic in the construction and interpretation of tests of aptitude for skilled trades, clerical occupations, executive positions, learned professions, and artistic pursuits.

In the chapters which follow we shall examine the assumptions inherent in the idea of aptitude, and the evidence that these assumptions are not unwarranted. It will then be apparent why judgments regarding a person's aptitude for a specified occupation are expressions of likelihood but not of certainty—appraisals of predisposition, inclination, readiness, suitability, or aptness for the pursuit in question, as indeed the root meaning of the word "aptitude" would suggest. As such, it will be evident that these judgments are necessarily expressed in comparative terms and, when feasible, as statistical probabilities.

Chapter III

THEORY OF APTITUDE (*Concluded*)

HOW PEOPLE DIFFER

1. Assumptions implied in the concept of aptitude. Differences within the individual. 2. Differences between individuals. Nature and characteristics of the distributions of these differences. 3. Their significance. 4. How persistent are differences in aptitude?

I

THE concept of aptitude carries within it certain assumptions. These articles of faith underlie the thinking of anyone who ventures to deal with the problem of how to ascertain an individual's capacities in the hope of clarifying his ideas as to his fitness to undertake training for some occupation. They permeate both research and practice in aptitude-testing. We shall find justification for them in the facts of human nature, and particularly in three generalizations of differential psychology which may first be baldly stated and then developed in turn:

An individual's potentialities are not all equally strong. One can learn to do certain things more easily and better than other things, and can develop greater interest and satisfaction in some kinds of activity than in others.

Individuals differ one from another in their potentialities.

Many of these differences are relatively stable. They tend to persist. Any changes which subsequently take place in an individual's potentialities occur within limits imposed by his present constitution.

That there are usually wide inequalities among an individual's various talents can scarcely be questioned, least of all by employers, educators, or others who have been called upon to shift a person from one situation to another in search of some activity in which he might excel, and who, in the process, have experienced the keen satisfaction of helping him to discover a real aptitude.

Almost anyone can perfect some kinds of response more easily than other kinds, can acquire certain skills and appreciations with more facility, or certain varieties of knowledge more quickly and thoroughly, and hence adapt himself to some educational and occupational fields more readily than to others. Even Leonardo da Vinci —extremely versatile engineer, musician, painter, sculptor, architect, natural philosopher, designer of airplanes and submarines—was not equally gifted in all the directions toward which he focussed his great originality and powers of concentration; nor was he able to develop the same degree of zest and absorption in each of these kinds of employment. He was not equally superior in every trait.

At the opposite extreme, no one in a quandary as to the field of occupation for which he might prepare is equally unsuited for all vocational pursuits. The average of his potentialities may be low with respect to the average of the population; but some of the traits which go to make up his average are better than others.

There need be little argument on this point. The question of fact is only as to the size of these trait differences. By what amounts do an individual's best and worst capacities differ from his own average? If the range is relatively small, it matters little, so far as his own make-up is concerned, whether he chooses to prepare for one field of occupation or another within the level of his average capacity. In that event his main concern would be to ascertain his general level; and then, within that zone, let his selection of an occupation be determined by economic or social considerations or by sheer opportunism. How common this practice is, every counselor is well aware. But the evidence points to the conclusion that the differences between a person's best specific capacities and his poorest are with rare exceptions so large that they are of the utmost practical moment in his occupational planning.

These facts about intra-individual differences—trait differences *within* the individual—will be enlarged upon after equally important facts regarding differences *between* individuals have been reviewed.

2

Individuals differ one from another. People do not all inherit the same endowments, nor develop equally. Contrasts between the feeble and the strong, the flighty and the poised, the submissive and the masterful, the fool and the genius, have been patent since the dawn of human society; but only since Sir Francis Galton, brilliant and inquisitive half-cousin of Charles Darwin, demonstrated more than half a century ago the possibility of measuring the magnitude of such differences and ascertaining the relationships between them, has a science of differential psychology been attempted. This science underlies the theory of aptitude-testing. Slowly it has forged the necessary experimental and statistical tools of research. It has learned to standardize and to control the conditions under which observations and measurements of behavior are made, and to isolate and weigh—by such means as correlational statistics—certain factors which determine the observed differences in behavior. This young science confronts vast areas of research not yet explored. It nevertheless has already confirmed the conviction back of any search for aptitudes, that the differences between individuals are such as to be of enormous significance to them and to society. In vocational planning, these differences are basic. The boy who wants to discover his bent is correct in supposing that his aptitudes are distinctive of him—not just like those of all other boys.

To be sure, narrow differences between individuals have been found to occur much oftener than wide ones. With respect to almost any measurable ability or trait—musical sensitivity, output of energy, educability, mechanical ingenuity, or the speed with which one can lift one's foot from the accelerator of an automobile after seeing a red light—most of us differ but little from the average of the general population; some differ by moderate amounts; and relatively very few are found near either limit of the range.

The frequency distribution of such differences throughout the population is quite like the frequency of occurrence of differences in anatomical or other biological characteristics, such as size of foot, to take a homely instance. When "the average man" goes to buy a pair of shoes he is fitted with a size 8½. Of 500,000 pairs sold to men in one retail store during the past forty years, more of this size have been bought than of any other. Nearly the same number of 8's and a great many 9's have been purchased. Together these three half-sizes have met the needs of 52 per cent of the customers. Fourteen per cent required 9½'s or 10's; and 14 per cent, 7½'s or 7's. There has been still less demand for the other sizes, very large and very small shoes being least often required; and at the extremes of the range only one customer among the half-million—Primo Carnera, then the world's champion heavy-weight boxer—needed a size 17;

and only one—a midget from Coney Island—could wear a child's size 6.

The same close clustering about the average, the same falling off in frequency of occurrence as the amount of the difference from the central tendency increases, has been observed over and over again when the distributions of scores in psychological tests have been plotted. The greater the difference from the average, the less often it occurs.

In speaking of "common people," Lincoln remarked that "the Lord . . . makes so many of them." Meanwhile, of Abraham Lincolns we have had but one.

Such facts regarding the distribution of individual differences emphatically do not permit pigeonholing everyone into contrasted types on the assumption that a person must be either quick *or* slow, introvert or extravert, dominant or submissive, distinctly college material or clearly unable to profit by a liberal education. Much more frequently he is found to be able to do fairly passable work in only the less exacting courses of study; just moderately speedy in his reactions; ambivert rather than definitely introvert or extravert; and submissive in some social situations while dominating in others. To indicate a person's status with respect to an important ability or other trait, we need, not two opposed categories under one of which he is to be classified, but a continuous scale. His performance in a test of self-sufficiency, let us say, may be average: he stands at the midpoint of an unbroken continuum extending from extreme dependence to extreme independence. Similarly, his aptitude for foreign languages (or for mathematics, or for chemistry, or for track athletics) is not an "all-or-none" characteristic, a unitary trait which is either present or absent in his make-up, but a power or combination of powers which he exhibits in greater or less degree than other people. As such it can be measured within ascertainable limits of precision and located on an appropriate linear scale. If he does better than only twenty per cent of entering freshmen in the Iowa test of aptitude for chemistry, his comparative standing in this trait, relative to other freshmen, is readily indicated by his position on a percentile scale.[1]

When a large representative sample of the population is measured

[1] For use when counseling, Standard Scales (so called because the unit is the Standard Deviation from the Average) have advantages in comparison with the decile and percentile scales more commonly employed. Standard Scales avoid one disconcerting feature of any decile or percentile scale, namely, that percentile units of difference within the middle range are much smaller than at the extremes. (See pages 248ff.)

with respect to a vocationally significant trait, we have seen that scores which differ but little from the average occur more frequently than those which differ widely. The actual distribution of the scores is not, however, necessarily a normal, bell-shaped, symmetrical, so-called "chance" distribution. It may, for instance, turn out to be bi-modal (with two humps). It may be asymmetrical, the frequency surface tailing off toward the very high scores (positively skewed) or toward the low end of the scale (negatively skewed).

It is important to bear in mind what may be implied by such characteristics of the distribution of individual differences in a trait. For example, positive skewness, a bunching of the scores toward the lower end of the scale, may merely mean that the test is on the whole too difficult for the population measured. Or it may serve to call attention to an error in sampling; the population examined may not be strictly representative of the total population. Other peculiarities in the distribution of scores may bring to light unevennesses in the grading of the difficulty of the items, or errors in weighting, and so lead to improvements in the instrument of measurement.

The form of a frequency distribution varies also with the nature of the units in which the measurements are expressed. One symptom of aptitude for track athletics is the time a young man takes to run a hundred yards. His score may be recorded in units of time—seconds and fifths-of-a-second required to run that distance. Or the same performance may be expressed as a reciprocal of that measure, namely, the number of yards he runs per second. When the speed of a large number of candidates of approximately the same age and inexperience in track training is measured and expressed in units of distance—the number of yards run per second—the distribution of the differences in ability is very nearly normal; but when the same data are expressed in the other equally correct way, the form of the distribution is negatively skewed. The choice of units is arbitrary. It is for the investigator to say whether or not he wants to express his measurements in units which favor a normal distribution.

It should, moreover, be remembered that a normal, chance distribution of an ability is theoretically to be expected only when certain conditions maintain. The chief of these conditions is that the dice be not loaded; that the trait measured be a product of many independent determiners *no one of which is prepotent.* Deviations from the normal form of distribution are to be expected whenever the strength of the trait is due in greater part to one or two of its determiners than to the many others—when the surfaces of the dice are not all equally smooth, as it were.[2] It is a gratuitous assumption to suppose that every biological characteristic, including every vocationally significant aptitude, should be spread throughout the population strictly according to the law of chance.[3]

The distribution throughout the general population of differences in a vocationally significant ability stands in sharp contrast with their more restricted distribution among those who follow an occupation which calls for that ability.

For example, in Fig. 1 is pictured the frequency of occurrence, in a general population of male workers, of different levels of ability in number checking as measured by one part of the Minnesota Vocational Test for Clerical Workers.

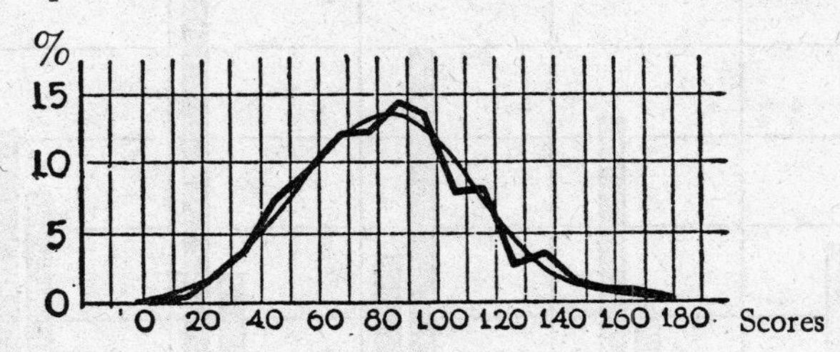

Fig. 1. A Nearly Normal Distribution

Showing, for a standard population sample of 491 men, the distribution of scores in a Number Checking Test, Part One of the Minnesota Vocational Test for Clerical Workers, compared with a normal distribution. From Green, Berman, Paterson and Trabue, *A Manual of Selected Occupational Tests*, page 82.

The task is simple enough: to make quick and accurate comparisons of two columns of numbers and to check each pair the members of which are exactly alike. Eight minutes is allowed in which to compare 200 pairs, half of which are the same and half, different. The score is the number right minus the number wrong, so the highest possible score is 200. The group examined consisted of 491 men of various ages and callings, so chosen as to furnish a representative sample of the entire male occupational population of the Twin City region. Only one man scored over 170; and only one, less than 10. Between these extremes, the scores cluster about the central tendency for the group, which is 83. The distribution of these measures is not precisely that of the normal bell-shaped

[2] With many traits, the distribution of differences, while not normal, roughly approximates this form; sufficiently, at least, to warrant the construction and practical use of a scale, the unit of which is the Standard Deviation of the Distribution.

[3] E. L. Thorndike reviews the evidence regarding the form of distribution of intellectual abilities in Chapter VIII of his work on *The Measurement of Intelligence.* He shows that for such functions as are measured by the National Intelligence Examination A, the Otis Advanced Examination and the Haggerty Delta 2, the distribution is approximately normal at each age up to at least fifteen years. Among white adult males he finds indication of some positive skewness in the distribution; perhaps, as he suggests, because the abilities of certain individuals increase greatly as they approach maturity, while the abilities of others increase little if at all.

probability surface, but resembles it. When these raw scores are transmuted into Standard Scores and then into letter grades, the distribution takes the symmetrical form shown in the first chart of Fig. 2. The proportion of the group whose performance entitles them to an A is 7 per cent; B, 24 per cent; C, 38 per cent; D, 24 per cent; and E, 7 per cent. A quite different picture is seen when the test performance of a group of men clerical workers is plotted against this

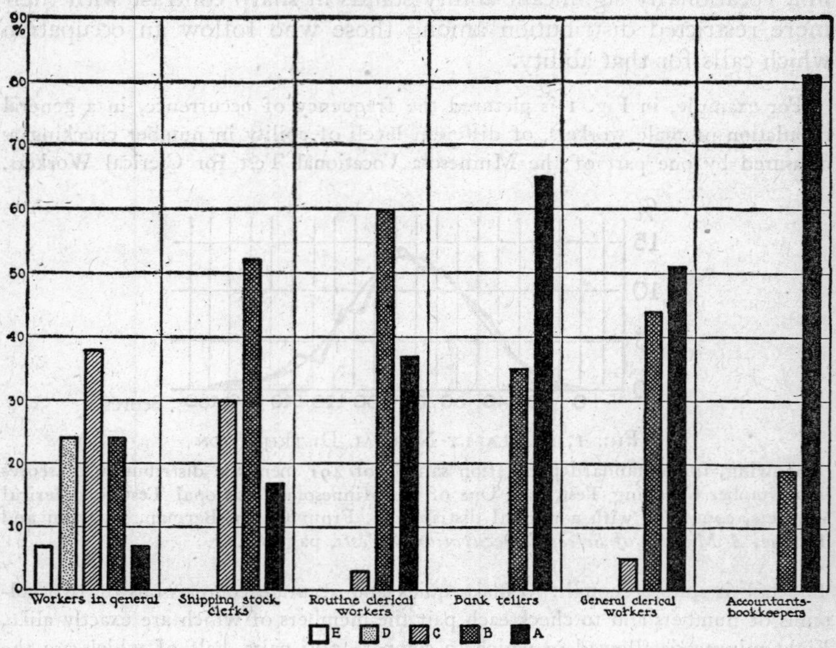

FIG. 2. DISTRIBUTION OF LETTER GRADES IN THE MINNESOTA NUMBER CHECKING TEST, FOR MEN WORKERS IN GENERAL, AND FOR GROUPS OF MEN CLERICAL WORKERS

same scale. In a group of 23 shipping clerks, none was found who scored D or E in this number comparison test. Among 17 bank tellers and 27 accountants and bookkeepers, none scored C, D, or E, and the large majority scored A; that is, they equaled the scores made on this test by the highest 7 per cent of men in general, as the accompanying figure shows.[4]

The fact that so few of the clerical workers made letter grades lower than B raises a presumption that a shortage of the abilities brought into play by this test is a handicap in clerical occupations, and that lower scores may be construed as symptoms of lack of one of the aptitudes needed in learning to do clerical work.

[4] See *A Manual of Selected Occupational Tests*, prepared by Helen J. Green and Isabel R. Berman, under the direction of D. G. Paterson and M. R. Trabue. Bulletins of the University of Minnesota Employment Stabilization Research Institute, Vol. II, No. 3, July, 1933, p. 82; and *Measured Characteristics of Clerical Workers*, by Dorothy M. Andrew and D. G. Paterson. *Ibid.*, Vol. III, No. 1, July, 1934, p. 30.

This presumption is strengthened by similar studies of both men and women clerical workers and of students succeeding and failing in courses of training for clerical employment, as we shall see in Chapter XIII. It is further confirmed by the finding that speed and accuracy in number checking are not greatly subject to improvement through clerical experience.

Inquiries such as these, into the distribution of individual differences throughout the general population and in occupational groups, throw into relief the traits to be looked for as symptomatic of specific aptitudes. They help to estimate the probabilities that an individual characterized by a certain level of ability as tested will remain in the occupation if he enters it. In the instance just described, the presumption is strong that a man with barely average ability in number checking will not continue permanently in clerical work. If in other respects also he is found to be deficient in abilities ordinarily found in men following clerical occupations (see Chapter XIII), it is incumbent on him and his counselor to search for fields of opportunity in which his chances of adjustment are greater.

3

Returning now to our first assumption, that there are important trait differences within the make-up of each individual, we find that the tendency of the abilities of individuals in a representative population to cluster around the average for that group is matched by a similar tendency for the different abilities of a single individual to cluster about his own average. When his abilities in mathematics, vocabulary, reaction-time, output of energy, physical strength, grit, and many other traits are measured, it is found that in the majority of these respects his scores do not differ very greatly from his own central tendency. However, in some of his traits, they do. The widest variations are apt to be in his various motor abilities which, indeed, bear but little relationship to each other. His different sensory and perceptual powers also do not tend to cluster as closely about his average as do his more complex and ordinarily much more important intellectual abilities. But here also, in certain respects he is deficient, and in others he is superior, as compared with his average. Hull, after reviewing the evidence on this point, arrived at the conclusion that the average person's best capacities exceed his poorest by nearly twice as much as his poorest are above zero. That is to say, on a scale of vocational aptitude efficiency, his best potentialities are almost three times as good as his worst. (See Fig. 3.) The spread is of course much wider in some individuals than in others. In a few people the range of difference between their strongest and their weakest aptitudes is relatively small. Hull's generalization refers to the average person.

Such quantitative estimates are necessarily very tentative. Only a sampling of the numerous distinguishable vocational aptitudes have as yet been measured with any degree of precision. For most of these the zero point on the scale of measurement—"just not any" of the aptitude in question—has not yet been rigorously located. And all too few of the available researches have been made on truly representative cross-sections of the entire adult population. With the progress of scientific inquiry, any present approximation to the facts about

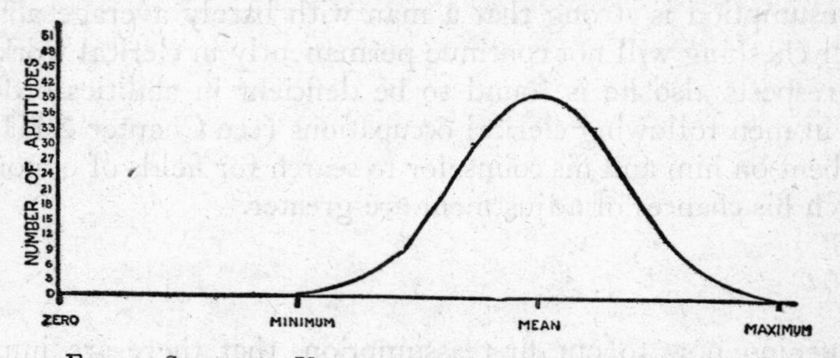

FIG. 3. SCALE OF VOCATIONAL APTITUDE EFFICIENCY[5]

Showing an approximate distribution of the average person's vocational-aptitude potentialities. In this figure the aptitude of maximum efficiency is placed at three times that of least efficiency.

the range between the average person's best capacities and his poorest will be subject to correction. But even if Hull's estimate should turn out to be somewhat too large, the fact would nevertheless remain that a person's chances of satisfactory occupational adjustment are notably heightened when he comes to realize what his different abilities are and prepares for an occupation in which his best potentialities may find full scope.

A counselor, then, is quite properly concerned with helping an individual to see clearly the differences between his various capacities, and also the differences between his capacities and those of other individuals—provided that our third assumption is correct, namely, that these differences are fairly stable. It remains to ask the extent to which a person's ability to acquire a specified pattern of occupational skills, knowledge, and interests—in other words, his aptitude for an occupation—is limited by his present constitution.

[5] From C. L. Hull, *Aptitude Testing*, p. 48. Yonkers: World Book Co., 1928.

4

The theory of aptitude implies that a person's potentialities are fairly stable. If he gives clear evidence today of ability to learn to play the flute and of inability to learn accountancy, we should be amazed to find tomorrow that his aptitudes in these directions were reversed. Human nature is never as unstable as that.

To be sure, we know that a person will not in all respects be exactly the same tomorrow as he is today; and five years hence he may quite conceivably have developed or retrograded in ways at present impossible to anticipate. Favorable opportunities may encourage the ripening of latent talents now unsuspected, while other aptitudes may lapse through lack of timely exercise. What at that time he will be able to learn to do is a function of his present capacities and purposes, and also of the experiences in store for him.

A theory of aptitude must not assume that each of the factors determining a person's traits is constant in the sense that it will not alter, more or less, with time. We must, however, assume—if the concept of educational and vocational aptitudes is to have any meaning at all—that the changes which undoubtedly do take place in the relative potency of these factors are seldom sudden, and that they occur *within limits* which can often be ascertained in advance.

In the chapters which follow, this question regarding the relative stability of a person's traits will be repeatedly raised. Within what range may his mental powers be expected to fluctuate? How persistent are his vocational interests, and his capacities for acquiring different kinds of skill? What degree of permanence, if any, can be counted upon, in each of the specific aptitudes ascertained, be they mechanical or clerical, social or intellectual, scientific or artistic, commercial or literary, manual or managerial, symptomatic of capacity for research or for selling or for any other pursuit? Regarding these matters informed judgment is necessary when counseling, as well as knowledge regarding the nature and amount of the individual differences which at present characterize the person whose plans are at stake. We shall turn first to the question as to the stability of a complex trait which is an important constituent of many aptitudes: intelligence.

Chapter IV

INTELLIGENCE AND APTITUDE

---

1. Variations in mental power. 2. Meaning of intelligence. 3. Measures of intelligence. Reasons for the inconstancy of the I Q. 4. Precautions to be taken when estimating mental abilities from school accomplishments and from test performance.

THE theory of aptitude rests, as we have seen, upon the facts of individual differences—differences symptomatic of later educational and occupational achievement and of capacity to find satisfaction in this achievement. The present chapter deals with differences in intelligence. As we consider the nature of intelligence and the differences which people exhibit in their ability to meet their problems intelligently, we shall not overlook the facts as to the relative stability of these differences, or their modifiability within limits. The possibility of throwing light on a person's academic and vocational aptitudes through study of his mental test records and other indications of his intelligence—verbal, mathematical, social, or mechanical—will then be taken up in connection with the findings as to the distribution of intelligence test scores in various occupational groups.

1

The capacities which differentiate an intelligent from an unintelligent person are obviously factors in many vocational and educational aptitudes. What are the facts as to the relative constancy or inconstancy of a person's ability to think and act intelligently? Does this ability mature at a predictable rate during childhood and youth? After maturity is reached, does one's intelligence score vary from time to time only within the limits of accuracy of the instruments of measurement? It is necessary to be clear in these matters in order that measures of intelligence may be properly interpreted when counseling.

Most of us have the conviction that we are not always equally clear-headed; that there are periods when we are prone to make an unusual proportion of stupid decisions; that at certain times we can work rapidly, accurately, at high pressure, and solve problems ordinarily quite too difficult for us, while at other times, try as we will, we cannot shine at our best. Our level of intelligence seems to us to fluctuate in cycles of long or short duration, somewhat like stock-market averages from boom to depression and back again, and also from season to season, from hour to hour.

Are these apparent variations in intellectual grasp, in ability to think clearly to a purpose, wholly illusory? Certainly not. We observe a man excessively fatigued by work and worry, and realize that his judgment will be much more dependable after a fortnight of relaxation in the woods. We see a lawyer befuddled by alcohol and wait until he is sober again before asking his considered opinion on an important point. Of course, when giving a test to measure intelligence or any other mental attribute we not only try to make certain that illness, fatigue, embarrassment, or other temporary incapacity is not interfering with the performance. We also like to repeat the test after a period of time has elapsed, to increase the probability of securing dependably representative samples of the person's ability. His test score tells how well he can do the task at the time. It more often indicates a lower than an upper limit to the range of his performance. The magnitude of the fluctuations in an individual's intelligence as tested is rarely as great as they appear to him to be; but they are sometimes serious enough. We shall return to this point after we have agreed, if possible, as to precisely what is meant by intelligence, and what intelligence tests measure.

2

In defining the term "intelligence," writers have used various phraseologies to say pretty much the same thing. Consider the setting in which the word is commonly used. We say that Jones is more intelligent than Smith; that officers in the navy on the whole show more intelligence than the sailors they command; that higher intelligence is needed in the skilled trades than in purely repetitive manual occupations; that elephants are more intelligent than horses, and white rats than guinea-pigs; or that the village fool is so very unintelligent compared with his associates that he really ought to be under the care of an institution. These comparisons have something in common. They all refer to the ability to achieve a purpose in spite of difficulties. We shall use the term "intelligence" to mean the ability of an organism to solve new problems or, as Warren puts it, "to meet novel situations by improvising novel adaptive responses."

Such a definition does not restrict the meaning of intelligence to those powers of thinking, of reflective judgment, of abstraction and generalization as aids in problem solving, in which, to be sure, the most intelligent minds outstandingly excel. Rather, these higher, more complex mental functions are elaborations of those simpler processes of learning and behavioral adaptation which we as human beings share with other organisms.

The simplest instances of human and animal conditioning and of learning by trial-and-error are evidences of intelligence, though of a lowly order. The solving of a problem by insight, by a sudden grasp of the meaning of an aspect of the situation, as observed in the behavior of anthropoid apes as well as of human beings, is a sign of higher intelligence which succeeds where even the most persistent random effort fails. In such behavior is clearly revealed the power to halt overt action, to inhibit habitual or instinctive or merely random responses, to differentiate parts of a total experience, and to apprehend the relations between these parts. Such abilities are most valuable in achieving a purpose intelligently instead of going at it blindly.

Still higher ability to deal intelligently with novel situations—to think a problem through to a solution in advance of trial-and-error attempts—requires the use of words and symbols as aids in abstracting significant aspects of the problem, seeing their relations, and manipulating them mentally, recombining them and testing the outcomes in thought preliminary to testing them in external behavior. The more successful a person is in using his head in this way to surmount difficulties, to avoid errors and to arrive at the right solutions of complicated problems, the more intelligent he is. Just how intelligent is measured in terms of (a) the level of difficulty of the problems he can solve, (b) the range or number of problems he can solve at that level, and (c) the speed with which he can solve them. These, then, are three dimensions of intelligence.

Without recourse to language, the processes of comparison, abstraction, generalization and mental organization would be limited indeed. With the aid of verbal symbols we can more easily wrestle with problems, manipulate meanings, and test possible solutions of our difficulties mentally before we act. Little wonder, then, that a good test of vocabulary is of use as an indirect measure of a person's verbal or conceptual intelligence, and for two reasons: first, the richer his store of words and meanings, the better his equipment for solving some of his problems promptly and correctly, that is, for showing intelligence; second, the more intelligent he has been since infancy, the greater the likelihood that he has gained command of a wide variety of correct word-meanings. Intelligence is far from being identical with the power to read understandingly, to speak aptly, or to write coherently and concisely. But the reciprocal relations between mastery of the mother tongue and ability to think intelligently should be obvious.

The same point holds with regard to command of the mathematical tools of thought. The brighter the boy, the more arithmetic and algebra he absorbs; and in turn the more easily he solves quantitative problems.

Mechanical intelligence as seen in the ability to adapt tools and mechanisms to a purpose, and social intelligence, ability to deal with people, are still other examples of innate powers of problem-solving that improve with use.

3

It is well known that the Binet-Simon scale had its origin in the need of the Parisian schools for an instrument with which to estimate a pupil's probable rate of progress and to segregate those who could scarcely be expected to benefit from the usual formal instruction. This scale and its revisions have been powerful instruments in individualizing education. The adjustment of school tasks to abilities has made for the less hampered progress of all, whether quick or slow, keen or dull, mechanically minded or verbally facile. Many paper-and-pencil tests have a similar purpose. In elementary school, in high school, and at time of college entrance, they have been of value in indicating the probabilities of subsequent success in mastering school subjects. The brighter pupils, as measured, for example, by the Stanford Binet, the Otis, the Terman, or the American Council examinations, ordinarily continue to lead their classes year after year, and those who show less mental power in test performance tend to lag behind. When discrepancies between a pupil's accomplishments and his mental test scores are observed, the specific causes may be sought and corrections made, or appropriate incentives brought to bear.

In contrast to the wide use of these common intelligence tests, such tests as have been proposed for measuring social intelligence have found little currency; and for good reason. Social intelligence, to be sure, is an important factor in many callings, but it is hard to gauge by means of standard samples of social behavior. Tests which provide actual situations calling for resourcefulness in dealing with persons are harder to arrange and to standardize than tasks involving only the manipulation of mechanical objects, while paper-and-pencil problems sampling a person's ability to manipulate concepts can still more readily be devised, arranged after trial in order of difficulty, and standardized as a test of conceptual or so-called "abstract" intelligence. This may explain in part why the testing of social intelligence has not progressed as far as the testing of intelligence in dealing with mechanical contrivances and with ideas. But there is still another reason why the greatest ingenuity and pains have been lavished on the improvement of ways of testing conceptual intelligence, namely, that such intelligence is a primary factor both in school progress and in occupational adjustment. A person's conceptual intelligence to some degree conditions his rate of advancement not only in humanistic and scientific courses of study, but also in trade and technical training, and in occupations of a social nature. No wonder that a counselor helping a person to plan his schooling and to choose a field of occupational specialization, wants to know his scores in intelligence examinations. They aid in appraising not only his scholastic educability, but his aptitude for various callings as well.

How stable are the traits measured by these intelligence tests?

The correspondence between intelligence test scores and rate of progress in school seemed quite striking when first brought out a generation ago. Wide fluctuations in a pupil's I Q from year to year were unusual exceptions to the general rule.[1] The coefficients of correlation between test and subsequent re-test were not zero, as would be the case if there were no fixity or stability whatever in the mental functions measured; they clustered around .85. The theory of the "constancy of the I Q" was advanced. It was even held that the tests measured *native* intelligence; and, moreover, that the level of intelligence with which a child was endowed by inheritance could not

[1] A child's Mental Age is his Binet mental test score expressed in terms of the age at which children on the average attain that score. His Intelligence Quotient—the ratio of his Mental Age to his actual chronological age—is then simply an index of the *rate* at which the mental abilities measured have improved since infancy. The IQ, the index of rate of growth in intelligence, should not be confused with the actual measure of intelligence on which it is based. Nor should it be forgotten that Mental Age scores above fourteen years are not mental ages in the above sense, but are points on an arbitrary scale.

at all be improved by appropriate environmental means. These were rather extreme deductions from the data, as we shall presently see.

There can be scarcely any doubt today that schooling and other educative experiences tend to increase a child's intelligence, or that lack of such opportunities limits his growth in this respect. Where such a doubt still exists, however, it is only necessary to review the facts as to the differences in intelligence between children of the same parents reared apart. Brothers and sisters separated in early childhood and placed in foster homes do not resemble each other in intelligence so closely as those brought up together. Those who have had the good fortune to be placed in slightly better home environments are found to average about 10 per cent higher on the intelligence scale than their less fortunate mates. A few striking instances of identical twins separated in infancy supply further light on the part played by environmental influences in modifying native intelligence. Still other pertinent facts have been brought to view by investigations of the intelligence of canal-boat children in England and of mountain-whites in remote hollows of Virginia, who are alike in lacking the benefits of any schooling. Not much below the average of other populations in intelligence up to age six, they thereafter fall rapidly behind. A satisfactory explanation cannot be found in the supposition that the tests used are too heavily weighted with tasks that children learn to do only in school. The most reasonable interpretation would seem to be that a person's position on the scale of intelligence is not unalterably fixed at birth. His ability to think and act intelligently is a product of at least three factors: native endowment, growth or maturity, and opportunity for educative experience.

Improvement in environment does produce a gain in intelligence, as Freeman and others have abundantly shown. To be sure, inherited capacities make a greater contribution than environmental influences to the ultimate outcome. We may agree in general with Barbara Burks, whose summary of the scientific evidence led to the conclusion that "probably close to 75 or 80 per cent of I Q variance is due to innate and heritable causes"; that "about 17 per cent is due to differences in home environment"; and that "home environment in rare extreme cases may account for as much as 20 points of increment above the expected, or congenital, level."

Such findings will be subject to some revision as more elaborately controlled studies are made. However, fortunately for the theory and practice of aptitude testing, it is not necessary to wait until the age-old controversy is finally settled as to precisely how much of an individual's talent may be credited to hereditary factors and how much to the environmental influences that have interacted with the native capacities. A person planning his educational and occupational future is looking forward, not back. How intelligent is he now? That is the first question. Then, what does that fact indicate as to his probable intelligence in the future? In other words, what is his ability to learn the things he will need to learn in order to enter this occupation or that, and what will be his ability to conduct himself intelligently and to make progress once he has begun? A counselor can form a useful estimate of such potentialities only on the ground of evidence as to the relative constancy or inconstancy of abilities already manifest.

The practical question is straightforward enough: within what limits may this person's capacity, as revealed to date, be expected to vary during the years ahead? If, for example, his I Q is 100 on entering high school at age 14, what are the probabilities that within the next four years it will vary as much as 12 points, say, and be only 88, or as high as 112? The evidence at present in hand indicates that there is about one chance in 22 that during a four-year period an I Q will either increase or decrease as much as this, and about one chance in three that it will change as much as 6 points. A counselor looking at the score on a student's cumulative record does not forget the one chance in 22, remembering also that I Q's of the brighter children more often are found to improve with time than to retrograde.

The possibility of locating and removing causes of mental retardation is also to be borne in mind. Here, for example, is a non-reader, a boy who after three years in the primary school still has not learned to attach the proper meanings to the queer symbols on the pages of his primer. His mental age is found to be lower than that of most other nine-year-olds. And then he has the good fortune to come under the instruction of a teacher who knows how to deal with special disabilities. She succeeds in teaching him to write and then to read. The tools of study are now at his command. He forges ahead in school work. His I Q likewise shows improvement.

Quite as striking are the changes in mental alertness that have been observed in a few children whose backwardness turned out to be an effect of extreme malnutrition or of a disordered thyroid gland. Only when the conditions of health and the influences of home and school environment remain substantially the same should it be expected that a child's I Q, or the intelligence of an older person, for that matter, would stay approximately constant. On the other hand, intelligence does not fluctuate at random. Very wide changes in scores not traceable to poor administration of the tests are rare indeed.

4

It should be noted that frequently it is quite possible for a counselor to make a rough but useful appraisal of his client's intelligence from data other than scores on standardized tests. Not, to be sure, from his appearance and manner, which are notoriously deceptive; but from ascertained facts as to his past achievements, his rate of progress through school, his grade-age ratio at the present time or at time of leaving school, his rank in class provided the standards of the school he has attended are known, and his demonstrated success at employments requiring mental alertness. One can confidently infer that a stupid-looking young woman with an impediment of speech is really pretty keen intellectually if she has graduated with honors from a good high school at age sixteen and published two articles for which editors have paid. Similarly, repeated failure in school is an indication of marked dullness, although a counselor will wish to ascertain, if possible, whether this retardation is really the result of inability to learn rather than of ill-health, poor eyesight, bungling instruction, home distractions, inefficient study habits, interests outside of school, or other remediable causes. Inferences as to intelligence, when based on records of school progress and accomplishment, should be made with appropriate reservations.

Caution is also necessary when inferring a person's mental power, alertness, or scholastic aptitude from his score on an intelligence examination. A relatively poor performance is generally indicative of low intelligence; but it may be due, instead, to temporary indisposition, visual defect, reading disability, personal antagonism toward the examiner, or other irrelevant cause. The story is in point of a somewhat precocious child of five whose parents wanted him to enter school six months before the customary minimal age, and arranged with the principal to have the boy tested. When he came back from the examination with an unfavorable report, his mother asked him what he had been doing. "Oh, a woman asked me a lot of fool questions and I thought up the silliest answers I could," which may or may not have been an intelligent way of responding to the Binet tests given in a stilted manner. In general, a low score is less certainly indicative of low intelligence than is a high score of high intelligence. But even a high score may possibly be attributable in part to previous familiarity with the test, to coaching, or to errors in administration. Whatever the results of the examination, a counselor will scrutinize all the available evidence of a person's ability to learn, rather than rely entirely on test scores.

The final score, whether expressed as a standard score, percentile rank, mental age, or intelligence quotient, is not all that an intelligence examination can tell. Knowledge of the particular sorts of problems in dealing with which a person shows the most intelligence supplements the information as to his average intelligence level. He may excel in dealing with verbal material or with mathematical problems. His mathematical intelligence, in turn, is a complex trait; for intelligence in manipulating spatial relations, as in geometry, does not always go with intelligence in manipulating numbers or algebraic symbols. The counselor wants separate measures of each of these sorts of intelligence. He knows that they are needed in varying degrees in different fields of occupation. The relative frequency of errors and omissions in the several parts of the examination should be noted. Scores on the sub-tests furnish symptoms of relative intelligence in dealing with space relations, with numbers, and with verbal meanings. For example, group tests of the Army Alpha sort may be inspected for indications of relative superiority in dealing with arithmetical problems, and with abstract verbal relations. A high-school pupil's scores in separate items of the Binet examination may also be grouped so as to portray his intelligence profile.

Intelligence examinations which stress the factor of speed are properly called mental alertness tests. Examinations the chief purpose of which is to ascertain the upper level of difficulty of the problems which can be successfully solved may be called tests of mental power.

5

Before taking up the vocational significance of performance in intelligence examinations we may briefly summarize. Intelligence has been defined as ability to solve new problems. This ability, while largely determined by heredity and maturation, varies also with the individual's condition. It is subject to substantial improvement through exercise and favorable environmental influences. It is not a single uniform ability, but is highly complex. It varies in the individual with the type of problem to which it is applied. And so in estimating a person's aptitudes it is worth while to ascertain whether he shows equal intelligence in dealing with a wide variety of problems, or excels in the solution of certain definite kinds of problems: mechanical, arithmetical, geometric, linguistic, or those involving personal relationships.

A close connection has been observed between educability and intelligence as measured by Binet tests and the better group examinations. Performance in such tests serves as a symptom of ability to progress in school work and to achieve the educational level deemed appropriate for entrance to various occupations and professions.

Intelligence tests are standardized tasks to measure resourcefulness in solving problems. They provide at best only carefully selected samples of a person's abilities in these respects and cannot yield perfect measures. Nor, indeed, are the abilities which they sample entirely stable. The range of probabilities that a person's intelligence as measured by the tests will improve or retrograde with time has been indicated. Ways of estimating intelligence from data other than standardized tests have also been described. They may be used to check the tests, as tests in turn are used as correctives of personal impression. The significance of measures of intelligence as indicators of suitability for various kinds of occupations will be treated in the following chapter.

Chapter V

INTELLIGENCE AND APTITUDE (*Concluded*)

1. Minimal occupational requirements: the army data. 2. Pond's data from a factory population of 9,000 men. 3. Minimal levels in the simplest occupations followed by women. 4. Intelligence requisite for business and for professions. 5. Wide range of intelligence in every occupation. What this means in vocational planning.

1

APTITUDE for learning from books, as we have seen, is partly, although not wholly, a matter of intelligence. We shall not forget that interest, or zest for learning, is also a factor in scholastic aptitude. Still other factors include specific abilities, such as ability to read easily and to command the concepts required in order to study the subject-matter in question. These last-mentioned factors are measurable by means of appropriate achievement tests. Intelligence examinations help to answer the question whether a person has the capacity to progress up the educational ladder to the level required by the occupation he is considering. They also throw light on his suitability for occupations known to demand certain minimal mental abilities of the sort measured by these examinations. The present chapter reviews evidence regarding the intelligence of various occupational groups, and considers the meaning of these facts for vocational adjustment.

Army Alpha, which the writer helped to develop during the great emergency of 1917, was an aid in estimating how promptly a recruit could be trained to follow directions as a soldier, or be prepared for a position of command. Although couched partly in military phrase, the mental abilities assessed were much the same as those which have since been measured with more precision by other group tests of intelligence—lusty progeny of the researches which were pooled to produce the army examinations.[1]

After the war, Army Alpha was for a time widely employed to measure scholastic aptitude. There are now better tests for this purpose; but since more is known about the vocational significance of performance on Army Alpha than of other tests of this kind, the accompanying scale of occupations arranged according to levels of intelligence is shown in terms of Alpha scores.

The data for this table are drawn from a study by Fryer,[2] who carefully analyzed the findings of the military psychologists and incorporated subsequent inquiries. Fryer ranked the occupations according to average score. For present purposes they have been arranged in order according to the score of the man who ranked at the *25th percentile*—the lower quartile—among men in his occupation. The 25th percentile has no magical significance. It merely means that three-quarters of the men following the occupation did better than this. But, pending the time when the minimal intellectual abilities essential to success in each occupation have been more precisely ascertained, these measures are well worth bearing in mind. A person who scores below the 25th percentile for the occupation he is considering need not necessarily be warned to look elsewhere for his vocation; but his counselor, in the light of what he knows both about the occupation and about the person, should weigh the probabilities that such a score may be an indication of ineptitude.

The table gives the average and the upper quartile scores for each occupation, as well as the point above which three-fourths of the men in the occupation scored. For readers who prefer to think in terms of standard scores, the same data are also expressed as points on a scale on which 5.00 is the central tendency, the general average score; while the unit 1.00 is the Standard Deviation of the population tested.

To counselors who are looking for suggestions regarding minimal occupational requirements, the Q1 column of Standard Scores is the

[1] Among the many forerunners of the army group intelligence tests may be mentioned the Trabue forms of the Ebbinghaus Completion Tests; the Woodworth and Wells Association Tests; the employment tests prepared by Thorndike for the Metropolitan Life Insurance Company in 1914; the early forms of Scott's group tests of intelligence; and Wells' number-series-completion test, made up of problems similar to those set by Yerkes' multiple choice apparatus. But by far the most useful contributions were from an unpublished dissertation by Terman's student, A. S. Otis, who had already brought nearly to completion his Group Intelligence Scale based on tests incorporated in what came to be known as the Otis Advanced Examination.

[2] Douglas Fryer, "Occupational-Intelligence Standards," *School and Society*, September 2, 1922, 16:273-277.

TABLE I. OCCUPATIONS AND INTELLIGENCE

Showing Army Alpha raw scores and standard scores of men following various occupations

	Raw scores			Standard scores		
Occupation	Q_1	Av.	Q_3	Q_1	Av.	Q_3
Clergyman	124	152	185	6.24	6.79	7.83
Engineer (civil and mechanical)	110	161	183	5.98	6.98	7.72
Physician	107	127	164	5.93	6.30	7.06
Accountant	103	137	155	5.85	6.48	6.85
Y. M. C. A. secretary	99	111	163	5.78	6.00	7.03
Teacher (public schools)	97	122	148	5.74	6.20	6.71
Chemist	94	119	139	5.69	6.15	6.52
Draftsman	84	114	139	5.50	6.06	6.52
Executive (minor)	81	109	137	5.43	5.96	6.48
Dentist	80	110	128	5.41	5.98	6.31
Nurse	78	99	126	5.37	5.78	6.28
Bookkeeper	77	101	127	5.35	5.81	6.30
Clerk (office)	74	96	121	5.28	5.72	6.19
Stenographer and typist	73	103	124	5.26	5.85	6.24
Clerk (railroad)	69	91	115	5.17	5.63	6.07
Conductor (railroad)	64	83	106	5.07	5.48	5.91
Foreman (construction)	62	80	114	5.02	5.41	6.06
Druggist	61	78	106	5.00	5.37	5.91
Clerk (postal)	60	81	106	4.97	5.43	5.91
Photographer	59	86	107	4.95	5.54	5.93
Sign-letterer	59	81	106	4.95	5.43	5.91
Foreman (factory)	59	77	107	4.95	5.35	5.93
Telegrapher and radio operator	57	85	110	4.89	5.52	5.98
Musician (band)	57	82	108	4.89	5.46	5.94
Electrician	57	81	109	4.89	5.43	5.96
Clerk (stock)	56	80	105	4.87	5.41	5.89
Graphotype operator	56	75	105	4.87	5.30	5.89
Clerk (receiving and shipping)	54	78	102	4.82	5.37	5.83
Farrier	54	72	99	4.82	5.24	5.78
Engineer (locomotive)	53	74	91	4.79	5.28	5.63
Auto assembler	51	68	97	4.74	5.15	5.74
Toolmaker	50	67	92	4.71	5.13	5.65
Carpenter (ship)	49	69	93	4.68	5.17	5.67
Gunsmith	49	66	86	4.68	5.11	5.54
Handyman (general mechanic)	48	69	94	4.66	5.17	5.69
Engineer (marine)	47	68	89	4.63	5.15	5.59
Telephone operator	46	70	95	4.61	5.20	5.70
Policeman and detective	46	69	90	4.61	5.17	5.61
Motorcyclist	46	63	88	4.61	5.04	5.57
Auto-engine mechanic	45	66	92	4.58	5.11	5.65
Laundryman	45	66	91	4.58	5.11	5.63
Plumber	44	66	88	4.55	5.11	5.57
Pipe-fitter	44	66	88	4.55	5.11	5.57
Lathe hand (production)	44	65	91	4.55	5.09	5.63
Carpenter (bridge)	44	65	88	4.55	5.09	5.57
Fireman (locomotive)	44	61	84	4.55	5.00	5.50

Table I. (*Continued*)

Occupation	Raw scores Q1	Raw scores Av.	Raw scores Q3	Standard scores Q1	Standard scores Av.	Standard scores Q3
Auto mechanic (general)	43	65	91	4.53	5.09	5.63
Chauffeur	43	65	91	4.53	5.09	5.63
Lineman	43	64	88	4.53	5.07	5.57
Tailor	42	65	89	4.50	5.09	5.59
Riveter (hand)	42	68	86	4.50	5.15	5.54
Brakeman (railroad)	41	63	86	4.47	5.04	5.54
Caterer	41	57	81	4.47	4.89	5.43
Machinist (general)	40	63	89	4.43	5.04	5.59
Butcher	40	61	85	4.43	5.00	5.52
Carpenter (general)	40	60	84	4.43	4.97	5.50
Baker	40	59	87	4.43	4.95	5.56
Farmer	40	58	83	4.43	4.92	5.48
Miner (general)	40	49	71	4.43	4.68	5.22
Blacksmith (general)	39	61	82	4.40	5.00	5.46
Mine drill runner	39	59	83	4.40	4.95	5.48
Horse-trainer	39	57	71	4.40	4.89	5.22
Shop mechanic (railroad)	38	60	94	4.37	4.97	5.69
Painter	38	59	81	4.37	4.95	5.43
Cobbler	38	56	76	4.37	4.87	5.33
Sales clerk	38	52	96	4.37	4.76	5.72
Concrete worker	37	58	85	4.33	4.92	5.52
Auto-truck chauffeur	37	58	83	4.33	4.92	5.48
Bricklayer	37	58	82	4.33	4.92	5.46
Printer	36	60	93	4.30	4.97	5.67
Engineman (stationary)	35	55	81	4.27	4.84	5.43
Horse hostler	35	55	77	4.27	4.84	5.35
Barber	34	55	78	4.23	4.84	5.37
Rigger	33	50	75	4.20	4.71	5.30
Actor (vaudeville)	31	62	94	4.13	5.02	5.69
Storekeeper (factory)	31	51	79	4.13	4.74	5.39
Boilermaker	31	51	74	4.13	4.74	5.28
Teamster	30	50	72	4.10	4.71	5.24
Aeroplane worker	26	51	77	3.95	4.74	5.35
Station agent (general)	21	48	89	3.73	4.66	5.59
Structural-steel worker	20	31	62	3.68	4.13	5.02
Hospital attendant	19	40	67	3.64	4.43	5.13
Mason	19	40	60	3.64	4.43	4.97
Shoemaker	19	35	57	3.64	4.27	4.89
Canvas worker	19	31	60	3.64	4.13	4.97
Fireman (stationary)	19	27	63	3.64	4.00	5.04
Lumberman	18	35	62	3.59	4.27	5.02
Textile worker	18	26	60	3.59	3.95	4.97
Cook	17	27	57	3.55	4.00	4.89
Sailor	16	32	59	3.50	4.17	4.95
Leather-worker	16	30	41	3.50	4.10	4.47
Sheet-metal worker	16	22	46	3.50	3.77	4.61
Fisherman	15	20	51	3.45	3.68	4.74
Laborer (construction)	13	21	47	3.37	3.73	4.63

most interesting. It is seen, for example, that the occupation of clergyman is the only one in which the lower quartile score is more than one sigma (one Standard Deviation) above the general average; while at the other end of the list, none of the lower quartiles, with the exception of those for fisherman and for laborer in the construction industry, falls as much as one and a half sigma units below the general average. To be sure, less than 7 per cent of the working population would be found to score below this point, 3.50; and only about 16 per cent, below 4.00 on the Standard Scale.[3] From these 16 per cent are drawn fully one-fourth of those who follow the least bookish—or should one say "paperish," or "schoolish," or "verbal"?—occupations.

At the upper end of the table, one notices that the engineers averaged higher than the clergymen, although the level below which 25 per cent of the engineers scored is not so high as the corresponding figure for the clergy.

Hospital attendants have the same average (4.43) and the same lower quartile score as masons, but their upper quartile score is higher; which suggests a question which ought often to be raised when counseling: "Do you prefer an occupation in which you will be one of the brightest in your group, or about average, or one of the less alert?" Anyone whose Alpha score is precisely at the general average[4] would find himself one of the more intelligent members of his occupational group if he were to become a sheet-metal worker, a sailor, a textile worker or a cook. As a blacksmith, butcher, or locomotive fireman, half of his fellows would be as bright as he; while if he chose to become a druggist, a postal clerk, or a factory foreman, the chances are that he would excel only a fourth of his competitors in the kind of mental alertness which Army Alpha samples. If his score is one-half sigma above the average, a similar comparison may be drawn between the occupations of carpenter, telegrapher, and draftsman. If it is one sigma above average, it excels the scores made by three-fourths of the postal clerks, one-half of the minor executives, and one-fourth of the physicians; while if it is one-third sigma below average, the occupations of construction laborer, station agent, and policeman may be mentioned in drawing attention to this question as to whether he prefers to follow a calling in which he will be one of its brighter members. When counseling a young man infatuated with aviation, determined to fly, the facts regarding his mental level compared with that of aviators and of workers in other occupations

[3] See Fig. 13 on page 251.

[4] Raw score, 61; Standard score, 5.00.

essential to the aviation industry may help him to come down to earth, without any injury to his self-regard. His test performance

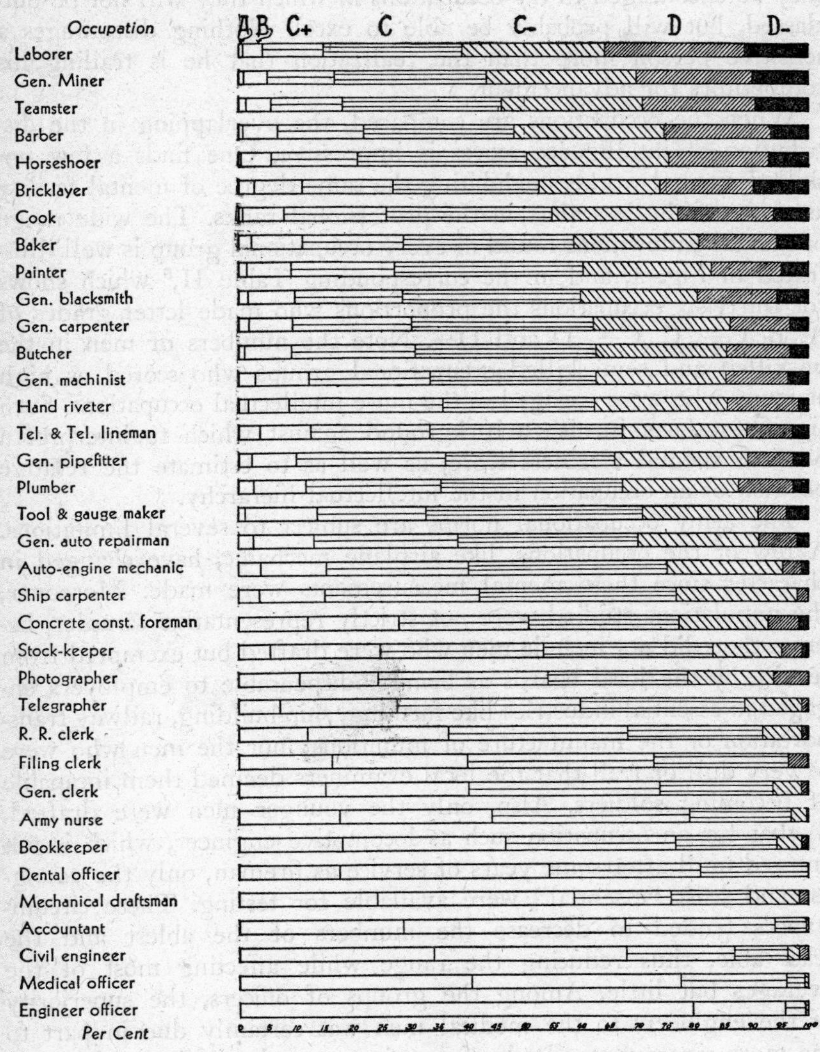

FIG. 4. DISTRIBUTION OF INTELLIGENCE SCORES

Showing for each of thirty-six occupational groups the proportion of soldiers receiving each letter rating.

is something objective, and so are the scores made by men in the various occupations he is considering.

In conferring with persons who lack confidence in themselves or who are subject to feelings of inferiority, it is especially desirable that they be encouraged to try occupations in which they will not be outclassed, but will probably be able to excel. Nothing discourages a sensitive person more than the realization that he is trailing his competitors for advancement.

When the occupations are compared, the overlapping in the distribution of intelligence scores is impressive. One finds a few unskilled manual workers exhibiting the same degree of mental facility as some of the less alert in the professional ranks. The wide range of mental endowment found in every occupational group is well illustrated in Fig. 4, and in the corresponding Table II,[5] which shows for thirty-six occupations the proportions who made letter grades of A, B, C+, C, C−, D and D−. Note the numbers of men in the unskilled and semi-skilled occupational groups who scored as high as many who were engaged in the more intellectual occupations. Such significant facts furnish a background against which to interpret a person's mental alertness score, as well as to estimate the relative position of an occupation in the intellectual hierarchy.

The army occupational norms are subject to several limitations. A few of the occupations, like airplane mechanic, have changed in character since these mental measurements were made. Moreover, the populations studied were not strictly representative samples, because they did not include men who were drafted but exempted from service by the local boards as being indispensable to employers engaged in essential industries like farming, ship-building, railway transportation or the manufacture of munitions; nor the men who were so very dull or frail that the local examiners deemed them incapable of becoming soldiers. Also, only the younger men were drafted, so that for an occupation such as locomotive engineer, which is not entered until after some years of service as fireman, only the youngest and least "essential" were available for testing. These circumstances tended to decrease the numbers of the ablest and the least able, thus reducing the range while affecting most of the averages but little. Among the groups of officers, the superiority of the engineers to the medical men was certainly due in part to the more rigorous standards of recruitment and selection maintained by the Engineer Corps. Most of the population samples are nevertheless fairly representative of the various occupational groups.

[5] Adapted from data regarding the intelligence scores of a population of 18,000 men, in *Psychological Examining in the U. S. Army*. R. M. Yerkes, editor. *Memoirs of National Academy of Sciences*, 1921, 15:828.

TABLE II. DISTRIBUTION OF INTELLIGENCE SCORES AMONG SOLDIERS REPRESENTING THIRTY-SIX OCCUPATIONAL GROUPS

Arranged in order according to median score, and showing for each group the percentage of men receiving each Army Letter Grade[6]

	Letter Grades						
Occupation	A	B	C+	C	C−	D	D−
Laborer	0.6	3.5	10.7	24.2	25.1	24.6	11.4
Miner	0.9	4.1	11.7	26.7	26.4	20.3	9.7
Teamster	1.3	4.3	12.5	27.9	24.9	19.7	9.4
Barber	0.8	6.1	14.9	26.3	26.5	18.8	6.6
Horseshoer	0.5	5.2	15.1	29.7	25.0	17.5	7.1
Bricklayer	2.9	8.2	15.9	25.6	21.3	16.4	9.7
Cook	0.7	7.3	17.9	29.0	22.1	16.8	6.2
Baker	2.4	8.7	17.7	29.5	22.4	13.7	5.5
Painter	1.5	7.7	18.2	33.0	22.5	12.2	4.8
Blacksmith	1.7	8.2	18.8	31.3	20.5	13.9	5.4
Carpenter	1.9	7.6	20.7	31.9	24.1	10.5	3.3
Butcher	1.1	8.3	21.6	31.8	22.8	11.3	3.1
Machinist	3.0	9.3	21.2	29.2	22.7	10.8	4.1
Hand riveter	1.8	7.1	26.8	26.8	23.2	12.5	1.8
Tel. & Tel. lineman	3.8	8.9	20.8	33.9	21.7	8.0	2.9
Pipefitter	2.3	7.8	26.1	29.8	23.4	7.8	2.8
Plumber	2.6	9.2	23.7	31.9	20.4	9.6	2.6
Tool and gauge maker	1.3	12.6	19.0	38.0	20.2	5.1	3.8
Auto repairman	2.8	10.6	25.1	31.7	21.2	6.7	1.9
Auto-engine mechanic	4.0	11.5	24.7	35.1	20.7	2.9	1.2
Ship carpenter	3.8	11.5	26.9	34.6	21.2	1.9	...
Concrete const. foreman	12.3	15.8	22.8	26.3	15.8	5.3	1.8
Stock-keeper	5.6	19.2	28.6	29.6	12.1	3.6	1.2
Photographer	10.6	13.8	29.8	24.5	14.9	6.4	...
Telegrapher	7.3	20.3	32.2	29.1	10.0	1.2	...
R.R. clerk	12.0	24.7	31.5	23.7	6.8	1.0	0.3
Filing clerk	16.4	23.6	32.7	23.6	...	3.6	...
General clerk	15.3	25.0	33.6	19.7	5.2	0.9	0.3
Army nurse	17.6	26.9	34.4	17.7	3.1	0.2	...
Bookkeeper	18.1	28.6	29.9	17.9	4.4	0.9	0.2
Dental officer	17.7	36.7	26.6	19.0	...	...	...
Mechanical draftsman	24.1	34.5	17.2	13.8	8.6	1.7	...
Accountant	28.7	39.1	26.2	5.5	0.5	...	...
Civil engineer	34.0	34.0	18.9	9.4	1.9	1.9	...
Medical officer	40.7	36.8	18.6	3.1	0.9	...	...
Engineer officer	79.6	16.3	3.6	0.4	...	...	...

2

The distributions of intelligence test scores of 44 occupational groups in a factory population of 9,075 men has been ascertained by Pond.[7] The examination she used is the Scovill Classification Test,

[6] Based on Table 378, *Memoirs of the National Academy of Sciences.* 1921, 15: 828.

[7] Millicent Pond, "Occupations, Intelligence, Age and Schooling," *Personnel Journal,* 1933, 11:373-382.

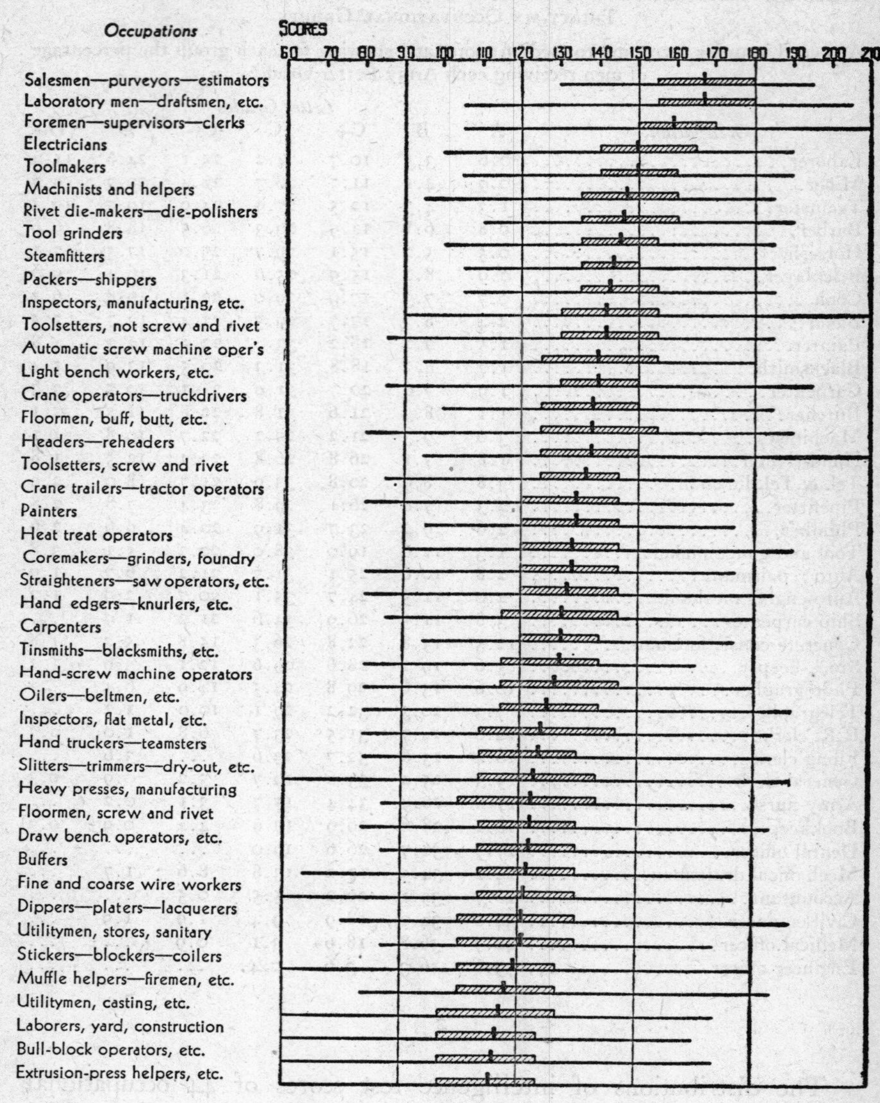

FIG. 5. DISTRIBUTION OF SCOVILL CLASSIFICATION TEST SCORES FOR MEN FOLLOWING FACTORY OCCUPATIONS

Showing total range, interquartile range and average score of 44 occupational groups arranged in order of average test score.

a battery well adapted for the purpose. It consists of eight paper-and-pencil tests, seven of them taken with slight modification from the army series. Four non-verbal tests, namely, picture completion, number checking, digit-symbol substitution, and geometrical construction, were adapted from the Army Beta examination which had been used in testing recruits who did not speak English or who could not read; and three of the best verbal tests from Army Alpha were included, namely, arithmetical reasoning, opposites, and analogies. The scores range from 60 to 210, with an average of 128.9. The sigma of the distribution is 22.58, which means that about two-thirds of the men scored between 106 and 152. For each occupational group the average score was ascertained; also the lower and upper quartiles, and the extreme range. In Table III the occupations are listed according to the degree of intelligence required to do the work as estimated by eight executives who had wide knowledge of these occupations, but who knew nothing of the scores. In the accompanying figure the occupations are arranged in the order of the mean scores. Note the differences, as well as the striking similarities, between these two lists.[8] Observe also the overlapping of the distributions, as in the army data. Counselors will probably be most interested in the lower quartile score for each occupational group. A man who scores below 135, let us say, which happens to be the lower quartile for steamfitters and tool-grinders, might make good in one of these occupations; but, other things being equal, it would seem to be more suitable for him to consider some occupation like toolsetter, painter, heat-treatment operator, or coremaker in the foundry, since in these occupations are larger proportions of men with intelligence similar to his.

Every applicant scores within the preferred range for some factory occupation or other. This is one of the most significant conclusions from Pond's researches. During periods of industrial activity, when many new employees are being hired, some opening can ordinarily be found which corresponds in its *intellectual* requirements to the abilities of each applicant as measured by the tests. No matter where he may rank on the scale of mental endowment, there is work that he can learn to do.

It is natural that a hierarchy of occupations arranged according to the average intelligence scores of the people who follow them is similar to a list in which they are ranked according to the amount of schooling ordinarily required. The two are not, however, iden-

[8] Miss Pond advances several good reasons for these differences on page 379 of the article cited.

TABLE III. INTELLIGENCE SCORES OF MEN IN A FACTORY POPULATION OF 9075

Showing the data for 44 occupational groups arranged in order according to the estimated degree of intelligence required. (Compare with the order in Fig. 5.)

Occupations	*N*	*Mean*	*Inter-quartile Range*	*Total Range*
Salesmen, purveyors, estimators	112	167.3	155–179	130–194
Laboratory workers, draftsmen, etc.	93	167.3	155–179	105–204
Foremen, supervisors, clerks	349	159.2	150–169	105–209
Toolmakers	165	149.7	140–159	105–189
Machinists and helpers	91	147.7	135–159	95–184
Tool-grinders	86	145.3	135–154	100–184
Toolsetters (not screw and rivet)	135	141.5	130–154	85–184
Electricians	57	149.9	140–164	100–189
Rivet die-makers, die-polishers	44	147.3	135–159	110–189
Steamfitters	51	144.3	135–149	105–184
Toolsetters, screw and rivet	71	136.7	125–144	85–174
Carpenters	61	130.5	120–139	95–174
Tinsmiths, ironworkers, blacksmiths	90	129.8	115–139	80–164
Painters	52	134.1	120–144	95–174
Crane operators, truck-drivers	152	138.2	125–149	100–184
Heat treat operators	100	132.5	120–144	90–189
Inspectors, mill and manufacturing	202	141.9	130–154	90–209
Packers, shippers	61	142.9	135–154	105–184
Miscellaneous machine operators, screw and rivet	87	139.7	125–154	95–179
Inspectors, rod, wire, flat metal, tube	147	125.6	110–144	80–184
Hand-screw machine operators	151	128.7	115–144	80–179
Crane trailers, tractor operators	146	134.2	120–144	80–174
Hand edgers, knurlers, automatic-machine operators	217	130.7	115–144	85–179
Buffers	291	122.1	110–134	65–174
Coremakers, grinders, helpers, foundry	142	132.5	120–144	80–174
Light bench workers, repair, etc.	321	139.5	130–149	85–194
Headers, reheaders	229	138.1	125–149	95–209
Straightener operators, helpers, saw operators	310	132.0	120–144	80–184
Fine and coarse wire workers	299	121.5	110–134	60–174
Draw-bench operators, helpers	89	122.8	110–134	85–179
Dippers, platers, lacquerers, etc.	276	121.1	105–134	75–189
Stickers, blockers, coilers	102	118.9	105–129	60–179
Slitters, trimmers, dry-out, etc.	1032	123.7	110–139	60–189
Heavy presses, manufacturing	145	123.2	105–139	85–174
Floormen, buff, butt, burner, etc.	300	138.2	125–154	80–189
Muffle helpers, firemen, moldmen, casting	328	117.0	105–129	80–184
Bull-block operators, pointers, rolls helpers	651	113.8	100–124	60–169
Extrusion-press helpers, utilitymen, mill	362	113.0	100–124	60–174
Oilers, beltmen, rolling-barrel operators, etc.	260	127.2	115–139	80–189
Floormen, screw and rivet	101	123.1	110–134	80–184
Utility men, casting, moldmen, floormen, foundry	469	115.3	100–129	60–169
Hand truckers, teamsters	237	125.2	110–134	80–184
Utility men, stores and sanitary department	119	121.0	105–134	85–169
Laborers, yard and construction	292	114.5	100–124	60–164
Total (average weighted by N)	9075	128.9	110–144	60–209

tical. Tool and die makers, cabinet-makers, and other mechanics or artisans representative of the skilled trades—the aristocracy of manual workers—may get on with less schooling than clerical workers of similar intelligence; but they ordinarily have four years of apprenticeship and need both practical and conceptual intelligence sufficient to enable them to master the intricacies of a trade during these years. Ability to think about spatial attributes of objects, their shapes, sizes and relations; resourcefulness in choosing tools, materials, and methods of manipulating them; good sense as well as accuracy in making measurements and numerical computations; all these the budding carpenter, glazier, or mechanic needs, as well as the ability to acquire trade knowledge through oral and printed instruction, and skill through imitation and practice. It follows that aptitudes indicative of capacity to profit from trade apprenticeships cannot be estimated very reliably from verbal intelligence scores alone. Test batteries like the Scovill Classification Test are better for this purpose. Such paper-and-pencil tests and also performance tests of mechanical intelligence—assembly tests and the less easy form boards—properly find a place in batteries designed to help a person to estimate his fitness for a mechanical trade. (See Chapter XI.)

3

Is it true, as is often alleged, that there are some kinds of work so simple and repetitive that they require absolutely no intelligence whatever because the worker is, actually, but a machine? The Vocational Adjustment Bureau of New York, engaged for many years in guiding and training young women with modest abilities, has noted the kinds of jobs for which mentally retarded girls can be prepared. After working with 375 problem girls between the ages of fifteen and twenty-two, with mental ages ranging from six years to seventeen, Burr[9] published her tentative conclusions regarding minimum intellectual attainments needed in such jobs as packing, labeling, hand sewing, operating power-driven sewing-machines, paper-box making, and millinery operations. She found, for example, that "the least exacting employment for which girls of a mental age of seven years and six months are satisfactory is the packing of small articles not easily damaged by careless handling. There are any number of such articles and the Bureau has placed several of its applicants in one job where the packing of powder puffs in individual oiled envelopes

[9] Emily T. Burr, "Minimum Intellectual Levels of Accomplishment in Industry," *Personnel Journal*, 1924, 3:207-212.

is the task demanded. When the packing involves the folding of the articles and the separation of each article from a large quantity not easily isolated, like the packing of hair nets, for instance, only such girls as measured nine years and nine months mentally, were found to be equal to the task. This fact was arrived at through the simple process of elimination, by having returned to the Bureau as unsuitable, girls of lower mental age for whom the work was too difficult. Here the placing of a single net in a sheet of tissue paper, the folding of the paper, and inserting of the simple package into an envelope, demands a degree of delicate manipulation which the packer of powder puffs is not required to exercise.

"When the requirements of such jobs as stock-keeping, labeling and checking had to be met, the lowest intellectual level that proved satisfactory was ten years and five months. On the other hand, the level of nine years and five months was found to be sufficient for employment in cut-out-pasting work where the occupation is almost mechanical and the chances for error slight. . . .

"In the assembling of parts, a certain amount of judgment is required and here it has been found that the lowest grade at which girls placed by the Bureau could keep such jobs ranked at thirteen years. Some girls of a lower level have been placed but none has remained for the standard three months' period."

These tentative minimum levels of intelligence were subsequently found to have been set too high. After several more years of experience in training and placing young women, it was found that some whose mental age was only five could be trained to succeed at the easiest packing jobs. Women with a mental age of six had been satisfactorily placed in light factory work; at seven, some had been trained for assembling parts, errand service, examining, and pasting jobs; at eight they could be taught to do cutting, folding, and garment-machine operating; at nine, hand sewing, press operating, filing, and care of stock; at ten, routine clerical work; and at the mental age of eleven, selling.[10] Such are probably the rock-bottom levels at which it is feasible to undertake to train mentally retarded girls for self-support in industry.

4

Toward the other end of the occupational scale, many studies have been undertaken to ascertain the minimum intelligence levels for

[10] Edna W. Unger and Emily T. Burr, *Minimum Mental Age Levels of Achievement.* Albany: New York State Department of Education, 1931.

admission to professional-training schools—teaching, nursing, dentistry, engineering, law, and medicine. Minimum levels of intelligence as measured by the more reliable examinations are without question factors in aptitude for successful mastery of what these schools teach. Since professional schools are the gateways to professional practice, the standards they adopt for admission are necessarily taken into account whenever a person's aptitudes for these professions are in question.

For a career in business also there is a minimum intelligence level: the general population average. Relatively few men and women carrying business responsibilities score below this average. The minimum for those who look forward to minor executive posts may be placed at a point roughly equivalent to 5.50 on the standard scale. Standards for different kinds of clerical work are considered in Chapter XIII. There we shall find that tests to measure specific clerical aptitudes tell but part of the story, and that intelligence in dealing with verbal and numerical materials, as measured by the very tests which are most indicative of a person's ability to make progress in school and college, is an even weightier factor in aptitude for office work.

5

We have seen that intelligence is to be reckoned with when estimating vocational as well as educational aptitude. Occupations differ greatly in the difficulty of the problems of adjustment they entail; and individuals differ in their ability to make these adjustments, to overcome the difficulties, to solve promptly and correctly the problems that arise—which is another way of saying that some people can think and act more intelligently than others. Intelligence is much the same as educability when that term is not restricted to mean merely the ability to learn school subjects but is used in its broadest sense: ability to profit by experience.

A person's relative position on a scale of intelligence may be approximately ascertained by sampling his ability to solve the problems set by intelligence tests—problems the relative difficulty of which has been carefully determined. So also, an occupation may be ranked in comparison with other occupations, either according to the average intelligence of the persons who follow it or according to the minimal level of intelligence required to succeed in it. There seem to be almost no occupations, however simple and monotonous the operations may be, that do not require the worker to be at least as intelligent as the average five-year-old child. As the scale of intelligence is ascended, the variety of occupations in which it is possible for a person to compete increases, at first slowly, then rapidly; so that, in so far as this factor of intelligence is concerned, most people have a wide range of callings from which to choose.

In every field of employment we have found not only workers with the minimal intelligence required, but many who far exceed this minimum. In other words, the range of differences among persons following any occupation is very great. When this fact is brought home to one in doubt about his choice of an occupation, it brings to a focus the important question as to whether he prefers an occupation in which he will find himself one of the more intelligent, or less intelligent, members of his calling. A counselor may say, for example, to a certain college girl with medical ambitions, "If you engage in medical practice, you will find that about three-fourths of your professional associates are brighter than you are; while in the occupations of nurse, oral hygienist, or technician in a bacteriological laboratory, you will be one of the mentally superior members of your calling. Which do you prefer?" The decision rests with the individual herself, not with her counselor; but it is a counselor's duty to see that the alternative possibilities are recognized. These considerations are peculiarly pertinent to the vocational plans of anyone who is likely to be a prey to feelings of inferiority if he finds himself one of the less able members of his occupational group.

When a person's status with respect to intelligence has been ascertained by standard tests or by reference to his school progress and achievements—preferably by both—his counselor may use the information to help in answering the vital question as to the likelihood that his client can master the school or college subjects prerequisite to his entrance upon the occupations he is considering, and also to bring to his attention other occupations in which he might find himself more congenially placed. In these connections, it is well to keep in mind not only the figures indicative of his mental age or his intelligence score, but also his relative excellence of performance in the different kinds of sub-tests which go to make up an intelligence examination. For intelligence is a complex, not a unitary, trait. The degree of intelligence a person exhibits varies with the kind of problem on which it is brought to bear. We have seen, for example, that it is well to distinguish intelligence in using verbal concepts from intelligence in solving mathematical problems, in dealing with spatial relations, in manipulating mechanisms, and in managing other people. Occupations as well as school subjects differ in the demands they make on these different kinds of intelligence.

In addition to the problem-solving abilities which we have called intelligence—the ability to meet new situations by improvising novel but adequate adaptive responses—many occupations call for highly specific abilities or special talents. Symptoms indicative of these capacities, and ways of measuring them, will be treated in subsequent chapters. But first we shall pause to consider another factor almost as weighty as intelligence in any estimate of individual aptitude: the factor of interest.

Chapter VI

INTERESTS AND APTITUDES

1. Although the strength of a vocational purpose cannot be precisely ascertained, vocational interests, at least, can be measured. Four reasons for undertaking this. 2. Meaning of "interest": its outer and inner aspects. Relation between interests and abilities. 3. Ways of ascertaining interests. The cumulative record. The ideal test. 4. The indirect, informational approach to interests.

I

"If there were an instrument by which to measure desire, one could foretell achievement."

So, at least, mused the professor in Willa Cather's novel, *The Professor's House.* He was thinking of the thousands of young men who had heard his lectures, and of the single student, no brighter than many of the others, who later had accomplished something really exceptional.

The strength of certain drives in animals has been compared in terms of the obstacles they are willing to surmount, the punishment they are willing to take, in order to satisfy those desires. A mother rat is a little more ready to cross an electric grid and suffer a mild shock in order to get back to her young than she is to reach a foodbox when hungry. Fernald's Achievement Capacity Test—a test of grit, of willingness to undergo increasing physical discomfort in order to make a good showing—was an earlier application of this same principle to the measurement of human desire.

But there are as yet no convenient instruments for measuring the strength and persistence of an intense focalized vocational purpose. Of this potent factor in future achievement the person himself must still be the judge. A counselor can only try to make certain that this crucial point is not overlooked but is given due weight in relation to the many other relevant factors.

Desire, however, is akin to interest; and interests can be explored and inventoried. They can also be at least roughly measured, either directly or indirectly. We usually want to do what we like to do; and we like to do what interests us. Since people tend to find the keenest satisfaction in those activities which challenge their sustained attention, there is abundant reason for canvassing their interests systematically and for helping them to arrive at a clear picture of their affective tendencies. This is the first and most obvious reason for attempting to measure a person's vocational interests: to find out whether he will probably like to do the work of the occupation in question.

A second reason is, to ascertain whether the personal relationships within the occupation will probably prove to be congenial. The man who is interested in the same things that interest his colleagues, who likes what they like and dislikes what they dislike, is apt to feel at home among them.

In the third place, it is known that there is some relationship—although the connection is far from close—between interests and abilities. More often than not, a person can learn to do best what interests him most, and, conversely, is likely to develop an interest in doing what he finds that he can do best.

A fourth reason for measuring a person's interests is that by so doing his attention is frequently drawn to possible fields of activity which might otherwise be overlooked.

2

Before examining means of measuring the relative strength of different interests, their stability or variability, and their relation to abilities, we must agree on the meaning of the term "interest."

Look at Smith and Johnson, electric welders at their benches, each engaged in building up and shaping the steel teeth on a huge bit for use in drilling oil wells. Smith is interested in this work while Johnson is not. You, the observer, notice the difference: Smith has every appearance of being concentrated on what he is doing, while Johnson's eyes wander toward other benches or toward the clock. Interest in an object or in an activity reveals itself in a heightening of attention to it. The interesting object is examined from every angle. The interesting activity is entered upon with promptness and zest, and is continued, perhaps even beyond the stage of excessive fatigue. The outward manifestations of interest, then, are concentration of attention and persistence of the activity.

An *interest* is a tendency to become absorbed in an experience and to continue it, while an aversion is a tendency to turn away from it to something else. Interests and aversions are dynamic. The tendencies are there even when one is busy with other things and has no chance to indulge them. It is the nature and strength of these *tendencies* which have meaning for educational and occupational plans. We therefore define interest not only in terms of the objects and activities which get attention and yield satisfaction, but also in terms of the strength of the tendencies to give attention to and seek satisfaction in these competing objects of interest.

An illustration will make clear this use of the term "interest" as meaning a tendency to engage in an activity as opportunity offers, to concentrate attention on it, and to prolong it because of the satisfaction it yields. A person with a keen interest in the reduction of automobile accidents notices relevant newspaper items which would escape attention if his all-absorbing interest were in the stock market or the drama. He talks about highway safety. He enjoys learning the fine points of automobile operation so that his own driving will be skillful and will create no hazards for other drivers. This specific interest may derive from more basic and general interests in personal security for himself and concern for the welfare of others. It may have been brought to a focus by the experience of having witnessed a gory tragedy. It may lead him in turn to explore related subjects, such as individual differences in accident proneness and the best ways of curing a driver of his susceptibility to accident. He may even delve into those chapters in social psychology, jurisprudence, automotive design, statistical method, and the principles of education which, when mastered, would aid him to undertake a career as safety engineer. Then if his interest continues, he may engage in the varied activities of that occupation with zest and satisfaction. In the same sense we speak of a person's relative interest in different school subjects, in social activities, in athletic sports, in the world of nature, in mathematics, in money matters, in the contemplation of beauty, in abstract thinking. The activities in which he engages because they appeal to him are *expressions* of his interests.

The outward and visible signs of interest are generally obvious in the behavior of the interested person. In posture and in movement he shows that he is giving his attention to the thing or the person or the job which interests him, and in so doing is shutting out competing stimuli which otherwise might draw his attention elsewhere. As interest wanes, attention wanders, or is held only with effort. The inward grace of which the attitude of attention is the outward sign is a feeling of pleasantness, a *liking* for the object, the person, or the task. Similarly, a feeling of unpleasantness characterizes experience of an object or an activity for which one has an aversion. These subjective aspects of a person's interests are revealed directly in his behavior toward the stimulating situation, and indirectly in what he says about his feelings with respect to it.

The capacity for achieving an interest in carrying on the work of any occupation is, then, a vital constituent of aptitude for it. Other things being equal, no one questions that a man is better fitted to undertake training for a calling that he will like than for one toward which he will feel either indifference or repugnance.

When an individual's present interests are ascertained, they are appropriately construed as symptoms of his probable future interests. They have even been regarded also as symptoms of future abilities; but the extent to which there is warrant for using measures of interest as clues to capacity for future accomplishment is a debatable question. We have said that a person is inclined to enjoy doing what he can do well. His vocational interests do tend in some degree to correspond to his potential abilities. But the relationship is not necessarily very close. Immaturity and lack of first-hand acquaintance with the kinds of activities involved in various pursuits tend seriously to depress whatever correlation there might otherwise be between a person's present interests and his future abilities. One dose of the drudgery involved may be enough to cure a boy's infatuation for a career as airplane mechanic, or a girl's obsession for the stage. The less familiar a young woman is with the actual duties of an occupation such as landscape gardening, the greater the likelihood that her eagerness to enter it will bear no relation to her ability to succeed. In such a case, ignorance is bliss. On the other hand, unfamiliarity with an occupation such as politics or plumbing or undertaking or dentistry or conveyor-assembly work is often a ground for unwarranted prejudice against it. Only after rich and varied opportunities to observe and to participate in different kinds of employment do a person's expressions of vocational interest approach their maximum reliability.

There is, indeed, in the minds of many counselors a good deal of doubt as to whether a person's interests are not so unstable—so subject to change with additional maturity, knowledge, and experience—that they are apt to furnish only tenuous if not misleading clues to aptitude. They have learned to discount what anyone, no matter who, tells them regarding his interests. To be sure, a person seriously concerned about his aptitudes is not inclined intentionally to falsify his expressions of preference. Discrepancies between his real interests and his reports about these interests generally arise from lack of familiarity with the activities in question, not from prevarication. But his experience of such activities may often be too meager to enable him to tell correctly whether they intrigue him or not; and so, what he sincerely says he likes to do and what he really would like to do are not always the same. Moreover, he is not always frank. Ask a representative sample of New Yorkers which daily paper they prefer to read. "The *New York Times*," is much the commonest reply. Actually, they bury their faces in the tabloids oftener than they choose to report, as subway counts and statistics of circulation clearly show.

Even when the probe has reached well beneath the surface and brought to view a clear picture of a person's interests, uncertainty still remains as to whether the pattern of these tendencies may not be radically altered within the space of a few months or years. The amazing plasticity of the affective constitution, the capacity of the human organism to learn to like activities and occupations which are at first distasteful, is certainly an aspect of human nature not to be ignored. With only a few exceptions, the many tests and questionnaires which have been offered as means of measuring educational and vocational interests have proved rather unreliable.

What then are the facts? Is there, indeed, scientific justification for the common practice of undertaking to help a person to discover and to understand what his real interests are? If so, how can it best be done? These questions are faced in the following pages. We shall first ask how interests are ascertained and how they may be measured. Then in the ensuing chapter we shall inquire how stable they are, and how the findings may be made of service in educational and vocational planning.

3

To ascertain his interests, a person's own description of the kinds of activities in which he most likes to engage, and of the growth and changes which have taken place in his ambitions, may be supplemented in several ways. Direct evidence of his preferences is found in the record of those activities, school subjects, recreations, and employments which have in the past captured his attention and absorbed his time. Next, his relative achievement in these different fields, furnishes a secondary or indirect but quite objective indication of his interest in them. Third, quantitative measures of certain significant aspects of his interests may be obtained. Fourth, clues may be secured from statements and ratings made by supervisors, teachers, or associates who have had ample opportunity to observe behavior expressive of his interests. Fifth, a systematic inventory, made with the aid of a well-designed questionnaire, supplies a useful picture of the pattern of his interests.

A student's cumulative record should contain many of the desired data. When conferring with an adult or with a youth who has unfortunately attended schools which as yet fail to maintain adequate records of their students, it is necessary for a counselor to glean in devious ways as much of the missing information as he can. He has to rely mainly on what he learns by interview; but he checks what is said against such other relevant data as can be secured. This information he files. He initiates what should in the future become a cumulative record; for it is not to be expected that decisions reached today will bring an end to the need for subsequent review and additional planning.

Fortunate is a student on whose cumulative record are several "behaviorgrams"—to use Bradshaw's word—notes of doings clearly indicative of interests. To illustrate such revealing items, the following are culled from observations of student behavior noted during the author's early teaching in secondary school and college. Jack "built a good birch-bark canoe." Margaret "organized a class orchestra." Beardsley "borrowed and read a text on differential calculus." Albert "sold the most advertising space in the Junior Annual." Henry "set himself the task of writing five sonnets a week and kept it up for three weeks." Roy "earned preparatory-school tuition by giving bird talks to women's clubs." William "has put in much time at the theater, backstage." Grace "spent her summer doing volunteer work in a hospital laboratory."

The reader can guess which of these eight students has now become Director of the American Museum of Natural History, and which ones undertook careers in business, manual training, medicine, literature, psychology, music, and motion-picture production. He will, as it happens, make not more than one error at most. Ordinarily an item of this kind, suggestive though it may be, is but a fragmentary indicator of interest. There should be several behaviorgrams on every cumulative record; and their relevance to the person's educational plans and occupational decisions should be viewed in the light of his school progress, his occupational and recreational history, his available test scores, his own narrative of his interests, and any other pertinent information. When doubt remains he should be encouraged to look about, to read, to talk with workers in the fields of occupation he is considering, and if possible to get the first-hand experience which is the one unfailing touchstone for revealing interest or aversion.

Before resorting to the decisive but time-consuming practical test—the actual tryout—a preliminary exploration of preferences may be carried through systematically with the aid of inventory blanks and interest questionnaires such as those described in the following chapter. Situations may also be arranged in which behavior revealing of interests can be noted and measured. Such situations, when standardized, are interest tests.

Tests of interest get at the facts regarding a person's tendencies either directly or indirectly. A direct objective test of interest is one that provides a standard situation with carefully selected samples of various appeals to interest, to which the person being tested will either give his attention or from which he will turn away, or otherwise react in a manner indicative of his usual response to such appeals. The anecdote was current in our grandfathers' day of the Connecticut father who wanted to find out whether his boy had the interests of a minister, a banker, or a farmer; so he left him alone with a Bible, a dollar, and an apple, to see which would most entice him and hold his sustained attention. On opening the door again, the father found the lad sitting on the Bible, with the dollar in his pocket, eating the apple, and instantly inferred that his interests resembled those of a politician. This ludicrous approach to the problem of interest measurement was in error neither in its purpose nor in its method of offering live alternatives, but rather in the unrepresentative character and the inadequate number of the behavioral situations provided. The father was correct in supposing that samples of actual preference are more valid indicators of likes and dislikes than verbal statements about them can possibly be. He wanted an objective test.

Ideally an interest test would first provide opportunity to become familiar with several typical kinds of activity, such as those in which a junior-high-school pupil engages in the various shops, studios, and laboratories of a prevocational tryout course. He would then be given a chance to put in more of his time in the shop or activity he likes best. His response to such an option, when uninfluenced by the advice or example of others, would be a true expression of interest. It is interest manifest. Similarly, the behavior of a person in a specially arranged museum could be noted—the length of time he spends looking into the case containing geological specimens, compared with the time devoted to cases containing gears and mechanical models, birds, animals, etchings, dolls, fine linens, specimens of typography, biological exhibits, and so on. Confronted with these options, the appeals which capture his attention and hold it longest are obviously the ones which, under the conditions of the test, actually get his interest. Practical considerations—the cost in time and money, and the difficulty of providing a satisfactory variety of alternatives—have stood in the way of developing this method of sampling an individual's interests up to the point where the results are reliable and significant. But the underlying principle is a sound one: instead of relying solely on what a person says are his interests, observe, if possible, that in which he actually takes interest.

4

When lacking the opportunity to ascertain the nature and strength of a person's interests by observing under experimentally controlled conditions the objects and activities toward which his attention spontaneously turns and by which it is held, he and his counselor may resort to other means. There are, for example, tests which measure interests indirectly, in terms of knowledge, abilities, or reaction tendencies which it is likely that only a person with real interest in the field in question would have acquired. These tests correspond to what Fryer in his comprehensive volume on *The Measurement of Interests*[1] has called measures of objective interests, in contrast with a person's *subjective estimates* of his feelings of interest, indifference, or aversion. As a matter of terminology, we prefer to speak of "objective measures" of interests, rather than of "objective interests," because the behavioral tendencies which we have called interests are what we want to know about, and they may be either objectively measured or subjectively estimated.

As indirect but objective and informing measures of interest, certain tests of information may be cited. The theory behind this informational approach is simple. It assumes that a person interested in any field—in mechanics, or bird life, or music, let us say—will have picked up in advance of any specialized training much more information about the subject than a person not interested in it. Such an information test has to be constructed so that it includes only items which could have been learned by almost anyone in the course

[1] Douglas Fryer, *The Measurement of Interests*. New York: Henry Holt and Company, Inc., 1931.

of his daily activities and general reading. There should be no items so technical that they would ordinarily be known only to specialists with training or experience in the field. A test of this sort measures interest indirectly, but in a manner useful in counseling.

The first informational test of vocational interests was, like many an invention, something of an accident. In 1916, the members of Walter Dill Scott's seminar at Carnegie Institute of Technology were working on the development of a battery of tests and forms for use in employing salesmen. When issued as "Aids in the Selection of Salesmen" for trial in cooperating business organizations, this battery included an application form, a model letter of reference to former employers, a man-to-man rating scale which shortly evolved into the Army Officer's Rating Scale, and five tests adapted for either group or individual administration. These five included a group intelligence test—one of several forerunners of the army examination—a test of linguistic ability, a card-sorting and filing test of clerical ability (an ability of which it was thought a salesman should have at least a minimum), a test of imagination, and a true-false test of range of information. This last test had been developed by one of the graduate students, E. S. Robinson, on the hypothesis that the wider a sales candidate's acquaintance with many varied topics, the more readily he could engage in conversation with possible purchasers. But before the mimeographed blank was issued in printed form, the writer suggested that it would be less likely to arouse resistance or to touch the pride of the men for whom it was intended if it were called a test of "Range of Interest." It was then so labeled. And a rough measure of range of interest it undoubtedly was. Administered to 800 high-school students, 200 college freshmen, and about 200 business people, salesmen and sales executives, the lower quartile scores of the business groups exceeded the upper quartile score of each group of students, while a small group of successful sales executives averaged higher than any of the others. Although it is likely that these differences were due in considerable part to the factors of maturity and ability, as well as to range of interest, the test illustrates how interests may be measured indirectly but objectively, in terms of the information the interested person has acquired.

This informational approach to the study of vocational interests has since been used by various investigators. O'Rourke's Mechanical Aptitude Test, described on pages 318-320, is an excellent example. It measures the amount of information a youth has picked up regarding tools and their uses. Such relationship as has been found between scores in this test and subsequent achievement in shop courses and in the work of machinist apprentices, is readily understood on the hypothesis that a young man's test performance is determined in part by the strength of his interest in tools and mechanical activities—an interest which has led him to acquire the information measured.

The most widely used tests of interest are in the form of paper-and-pencil inventories which a person checks, in a manner to indicate his likes and dislikes. They furnish objective records of subjective estimates of preference. To a consideration of these aids in ascertaining the pattern of an individual's interests we shall turn in the following chapter.

5

We have touched upon the reasons for finding out as fully and accurately as possible about a person's interests, and have considered various ways in which this can be done. A man's narrative of the growth of his interests has been mentioned as of value in securing a true picture of them, while special stress has been placed on the accumulation, over a period of time, of recorded data with respect to activities most revealing of those same interests. Objective methods of measuring interests, either directly or indirectly, have been illustrated.

We defined interest in an object, a person, an activity, or a field of occupation, as a tendency to give attention to it, to be attracted by it, to like it, to find satisfaction in it. Neither the inner aspects of interest nor its outward manifestations in observable behavior have been ignored. Both are pertinent. No wonder that the professor groped for "an instrument by which to measure desire"! Without the capacity to achieve a genuine interest in a branch of learning or in a field of occupation, without the likelihood that its pursuit will furnish the inward satisfactions of enjoyment, the capacity to acquire the necessary proficiency is but a cold and steely asset. Interest, then, is not only a symptom, it is of the very essence, of aptitude.

Chapter VII

INTEREST INVENTORIES

THEIR USE IN COUNSELING

---

1. Interest questionnaires may have stimulative as well as informative values. Three blanks described. 2. Reliability and stability of interest scores. 3. Inventories for specific purposes. 4. Primary factors in vocational interests. 5. Considerations governing choice of an interest inventory. Strong's blank compared with Thurstone's. 6. Interpreting interest scores in personal interview. The intrinsic significance of interests. 7. Recapitulation.

1

SIGNIFICANT symptoms of aptitude may be found in what a person says about his interests. These expressions, to be sure, do not always correctly represent his actual interests, nor do his real vocational interests always correspond with his capacity to perform. But even though their connection with subsequent achievement is remote, it is nevertheless worth while to explore systematically those clues to aptitude discoverable in verbal expressions of interest.

To this end, wide use has been made of paper-and-pencil blanks—interest inventories and questionnaires. By such methods, instead of measuring interests directly, or inferring them indirectly from tests of information, we study what a person says his preferences are. The best of these interest blanks have proved to be among the most valued aids in counseling. We shall note the limitations of this procedure, list both its obvious and its incidental uses, and describe several of the available forms, at the same time emphasizing the principles governing selection of the blanks best suited to particular needs in counseling. The very natural question as to the stability of a person's interests when ascertained in this way will be discussed;

also the possibility of disclosing certain important constituents or factors which enter into the make-up of his vocational interests.

Sources of inaccuracy in any procedure which has to rely on what a person says about his interests are chiefly of three kinds. These may be called the information error, the generalization error, and the prevarication error. A young man's statement that he dislikes working with tools at a carpenter's bench may be misleading as an indication of his most probable future attitude toward such work, because he has never had a chance to try it long enough to find out whether it is really distasteful or not—an information error; or because he dislikes the one shaky, poorly equipped bench in his attic at which he has worked—a generalization error; or because, although he has a sneaking fondness for just such work, he will not admit it because he thinks that nice white-collar people (of whom he hopes to be one) do not like it—a prevarication error. In spite of these undoubted sources of inaccuracy, and in spite of the difficulty of preparing lists of items which serve adequately as representative samples of the great variety of significant interests, paper-and-pencil inventories have served and will continue to serve two distinct purposes. The first of these may be called stimulative; the other, informative. These two functions of interest questionnaires should be kept clearly in mind when the merits of various blanks are being compared.

The stimulative function is illustrated in the use of a blank to encourage thoughtful self-scrutiny, in the very process of filling it out. A good blank leads a person to think about his interests, to notice his preferences for various kinds of activity, his satisfaction or dissatisfaction with different school subjects, types of reading and of recreation, varieties of work and conditions of employment, and his liking or dislike for various sorts of people; and to ponder the reasons for these indications of his interests together with their bearing on his educational and occupational plans. The blank should offer a representative sample list of items, educational, recreational, occupational, and personal, so arranged as to aid the individual who checks it in canvassing his different interests systematically. It will then draw his attention to interests which, without a planned review, he might overlook. It will also suggest to him some of the areas in which he might wish to develop interests hitherto dormant. In each of these ways the blank performs a stimulative function.

The informative function may be illustrated in the use of specially constructed blanks to disclose something otherwise obscure regarding a person's interests, such as the degree of similarity or dissimilarity between his interest pattern and the patterns characteristic of people pursuing certain fields of study or employment which he is contemplating.

For stimulating thoughtful consideration of interests by suggesting how to observe one's own likes and dislikes, Miner's "Analysis of Work Interests"[1]—a four-page folder developed at Carnegie Institute of Technology in 1918 and several times revised after extensive use—remains to this day (1936) one of the best questionnaires. Particularly with high-school students, it serves to focus attention on significant aspects of occupational interests. When a student's responses are later discussed in personal interview, he can gain an orientation toward the world of work in briefer time and more understandingly than is possible without the help of such a preliminary self-inventory.

A similar purpose led the writer to initiate in 1928 the preparation of a blank called "Aids to the Vocational Interview,"[2] designed for use with adults and advanced college students. This eight-page folder aims to draw out expressions of both vocational and avocational preferences, and to insure that they are passed in review in their relation to other vital facts, such as a person's finances, his home and family circumstances, his physical and mental condition, his traits of personality, and his abilities as indicated on his educational history and his record of work experience, due consideration being given also to the opportunities for employment, the financial and non-financial rewards and the facilities for training in the fields of occupation toward which he is drawn.

Strong's Vocational Interest Blank, described in detail on pages 354-357, is the most dependable means available for ascertaining the similarity between a person's interests and those of people actually engaged in specified occupations on the professional level. Strictly speaking, the scoring system shows whether the way in which a person marks the blank resembles the way in which people in each of the professions and occupations for which scoring scales are provided, have typically marked it. Strong has found in the course of his extensive researches that there are characteristic differences between the responses made by people representative of each of the specified

[1] Distributed by the C. H. Stoelting Company, Chicago. See J. B. Miner, "An Aid to the Analysis of Vocational Interests," *Journal of Educational Research*, 1922, 5:311-323.

[2] Distributed by the Psychological Corporation, 522 Fifth Avenue, New York. Described in full, with Manual of Instructions, in *How to Interview* by W. V. Bingham and B. V. Moore. New York: Harper & Brothers. Revised Edition, 1934, pp. 54-56 and 229-245.

occupational groups. That these responses are significant symptoms of interest pattern has been shown in several ways. Reference has already been made to the fact that occupational groups are differentiated by the scores, and it may here be added that most of the overlapping in the distributions occurs among occupations which are somewhat similar. Thus, when blanks filled out by chemists and architects are scored for resemblance to the interests of engineers, more than a third of them rate A; while scarcely any ministers, advertising men, or salesmen have this rating when their blanks are scored for engineering interest. In the second place, students in professional schools such as law, medicine, and engineering, have a high proportion of A or B ratings in their respective fields of interest. Thirdly, in so far as it has been possible to follow the subsequent vocational decisions of college students who have filled out the blank, it has been observed that a considerable number of them have eventually chosen to undertake training for the occupation in which they had the highest interest score; and of the others, a large proportion have chosen occupations not unlike those in which the blank had shown their interests to cluster. These facts encourage the belief that the scores tell something definitely pertinent to vocational planning.

2

Strong has ascertained the reliability of an interest score and its relative stability. This is of importance for the whole field of interest measurement, for if the pattern of a person's interests is quite unstable, if his likes and dislikes tend to fluctuate widely from year to year, there is little point in undertaking to help him to understand and appreciate just what his vocational interests are today. How closely, then, do his present scores predict what they will be a year hence, or after five years?

Of course a great many of one's expressions of specific likes and dislikes do change, some of them overnight. No one checks nearly all of the 420 items on the blank twice in the same way. But the majority of these inconstancies are in the responses to items which after all are not, for the person in question, the more significant indicators of his real interest pattern. Most of the items which for him really matter he tends to mark in the same way again and again. The dominant interests persist. If this were not so, it would be difficult to explain findings such as those in the accompanying table, which gives the correlations between scores obtained on test and re-test.

TABLE IV. CORRELATIONS BETWEEN TEST AND RE-TEST SCORES

Showing stability of interest over an interval of one year

	Scored for Interest of				
	Engineers	Physicians	Ministers	Lawyers	C.P.A.'s
247 college freshmen....	.91	.85	.79	.75	.62
150 high-school juniors..	.83	.73	.68	.65	.55

Over a five-year period the relative permanence of interest patterns has been ascertained by comparing the scores of 223 men tested with an earlier form of the blank in 1927 when they were college seniors, and again in 1932. For 21 occupational scales the average correlation between test and re-test was .75. These correlations are about as high as those which show the relative constancy of the I Q over a five-year period. Interest patterns do change with time, but rarely to such an extent that an A rating becomes a C.[3]

This generalization would seem to hold at least for adults and for younger people whose interests are fairly well informed and mature. As seen in Table IV, the correlations between scores on test and re-test after a year are uniformly higher for the college students than for the high-school boys, as is to be expected. Strong[4] presents evidence that interest patterns as measured by his blank change less and less as people mature, becoming fairly stable by age 25. Counselors quite properly place no great reliance on the scores of young people under 17, and when referring to these scores in interview, make appropriate allowances for inexperience and immaturity.

This does not mean that the blank should not be given to adolescents. When used to stimulate thought regarding vocational interests it has value in earlier years. Even when the blank is not scored, but is only inspected for indications of interests dominantly social or intellectual, scientific or linguistic, mechanical or commercial, it furnishes many a good clue to be explored in personal interview. The reasons for certain preferences and clusterings of interests can be inquired into, and discussed in their relation to impending educational choices as well as to more remote ambitions. A blank like Strong's is not simply an instrument of measurement: it can be an educational device as well.

3

Other interest inventories have been devised for various purposes. Manson's Occupational Interest Blank for Women, described

[3] For the precise meaning of these letter ratings, see page 356.

[4] E. K. Strong, Jr., *Change of Interests with Age.* Stanford University Press, 1931.

on page 358, is similar to Strong's in purpose, but is less searching and less reliable. Garretson and Symonds' Interest Questionnaire for High School Students, described on page 360, is designed for boys only, in the eighth and ninth grades, and can be scored so as to indicate the resemblance between a boy's interests and those of students in each of three types of high school—academic, technical and commercial. Hepner's Vocational Interest Test for Men undertakes the Herculean task of furnishing Vocational Interest Quotients indicative of the similarity of the man's interest pattern to that of the average experienced member of each of 20 skilled trades, 24 business occupations, and 24 professions; and for women, scoring keys for 24 equally disparate occupations. But because of the inclusion of many general non-diagnostic items among the 167 on the blank, and the small numbers in the occupational groups used in preparing the scales, the resulting V I Q's do not differentiate well between occupational groups, and their use in guidance cannot be recommended. For a blank known as the Oberlin Vocational Interest Inquiry, Hartson and Bretlinger[5] selected 190 pairs of contrasted specific activities which the student compares. These have been so chosen as to bring out preferences for major occupational activities in a manner illuminating to both student and counselor. Brainard and Stewart's Specific Interest Test,[6] calls for an estimate of the degree of enjoyment found in each of many specific activities. These in turn are grouped under twenty headings such as "Skilled Manual—Likes to use hands"; "Physical—Likes to do work involving bodily exertion"; "Social—Enjoys group activities, prefers not to work alone," etc. The interest profile thus secured need not be regarded as a very reliable measure of enduring interests; but the blank has proved to be an aid in sharpening a student's thinking about his trends of interest.

4

To simplify the measurement of interests and at the same time to make the results precise and significant, it is highly desirable to be able to identify not only a person's specific likes and dislikes, but also the major trends of interest, and particularly, if possible, the primary factors which, in combination, account for these trends. It is reasonable to suppose that running through numerous specific interests are certain fundamental ones—"primary factors," so-called—

[5] *Cf.* Douglas Fryer, *The Measurement of Interests*, pp. 38-41.

[6] Available in four forms: B, for boys (high-school students and college entrants); M, for men; G, for girls; and W, for women.

which contribute in greater or lesser degree to the interest pattern. That these factors may be few in number has been pointed out by Thurstone.[7] Using a table of intercorrelations of interest scores for eighteen occupations supplied by Strong, he showed that nearly all of the relationships between these scores can be accounted for by assuming four factors. He then worked out the loading of each of these four factors for each of the eighteen occupations. It would be most illuminating if we could identify and measure in an individual the strength of these four interest factors. What are they? Factor X_1 —whatever it may eventually come to be called—has high positive loadings in the professions of chemistry, engineering, psychology, architecture, agriculture and medicine; and negative loadings (dislike) in the professions of advertising, life insurance selling and real estate selling. It seemed to Thurstone that scientific interest is probably a factor that would differentiate these professions in the manner indicated, and so he tentatively named this factor "interest in science." Following the same procedure, he chose as possibly appropriate names for factors X_2, X_3, and X_4, "interest in language," "interest in people," and "interest in business." Factorial analysis of other tables of intercorrelations based on data which include responses to items different from those in Strong's inventory, and starting with a different principal vector, may sometime bring into prominence factors appropriately named "interest in beauty," "interest in nature," "interest in mechanical manipulation," "interest in intellectual activity," "interest in money values," and so on. Measurement of the strength of such factors in the interests of people pursuing each of the leading fields of occupation would then furnish bases of comparison with an individual's interest profile. When psychologists have analyzed vocational abilities into a relatively small number of primary abilities—a task on which they are also hard at work—it may appear that there is definable, corresponding to each primary ability, a primary interest.

Thurstone is now (1936) in the midst of an inquiry into the factors of vocational interest. He selected eighty occupations for a Vocational Interest Schedule which 3,400 college students checked, expressing their liking, indifference, or dislike for each occupation in the list. Their interests as thus recorded were then examined by the centroid method of factorial analysis described in his volume, *The Vectors of Mind*.[8] He wished to test the hypothesis that these

[7] L. L. Thurstone, "A Multiple Factor Study of Vocational Interests," *Personnel Journal*, 1931, 10:198-205.
[8] Chicago: University of Chicago Press, 1935.

vocational interests are not independent, but that the strength of each one can be expressed as a linear function of a relatively few reference interests. Eight factors proved sufficient to account for the relationships between these eighty vocational interests. In other words, an individual can be described—in so far as his interests are expressed by the manner in which he checks the blank—in terms of eight scores. Each of the eight reference factors is best defined in terms of the vocations that have significant projections on it. Thus, he says,[9]

A commercial interest factor has significant positive loadings in the following vocations: advertiser, auto salesman, banker, building contractor, certified public accountant, landscape gardener, manufacturer, office manager, club secretary, factory manager, florist, printer, private secretary, retail merchant, sales manager, stockbroker, tax expert, and business manager. There can hardly be any debate about the naming of this factor.

A legal interest factor has significant and positive loadings in the following occupations: judge, criminal lawyer, corporation lawyer, clergyman, congressman, diplomatic service, economist, foreign correspondent, public speaker, banker, historian, tax expert, stock broker. The naming of each of these reference factors is determined also by inspection of the size of the projections. The largest projections on this factor are the definitely legal professions.

An athletic factor seems to have as its principal characteristic an interest in physical activity. The occupations which have large positive projections on this factor are as follows: athletic director, cattle-rancher, newspaper reporter, explorer, forest ranger, press agent, professional athlete, radio announcer, secret service, ship officer, army officer.

An academic factor seems to have as its principal characteristic an interest in books. The vocations with large positive projections on this factor are as follows: historian, librarian, mathematician, philosopher, college professor, economist, high-school teacher, psychologist, sociologist, vocational counselor.

One of the most general interest factors we have called "descriptive" in that it seems to be characterized by a general interest in people and in things. It seems to be largely verbal in character and rather less analytical than some of the subsequent factors. The occupations with positive loadings in this factor are as follows: actor, advertiser, art critic, artist, journalist, musician, reporter, novelist, orchestra conductor, philosopher, explorer, foreign correspondent, poet, press agent, psychologist, printer, radio announcer, sculptor, secret service, diplomatic service. It has been suggested that this factor be called "humanistic."

A biological factor has positive projections of the following occupations: biologist, botanist, chemist, pharmacist, physician, dentist, geologist, scientist, surgeon.

A physical-science factor has positive projections of the following vocations:

[9] "Factorial Analysis of Vocational Interests," a paper read at a meeting of the American Psychological Association in Ann Arbor, September, 1935.

architect, astronomer, building contractor, chemist, inventor, manufacturer, mathematician, engineer, philosopher, physicist, scientist. This interest factor differs distinctly from the biological group, and it seems necessary to conclude that the interests of college students in physical science and in biological science are rather distinct entities.

An art factor is indicated, but the schedule did not contain a sufficient number of the art occupations to make its determination with certainty. In further experimental schedules the list of art occupations will be extended in order that the existence of a separate art factor may be determined.

These reference factors are not all uncorrelated. Several of them have intercorrelations of .25 or .30 in the experimental population, but most of them have zero intercorrelations.

In arranging the schedule for practical use provision has been made for plotting a profile of each subject showing his positive or negative rating on each of the eight reference interests. This profile would be of aid in vocational and educational counseling.

5

Thurstone's factorial approach to the problem of interest measurement is most promising. It is too early to say how useful his present blank and the interest profile it yields will prove to be in connection with the counseling of college students and adults, but we may compare it with Strong's in order to illustrate several points to be kept in mind when selecting any blank for practical use.

Here, as in any similar comparison of available blanks, we may ask first: Which is the more effective in inducing thoughtful self-appraisal on the part of the student who fills it out? Which blank, as it is being checked, draws attention more sharply to the fact of differences in appeal of various occupational fields, and helps the student to recognize his own preferences for different kinds of vocational activity, conditions of work, and personal associates? In short, which of these blanks excels in stimulating the student?

Next, which is the more informing? What do the scores tell? Is one of the blanks superior to the other in the nature and accuracy of the facts it brings out regarding important factors in the student's interests, and the similarity or difference between his constellations of interests and those of people engaged in occupations he may be considering? How relevant are these facts to his educational and occupational planning?

Third, which blank offers more aid during the counseling interview, not only in the final scores it provides but also in the specific responses, inspection of which may bring forward points to be reviewed with the student personally? Which blank is the more likely to draw attention to vocational areas of probable interest which otherwise might escape consideration?

Finally, which is the more convenient to use, the more economical of time and money?

With these questions in mind, we note, first, that Thurstone's blank undertakes just one thing: to measure the strength of each of seven relatively independent factors of vocational interest.[10] The bearing of these scores may then be discussed during the interview. Strong's scoring system, on the other hand, measures the similarity between a person's interest pattern and that of people following each occupation for which the blank is scored. It puts the question, "Does this person tend to like the same things that people following these occupations like?" The strength of certain interest factors—social, commercial, linguistic, scientific—may be roughly estimated by inspection of the groups of similar occupations within which the person's high scores tend to cluster. A grouping of occupations according to similarities of interest pattern is found on page 355.

Secondly, Thurstone's blank takes less time to administer. In its present form it lists 72 occupations and within the space of a few moments a student can record his reactions to these items, checking those he likes, those he dislikes, and those to which he is indifferent. Strong makes use of 420 items: 100 occupations, 54 amusements, 39 school subjects, 52 activities, 53 peculiarities of people, all to be checked L, I, or D ("like," "indifferent," or "dislike"); also 10 activities from which are to be chosen the 3 that the person would most enjoy and the 3 he would enjoy least; 10 factors affecting work, from which the 3 considered most important and the three least important, are to be checked; 10 eminent names, to be checked to indicate "the 3 men you would most like to have been; also the 3 you would least like to have been"; 10 positions in a club or society, to be similarly evaluated; 42 pairs of items to be compared as to interest; and self ratings on 40 characteristics. Even when a person follows the instruction to work rapidly, he needs at least twenty or thirty minutes in which to complete the blank.

Thirdly, Strong's blank is much more tedious and expensive to score, even when all that is desired is to ascertain the rating for a single occupation. Thurstone's is a model of simplicity and convenience.

[10] The current edition provides seven scoring stencils, no attempt being made at present to score the eighth factor, interest in art.

However—and this fourth point is crucial—much more is known today about the meaning of the Strong scores than about the Thurstone profile which must be interpreted with extreme caution until the facts are ascertained as to the stability of the factors measured and their weights in the vocational interests of people actually entering and following the various occupations.

Finally, compare the usefulness of the two blanks during the vocational interview itself. Either furnishes a good point of departure. The student who has filled it out is keen to discuss his interests further. When shown his scores, he is likely to recognize some of the characteristics brought into relief. He may question their pertinence, but he will probably leave the interview determined to observe his own preferences closely, and before undertaking preparation for any field of occupation, to learn enough about it so that he will feel confident of his capacity to learn to like the work and the associations it involves. Both before and during the interview, inspection of the way individual items have been checked—as well as the numerical scores—will suggest to the counselor certain points to be raised. For this purpose Strong's blank is rich in resources which Thurstone's lacks.

No one blank can be all things to all counselors. Nor to all clients. Neither of these blanks is satisfactory for the less mature pupils in high school, nor for persons whose vocational future probably will be in the manual occupations or the more routine clerical fields. Both are for students and adults of college calibre. When so employed, it seems clear that each to some extent performs both stimulative and informative functions; but that Strong's—in spite of the cost in time required to administer and to score it—is today much the more serviceable aid in counseling. In some situations both blanks might advantageously be employed: Thurstone's as a quick, convenient means of ascertaining the strength of certain factors presumably dominant in the individual's vocational preferences; and Strong's, for a more detailed inquiry.

6

Such are the main considerations which govern choice among questionnaires and tests offered for use in helping a person to clarify his understanding of his vocational interests. After they have been administered, the results should be conservatively interpreted in personal interview (or, if time presses, in a group conference), as follows: the counselor emphasizes that while a person's specific interests are subject to wide fluctuation, their general pattern becomes fairly stable as he approaches maturity. His degree of interest in the kind of work he plans to undertake is one symptom of his aptitude for it. The tests may help him to a clearer realization of the nature of his present preferences. In the light of this understanding he may then be encouraged to widen his interests, to concentrate on the more intensive cultivation of those specific interests which are seen to be most in harmony with his capacities, or to seek opportunity for observation and experience that will further clarify his self-understanding.

The decisive test of interest—as of ability—will always be the occupational tryout. So counselors wisely urge students to make full use of opportunities to find out how it actually feels to be doing work of the sort they think they would enjoy.

The notion that interest may be safely construed as an indication of potential ability may well be discounted, and the point stressed that evidences of capacity should be looked for elsewhere. Interest inventories have their chief informative value in hinting at an answer to the question as to whether, granted that a person has the necessary talents, he will probably find the field of occupation he is considering a congenial and pleasant one. Even though a man could learn to be a highly competent watchmaker or sailor or circus performer, it does not necessarily follow that he would like the work, or that he would enjoy the privilege of close association with his fellows in that occupation. But when he finds evidence that he does like the same things that most people in a given occupation like, and expresses a distaste for the very things they dislike, the inference naturally follows that he would probably find this calling congenial.

For, after all, the degree of satisfaction a person finds in his daily employment is for him quite as important as is his proficiency in it. America has been prone to overemphasize the economic and social values of productivity, efficiency, competence; while the values attaching to an individual's enjoyment of his work have been too frequently forgotten. When looking for indications of capacity to learn to do well the tasks of an occupation, we should not forget to search also for symptoms of capacity to develop a liking for them. Even though tests of interest may be of trivial use as indicators of *ability*, they nevertheless have worth in their own right; for they do furnish symptoms of capacity for realizing those deep-seated personal values of *enjoyment* accruing only to the man who likes his work.

7

To recapitulate: The measurement of a person's present interests is intended to provide symptoms indicative of what his interests are likely to be in the future. This information is sought because, when reliably ascertained, it has four possible uses: first, to indicate whether he will probably *like the actual work* of the occupation he is considering well enough to become absorbed in it and stick to it; second, to indicate whether he will probably find himself among *congenial associates*, with interests similar to his own; third (and this is a remote third), to provide symptoms of his future *abilities*; fourth, to suggest *alternative fields* of occupation which may not yet have been seriously considered.

Stated in terms of the person's own concern, expressions of interest skillfully elicited have value chiefly as symptoms of his capacity to acquire a liking for the work in question; next, as symptoms of congeniality with others in the occupation; and only incidentally, as indicators of capacity to acquire the needed proficiency, without which, to be sure, there can be little enjoyment of the work.

For the counselor, interest inventories and the scores they yield are of assistance in focusing attention on the problem, furnishing points of discussion in the vocational interview, and indicating specific needs for further experience as a basis for making in the future more dependable appraisals of the person's real interests.

Chapter VIII

ACHIEVEMENT TESTS AS INDICATORS OF APTITUDES

1. Past accomplishments indicate present capacities. When achievement tests are used to estimate ability to make further progress, they serve as tests of aptitude. 2. Measures of occupational proficiency: trade tests. 3. Tests of scholastic achievement: Iowa Placement tests; Cooperative Test Service tests; other representative examinations. 4. Conclusion of Part One.

1

THE range of choice among tests for use in measuring aptitudes is not limited to those which happen to have been called tests of aptitude. The whole gamut of educational achievement tests, occupational proficiency tests, trade tests, intelligence tests, interest tests, personality tests, and character tests—all are available for consideration. It is not the name of the test that matters, nor the purpose for which it was first prepared; but the closeness of correspondence between scores in the test and subsequent achievement in the type of activity demanded by the occupation in question. If it is known that those who do well in the test are more likely to succeed in the occupation than those who do poorly, it can be used as a test of aptitude, whatever its designation.

It is peculiarly unfortunate that writers about tests have left the impression in some quarters that a sharp line must be drawn between tests of achievement and tests of aptitude. The difference really lies, not in the tests themselves, but in the uses to which they are put. As a matter of fact, many achievement tests are at the same time very good tests of aptitude. An achievement test in physics, a trade test in automobile valve-setting, and a proficiency test in the use of a slide rule are alike in measuring acquired abilities. They indicate how well certain things have been learned. Of course. But that is no bar to the use of a person's scores in these very tests in estimating his aptitudes for learning something more. When a young man scores high in each of these three achievement tests—physics, valve-setting, and manipulation of the slide rule—one is justified in hazarding the opinion that he has some aptitude for engineering work.

Two pattern-maker apprentices after a year in the same shop take a trade test to measure the proficiency they have gained. One scores very high, giving the foreman ample reason to infer that he has more aptitude for pattern-making and will probably be able to do the work of a journeyman several months sooner than his fellow apprentice who makes a low score on this trade test.

We give an achievement test in arithmetic at the close of a school term. We note how well a pupil has mastered the topics covered and which ones he ought to review. He receives a mark of D, indicative of less than average achievement under the conditions which have prevailed. A principal who has observed that pupils in his school with a record of several D's in arithmetic rarely pass in algebra courses, would be warranted in using this achievement test as a means of appraising aptitude for algebra; just as an employer uses it as one symptom of an applicant's aptitude for becoming a satisfactory pay-roll clerk. The term "aptitude test" must not be restricted in its use to those tests designed to measure individual differences in advance of any training in the function tested. Any test, whatever its label, is a test of aptitude in so far as the scores are known to be indicative of future potentialities.

To be sure, tests which have been constructed primarily to measure a person's abilities before there has been opportunity for special training of those abilities are usually called aptitude tests; while those which have been designed to measure the results of training are not inappropriately designated as tests of achievement or proficiency. But a person's capacity to profit from further training is disclosed by the ratio of his present accomplishment to the amount of training he has received to date, as well as by the abilities he may show in advance of training. It follows that any achievement test, when used for this purpose, becomes also a test of aptitude.

Moreover, it must not be forgotten that aptitude tests in the narrower sense of the term—tests intended for use in advance of any special training in the abilities measured—tell us what the individual does or achieves under the conditions set by the examinations. They are properly called aptitude tests only when the measures they yield are known to be indicative of probable levels of future attainment. This generalization holds equally of all kinds of measures of individual differences whether called tests of personality, knowledge, interest, proficiency, character, æsthetic judgment, educability, intelligence, or special ability. Any one of them is an aptitude test if the scores have been shown to be indicative of subsequent educational or vocational progress.

2

Achievement tests most likely to be of value in counseling are of two sorts: measures of occupational proficiency, usually called trade tests, and standardized examinations in school subjects.

Trade tests have been developed as aids in ascertaining the extent to which a person claiming experience in an occupation already possesses the technical knowledge and proficiency of an expert in it, or of a journeyman, an apprentice, or a mere novice.[1] Many of these tests are oral, consisting of a battery of questions which call for no elaborate replies, but which can be answered in a word by the person who really knows the trade, while the novice, no matter how bright he may be, is at a loss. Some trade tests make use of pictures of the tools or apparatus of the occupation to facilitate the questioning. Still others are performance tests. The examinee is provided with specified materials and tools of his trade, and asked to turn out designated products which can then be objectively scored for excellence by compari-

[1] A reader wishing to familiarize himself with this field may well begin with the volume by J. C. Chapman, *Trade Tests*, New York: Henry Holt and Company, Inc., 1921. While giving the theory of trade test construction and administration, this book describes in detail oral trade tests for carpenter, bricklayer, pipe-fitter, plumber, structural-steel erector, electrician, lineman and cableman, foundryman, automatic-screw-machine operator, die-sinker, drop-forger, butcher, typewriter maker and repairman, compositor, surveyor, tailor, radio operator, and oxyacetylene welder; picture tests for carpenter, electrician, lathe operator, horseshoer, boilermaker, cobbler, and welder; and performance tests for pattern-maker, steam-fitter, sheet-metal worker, interior wireman, bench hand and assembler, lathe operator, blacksmith, typist, stenographer, and truck-driver; and a written group test for bricklayer.

A volume descriptive of oral and picture trade tests less rigorously constructed than the army tests described by Chapman, but up to date in terminology and a convenient help in interviewing persons with trade experience, is *Interview Aids and Trade Questions for Employment Offices*, by L. A. Thompson, Jr., New York: Harper & Brothers, 1936. The U. S. Public Employment Service is supplying its interviewers from time to time with tests developed by its Division of Standards and Research. The director of this Division, W. H. Stead, informs us that the preparation of trade tests for jobs in the construction industry is progressing. Oral tests for forty-five occupations have been given preliminary trial at research centers in seven cities. Final standardization of the questions is in progress and questions for about twenty construction jobs have been made available for employment interviewers.

son with a scale of norms; or he is directed to do a specified task and is graded on the speed and skill with which he does it. A standard test of proficiency in typing from rough copy, such as the one included in O'Rourke's Civil Service Examination for Stenographers and Typists,[2] furnishes a good example of a performance trade test.

3

In drawing attention to representative tests of school achievement and of aptitude for special subjects of study, we shall first mention the Iowa Placement Examinations issued by the Bureau of Educational Research and Service at the University of Iowa under the direction of G. D. Stoddard; and the achievement tests currently made available by the American Council on Education, through the Cooperative Test Service of which Ben D. Wood is director. These tests are particularly valuable when counseling high-school seniors and college freshmen regarding their academic work. Some of the scores have obvious bearing on vocational decisions also.

The following extracts descriptive of the Iowa Placement Examinations and their uses are from "Suggestions for Testing Programs at the College Level."[3]

The examinations consist of two series—*aptitude tests* which measure the particular mental abilities related to subsequent success in a subject, and *training tests* which are essentially standardized achievement tests of sufficient scope and difficulty to be valid and reliable at the college level. The aptitude examinations, by the nature of their construction, more closely approach the usual mental-ability tests. However, they draw upon learned elementary materials when these are of value in predicting subject-matter success. . . .

The *Iowa Placement Examinations* may be had in four series, A and B, X and Y. Eleven examinations are available in forms A and B, covering aptitude and training in English, mathematics, chemistry, physics, French, Spanish, and general foreign-language aptitude. In the X and Y series the tests are available for chemistry aptitude and chemistry training, English training, mathematics aptitude, French training, and Spanish training. The reliability coefficients for the examinations range from .89 to .94. Each test has been carefully validated. For the prediction of achievement in single subjects, correlations between single examinations and course grades run from .51 to .66. When used in battery form for the prediction of general college achievement, correlations with first-year achievement have been secured as high as .75, with the average about .70.

[2] Obtainable from the Psychological Corporation. See page 157.

[3] A pamphlet by D. E. Feder, distributed by the Bureau of Educational Research and Service, University of Iowa, Iowa City. The price of each of the Iowa Placement Examinations is $3.50 a hundred, including manual of directions, key, and norms.

Complete norms based on the performance of college freshmen are furnished with all four series. . . .

A battery of tests which has yielded highly satisfactory results is the following:

1. Iowa High School Content Examination[4]
2. English Training Examination
3. Iowa Silent Reading Test[4]
4. Mathematics Aptitude Examination

From such a battery it is possible to derive a highly meaningful composite score which may be transmuted into percentile ranks, T-scores or standard scores. The individual tests may be variously weighted in making up the composite. At the University of Iowa the usual practice has been to multiply the Mathematics Aptitude Test score by three and leave the others unweighted. The composite score thus obtained correlates about .95 with tests of general mental ability at the college level. However, the composite itself and its components are much more valuable than a single general mental-ability score because they take direct account of the abilities involved in college work of various types. The importance of this may be seen not only in the higher correlations with actual achievement when the Placement Examinations are used, but also in the greatly increased effectiveness for diagnostic and remedial work. With these results at hand, personnel departments are able to judge the relative efficiency of a student, to make suggestions as to the kind and amount of work he should carry, etc. . . . The tests are also being used for vocational guidance, with a noticeable degree of satisfaction. . . .[5]

The placement examinations may serve as diagnostic tests to reveal special sources of difficulty and as prognostic tests for the indication of the quality of work which may be expected from each individual.

A battery of tests such as outlined above may be employed with confidence in the following ways:

1. To aid in selecting and admitting students.
2. To afford a basis for prediction of the character of the work that each student will do in college.
3. To assist in deciding how much work a student can carry.
4. To section classes for instructional purposes on the basis of mental ability.
5. To deal more effectively with students who are not well oriented in their college work; e.g., students who fail their work but possess adequate mental ability; students who work hard but do not succeed; students who lack interest in their work; and students on probation for various delinquencies.

[4] These are not in the Iowa Placement Examination series, but may be purchased from the Bureau of Educational Research and Service, University of Iowa, Iowa City.

[5] See, for example, Henry C. Link, "Vocational Guidance in Practice Today." In *Our Children: A Handbook for Parents.* Edited by Dorothy Canfield Fisher and Sidonie Matsner Gruenberg. New York: Viking Press, 1932. Pp. 268-281.

6. To give scientific aid in vocational guidance and placement.
7. To furnish a basis for the diagnosis of individual and class weaknesses.
8. To enable comparative studies of intellectual levels as between classes, colleges, and college years.
9. To enable high schools and preparatory schools to survey their seniors or graduates in order to determine probable fitness for college studies.

The Cooperative Test Service prepares and issues each year, about May 1st, examinations in the fundamental subject-matter of many courses taught in junior and senior high school and in college. The great advantage of these tests is that, being available in several equivalent forms, they make possible the measurement of individual growth year after year. Nearly all of these examinations have reliabilities above .90 and may appropriately be used for individual counseling. All are distinctly superior in this respect to ordinary examinations, as well as to school marks.[6]

Representative of tests for use in upper elementary grades and junior high school is the New Stanford Achievement Test (Advanced Examination).[7] The ten examinations which constitute this battery, each available in five equivalent forms, cover the following subjects:

1. Reading: Paragraph Meaning
2. Reading: Word Meaning
3. Dictation: Spelling
4. Language Usage
5. Literature
6. History and Civics
7. Geography
8. Physiology and Hygiene
9. Arithmetical Reasoning
10. Arithmetical Computation

Of these examinations, the ones most likely to be of interest when counseling with reference to aptitudes are the tests in reading, spelling, and arithmetic; and these, fortunately, have the highest reliabilities. The scores in Test 4, Language Usage, are also of importance but are less reliable and should not be used in individual guidance unless supplemented by other measures; for example, those pro-

[6] A list of the examinations currently issued by the Cooperative Test Service is given on pages 362-364.

[7] By T. L. Kelley, G. M. Ruch, and L. M. Terman. Yonkers: World Book Co., 1929. $2.00 for 25. Guide, 15 cents, contains norms, reliabilities, and suggestions regarding use and interpretation of results.

vided by O'Rourke's Survey and Achievement Tests of English Usage,[8] or by scores in other school achievement tests.[9]

4

The conclusion of this chapter on achievement tests is a convenient stopping-place from which to look back over the road we have been traveling.

As we have just noted, measurements of past accomplishments both in and out of school, when judged in relation to the length and character of the training or experience which has preceded them, provide the surest ground for estimating the possibilities of further progress. Hence the importance of using the most reliable achievement tests to be had, and of maintaining over a period of years a cumulative record of the scores.

These measures do not, however, supply all the information needed. Interests—as we saw in the chapters immediately preceding—should also be ascertained, their growth facilitated in so far as possible, and any changes in them made part of the record.

[8] For Grades 7 to 13. Three forms available; 2 cents each. Industrial norms as well as school grade norms are given in L. J. O'Rourke, *Rebuilding the English Usage Curriculum*, price 50 cents. Obtainable from the Psychological Corporation, 522 Fifth Avenue, New York, or from the Psychological Institute, 3506 Patterson St., N.W., Washington, D. C.

[9] A complete list of scholastic achievement tests is not in place in this volume. Many are described in the catalogs of the publishers and distributors of tests listed on page 362. The following tests are among those available through the Psychological Corporation:

The Metropolitan Achievement Tests (by R. D. Allen and associates), Advanced Battery, for grades 7 and 8, include tests in spelling, reading, vocabulary, arithmetic fundamentals and problems, English, literature, history and geography. $2.00 for 25. Supervisor's Manual, 25 cents.

The Modern School Achievement Test, for elementary grades, is a battery of ten examinations, in reading comprehension, reading speed, arithmetic computation, arithmetic reasoning, spelling, health knowledge, language usage, history and civics, geography, and elementary science. Two forms. $7.55 a hundred. A shorter battery comprises the examinations in reading, arithmetic, spelling, and language usage. $5.25 a hundred.

The Progressive Achievement Tests (E. W. Tiegs and W. W. Clark) furnish a diagnostic profile of the student's abilities in five tests and nineteen sub-tests of reading vocabulary, reading comprehension, arithmetic reasoning, arithmetic fundamentals, and language. The price of the Intermediate Battery for grades 7 to 9 is $1.25 for 25; of the Advanced Battery for high school and college, $1.50 for 25.

The Sones-Harry High School Achievement Test is in four parts: language and literature, mathematics, natural science, and social studies. Two forms, $1.90 for 25.

The Carnegie High School Achievement Examination, constructed by Cleeton and Shaffer for use with high-school students and college freshmen, is a sixteen-page booklet to measure ability in reading, English, mathematics, sciences, social studies, German, French, and Spanish. Two forms. 10 cents.

The unfolding of intelligence, too, should be measured periodically. In the absence of dependable measures of an individual's linguistic, mathematical, and mechanical intelligence, not only may the significance of his school achievements be misconstrued, but the guidance of his educational and vocational ambitions misdirected.

Intelligence, interests, past achievements—what other information is needed in order that educational plans may lead in the direction of a suitable vocational goal? This information is of three kinds: first, acquaintance with the fields of occupation; second, knowledge of the abilities and training they demand; and third, the facts about the individual's specific aptitudes. His special talents must be ferreted out—as we saw in Chapter I—if he is to gain a clear realization of his fitness for entering a particular course of training. His counselor must help him to secure and to assimilate such information, as well as the facts about his intelligence, his interests, and the significance of his past accomplishments.

How is this to be done?

Within the confusing welter of occupations which people actually do follow, there must be some feasible means of orientation. To the discovery of such means, Part Two of this book is devoted. The first chapter simplifies the preliminary task of classification. Succeeding chapters canvass, one after the other, the main fields of occupation in quest of the aptitudes which they require. In each instance the question will be raised as to the availability of tests and other aids which might be of assistance in disclosing such aptitudes.

Only after completing this excursion through the world of work shall we venture, in Part Three, to give a more technical description of the practice of testing, in order to formulate the general principles which govern the choice of specific tests, the manner of administering them, and the interpretation of the measures they yield.

PART TWO

ORIENTATION

Within the World of Work

Chapter IX

THE WORLD OF WORK

1. How occupations may be classified. 2. Hierarchies arranged according to educational requirements; intelligence; earnings; prestige; numerical importance. 3. Changes of trend in occupational opportunities. 4. Cultural and practical reasons for the study of occupations. Facts which challenge students' attention.

1

If it were possible to look at a cinema showing people actively pursuing all the various callings by which livelihoods are earned—in mines and marts, on farms and fishing-banks, before the microphone and the footlights, at the bench and at the linotype; in police courts, embassies, textile-mills, beauty shops and churches; harvesting, embalming, legislating, riveting, teaching, cooking, inventing, boxing; leading soldiers into battle, ministering to the insane, polishing silver, painting portraits, catering to weddings, fighting fires, planting forests; or managing universities, prisons, lunch wagons and stock exchanges—the bewildered spectator might well exclaim, "How is it possible to schematize these thousands of occupations, to bring them into some semblance of order, so that the vocational aptitudes which they require may be compared?" To this question the present chapter is dedicated.

It may be granted instantly that no description of the world of work can do justice to the richness of its variety. The Federal Bureau of the Census recognizes 557 separate occupational groups under which are classified upwards of 25,000 occupational designations; and certain of these titles, such as "mechanical engineer," "trained nurse," or "automobile repairman," actually are blanket terms, each applicable to a number of easily distinguishable pursuits.

Moreover, within any occupation—surgeon, steam-shovel operator, manicurist, editor—the actual work performed varies from one position to another. It is not standardized. Even among the manicurists holding identical positions in a single barber shop may be found a wide range of methods of operation and of individual skills. An occupation is not a static, stereotyped way of earning a livelihood, nor are all who follow it equally gifted and competent. They do not all do precisely the same things or operate in identical ways. The closer one looks at people at work, the more heterogeneous their occupations appear.

The thousands of callings may nevertheless be examined from a few very significant angles; and when this is done, order replaces the apparently baffling chaos. The differences that really matter are one after another brought into focus.

The best clues to a systematic and useful survey of the world of work are furnished by the questions most often raised when a person is planning his future in the light of his fitness for a certain occupation.

These questions were listed on page 5 of the introductory chapter. They dealt with the level of general education expected of people who enter a given occupation; the length of the time required for specialized training; the minimal and optimal intelligence levels of the people who follow it; the special talents needed; the kinds of work to be done, and the surroundings, which may be congenial to one person and not to another; the remuneration, financial and non-financial; the security of employment, opportunities for advancement and keenness of competition; and the social prestige attaching to the occupation. Such questions, we observed, can be answered if at all in comparative terms. The occupation is more, or less, social—or overcrowded, or stable, or esteemed—than certain others. It may, therefore, be ranked in comparison with them—assigned its position within a hierarchy—with reference to the particular aspect under discussion.

2

A schematic picture of the world of occupations ought, then, to reveal them in a series of scales, dimensions, or hierarchies. At different levels on one of these scales are representative occupations arranged according to the average earnings of those who follow them. On another, an age scale, these same occupations are regrouped to show at a glance the age range within which people most appropriately enter each one. The total amount of schooling, including the background of general education ordinarily expected of persons following that calling plus the period required to complete the necessary specialized education, furnishes the basis for a third arrangement. A similar hierarchy lists the occupations according to the educational level at which the specialized vocational preparation ordinarily begins. Another shows the length of time in weeks or years required to complete this special preparation. Other desired groupings are in terms of the relative demand and supply of workers, the relative importance of special talents in the occupation, the range of opportunities which it opens up, the level of general intelligence characteristic of the majority of the people who follow it, and the prestige which attaches to it. Still other useful schemes of classification will occur to every student of the subject.

At the upper end of the educational scale, for example, are the learned professions: medicine, law, divinity, scientific research; and at the other, such occupations as barber or fisherman which can be learned readily enough without any general schooling whatever. In between are grouped the occupations which ordinarily require a background of elementary schooling, junior high school, senior high school, or some college work, as the case may be, before entrance on specialized professional education or vocational training. Every counselor has such a hierarchy in mind. He may put it in the form of a chart designed to answer the student's question, "What kind of occupations is it appropriate for me to consider if I can first achieve a specified level of general education?" Or, "What amount of general education should I plan to complete before beginning to specialize in preparation for a specified occupation?"

The first answer to such questions is naturally in terms of minimal educational requirements; but whenever family circumstances and the scholastic aptitudes of the client indicate that he may well undertake to secure more than this minimum of general education before specializing, the counselor encourages him to continue. His range of possible vocational choice is thereby widened. The occupations farther down the scale will still be open for his consideration. Men who have graduated from a university have earned a good livelihood at stenography. A college woman who does not choose to teach, or who finds that profession for the time being overcrowded, may go behind the sales counter or manage a tearoom in competition with people who never finished high school. To be sure, the number of persons eligible to compete for work in the lower-level occupations is in general greater than in the higher-level fields of employment, and the prevailing rate of earnings in them is correspondingly depressed. But, general education beyond the minimal requirements for occupational success adds to the richness of life, and, within limits, enhances the likelihood of ultimate advancement within the occupation finally entered. These are weighty reasons for encouraging nearly everyone to secure as much general education as his endowment of scholastic aptitude indicates that he can profitably assimilate—provided, of course, that he can plan so that he will not have to leave school and seek employment before he has finished both the general and the vocational phases of his educational program. At the completion of the entire span of his formal schooling he should not find himself unprepared to compete for employment in the occupational field of his choice. Such points as these are convincingly brought home by a counselor who keeps in mind a schedule of typical occupations arranged according to an educational scale.

An educational-vocational scale ought to be expressed not only in terms of school attainment requisite for the successive levels of occupation, but also in terms of the aptitudes for acquiring these designated levels of formal education; for an inquirer is interested to know not only what academic preparation is necessary if he is to enter a certain field of work; he wants quite as much an estimate of his chances of progressing up the educational ladder to that point. Tests of scholastic aptitude have here an obvious vocational significance.

The hierarchy of occupations on a scale of intelligence has already been illustrated in Chapter V. As we there observed, a comparison between a person's intelligence as measured by standard tests and that of groups representing different occupational fields may be of real help to him in choosing an occupation in which he is likely to find himself satisfactorily placed, and gives emphasis to the often-neglected question as to whether he would really find himself happier in an occupation in which he would be more intelligent than the majority of his associates, or less intelligent.

Even the most cursory inspection of the world of work cannot overlook its economic dimension—comparative financial rewards. The facts regarding actual annual earnings of the people who follow different callings are not easy to ascertain. It is hard enough to find out the nominal hourly or weekly wage rates or monthly salaries; but these, especially in seasonal occupations or in unstable industries, are not closely related to annual incomes. A sample scale, showing the salary range of office occupations at each level from errand boy to actuary, is found on page 147.

While the order in which occupations are ranked on any scale of earnings would appear to be quite similar to those in the lists previously mentioned, the differences apparent on closer inspection emphasize the fact that society does not always remunerate those who serve it in direct proportion to their intelligence, special talents, or schooling. There are ways other than financial in which service may be rewarded. The girl who lays aside her factory apron to take a lower-paid job in an office; the successful financier who turns diplomat; the scientist who seeks eminence in pure research instead of trying to invent marketable gadgets, all weigh social approval against financial gain. Prestige counts, as well as pay.

For gauging occupational rank according to the prestige which is generally accorded to workers in the various fields, Beckman[1] has used a scale of five grades:

I. Unskilled Manual Occupations
II. Semi-skilled Occupations
III. (a) Skilled Manual Occupations
  (b) Skilled White-collar Occupations
IV. (a) Sub-professional Occupations
  (b) Business Occupations
  (c) Minor Supervisory Occupations
V. (a) Professional (Linguistic) Occupations
  (b) Professional (Scientific) Occupations
  (c) Managerial and Executive Occupations

Beckman's purpose was to prepare a grouping which would readily indicate the rank of an occupation on the basis of the intelligence, capacity or skill, education and training required for its pursuit, at the same time reflecting the socio-economic prestige attached to it. Table V lists representative occupations in each grade of this prestige scale—another chart to use in finding one's orientation within the panorama of the world at work.

Other lists which a counselor will find of value include the comprehensive classification in Parker's bibliography, *Books About Jobs*, published by the American Library Association for the National Occupational Conference; Sir Michael Sadler's classification of occupations followed by university graduates in his *Handbook of Oxford University*; the Barr Scale of Occupations arranged according to estimates of the intelligence required; the Minnesota Occupational Rating Scales, showing occupations rated in terms of abstract intelligence, mechanical ability, social intelligence, artistic ability, and

[1] R. O. Beckman, "A New Scale for Gauging Occupational Rank," *Personnel Journal*, 1934, 13:225-233.

TABLE V. BECKMAN'S LIST OF REPRESENTATIVE OCCUPATIONS IN EACH GRADE OF THE OCCUPATIONAL SCALE

Grade 1—Unskilled Manual Occupations

Farm laborers
Lumbermen, raftsmen, and woodchoppers
Laborers (construction, manufacturing, road, warehouse, etc.)
Longshoremen
Sailors and deckhands
Garage, trucking, and stable hands
Deliverymen
Newsboys
Soldiers, sailors, and marines
Attendants (poolrooms, bowling alleys, golf clubs, etc.)
Charwomen, maids, and cleaners
Janitors and sextons
Porters
Messengers and office boys and girls

Grade 2—Semi-skilled Occupations

Fishermen and oystermen
Mine operatives
Filers, grinders, buffers
Stationary firemen
Furnace and smelter men
Oilers
Operatives in
- chemical and allied industries
- brick, tile, lime, and cement works
- foods, beverages, and tobacco
- blast furnaces, rolling mills, iron and steel factories
- tin and enamel ware
- leather industries
- planing, woodworking, and paper mills
- cotton and other textile mills

Draymen and teamsters
Baggagemen
Street railroad and bus conductors
Switchmen, flagmen, and yardmen
Truck-drivers and chauffeurs
Firefighters
Guards, watchmen, and doorkeepers
Policemen
Housekeepers and stewards
Laundry workers
Waiters

Grade 3A—Skilled Manual Occupations

Farm owners and tenants
Apprentices to building and other skilled trades
Bakers
Blacksmiths, forgemen, boilermakers
Building trades mechanics
Printing and publishing trades mechanics
Dressmakers and seamstresses
Electricians

TABLE V. (*Continued*)

Engineers, stationary and locomotive
Jewelry workers and watchmakers
Machinists, millwrights, and toolmakers
Transportation mechanics
Milliners
Molders, founders, and casters
Painters and glaziers
Paperhangers
Pattern and model makers
Shoemakers and cobblers
Tailors and tailoresses
Operatives in
  glass and pottery
  clothing industries
  automobile factories
  furniture, piano, and organ factories
  electric light and power plants and supply factories
Railroad firemen and brakemen
Motormen
Barbers, hairdressers and manicurists
Practical nurses and midwives
Cooks (hotels, restaurants, etc.)

Grade 3B—Skilled White-collar Occupations

Freight and express agents
Mail clerks and carriers
Radio, telegraph, and telephone operators
Clerks in stores
Inspectors, gaugers, and samplers
Canvassers, demonstrators, and sales persons in stores
Marshals, sheriffs, detectives, etc.
Dentists' and physicians' assistants
Boarding and lodging-house keepers
Collectors
Bookkeepers and cashiers
Office clerks
Stenographers and typists

Grade 4A—Sub-professional Occupations

Opticians
Undertakers
Actors and showmen
Designers, draftsmen and apprentices, and inventors
Photographers
Trained nurses
Apprentices to various professional persons
Healers (not elsewhere classified)
Religious workers
Technicians and laboratory assistants

Grade 4B—Business Occupations

Owners and proprietors of garages, truck, and cab companies
Conductors (steam railroads)
Postmasters

TABLE V. (*Continued*)

Advertising agents
Commercial brokers and commission men
Loan brokers and pawnbrokers
Commercial travelers
Decorators, drapers, and window-dressers
Insurance agents
Proprietors of employment agencies, grain elevators, warehouses, etc.
Real estate agents
Retail dealers
Sales agents and auctioneers
Wholesalers, importers, exporters
Billiard-room, dance-hall, theater, and amusement-resort keepers, etc.
Hotel keepers and managers
Laundry owners, managers, and officials
Restaurant and lunchroom keepers
Credit men and purchasing agents
Floorwalkers and foremen in stores

Grade 4C—Minor Supervisory Occupations

Farm managers and foremen
Mine foremen and overseers
Manufacturing foremen and overseers
Captains, masters, mates, pilots
Foremen, overseers, and inspectors, transportation and communications
Foremen, miscellaneous trades
Keepers of charitable and penal institutions
Cemetery-keepers

Grade 5A—Professional Occupations (Linguistic)

Authors, editors, and reporters
Clergymen
College presidents and professors
Lawyers, judges, and justices
Musicians and teachers of music
Teachers
Librarians
Social and welfare workers and related occupations

Grade 5B—Professional Occupations (Scientific)

Architects
Artists, sculptors, and teachers of art
Chemists, assayers, and metallurgists
Dentists
Physicians, surgeons, osteopaths
Technical engineers (civil, electrical, etc.)
Veterinary surgeons
County agents, farm demonstrators, etc.
Accountants, auditors, and actuaries

Grade 5C—Managerial and Executive Occupations

Owners and managers of log and timber camps
Mine operators, managers and officials
Manufacturing managers and officials, and manufacturers
Garage, transfer, and cab company managers and officials

Table V. (*Continued*)

Railroad officials and superintendents
Other transportation proprietors and managers
Bankers and bank officials
Stock brokers and promoters
Managers and officials, insurance companies
Managers and officials, real estate companies
Government officials and inspectors

musical talent, given on pages 365-380; and the lists in Chapter V of this book.

From the volumes of the U. S. Census of Occupations may be drawn off lists of occupations arranged in order according to the numbers following them. The leading professions, for example, have the relative numerical importance shown in Table VI.

Table VI. Occupational Distribution in 1930

Professional Service

Occupation	*Number*
1. Teachers	1,125,000
2. Technical engineers	507,000
3. Trained nurses	294,000
4. Musicians and music-teachers	165,000
5. Lawyers	161,000
6. Physicians	160,000
7. Clergymen	149,000
8. Draftsmen and designers	103,000
9. Dentists	71,000
10. Artists and art teachers	57,000
11. Chemists and metallurgists	47,000
12. Actors	38,000
13. Librarians	31,000
14. Architects	22,000
15. Veterinarians	12,000
16. Authors	12,000

When such data are compared with those for previous decades, significant changes of trend in occupational opportunities will be observed. In Figs. 6, 7 and 8, it is clear that some of the occupations have been declining, either rapidly or slowly, in comparison with the general upward trend of population; while others have been increasing. Changes that have been taking place both nationally and locally are illustrated in *Occupational Trends in New York City*, prepared under the author's supervision and published by the National Occupational Conference in 1933. We quote the following summary from page xiii of this brochure:

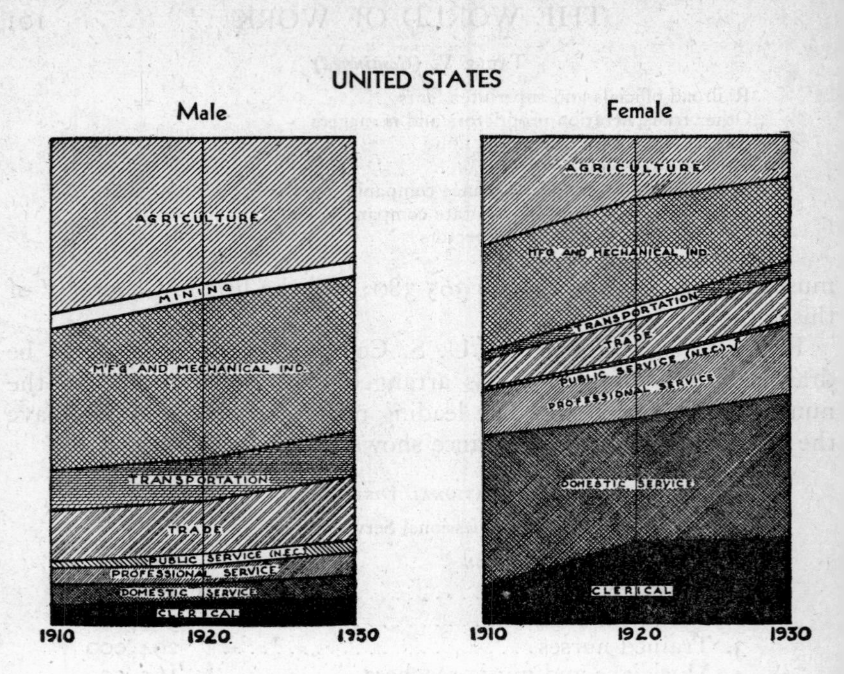

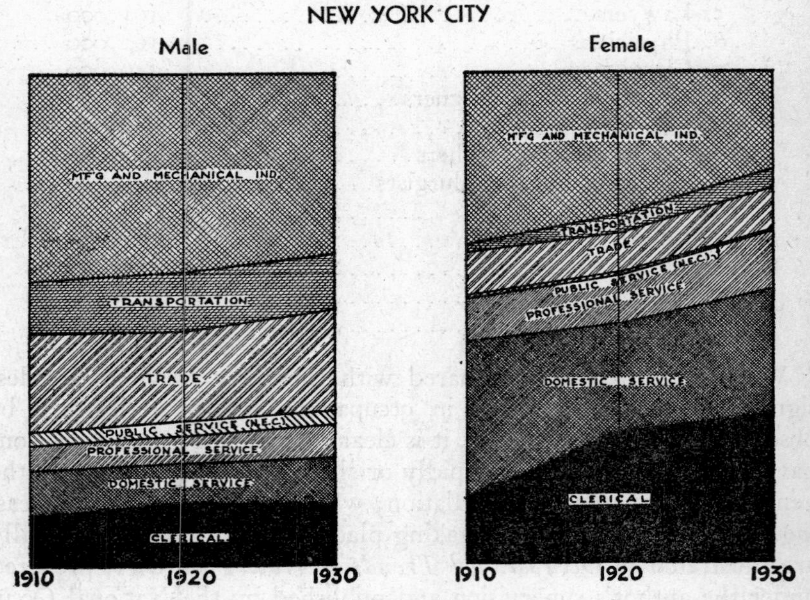

FIG. 6. CHANGING PROPORTIONS IN MAJOR OCCUPATIONAL GROUPS, 1910-1930

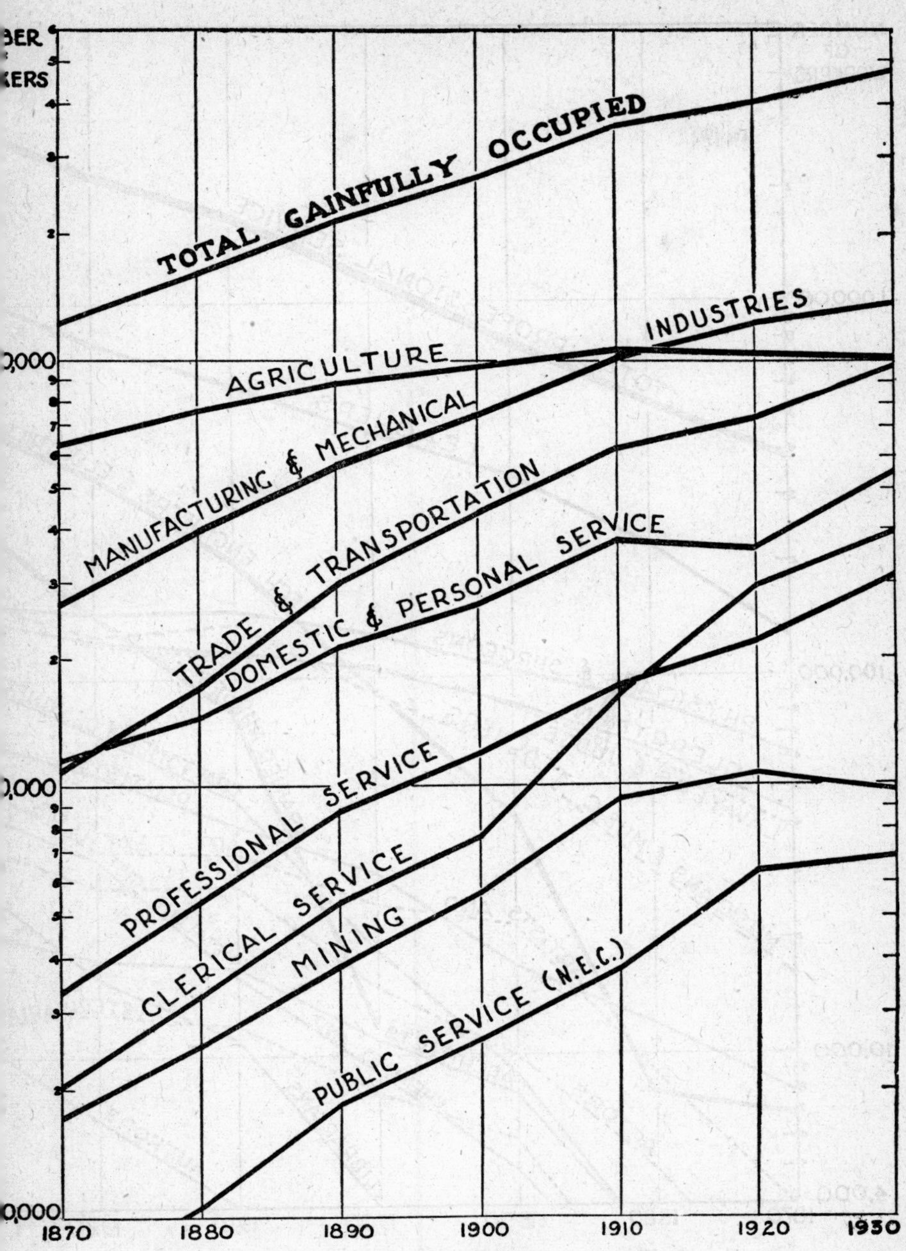

FIG. 7. TRENDS OF OCCUPATIONS IN THE UNITED STATES, 1870-1930

From U. S. Census data analyzed by R. G. Hurlin.

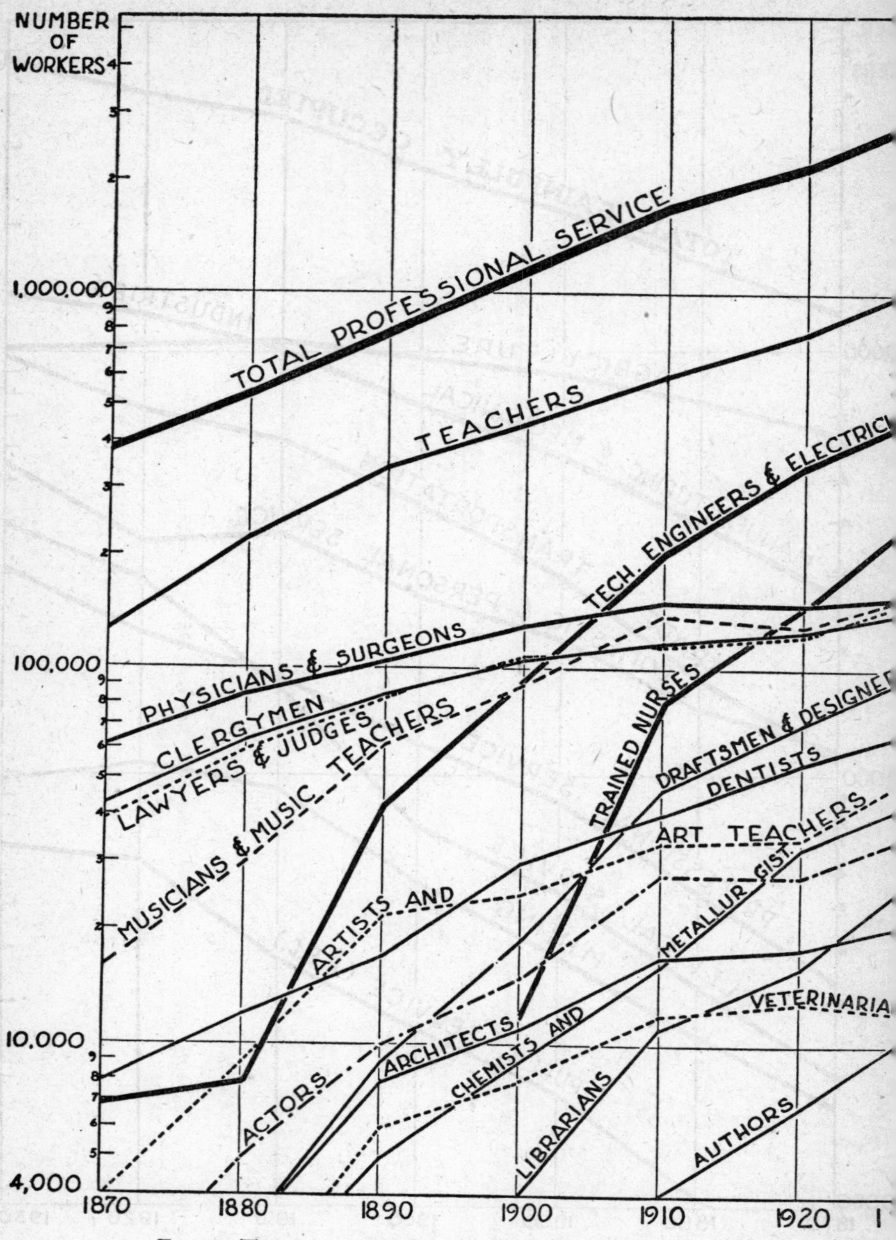

Fig. 8. Trends among Professional Groups, 1870-1930

From U. S. Census data analyzed by R. G. Hurlin.

Table VII. Occupations Showing an Upward Trend

The following list includes those leading occupations or occupational groups in which the proportion of gainful workers increased during the period from 1910 to 1930, either in the country as a whole or in New York City.

The letters after the name of an occupation indicate whether the increase applies to the country as a whole or to New York City, and whether this upward trend has been noted for *men* alone, M; for *women* alone, F; or for *both* men and women, B. Capital letters refer to the United States as a whole; small letters to New York City. Thus, "Bakers—B" means an increase in the proportions of *both* men and women bakers in the country as a whole, but not in New York City. "Electricians—M m" means an increase of *male* electricians in the country as a whole and also in New York City.

MANUFACTURING AND MECHANICAL INDUSTRIES

Bakers—B
Cabinetmakers—M
Compositors, linotypers, and typesetters—M
Electricians—M m
Engravers—M
Mechanics—M m
Milliners and millinery dealers—m
Painters, glaziers, varnishers, etc.—B m
Plasterers—M
Structural ironworkers—M m
Toolmakers, die setters and sinkers—M
Upholsterers—M m
Operatives (not otherwise specified)
- automobile factories—B
- building industry—m
- chemical and allied industries—B m
- clothing industries—F
- electric light and power plants—M m
- electric machinery and supply—B b
- furniture factories—B f
- knitting mills—M
- shoe factories—m
- silk mills—M

TRANSPORTATION AND COMMUNICATION

Chauffeurs, truck and tractor drivers—B m
Mail-carriers—M m
Sailors and deckhands—M
Telegraph and telephone linemen—M m
Telephone operators—B f

TRADE

Commercial travelers—B
Decorators, drapers, and window-dressers—B b
Floorwalkers and foremen (stores)—B
Insurance agents—B b
Real estate agents and officials—B b
Retail dealers—B
Salesmen and saleswomen—B m
Stock brokers—B b
Undertakers—B
Wholesale dealers, importers, exporters—F

PUBLIC SERVICE (Not elsewhere classified)

Firemen (fire department)—M m
Policemen—B b

PROFESSIONAL SERVICE

Actors and actresses—F
Architects—M
Artists, sculptors, and teachers of art—B b
Chemists, assayers, and metallurgists—M m
Clergymen—F
College professors and presidents—B b
Designers—F
Dentists—M m
Draftsmen—M b
Editors and reporters—B b
Lawyers, judges, and justices—B b
Librarians—B b
Musicians and teachers of music—m
Photographers—b
Teachers—B b
Technical engineers—M m
- civil engineers and surveyors—M m
- electrical engineers—M m
- mechanical engineers—M
- mining engineers—M m

Trained nurses—F f

TABLE VII. (*Continued*)

DOMESTIC AND PERSONAL SERVICE

Barbers, hairdressers, and manicurists—B f	Janitors and sextons—M
Cleaning, dyeing, and pressing shop workers—B	Laundry operatives—B b
Cooks—M m	Porters (except in stores)—M m
Elevator-tenders—B m	Servants (except cooks)—m
	Waiters—B b

CLERICAL OCCUPATIONS

Accountants and auditors—B b	Clerks (except "clerks" in stores)—B b
Bookkeepers and cashiers—F f	Stenographers and typists—F

3

Study of occupations has several purposes. No matter what direction one's career may take, it is part of a liberal education to become aware of the nature and variety of the world's work. Moreover, it widens a student's outlook when the time comes for him to select a calling. It may serve to draw his attention to his aptitudes for some of the kinds of work brought to his notice. His educational plans and occupational decisions can be more intelligently shaped within the framework of this broad survey.

When students who have neither studied occupations systematically nor thought very seriously about their own aptitudes are asked to report their occupational choices, their expressions of preference bear only a scant resemblance to the fields of employment they ultimately enter. This holds to a distressing extent with regard to college men and women as well as to boys and girls of fourteen.

In order to bring home to a class or to a high-school assembly the desirability of looking afield beyond one's first casual choice and searching for possibly more suitable kinds of employment, one device is to display a chart on which the distribution of students' choices is shown side by side with the distribution of occupational opportunities. Such a chart[2] is shown in Fig. 9. Here the frequencies of occupational choices among 1,000 girls in the 7B grade of junior high school in New York City are placed beside the frequencies of women workers actually following those occupations in this city.

The chart carries its own admonitions. Girls who have expressed a preference for typing and stenography instantly recognize that a great many of them will doubtless need to find employment in other kinds of office work, such as bookkeeping, filing, computing, cashiering, or acting as telephone girl and receptionist. They begin to ask

[2] Adapted from data supplied by Jessie B. Adams of the Division of Guidance and Placement of the New York Schools, Charles B. Smith, director.

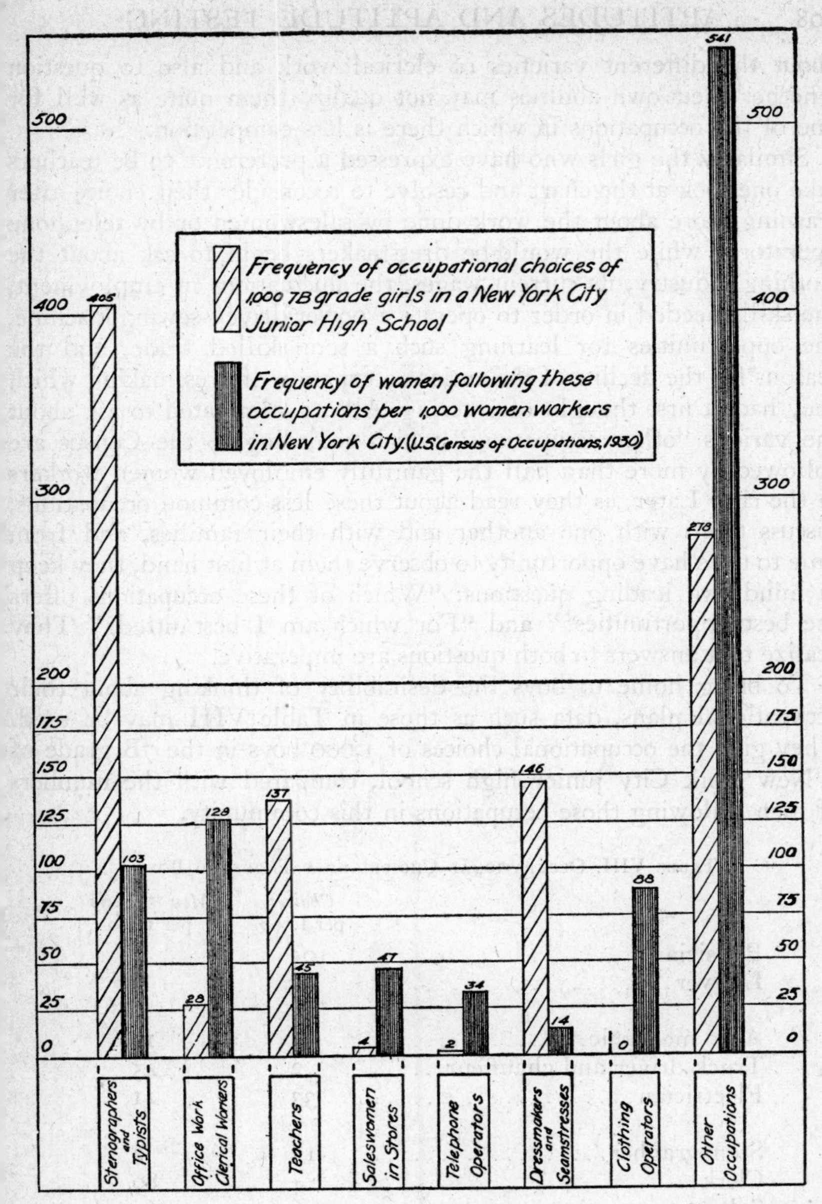

FIG. 9. DISCREPANCIES BETWEEN EXPRESSED PREFERENCES AND OCCUPATIONAL OPPORTUNITIES

Showing, for a group of 1,000 girls, the number who said they would choose each occupation, compared with the number in each 1,000 women workers in the same city following that occupation.

about the different varieties of clerical work and also to question whether their own abilities may not qualify them quite as well for one of the occupations in which there is less competition.

Similarly the girls who have expressed a preference to be teachers take one look at the chart and resolve to reconsider their choice after learning more about the work done by saleswomen or by telephone operators; while the would-be dressmakers begin to ask about the clothing industry, its current wages, the fluctuations in employment, the skills needed in order to operate a power-driven sewing-machine, the opportunities for learning such a semi-skilled trade, and the reasons for the decline of the ancient occupation of dressmaking which they had at first thought of entering. All are stimulated to ask about the various "other occupations" which according to the Census are followed by more than half the gainfully employed women workers in the city. Later, as they read about these less common occupations, discuss them with one another and with their families, and from time to time have opportunity to observe them at first hand, they keep in mind two leading questions: "Which of these occupations offers the best opportunities?" and "For which am I best fitted?" They realize that answers to both questions are imperative.

To bring home to boys the desirability of thinking about their occupational plans, data such as those in Table VIII may be used. They give the occupational choices of 1,000 boys in the 7B grade of a New York City junior high school, compared with the numbers of men following those occupations in this community.

TABLE VIII. OCCUPATIONAL CHOICES OF A THOUSAND BOYS

	Choices per 1,000	*Men Workers* per 1,000
Physician	105	5
Lawyer	64	8
Auto mechanic	51	19
Truck-driver and chauffeur	2	45
Electrician	33	11
Stenographer	13	2
Clerk	4	89
Salesman	6	67
Retail dealer	5	64
Barber	5	10
Other occupations	712	680

The present chapter has rapidly boxed the compass by which a person reads his direction and finds a course when making an exploration through unknown fields of work. Nothing has here been said, however, about special talents or aptitudes which certain kinds of occupations require. To these we now turn. We shall first ask whether any special qualifications are necessary in order to follow successfully the occupation of heavy manual labor.

Chapter X

APTITUDES FOR MANUAL OCCUPATIONS

1. Manual aptitudes and also other aptitudes are needed in the majority of manual occupations. 2. Machine-tending. 3. Aptitudes for heavy manual labor. Opportunities for advancement from heavy labor jobs. 4. Aptitudes for bench work. Operations common to many repetitive jobs. Elements of expertness. Frazier's study of manual versatility. 5. Tests of aptitude for bench work.

1

THE task of estimating a person's aptitudes for earning a livelihood with his hands is faced now and then by every counselor. Manual skills of one sort or another are factors in the success of assemblers, inspectors, and other workers at the bench, of artisans and craftsmen, dentists and surgeons, portrait-painters and violinists.

To be sure, the nature of the hand work to be done differs strikingly from one manual occupation to another. The requisite skills are highly specific. Then, too, a person's ability to succeed in any one of these callings is a product of several more or less independent factors, and is the result not alone of a single talent, whether called dexterity, motor coordination, manual ability, or aptitude for acquiring manual skill. Powers of visual and tactual discrimination may also be of importance, as in house-painting or hand weaving; perception of spatial relations, as in mechanical assembly work or in sculpture; kinesthetic sensitivity and auditory acuity, as in piano-tuning. Coolness under dangerous conditions is needed by an operative in a copper-refinery; knowledge of words, in typesetting or typewriting; musical talent, in a pianist; understanding of anatomy and pathology, in an operating surgeon; artistic abilities, in an etcher; and so on throughout the gamut of vocations in which manipulation of concrete materials is carried on. Manual aptitudes, desirable in several of the professions, in the skilled trades and in thousands of semi-skilled operations, are not, however, the sole determinants of a person's fitness to undertake a manual occupation.

Passing in review a number of more or less typical callings, we shall take note of operations and kinds of activity common to several varieties of manual work. We shall then be able to identify some of the factors which condition the abilities exhibited by the hand workers who follow these occupations, whether these factors are physical or mental, sensory or motor, affective or intellectual.

2

It may first be observed that there are uncounted jobs to be done that are quite unskilled and require neither quickness of fingers, nor strength, nor wits. Many machine-tending jobs—and their number has been increasing for three or four decades—demand no skill whatever, but only faithfulness in attendance. A responsible workman who can be counted upon always to be on hand promptly when the whistle blows, and not to neglect his duties such as they are, qualifies quite satisfactorily for many of these posts. Such considerations as this have led to the broad generalization that modern industry places a premium on "character," meaning dependability on the job, a trait to be appraised from past performance rather than from scores on any character tests. The watchman who stays all night near a cache of building materials to discourage anyone who might be inclined to make off with a few boards or a sack of cement; the guard at a railroad crossing or at the entrance to a safety deposit vault; the operator of any one of many kinds of converters, vats, compressors, stills, transformers, and other devices in chemical plants, chocolate factories, soapworks, refineries, steelworks, foundries, and power plants—each of these workers is essentially a watchman, an observer, like the lookout in the crow's nest of a cruiser, or a fire warden in his forest tower. He has to be continually on hand, awake, his eyes wandering now and then over the horizon or over the gauges of his machine, ready to notice and to report anything out of the ordinary.

Occupations like these, however, usually include among the duties to be performed a few which do require a modicum of special knowledge, judgment, skill, strength, mental alertness, or a combination of dexterity and decision, as well as faithful observation. The zone of unskilled work shades off rather rapidly in these directions. In addition to dependability on the job, the employment officer may inquire into the candidate's fitness for dextrous manipulation of tools, of machines, or of materials; or into his capacities accurately to discriminate textures, odors, sizes, or shapes; or his ability to maintain cool composure under conditions of surprise and sudden stress. These and many other components of personal endowment are then to be reckoned with, in estimating suitability for different kinds of manual occupation.

The sections which follow describe in succession several zones of occupational differentiation, beginning with the labor occupations in which strength, physical endurance, and skills in the use of *heavy tools* are indispensable.

3

"A strong back and a weak mind" have been alleged to be the chief requisites for successful and contented employment at heavy manual labor. Is this a correct or adequate specification of the qualities a man should have if he is to earn a livelihood at pick-and-shovel work in heavy industries like the manufacture of steel and the refining of lead, or in coal mining, quarrying, excavating, road construction, and railway-track maintenance? What are the requirements for becoming a longshoreman, a freight-rustler, a furniture-mover, a hodcarrier, a trucker in a factory, a laborer in a sawmill or a lumber-yard? Are hewers of wood and drawers of water selected for these laborious occupations chiefly by virtue of their physical strength and low intelligence?

Such questions may seem remote from the interests of educational and vocational counselors. The assumption has prevailed that no one who could do anything else would voluntarily choose heavy physical labor; that semi-skilled factory occupations not involving muscular strain are universally preferred; that the ranks of unskilled labor are filled to overflowing with the human residue from the relentless sieve of occupational differentiation; that these laborers, lacking aptitude for anything else, have no alternative if they are to find employment at all. This assumption must be challenged, for it colors one's attitude toward a vast field of occupations furnishing employment to about one in five among the male working population.

It is the purpose of this section to consider briefly the nature of the work done in the heavy labor occupations, and to bring together suggestions regarding aptitudes for this kind of work and openings to which it may lead.

Let it be emphasized at the start that heavy manual labor is not necessarily a blind-ally occupation. Quite the contrary. High-school and college graduates who can qualify for such physically exacting employment have not infrequently found it a direct road to steady advancement. Two or three personal observations, while unusual, picturesquely illustrate this point.

Ten years ago, in a large factory near New York, I saw a young graduate of an Eastern university, a football hero who had made a good scholastic record, pushing a hand truck and unloading from it heavy coils of copper wire. Why was he in such a job? He had decided that this particular concern was the one in which he wished to work out his career. At that time the employment office had only one vacancy, that of trucker; and to the surprise of the interviewer the applicant insisted on being given a chance at this work. In two months his energy and his friendliness with the many employees to and from whose benches he carried materials had brought him to the notice of supervisors, foreman, superintendent and even the general works manager; and although nothing had as yet been said to him about the matter, a tentative line of promotion had been planned. During the years that followed, he advanced rather more rapidly than most of his classmates who went from college directly into an office.

Another young man with a superb physique, on graduating from a venerable university in the South, worked in the industry of his choice for seven months at heavy pick-and-shovel labor in order to qualify as an employment interviewer assigned to the duty of hiring this grade of labor. Today, at an early age, he is a vice-president, not of the company in which he started, but of that giant industry, the United States Steel Corporation. Another vice-president of this same corporation went directly into the steel works as a laborer on graduation from high school. Employment at heavy manual labor, it seems, may open one of the obvious but usually neglected gateways to supervisory and managerial advancement.

Who, then, may qualify for a heavy labor job?

Large stature is not essential. A small wiry man may fill the requirements and hold his own with stockier and perhaps more stolid workers. But physical endurance beyond the limits demanded in most other occupations is indispensable if the laborer is to maintain his pace along with seasoned employees after the first hour or two. Muscles of back and arms and legs must be hardened. A palm that blisters easily is a disqualification, as is an abdominal wall that might rupture under the strain of heaving a load. Any distaste for overalls and grime must be swallowed. Moreover, the novice—the really *unskilled* laborer—quickly discovers that this is not in any strict sense an unskilled occupation, after all, but that there are certain knacks that must be learned before he can properly wield a pick, or be trusted with an ax, or toss high a shovelful of gravel, or trundle a loaded wheelbarrow up a ramp, or safely swing a sledge hammer, or manipulate a crowbar with an efficiency comparable to that of his fellow workers. And unless he soon becomes really competent in the use of such heavy tools, he is the first to be dropped from the payroll at a time of layoff, to find his way back toward the overcrowded ranks in the casual labor market.

Many a semi-skilled operation, so called, can be mastered in less time than it takes to become a competent "unskilled" laborer.

To be sure, only a modicum of intelligence is needed to acquire the essential skills. Morons can learn them, just as they can learn to drive an automobile, or to wait on table, or to operate a drill press, or to perform many of the repetitive operations on an assembly line. Morons can also learn to load and fire a deadly automatic pistol, or to jimmy a window. If they have the necessary physique, how much better it is for them and for society when they learn to surpass their mates in the wielding of spades and crowbars, of axes and cant hooks, instead of themselves becoming the tools of gangsters! A teacher of backward boys overlooks an opportunity when he neglects to develop in some of them an interest in the possibility of excelling in the use of heavy tools.

Then there are heavy labor occupations which definitely offer scope for more than a minimum of intelligence and prowess, and for other valuable abilities, as well as for physical endurance. The longshoreman rustling bales and casks aboard a freighter may become a stevedore, aristocrat of the waterfront, expert in the stowing away of great cargoes. The digger panning gold in a placer mine may turn prospector. Watch this trio of piano-movers at their work. They each weigh two hundred pounds or more, mostly bone and muscle. They move a little slowly, but somehow very expeditiously, with no false movements, as they rig the tackle to the roof of the house and hoist the bulky instrument to the upper-storey window. Notice the apparent ease with which they heave it across the sill, passing the weight from one to another, balancing it, resting it, up-ending it onto a cradle which they call a "dolly," and finally lifting it into the desired corner without a scratch on the polished surface. Must a piano-mover be strong of back? Of course. But that is only the beginning. His trade knowledge of just what to do and when to do it is indispensable.

Equally essential are his skills and knacks in doing these things adroitly, not to mention his cool head, his "nerve."

So it is with literally hundreds of heavy-labor occupations. Each has its own techniques. Because they necessitate the use of hands and the larger skeletal muscles we speak of them as "manual" labor and tend to forget that they make more continuous demands on the mind than many a routine white-collar job. Is it any wonder that such capable and sturdy workers have a fine pride in their calling, or that they occasionally look down on a puny clerk bending over a desk at routine copying which calls for less practical intelligence than theirs?

Not all laborers are dull. According to the army intelligence data,[1] at least one-fourth of those who had reported their occupations as Laborer, in the sample population studied, did better than the median of the total army population. The percentage distribution of letter grades among these 1,453 Laborers was as follows:

A	B	C+	C	C–	D	D–
0.62	3.5	10.7	24.2	25.1	24.6	11.4

The distribution of intelligence scores in a factory population of 9,000 men has been analyzed by Pond.[2] The range of scores in each occupation was found to be wide. The scores of the men in certain labor groups, working as utility men, yard construction laborers, bull-block operators and extension-press helpers varied all the way from 60 to 169 on the particular examination used; and while the median score for these groups, about 112, was slightly lower than for any other groups in the factory, it is worth noting that there were among the laboratory men and draftsmen, and also in the group of foremen, supervisors and clerks, individuals whose scores were lower than this median. There were laborers whose scores exceeded the median performance of the most intelligent occupational group in the population studied. A keen-minded man working as a laborer in such a plant is not thereby cut off from all association with fellow workers as intelligent as he.

A counselor of bright young men may well remind them that heavy labor jobs furnish a good opportunity to learn at first hand some of the fundamentals of industrial relations, of labor management, and of team work or cooperative effort in production.

The first step in advancement may be to a position as timekeeper; but this is ordinarily a blind-ally occupation. It is preferable instead, to become a machine operative, or a helper to an experienced crafts-

[1] *Memoirs of the National Academy of Sciences*, 15:828, 829.

[2] The Scovill Classification Test used in this study is described on pages 333-334.

man, or to earn the post of a gang boss. There is also the possibility of an opening in time study, rate setting, motion-economy studies, or safety engineering. Good sense and ingenuity in the organization of work and in the improvement of methods are assets. A real understanding of people coupled with the other traits of personal leadership may open the way to supervisory responsibilities and finally to executive positions.

Any young man with a sound physique should canvass the field of heavy labor, to see whether he cannot find a congenial occupation which will permit him to capitalize his superior physical endurance, as well as his other aptitudes. Mere bigness of frame, as has already been observed, is not always necessary. Men of medium build and even those of small but wiry constitution have been able to master the knacks of handling heavy tools and to stand the muscular strains without injury.

No standard tests of aptitude for heavy manual labor are here suggested. Strength of grip as measured with a hand dynamometer bears but little relation to aptitude for heavy manual work. Performance in dynamometer tests which measure strength of back and legs does have a definite relation to this aptitude; but these tests are seldom used, partly because the measures are not very reliable and partly because there is danger of physical injury while taking the tests. Aptitude for heavy labor is preferably estimated from observations regarding prowess in strenuous athletics such as wrestling, football, weight-throwing, and long-distance running.

4

Observe now the work being done at the bench by assemblers, packers, wrappers, polishers, paper-folders, cutters, egg-candlers, makers of artificial flowers. Note the quickness and apparent ease with which the movements are made. Here the larger muscles of the body are not brought into play. Fingers and hands do the manipulating. What activities are common to these different kinds of bench work?

In a multitude of such occupations the work includes as its main feature a repetition over and over again of a series of hand movements, as follows: reaching, picking up, transporting, placing in position, and releasing; reaching again, picking up, transporting, positioning, and releasing. This chain of acts constitutes the matrix of manual activity in many an operation at the workbench. The faster and more accurately this series of movements can be made, the more proficient is the worker. To be sure, each kind of operation introduces its own variants and demands its own additional skills. The packer of candies must choose in each instance which bonbon to reach for and where to put it in order to complete the standard pattern of the assortment she is packing. The packer of dates must estimate size and be alert to notice and reject defective fruits. The packer of eggs in the candler's dark room picks them up, two or three in the fingers of each hand, and clicks them together to detect by sound and feeling any cracked shell, meanwhile twirling them adroitly before the little window of the candle-flame box while he notices any tell-tale shadow floating across the translucent pink oval, indicating that an egg is a bit stale. Only after making these successive decisions does he deposit each egg in its proper container, "strictly fresh," "fresh," "seconds," or "rotten," that is, suitable only to be sold to a tannery. But how swiftly the adroit candler does all these things! His is typical of many manual occupations that call for the abilities of inspector and sorter as well as packer.

One notices within any group of workers doing the same hand operation marked differences in speed even after all of them have reached their limits of practice. On inquiry we find that some of them have achieved their maximum pace only after a relatively long period, while others have been adept in making progress and have early earned a bonus, "gotten into the money," as they say. Individual differences in (1) initial ability, (2) rate of learning, and (3) ultimate level of proficiency attained, are not very closely related to one another. Nor are these three aspects of a person's manual abilities of equal importance in all situations. Their relative significance under various circumstances is obvious as soon as the nature of the work to be done is examined.

Here, for instance, is a woman who takes a spool of photographic film, wraps it in a sheet of foil, twists the ends tight, and tosses the spool into a tray ready to be inserted in its yellow pasteboard container. She likes to do this all day long. For years she has far excelled all other wrappers at this task and is proud of her supremacy. Her agile fingers fly so fast that the observer's eye is baffled in the attempt to note the details of her movements. When necessary she can also put the spools into the boxes; and there her special competence ends. She has not asked the privilege of learning to do anything else, and there has been no necessity for her to do so. What matters it whether this worker was or was not initially adept, or whether she acquired her amazing skill quickly or slowly? It is her ultimate level of proficiency that counts.

Elsewhere in this plant are women doing equally simple manual operations, over and over again; but the exigencies of the manufacturing schedule require them occasionally to shift from a familiar operation to one which, though superficially similar, cannot be performed very rapidly until it has been practiced for a considerable period. Here there is a premium on manual versatility. In plants where such job changes are frequent, a worker's initial ability on undertaking a new manual operation, and his rate of improvement during the earliest stages of learning it, are more important than his ultimate level of skill, a level which he rarely can approach before a fresh task is set.

Superior initial ability is peculiarly needed in those manual occupations in which a novice or a bungling learner is apt to ruin an expensive tool, spoil costly materials, or even injure himself by accident.

A high level of ultimate ability is relatively more important in operations that are to be worked at for a long time after the learning period is over; while in estimating a person's aptitude for a manual occupation in which the nature and the difficulties of the work vary from week to week or from hour to hour, the problem is to predict his manual versatility, his rate of learning to do unfamiliar manual operations similar to those in the occupation, rather than to predict his terminal ability, his performance after the period of learning a particular skill has been completed.

The occupation of paper-box making, which calls for just such manual versatility, was described as follows by L. R. Frazier[3] when he was psychologist at the Dennison Manufacturing Company:

"The occupation studied was that of general box-maker. Until a year previous to the first experiment, the hand work connected with the making of boxes was divided into two important trades, known as 'boxmaking' and 'lining.' The first consisted of making the box proper, using cardboard and papers properly cut and glued. The second consisted of lining the interior of the box with satin or velvet by glueing this material to the boxes as made by the box-maker. Due to the delicate manipulation required, and especially to the wide variety of shapes, sizes, and styles, six months were necessary to become reasonably proficient at either job, and those few girls who succeeded in becoming all-round experts usually spent almost two years in acquiring their skill.

"Through analysis of the work, industrial engineers were able

[3] In an unpublished *Study of Manual Versatility*, on file with the Personnel Research Federation.

for each type of box to split the work of making and lining into a number of separate operations. Each of these operations can now be performed repetitively by a single employee until the order is finished. This may be a matter of hours or days. At the end of that time the employee is assigned to an operation on another box. This next operation is rarely identical with the first because of the great diversity in style and type of product. Sometimes it resembles the previous operation in a general way, but differs in respect to size, shape, materials, or quality of work demanded. In such a case the training on the first operation may be of some help on the second. At other times the new operation holds little or no resemblance to the preceding one and the employee has to begin almost at the beginning without being able to profit appreciably by his experience on the first operation.

"Preparatory to the selection of tests for tryout, the operations on the job were carefully observed upon several occasions, and the supervisors and some of the girls were questioned as to the parts of the work which gave them the most trouble. The work required the repetitive hand manipulation of relatively small, light-weight materials such as fine paper, satin, and cardboard in a variety of ways. The manipulation was not very intricate, but called for considerable precision such as in placing a narrow strip of glued paper evenly around the edge of a box, or in applying glue to the inside edges of a box while holding it in the hand without getting the glue on the other parts of the box. Both hands were used, sometimes doing almost identical operations, but more often not. There was considerable pressure for high production, and it was necessary to acquire as high a degree of speed as possible upon whatever operations a girl might be placed. The operations which an employee was called upon to do were sufficiently different from one another to cause the production curve to fluctuate violently from week to week.

"No attempt was made to list in detail the abilities or characteristics which appeared important. Instead, attention was given to noting the many different operations that the girls were called upon to do. As an illustration, the operation, 'pad-making'—*i.e.*, for interiors of fine boxes—is described as follows: Reaches for glue-brush with right hand, grasps handle, dips in glue-pot, removes excess glue by wiping against edge of pot; with left hand reaches for cardboard base of pad, grasps same and holds it in center; with right hand applies glue near all four edges, twisting cardboard with left hand; deposits cardboard on bench, glued side up; picks up another cardboard with left hand while dipping brush in glue with right hand; prepares several cardboards in this way; then deposits brush and wipes hands; reaches for strip of satin or velvet with left hand and places on bench while picking up glued cardboard with right; places cardboard in center of cloth and folds over the edges firmly with right hand; repeats, etc."

Aptitude for such an occupation, as we have seen, is indicated by symptoms of ability to adjust fairly quickly to the requirements of a relatively simple task at the bench. Versatility in the acquisition of specific skills, as well as mere speed of movement, is needed. To aid in measuring this aptitude—manual versatility—Frazier used a battery which included a pin-placing test adapted from a peg-board long in use at the Eastman Kodak Company, a card-assembly test requiring serial discrimination, a simple card-sorting test, and a series of card-dropping tests especially devised for inclusion in this battery.

The card-dropping tests are of special interest.[4] On a bench before the worker to be examined are two containers, each holding a stack of fifty playing-cards in a nearly horizontal position. These conveniently accessible cards are to be picked up one at a time and dropped through a narrow slot in the bench. The examiner records the time required to complete the task with the preferred hand; then, with the other hand; then with both hands working together, making use of two slots; and finally with the two hands working alternately. Simple tasks. And yet there are considerable differences in the manual versatility of workers as measured by their ability to excel on each of these four moderately varied operations. Furthermore, these differences are significantly related to their success at an occupation which requires them to shift readily from one box-making job to another which is similar to but not identical with it.

To understand the reason why a series of four simple card-dropping tests has proved useful as one measure of versatility in bench work, it is necessary only to observe closely the behavior of those who do poorly on the tests and of those who do well. Several differences in method and in promptness of adjustment to the various test situations are seen to characterize a superior performance. The girl with a high degree of manual versatility is apt to learn almost immediately to use only slight pressure of the thumb and to grasp each card lightly in picking it up, in order not to disturb the rest of the pile. She uses her third finger as well as the others. In putting a card into the slot, she inserts one corner first, instead of centering it first. She learns not to force the card through the opening, as an awkward girl does, but to let it drop. She looks directly at the spot where she is about to place a card, but is aware of other activities in indirect vision.

[4] For detailed specifications and norms, see page 287.

She quickly establishes a rhythm. Upon changing to the non-preferred hand she adopts methods which were found useful in working with the preferred hand. When using both hands at the same time, she lets her better hand lead slightly, setting the pattern of movement, the rhythm, and the tempo for her other hand. While these differences in adjustment to the test situation are evident, there are doubtless also other more subtle adjustments, difficult to observe and to define. In any event, a counselor appraising a person's aptitude for fine assembly jobs and for many other kinds of work at the bench should not be content to measure dexterity in doing only familiar tasks, or capacity to acquire a high level of skill at some one operation. He uses, instead, several tests, and looks for symptoms of manual versatility.

5

Mention may here be made of several performance tests which have been current in employment offices as aids in appraising the abilities of candidates for bench work of certain kinds.

The match-board or peg-board, popularized by Kemble[5] about twenty years ago, contains rows of holes into which wooden matches or metal pegs may be inserted. With it the examiner can measure speed in a variety of manual tasks, for example, in filling certain rows with one hand; then with the other; then with the two hands working together; then alternately; then in a manner to complete prescribed patterns; then under distraction or while performing a simple mental task, and so on.

O'Connor's Finger Dexterity Test, a modification of the peg-board, uses three hundred standard metal pegs or pins, an inch in length, and a metal plate with one hundred holes each large enough to take easily three of these pins. The pins are picked up three at a time and inserted until all the holes are filled. Another variety of manual aptitude is sampled by means of his Tweezer Dexterity Test which requires use of an implement in picking up and inserting pins in a peg-board. (See pages 281-286.)

Speed of hand movements common to many sorts of packing operations has been measured by simple spool-packing and block-packing tests, and by placing tests like the Minnesota Manual Dexterity Tests, the apparatus for which consists of a board with fifty-eight circular holes into which cylindrical blocks are to be placed (see page 278).

[5] W. F. Kemble, *Choosing Employees by Mental and Physical Tests*, p. 13 and Ch. XIV. New York: Engineering Magazine Co., 1917.

This test differs from a form board in that it requires no spatial discrimination, and so measures only the factor of manual speed in such a placing task.

Form boards have also been employed in estimating aptitudes for manual work at the bench. The time required to place variously shaped blocks in the proper cut-out spaces is a measure of a complex ability of which prompt, accurate perception of similarities or differences in shape and size is the main factor, while manual speed in picking up and placing the blocks is secondary. Ever since Link published a description of his form boards in 1919,[6] they have had a place in employment practice. This test, lengthened and restandardized as the Minnesota Spatial Relations Test, is described on page 309. The Kent-Shakow Industrial Form Board furnishes a discriminating and dependable measure, and is recommended for further experimentation in connection with employment and guidance practice.

Dotting with a lead pencil, tapping with a stylus on a tapping-board, and tapping with a telegraph key are illustrative of tasks used to measure quickness of voluntary movements with the hand and wrist. Accuracy or steadiness of voluntary hand movements is measured with a tracing-board. Steadiness of hand as indicated by absence of involuntary movements is measured by means of a steadiness-tester consisting of a brass plate in which is a series of holes of decreasing diameter, and a stylus which must be held for fifteen seconds in one hole after another without touching the plate.[7] The Scott Three-Hole Test, in which the task is to put a stylus into the holes one after another as fast as possible, is another manual test which has had some industrial use. These tests are not described here in greater detail because the abilities measured are highly specific and their vocational significance obscure.

The apparatus known as the Stanford Motor Skills Unit,[8] developed by Robert H. Seashore, is conveniently arranged for giving a battery of six tests designed to measure representative types of motor performance. It includes the Koerth Pursuit Rotor, to measure accuracy in following with a stylus a small target moving rapidly in a

[6] H. C. Link, *Employment Psychology*. New York: The Macmillan Company, 1919.

[7] Standard apparatus, available through the C. H. Stoelting Company, Chicago, is described by G. M. Whipple, *Manual of Mental and Physical Tests*. Second edition, 1:130-160. Baltimore: Warwick and York, 1914.

[8] R. H. Seashore, "Stanford Motor Skills Unit." *Psychological Monographs*, 1928, No. 2, 39:51-66. (Detailed specifications are given on pp. 55-65. The apparatus is obtainable through the C. H. Stoelting Company, Chicago.) See also "Individual Differences in Motor Skills," *Journal of General Psychology*, 1930, 3:38-66; and "The Aptitude Hypothesis in Motor Skills," *Journal of Experimental Psychology*, 1931, 14:555-561.

circle; the Miles Speed Rotor, to measure speed of rotary arm, wrist, and finger movements in turning a small hand drill; the Brown Spool Packer (Seashore-Tinker modification), to measure speed of packing spools in a box, using the two hands; the Motor Rhythm Synchrometer, to measure precision in reproducing on a telegraph key a regular rhythmic pattern; the Serial Discrimeter, to measure speed in making discriminating reactions to signals which change as fast as they are reacted to correctly; and finally a test which measures speed of tapping on a telegraph key. The complete battery can be administered in about two hours. Scoring is objective and automatic. This battery does not measure "general motor ability." Indeed, it is most improbable that there is any such general ability. Instead, the tests measure several relatively independent motor skills which may indicate aptitudes for vocational tasks requiring these specific skills. Unfortunately, the data which counselors need in interpreting the vocational significance of these tests are not available. A start in this direction is described in the second and third references cited.

Having considered in Chapter V, pages 44-57, the minimum intelligence levels of operatives doing various kinds of manual work, it is here necessary only to recall that the kinds of tests most suitable for ascertaining whether a person has the intelligence desired are non-verbal paper-and-pencil examinations like Army Beta, and tests like the Stanford-Binet Scale. The non-verbal parts of the Scovill Classification Test are well adapted for this purpose.

Among the measurable factors which have been found to contribute to aptitude for certain kinds of bench work are visual acuity, kinesthetic sensitivity, delicacy of touch, strength of grasp, and ability quickly to adopt a rapid easy rhythm of movement.

Yet another trait valuable in some semi-skilled operations, but not by any means in all, is mechanical ingenuity. The Stenquist Assembling Test, the Minnesota Mechanical Assembly Test and other aids in estimating mechanical aptitudes will be described in the following chapter, where attention is drawn to important differences between aptitude for semi-skilled manual work and aptitude for learning a trade.

The aptitudes of women and girls for various sorts of bench work and other manual occupations in industry have been measured by means of the tasks set by the I. E. R. Assembly Test for Girls, developed by Toops[9] and recently shortened and restandardized by Burr and Metcalfe of the Vocational Adjustment Bureau (see page 290).

[9] H. A. Toops, *Tests for Vocational Guidance of Children 13 to 16*. Teachers College, Columbia University, Contributions to Education, No. 136, 1923.

Temperamental qualifications, such, for instance, as insensitivity to the monotony of repetitive operations, are scarcely susceptible of measurement and must ordinarily be appraised in interview after the worker has had sufficient experience to be able to describe his reactions to long-continued repetitive manual work such as knitting, crocheting, packing, or sorting. Many workers like manual activity of this repetitive sort because it leaves their minds free to carry on pleasant reveries; while other workers are put under a strain which induces a condition of irritation and eventually leads to a nervous breakdown popularly known in Detroit as Forditis. And so an effort should be made to ascertain a person's susceptibility to manual monotony before arriving at an opinion as to his aptitude for working at a conveyor assembly belt or at a bench where the operations are highly repetitive.

To choose from among tests like those which have been mentioned a battery for use in estimating aptitude for any particular kind of bench work, it is clearly advisable to observe the nature of the work to be done and to analyze it, much as Frazier did before selecting tests to use in estimating the manual versatility of paper-box makers. Only then can a judicious opinion be formed as to the relative importance of the different factors which should be measured. The nucleus of such a battery is almost certain to include tasks involving speed of hand and finger movement in picking up and placing objects, and accuracy in the perception of the spatial relations of the objects handled. The other tests in the battery will then be selected in the light of the analysis of the particular operations to be performed, and of the differences between the workers who have failed at the job and those who have succeeded and found the work to their liking.

Explanation of Plate I

1. Card-dropping Test (Frazier).
2. Two-hand Test.
3. Pursuit Meter and Reaction Apparatus (Viteles), used in testing aptitudes for work of electrical sub-station operator, as described in M. S. Viteles, *Industrial Psychology,* Chapter XIII. New York: W. W. Norton, 1932.

Explanation of Plate II

1. Minnesota Mechanical Assembly Test, Box C.
2. Minnesota Spatial Relations Test, Board C.
   Courtesy of University of Minnesota Press.
3. Western Electric Audiometer, Type 4A.
   Courtesy of Graybar Electric Company, New York.

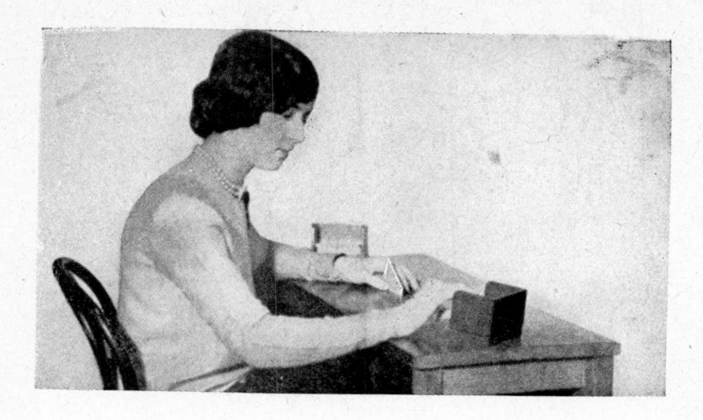

Plate I

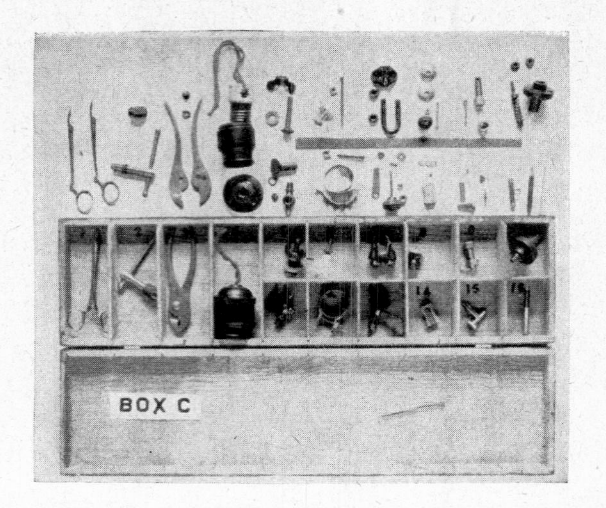

Plate II

allowances that must be made. He ranks high in manual skill largely in the sense that his versatility commands many distinguishable skills, and not necessarily in the sense that his skillfulness in any single operation is superior to that of a so-called semi-skilled worker who specializes in that one operation.

So it is in the trade of lather, stone mason, or welder; of ship carpenter or millwright; of locomotive engineer or airplane mechanic. The "tricks of his trade," hard-won possessions of every journeyman, are items of knowledge more often than feats of dexterity. When your automobile seems to be losing power, you want first a real mechanic who knows how to locate the difficulty, however obscure, whether in the distributor, carburetor, spark-plugs, feed line, valves, or transmission, rather than some one who is only expert with his hands in making the particular repair after he has been told what to do. The electrician diagnosing the illness of your short-wave radio, the painter mixing the exact color and shade you have specified for the trimmings on your house, the paperhanger cutting and matching the rolls without waste, the jeweler locating a worn pinion in your watch, all are applying their special knowledge. The typesetter needs quick fingers and keen eyes; but how long would he hold his job if his mind were not well stored with information—about the proper way to syllabicate every long word that has to be split at the end of a line, for example? Brains superior to those needed in strictly routine white-collar work and in most semi-skilled occupations are among the constituents of aptitude for a craft.

It is not inappropriate, when counseling a would-be apprentice, to make certain that his mental qualifications are of the right sort before inquiring into his motor coordination, his clumsiness or skill of hand.

Vital also is the question as to the strength and permanence of his informed interest in doing the work of the trade he thinks of undertaking. His decision to enter the army of skilled tradesmen and his choice of a particular craft for which to qualify may well be deferred until he knows his own preferences with an assurance grounded in close familiarity with the occupation that has attracted him. While associating with craftsmen and occasionally helping them in the work they are doing, he can learn how strongly such work and surroundings appeal to him. He may also pick up fairly definite impressions regarding other considerations to be weighed: trends of employment opportunity in the trade, wage rates and annual earnings, advantages and disadvantages of trade-union affiliation, hazards of health and safety, chances of securing an apprenticeship, opportunities for ultimate advancement beyond apprentice and journeyman status to that of master mechanic or foreman, or perhaps for eventually having a little business of his own, and the like.

A counselor's chief assistance often takes the form of supplementing his client's knowledge about the different trades and suggesting additional sources of information and opportunities for tryout experience. A vocational-interest inventory blank may serve well to initiate a counseling interview, but the interest scores are suggestive only. A person's account of his attitude toward a trade if made after observation and tryout, furnishes firmer ground for estimating the probability that he will like the occupation and find satisfaction in it.

The frequency with which final decision to master a trade is deferred, is reflected in the average age at which men actually enter the skilled trades. More carpenters have achieved their trade status after they were 35 years old than before. New recruits in considerable numbers have joined this venerable army at age 40, 45, 50 and 55. The tendency among electricians has been to take up the trade at a younger age. But even here, about half of them do not qualify until after they are 27. Only a relatively small fraction of those who eventually enter a trade definitely elect before age 18 the trade for which to prepare, and complete their training by the time they are 22. This is unfortunate. It is one indication of the long road American education still has to travel before it can be said to meet fully its responsibilities in the matter of vocational orientation and guidance.

A person's aptitude for a skilled trade is in part a matter of his interests and preferences; in part, of his facility in acquiring manual expertness in the kinds of skills required; and in part also, of his abilities in acquiring knowledge and exercising good sense in the decisions he makes. He is not likely to find satisfaction in a trade which is extremely difficult for him to learn. Nor is he likely to find opportunity to enter on an apprenticeship or be allowed to continue in it, if he is dull and inept. Evidences of likelihood that a young man has the ability to acquire trade knowledge and to exercise practical judgment as well as to become expert in the manual manipulation of tools, are needed before encouraging him to spend much time in canvassing the possibility of taking up a skilled trade. His aptitude may be fairly obvious after considering his past achievements and expressed preferences. But if there is still doubt regarding his fitness, his performance in tests such as we shall shortly describe, may well be reviewed. If the results from these tests furnish indications that he has manual aptitude but probably lacks the required mental endowments, his attention may be drawn to the many possibilities in semiskilled occupations. He may be reminded that an apprentice is paid scarcely as much as an unskilled laborer; while in many semi-skilled employments it is possible to earn more than a minimum wage after a learning period from two weeks to six months in length. Also, employment at semi-skilled operations is no bar to subsequent entry on preparation for a skilled trade, if the desire persists. Indeed, the gaining of experience in several different jobs related to a trade is a common way of securing part of the preparation for it.

To repeat: the more significant differences between aptitude for a skilled trade and aptitude for other manual occupations are found within the area of the mind. To be certain that a candidate has the requisite mental abilities is then one of his counselor's chief concerns.

When a backward youth has been doing poorly in his school work there is always a possibility that his aptitudes include greater fitness for working with concrete materials than with verbal symbols of abstract concepts. But his practical intelligence and his capacity to learn a skilled trade cannot be taken for granted. The lack of ability to master traditional academic subjects is no indication of aptitude for learning a skilled trade. On the contrary, it raises some presumption of probable lack of mechanical aptitude also. Counselors experience difficulty even today in convincing some teachers of this fact, and in persuading them of the desirability of seeking out positive evidence of the necessary aptitudes before encouraging a young man to focus his ambitions on a trade, rather than on a less exacting manual, commercial or personal-service occupation that is more probably within his capacities.

An individual's cumulative record, gathered over a period of years, contains relevant items. His standing in the school subjects he has taken may be scrutinized for indications of ability to acquire and make good use of a rather large stock of trade information. Here, too, should be found scores attained on achievement tests in arithmetical operations, arithmetical problems, algebra, and geometry. All are pertinent. Also his marks in drawing and industrial arts. His relative standing in mathematical and scientific courses when compared with his marks in the more strictly verbal subjects will throw light on his trends of ability and interest. They should, if possible, be compared with the school achievements of his predecessors who have eventually found satisfactory adjustment in a skilled trade.

If the cumulative record lacks scores on dependable tests of intelligence, possession of the requisite level of verbal intelligence may be roughly estimated by reference to school marks and rate of school progress.

When progress in school has not been entirely satisfactory—due perhaps to a strong distaste for the particular subject-matter which the curriculum has imposed—one or two intelligence tests should be given; for a person is quite likely to have some trouble in learning the technical information of a trade if he has a Binet Mental Age score of less than 14 years; an Otis Higher (20 minutes) score of less than 26; an Army Alpha score below 63; or a Beta score below 70. To be sure, a few employers, when engaging apprentices for the more difficult trades, set standards higher than these; while in other trades the minimum safe level—in the kind of mental abilities which these tests sample—is somewhat under the figures cited. These scores, however, may serve to define the borders of a danger zone, or at least a zone of doubt.

The accompanying Table IX lists a number of the trades included in the army occupational intelligence study, together with the Binet Mental Age scores corresponding roughly to the lower and upper quartile scores of men reporting these as their occupations. It is suggested that scores less than these lower quartiles be construed as warnings.

TABLE IX. LOWER LIMITS OF THE SAFETY ZONE

Showing certain skilled trades arranged in approximate order according to minimal requirements of ability to learn, as measured by tests of intelligence, and showing both the lower and the upper limits of the middle 50 per cent of men following the occupation. (From army data.)

Mental Age, 14 to 17
- Photographer
- Telegrapher
- Electrician

Mental Age, 13.5 to 16
- Farrier
- Locomotive engineer
- Toolmaker
- Ship carpenter

Mental Age, 13 to 15.8
- Marine engineer
- Auto-engine mechanic
- Plumber
- Pipefitter
- General auto mechanic
- Lineman
- Tailor

Mental Age, 12.5 to 15.5
- General machinist
- General carpenter
- Baker
- General blacksmith
- Railway shop mechanic
- Painter
- Cobbler
- Bricklayer
- Stationary engineer

Mental Age, 12 to 14.5
- Boilermaker
- Structural-steel worker
- Mason
- Stationary fireman

As to intelligence quotients found on the cumulative record, a single figure of 80 or 85 need not be taken very seriously if it is out of line with other indications of the young man's capacities, especially if it was based on a group test, or recorded a few years previously during the elementary school period. But two or more of these I Q's, each less than 90, carry an admonition to find out whether they now fairly represent the candidate's ability to learn; for if they do, the more difficult of the skilled trades will probably be beyond his grasp. For such trades a Stanford Binet I Q of 92 is a safer minimum, and 84 for the less difficult.

Another reason why a counselor wants to ascertain his client's intelligence has already been suggested. It may make quite a difference in the degree of satisfaction he eventually finds in his occupation if he chooses a trade in which he is one of the more intelligent rather than one of the less intelligent members of his group. A young man whose I Q is 110, for example, and who wants to be one of the leaders among his associates, would probably be more congenially situated in a skilled trade than in an engineering profession.

One use of a Binet test, when estimating fitness to undertake a skilled trade, appears when performances in the separate tasks set by the examination are compared. A profile indicative of superiority in the arithmetical, spatial and mechanical items usually goes with technical interests and aptitudes, even when performance in the verbal items is not up to par.

The differences a counselor finds in his client's abilities to deal with various sorts of problems—linguistic, mathematical, spatial, social, practical—remind us that as many varieties of intelligence may be distinguished and defined as there are kinds of problems. Persons of the same general level of intelligence may differ widely in their ability to solve two problems which are on the average, for the majority of people, quite alike in difficulty. So, for example, a person may do much better in a non-language paper-and-pencil test like Army Beta than he does in Alpha; or better in a series of manual performance problems than in either Alpha or Beta. As a rule, intelligence examinations like Army Beta or the non-verbal parts of the Scovill Classification Test furnish more dependable indications of ability to master a trade than do tests heavily weighted with verbal problems.

This does not mean that available scores on verbal tests of intelligence such as the Otis should be ignored, but rather that relatively low scores should not be interpreted as decisive. Non-verbal tests may tell a different story. Tests known to be indicative of mechanical intelligence, like those about to be described, are here of special value. They are a distinct help in distinguishing persons with aptitude for learning a trade from those whose best aptitudes are for semi-skilled manual occupations.

3

The essential difference between aptitude for a skilled trade and aptitude for a semi-skilled occupation should stand out in clear relief. A trade requires the ability to think through the problems of the craft as they arise and to decide what operations must be performed; while for many a semi-skilled occupation the ability to perform the necessary operations is enough. To succeed in a semi-skilled occupation, the first requisite may be an aptitude for acquiring manual skill, for learning to do the operations rapidly and dextrously; but a skilled trade demands also a degree of problem-solving ability—of intelligence, mechanical, mathematical and verbal—above the level of many an operative competently working at a repetitive manual occupation.

The distinction between aptitude for solving mechanical problems and aptitude for acquiring manual skills is illustrated in the following comparison between a mechanical aptitude test and a manual aptitude test. The same materials will serve for both tests. They consist of the parts of an electric lamp socket: porcelain core, knob, contacts, screws, washers, cardboard insulation, brass casing, and other pieces ready to be assembled. Ask a young man to fit them together so that the device will work. If he has never done this particular puzzle before, he must first study out how the parts fit, and the order in which they must be put into place. It challenges his mind—his mechanical intelligence, not his manual ability. The powers which he brings to bear upon the problem have been called by various names: sense of form, ability to visualize three-dimensional structure, perception of spatial relations, mechanical ingenuity, inventiveness, engineering aptitude, ability to deal with things, manipulative intelligence, practical intelligence. However labeled, the abilities he uses in solving problems like this are symptoms of what we shall call his *mechanical aptitude*. A graded series of such problems, beginning with tasks no harder than fitting together the three parts of a wooden clothes pin or a metal paper clamp, constitutes a mechanical assembly test of a kind frequently used as one means of estimating mechanical aptitude.

Suppose now that instead of asking the young man to think out the way in which the parts of the lamp socket should be assembled, we first show him just how to do it most easily and quickly, and then see how rapidly he can do it. His success under these circumstances is a symptom not of mechanical aptitude, but of *manual aptitude*. A person with little or no mechanical aptitude, but with good motor coordination, may learn to excel in the routine work of assembling lamp sockets. He may become highly proficient in the operations he learns to perform. But he will surely experience difficulty in mastering a mechanical trade; for his manual ability must here be guided by intelligence of the sort used in thinking through mechanical and arithmetical problems and in acquiring technical information. Granted that manual aptitudes of which the symptoms are good coordination of eye and hand, dexterity of fingers, steadiness and quickness of movement, ability to acquire a high degree of skill, are valuable assets in a candidate for an apprenticeship as well as in an applicant for training in a semi-skilled operation, it is nevertheless insisted that manual aptitudes are not enough. Skilled trades demand also mechanical aptitudes.

4

Certain tests designed to aid in estimating manual dexterity and versatility have been described in the previous chapter. The tasks they set are varied: spool-packing, block-packing, block-placing, card-placing, sorting, tapping, tracing, dotting, aiming, putting pins in a peg-board with fingers or with tweezers, turning a handle, maintaining steadiness, balancing, following with a pointer an irregularly moving target, and the like. The correlation between the different motor abilities measured by such tests is low. Motor tests, it must be remembered, are of use chiefly when there is a question as to a person's manual aptitude for learning an operation closely similar to the one involved in the particular test selected, or when success in a number of tests is used as an indication of manual versatility.

Keenness of eye, both in seeing fine details and in judging positions and distances, may be important in the operations to be learned; also kinesthetic sensitivity—the delicacy of feeling which enables one readily to judge distance of movement or snugness of fit when tightening a nut with a wrench, turning the handle of a cutting-machine, adjusting a gauge or micrometer, or manipulating other tools. Both motor and sensory abilities are factors in manual aptitudes. They are assets in a skilled trade such as woodworking or one of the metal trades, as well as in many a semi-skilled operation.

Our first concern, however, in estimating aptitudes for skilled trades is not with tests to measure motor abilities or sensory acuities. These questions may be deferred until after the evidence as to mechanical aptitudes and intelligence has been considered. We have already referred to the use of tests of abstract intelligence—verbal and mathematical—and have indicated the levels of performance below which a person's scores may be construed as contraindications of aptitude for learning a trade. Other significant factors are brought to light by means of mechanical assembly tests, form-boards, and paper-and-pencil tests specially designed to reveal mechanical—as contrasted with manual—aptitudes.

An early example of a standardized mechanical aptitude test is the Stenquist Assembling Test, variously known in the army in 1918 as the Stenquist Construction Test and the Stenquist Skill Test. Each form consists of a series of ten disassembled devices. The final score is a function partly of the correctness with which the objects are assembled and partly of the speed with which it is done. During the two decades since this test was first developed it has undergone several revisions and is one of the best of its type. The adaptation known as the Minnesota Mechanical Assembly Test is described in detail on page 294. This form of the test, when used to predict the success of junior-high-school boys in shop courses, was found to yield better results than most of the other tests in the Minnesota battery of mechanical ability tests. It is less reliable when given to men than to boys, perhaps because of greater differences in previous familiarity with some of the objects to be assembled.

One possible shortcoming in such a test when used to estimate whether a person has the kind of intelligence needed in learning a mechanical trade, resides in the fact that his score is due not alone to his mechanical insight but in part also to his manual dexterity. It is not exactly a pure test of mechanical intelligence. This same consideration has been raised with reference to other mechanical aptitude tests involving manual manipulation: the Ruger mechanical puzzles, the Healy Puzzle Box and the O'Connor Wiggly Block; also the various form boards such as the Minnesota Spatial Relations Test and the Kent-Shakow Industrial Form Boards which have been used to measure ability to recognize similarities of size and shape and to deal with spatial relations. Theoretically it should be possible to introduce proper allowances for individual differences in manual ability by measuring the time it takes a person to do the task both before and after he knows just how to do it; but this refinement has rarely been attempted because of the difficulty of equating levels of practice; and in any event the manual-ability factor is, after all, not of great consequence in determining a person's performance on tests like these. The Minnesota Mechanical Assembly Test and the Minnesota Spatial Relations Form Boards are at present the most dependable performance tests for use in measuring mechanical aptitude. On either of these tests, a Standard Score of less than 5.0 may well be construed as a precautionary signal.

There are numerous performance tests in which it is clear that success calls for both mechanical and manual aptitudes. One of these is selected for description here because it undoubtedly has some merit as an index of aptitude for drafting, woodworking, and the metal trades. It is the Two-Hand Test, a tracing test known in England as the Compound Slide Rest Test. The apparatus, illustrated on page 124,[1] consists of a small platform so mounted that it can be moved in any desired horizontal direction by turning two screws at right angles to each other. The direction of movement is governed by the relative speed with which the screws are turned, just as the cutting tool of an engine lathe is controlled by the operator. A paper on the platform rubs against the point of a fixed pencil, so that, as the screw handles are moved, a tracing is made. The task is to keep this mark within the narrow limits of a prescribed path shown on the paper, and to complete the tracing as soon as possible. The speed and accuracy with which this is done is taken as one indication of mechanical aptitude.[2] (See Fig. 10, page 136.)

The relative extent to which ability in this test is symptomatic of aptitude for different trades is suggested by the following correlations between test performance and trade ability as reported by the late Max Tagg, who was principal of a London technical school.

Pattern-making	.39
Draftsmanship	.42
Fitting (bench work in machine shop)	.55
Machine-operating	.57
Toolmaking	.59
Turning (lathe work)	.62

Mention may be made, in passing, of Rupp's two-hand adaptation of the pantograph, the operation of which seems to call for abilities similar to those measured by the Two-Hand Test here described.

5

Paper-and-pencil tests of mechanical aptitude also find a place in the testing program, particularly when groups are being examined

[1] From *Procedures in Employment Psychology*, p. 107, by W. V. Bingham and M. Freyd. New York: McGraw-Hill Book Company, 1926.

[2] Patten's test known as the Wisconsin Test of Engine Lathe Aptitude is similar in principle to this Two-Hand Test. See C. L. Hull, *Aptitude Testing*, p. 68. Yonkers: World Book Co., 1928. Patten reports a correlation of .42 between ability of engineering-college students in this test and the quality of the lathe work turned out in their shop practice course.

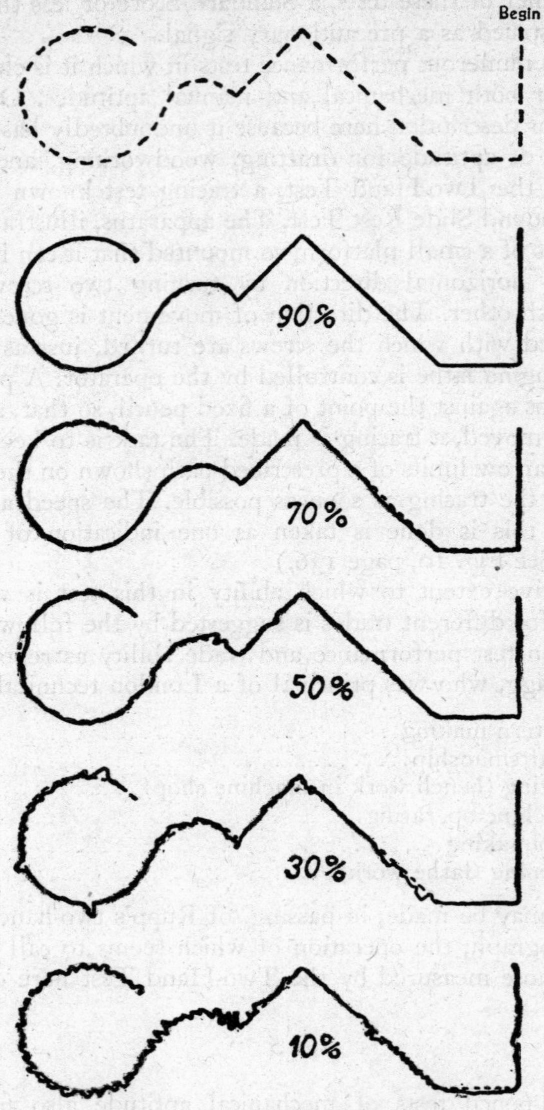

FIG. 10. SCALE OF PERFORMANCE

Showing a pattern to be traced and five samples of performance used in rating ability in the Two-hand Test (Compound Slide Rest) pictured on page 124. Adapted from W. Moede, *Arbeitstechnik,* page 130. Stuttgart: Ferdinand Enka Verlag, 1935.

for purposes of preliminary appraisal. Ability not only to perceive the spatial relations of objects but to think correctly about these relations is obviously an important factor in mechanical aptitude. Indeed, it is so essential for many kinds of work that numerous blanks and forms have been developed for use in measuring this kind of ability. One of the most convenient of these is the geometrical construction test known as the Minnesota Paper Form Board recently improved by Likert and Quasha. (See page 312.) This is essentially a test of *speed in recognition* of forms and space relations. It does not measure accurately the level of *difficulty* of the space problems which a person is able to solve. That requires a more searching examination with less emphasis on speed—such, for example, as the Yale Spatial Relations Test, developed as an aid in estimating aptitude for engineering, or Part I of O'Rourke's Geometrical Construction Test.

The MacQuarrie Test of Mechanical Ability has been widely used to furnish a first rough appraisal of both manual and mechanical abilities. Three of the seven sub-tests—tracing, tapping, and dotting—are manual. The others, of more interest as indicators of mechanical aptitudes, require some intelligence and quickness in dealing with forms, patterns, and relations in space. As suggested on page 314, counselors using this blank will ordinarily wish to note the relative excellence of a person's performance in these sub-tests. Then, if certain of the sub-scores are high or low, the particular abilities which they sample may be measured by means of other tests in order to learn whether the apparent superiority or inferiority is real.

Mechanical aptitude reveals itself in habits of noticing mechanical devices, how they are constructed and how they work. People with a mechanical bent pick up a varied stock of information about tools and common mechanical objects. Tests to measure familiarity with the uses of a large number of pictured tools and of ability to identify the objects and materials with which these tools are used, yield scores significantly related to other measures of mechanical aptitude.

O'Rourke's Mechanical Aptitude Test, Junior Grade, is a good example of such examinations. Part One consists of pictorial items; Part Two, of verbal informational items. The higher scores are ordinarily made only by young men who have evinced a continuing interest in mechanical things (see page 318). The author reports a correlation of .64 with ratings as machinist apprentice and correlations as high as .84 with ratings in vocational training courses. Stenquist's Mechanical Aptitude Tests (not to be confused with his Mechanical Assembling Tests) use pictorial and diagrammatic problems exclusively. The Detroit Mechanical Aptitudes Examinations (one for boys and one for girls) contain eight sub-tests, three of which call for an acquaintance with common tools, mechanical devices, and their uses; one is a paper form-board; one is a more difficult spatial relations test; one calls for comparison of sizes of simple figures; one is a pictorial sorting test; and one, a manual test of ability to trace a line within a narrow irregular path. Scores on these sub-tests as well as total scores are of interest in individual diagnosis.

6

The practice of those industries which exercise special care in the selection of trade apprentices is suggestive of standards to be kept in mind by counselors. The employment managers and foremen who make the selections place weight on evidences of mental as well as manual ability. Sometimes they have had opportunity to observe the candidate over a period of time while he has been working in the shop as an operative or a helper. The ease with which he has learned to do the work assigned and the care and diligence with which he has done it; his familiarity with tools; his age; his physical fitness; and his interests and personality as judged in interviews—all are given consideration. Inquiries are made as to his previous employment experience, his schooling, his rate of school progress, and his success in mathematics and drafting, as well as in any shop courses he may have taken. When examinations are given they are apt to contain arithmetical problems. When tests of intelligence are used, the minimum standards are not lower than those for routine clerical workers.

The Scovill Manufacturing Company has used in its employment office Pond's battery known as the Scovill Classification Test, consisting of three verbal and five non-verbal tests as described in Chapter V. When selecting toolmaker apprentices, a scientifically weighted score based on age and on performance in the five non-verbal tests has been found to be discriminating. Those to be hired are chosen by interview from among the applicants whose test performance comes up to the standards set. Eighty-three of these carefully selected apprentices have taken also four other tests. Their lower quartile scores are shown in Table X. It is suggested that counselors might well construe scores below these lower quartiles as precautionary signals when fitness for a trade as exacting as that of toolmaker is in question; but a very low score in only one or two of these tests need not be regarded as a serious deterrent, for among the candidates who were employed and definitely made good are a few whose scores on at least two of these tests were much below the levels indicated in the table.

TABLE X. LOWER QUARTILE SCORES OF TOOLMAKER APPRENTICES

Showing, for tests taken by 83 apprentices of the Scovill Manufacturing Company, the 25th percentile scores

Test	Q_1
1. Scovill Classification Test (final score)	150
2. Apprentice Scale	417
3. Otis Higher (20 minutes)	32
4. MacQuarrie Mechanical Ability	53
5. O'Connor Wiggly Block	6′48″
6. Kent-Shakow Form Board	60

The Classification Test score of 150 happens to be the lower quartile for men clerical workers in this plant, as well as for this group of toolmaker apprentices. The score of 417 on the Apprentice Scale is now considered the lower limit of the preferred range for toolmaker apprentice candidates. A score of 32 on the Otis corresponds roughly to a Binet Mental Age score of at least 15. A MacQuarrie score of 53 equals the average score for age 14, and is not far from the lower quartile for adults. The score on O'Connor's Block is the average time for three trials, corrected for age and for practice effect, and is not quite as good as his lower quartile mark which is 6′ 8″. The Kent-Shakow scores were computed according to the procedures first recommended by the authors of the test.

7

Before summarizing the main points with reference to trade aptitudes and ways of ascertaining them, the topic "Father's Occupation" deserves a word.

This is not the fourteenth century. And yet there are a few crafts—like that of glove cutter—in which one qualification ordinarily required of a candidate for an apprenticeship is that he have a father who is a journeyman of the craft. The remunerative goldbeater's trade is one of these. Blowers of Venetian glass and makers of elaborate ornamental candles are also said to maintain this tradition. Openings are filled by legacy as it were, quite like the presidency of many a bank and the management of certain New England cotton mills.

There are, indeed, even in a democratic society, some things to be said in favor of giving weighty consideration to the matter of heredity at times of vocational decision. It is not beside the point that the item "Father's Occupation" appears near the top of most personal history questionnaires. A young man who takes up his father's trade knows what he is doing. He brings to his training a background of familiarity with the work which other novices lack. Then, too, the chances are that a son has inherited his father's aptitudes. When this is not the case, who, except the youth himself, is more likely to be aware of the fact than the father who has doubtless often enough observed the boy's ineptitude when given opportunity to help in the day's work?

Other things being equal, the presumption is in favor of probable success if a son enters the craft which his father has satisfactorily pursued. But if either of them thinks that the requisite aptitudes are lacking, surely decision should be deferred until there has been a canvass of other fields.

8

We have seen that while aptitudes for the semi-skilled manual occupations are largely matters of manual versatility, of aptness in learning to make rapid dextrous movements of fingers or hands, aptitudes for skilled trades are more complex. They require in general a higher order of intelligence—mechanical, mathematical, and verbal—than do most of the semi-skilled occupations, but not so high as is expected of professional engineers.

To appraise these aptitudes, school marks and scores in scholastic aptitude tests and in performance tests of intelligence furnish the first sources of information to be canvassed. Scores in achievement tests, particularly in mathematical subjects, should also be considered. Then, mechanical aptitudes as revealed by available scores in such paper-and-pencil tests as the O'Rourke, Detroit, MacQuarrie, Stenquist, and Minnesota Paper Form Board, may well be passed in review. If doubt remains regarding the candidate's mechanical intelligence, his ability in tests such as the Minnesota Spatial Relations Form Boards, the Kent-Shakow Industrial Form Boards, and the Minnesota Mechanical Assembly Test, should be ascertained. When counselor and client are satisfied that he has a real interest in learning a trade and also the requisite verbal, mathematical, and mechanical capacities of mind, the question is appropriately raised as to whether there are any serious handicaps—poor motor coordination, or limited sensory acuities, visual, tactile, or kinesthetic—for ability to perceive fine details and to acquire numerous manual skills is needed, as well as ability to master items of technical knowledge. Finally, the special requirements of the particular trade under discussion are scrutinized. These may include such diverse considerations as the candidate's æsthetic judgment, of value in crafts like cabinet-making or wrought-iron work; unusual facility in translating two-dimensional data into three-dimensional structure, in pattern-making and the sheet-metal trade; strength of arm and back in stone masonry; high degrees of kinesthetic and auditory sensitivity in piano-tuning; indifference to disagreeable odors and sights in the slaughter-house trades; exceptional steadiness of nerve in structural-steel erecting; and the like. Indications of aptitudes for specific kinds of tasks as well as of the aptitudes generally sought in candidates for any trade apprenticeship will be scrupulously searched out.

So much for the skilled trades. The field of clerical occupations, to which attention now turns, differs, as we shall see, from the one we have been reviewing, not so much with respect to the level of general ability required as to the fact that clerical work ordinarily makes fewer demands on manual and mechanical aptitudes, and more on verbal facility.

Chapter XII

THE FIELD OF CLERICAL OCCUPATIONS

---

1. Reasons for interest in this field. The nature of clerical work. 2. Bills' classification of clerical positions. Range of salaries at each level. Responsibilities carried. Large proportion of clerical workers in the middle and upper ranks. 3. Typical activities. Four kinds of ability employers look for. 4. Mental alertness, a symptom of clerical aptitude. Resemblance between prognostic tests and tests of clerical proficiency.

1

THE clerical field embraces a large group of occupations. Aptitudes for clerical work can be fairly appraised only when the nature of the work done in the various kinds and levels of clerical employment is clearly understood. We shall therefore first survey the clerical scene in all its variety, classify the positions which clerical workers occupy, and describe the abilities, both general and specific, which these workers exhibit. Against such a background it will then be feasible to inspect selected tests of clerical aptitude and to judge of their worth.

Measurement of clerical aptitudes has received intensive study. This is fortunate. The number of people engaged in employments of a clerical nature has risen rapidly since 1900, and in 1930 the census enumerators found nearly 4,000,000 people who reported their occupations as clerical. Taking the country as a whole, 5.4 per cent of the men and 18.5 per cent of the women having gainful occupations were in this category. The proportions in the cities were even larger. In New York, for example, 30.1 per cent of the women following gainful occupations were clerical workers. Tests to help in estimating the probabilities of success in these occupations are therefore among the most desired aids in counseling.

The need for measures of clerical aptitudes is emphasized by the fact that the number of young people attracted toward such callings is vastly greater than the number of opportunities. From every educational level—grammar grades, secondary schools, colleges, and universities—streams of candidates for clerical employment pour into the vast pool of the white-collar labor market. Many of these young people make satisfactory adjustments. A great many, however, do not. Either they meet more able competitors for the vacanices which arise, or, having secured clerical work, they do not make progress in it, and eventually turn elsewhere. While planning their education and their search for work, they had in some instances assumed that their industry and ambition would fully compensate for any deficiencies in the abilities required. But they actually had little aptitude for the kinds of work done by clerical employees, or else they had not secured adequate training. Such mistakes a guidance service aims to forestall.

The occupational choices of pupils in school and at time of leaving show an unduly large proportion of expressed preferences for the more common clerical occupations. Huge numbers choose to prepare for typing and stenography. The occupation of bookkeeping, also popular, exhibits perhaps the most startling disparity between preferences and opportunities. There are reported to be at the present time about as many students who have elected to study bookkeeping as there are bookkeepers in the entire country! Obviously a large majority of these students will never earn a livelihood at keeping books or accounting. They may use their knowledge to some extent in other occupations; but they should at least have a second string to their bow. It is a counselor's privilege to help those with little or no aptitude for such clerical work to ascertain the fact some time before they finish their schooling, and to turn their attention toward stores or gardens or factories where there are occupations which may prove to be for them more promising.

The responsibilities placed on the shoulders of clerical workers are frequently heavier than an outsider realizes. Clerical duties in a modern office, as Marion A. Bills has pointed out, "include the gathering, classification, and preservation of data of all sorts, and the analysis and use of these data in planning, executing, and determining the results of operation." Such a description of the clerical field recognizes that clerks—at least those whose duties are not of the most elementary sort—are often called upon to make decisions similar to those of a minor executive, and in many instances to take part in the more exacting activities of the executive higher up the scale.

The late W. H. Leffingwell, distinguished industrial engineer who specialized in office problems, said that all clerical work consists of three functions only. The first of these functions is planning—determining what is to be done and when and where it is to be done. The second is communication—corresponding and interviewing both within the office itself and between the office and outsiders. The third, accounting and record-keeping, includes computing, recording and filing of all sorts. Of these three, planning the work is often thought of as an executive rather than a clerical function; but counselors should bear in mind that to some extent planning is required in all clerical work except the most routine, and is an essential feature of clerical activities in the middle- and higher-level positions. There is a wide range in the difficulty, the complexity and the responsibility of clerical positions, extending all the way from the clerk doing the simplest sorting to the clerk who has to make decisions, binding on his employer, involving thousands of dollars.

2

The steps up the promotional ladder, as well as the variety of clerical duties to be performed in a large office, are well illustrated in the classification of clerical positions developed by Bills in 1923 and now used for purposes of wage and salary standardization by many banks, insurance companies, chain stores, and manufacturing concerns.[1]

This classification of positions is based on the assumption that every clerical operation consists of three definite phases: (1) doing the work, (2) checking it, and (3) supervising it; and that each phase constitutes a step above the preceding one. Furthermore, the theory is that the difficulty of the job can be measured in terms of *the number and the kind of decisions to be made.*

The jobs are first divided into two groups, according to the kind of information the clerk must have. The first group includes jobs calling only for a knowledge of certain definite and specific rules covering practically all cases to be handled, any exceptions being referred to the supervisor. The second group comprises jobs in which decisions are made by reference to certain general principles rather

[1] Cf. W. V. Bingham, "Classifying and Testing for Clerical Jobs," *Personnel Journal*, 1935, 14:163-172.

than to specific rules, requiring, therefore, intensive knowledge of an entire field.

Each of these general groups of clerical positions is then subdivided into two classes. The first group is divided according to the number of rules the clerk must know; and the second, according to whether the necessary field of information is limited, or is large or technical.

The relative difficulty of the supervisory positions is then defined, either in terms of the number of people, or the kind of work, supervised. The supervision of thirty or forty office boys is classed according to the number in the group, while the direction of a few clerks engaged in technical work is classified by the kind of work they do.

A clerical position calling for two types of work receives a dual classification, and for salary purposes is assigned to the class carrying the higher maximum.

A separate scheme of classification is used for typists, stenographers, dictating-machine operators, secretaries, comptometer operators, and those using other business machines. The eight categories in this classification are shown in Table XI.

The main classification, shown in Table XII, specifies fourteen definite grades of clerical workers, ranging from the level of office boy to that of actuary.

The salary standards indicated are not those prevailing in any one company, but correspond fairly closely to the present practice of representative offices, and serve to illustrate the relationships which have been found to hold between the salaries earned by workers in the various grades of clerical occupation. Basic rates, particularly entering salaries on the lower levels, are found to vary somewhat from these figures in different lines of business and in different communities; but these differences do not seem to correspond to the size of the city, or to the part of the country in which it is located, or to the cost of living there. Fluctuations due to the status of the labor market and to changes in the cost of living are in general much narrower than would be expected. Throughout the most serious of business depressions the scale of clerical salaries paid by most large offices shifted, on the average, within a range of only 12 to 15 per cent.

The nature of the responsibilities carried by clerks on the different levels of this classification is illustrated in the following examples. The first describes work done in an insurance office by a clerical employee whose position is classed as B 1:

John Smith, working in a factory building, has slipped on the floor and broken his leg, and his employer has made a claim under the accident policy he carries with the insurance company. A memorandum giving the details of the accident and the resulting claim is relayed to this clerk, who checks the memorandum with his card file. He finds out whether the injured man's employer was insured and, if so, whether the policy covers broken legs caused by accidents inside the factory. If his file does not contain any card showing such insurance in force, he refers the notice to his supervisor for investigation; but, finding the policy in force and the accident covered, he enters the details on his card, together with the adjuster's estimate of the amount the company may be called upon to pay. Later, the claim adjuster finds that the sum to be paid may differ from the first estimate, and then the clerk receives a second memorandum and makes an additional entry on his card. Finally, after settlement with the policyholder and payment of doctor's bills and hospital charges, the clerk gets notice of the payments and enters on his card the required data.

TABLE XI. CLASSIFICATION OF "S" CLERICAL POSITIONS

i.e., Typing, Stenography, Secretarial, etc.

Class	*Description of work*	*Salary range* minimum	maximum
S1.	Transcribing on typewriter or other machine..........	$ 728	$1,040
S2.	Typing, combined with some stenographic or dictating-machine work; or difficult typing such as setting up schedules and tables..............	780	1,200
S2a.	Operating bookkeeping or Elliott-Fisher machine........	780	1,200
S3.	Typing from dictating machine..................	960	1,500
S3a.	Comptometer work..................	960	1,500
S4.	Stenographic work..................	1,200	1,800
S5.	Stenographic work with some secretarial duties..........	1,440	2,460
S6.	Secretarial work..................	1,740	3,200

An instance of a clerical position classified as C 1 is that of the Experience Clerk:

The Experience Clerk is the man who does the detail work needed in order to determine the rate you will pay for your automobile insurance next year. This means accumulating information about such cars as yours, insured in your state, of the same age as yours and carrying the same type of insurance. The amount you and your fellow car owners have paid for premiums must be learned, and also how many accidents you have had, how much property has been damaged, what personal injury has resulted, and how much the company has paid out to settle claims involving you and your fellow drivers. When your car is smashed up in an accident the insurance company is sometimes able to sell some of the good parts. The Experience Clerk records the amounts salvaged. If your car is damaged in a collision and the insurance company collects from the owner of the other car, that amount also goes into the credit account.

In addition to what the Experience Clerk has to do in gathering facts for his own company, he must meet the demands of the various state insurance de-

TABLE XII. CLASSIFICATION OF OTHER CLERICAL POSITIONS

Showing levels defined in terms of the nature and difficulty of the operations performed, and typical salary range for each level

Class	*Description of work*	*Salary range* minimum	maximum
A.	Messenger service jobs. Frequently combined with sorting and the operation of simple machines, to fill in time; but the messenger service is the chief duty, characteristic of the class	$ 728	$ 832
B.	Manual clerical operations requiring knowledge of a limited number of well-defined rules. This class includes some of the filing jobs, some of the identification work, some of the posting and computing; and, in general, those jobs where only a definite and specific change is made in the material handled.		
B1.	Doing the work, subject to check	728	1,040
B2.	Checking the work, or doing the work without subsequent check, or having charge of a small unit of the work	780	1,200
BB.	Supervision of B workers in small groups	900	1,380
C.	Positions in which the operations require knowledge of a large number of rules which are, however, precise and explicit. Any points not clearly covered by these rules are referred to the supervisor.		
C1.	Doing the work, subject to check	960	1,500
C2.	Checking the work, or doing it without subsequent check, or handling the more difficult C details, or having charge of a small unit of C work	1,200	1,800
D.	Supervision of A, B, S1 or S2 workers in large groups or of C or S3 workers in small groups	1,200	1,980
E.	Positions in which the operations require complete and intensive knowledge of a restricted field and action on questions not previously raised, calling for application of a general rule to a particular transaction.		
E1.	Doing the work, subject to check	1,400	2,340
E2.	Checking the work, handling doubtful papers requiring adjustment of difficulties, making special calculations or doing the more complicated E work	1,716	3,200
F.	Direction and supervision of a small unit of work in Class E or a large unit of lower grade work, or assisting in the supervision of a large unit of E grade work or lower	2,080	3,400
G.	Positions calling for technical training, professional background, or knowledge of the general principles of the business.		
G1.	Doing the usual work on this level	2,500	3,600
G2.	Handling the more complicated problems	3,000	4,800
H.	Supervision of G work, or of a large unit of lower work	3,200	5,000
I.	Supervision over H workers, or doing highly technical work for which special background and training is necessary	4,000	6,400

partments for much information of the same character. Lack of uniformity in the requirements of these departments multiplies the details. Moreover, the several associations in which the company has membership need similar records in their work of compiling data on accident experience. This clerk assembles all the material, prepares the reports, and finally arrives at a figure which may be used as a base in determining the rate for insuring your car. If at any stage of the work he finds himself at a loss to know how to proceed or how to interpret instructions, he consults his supervisor.

A typical E job in an insurance company is that of Underwriter:

In the Marine Division, for example, is a man who is obliged to know the various steamship lines, the individual ships, and the desirability of certain types of cargo, so that over the telephone he can say that the company will insure or decline to insure a cargo of refrigerators going from New York to South America on a certain steamer of a certain line. He may never before have had to deal with precisely the same set of circumstances with respect to merchandise, ship, etc.; but knowing the general principles of marine insurance, the company practice, and the ratings of the ships and lines, he must decide whether to accept the risk.

The men doing clerical work on the G and I levels in an insurance company are professional men such as actuaries (those who have passed specific examinations and have a recognized standing in actuarial societies), attorneys (those who have passed their bar examinations), engineers (technical college graduates), or others whose work requires definitely technical or professional background.

It is impossible to say how many clerical positions in the country at large are of the S 1 or B 1 sort—that is, requiring ability to do straight typing from copy, or to follow a relatively small number of clearly stated rules or, at the other extreme, how many there are on the G and I levels, filled only by graduate engineers, physicians, lawyers, or others with professional or equivalent advanced training or with long experience in a particular kind of technical work. Nor are we certain of the proportions in the several intermediate clerical grades—in secretarial positions, for instance, in contrast with the stenographic posts. Such estimates are difficult, because in only the more progressive of the larger offices are the gradations of clerical duties and qualifications clearly defined. The figures for a single company which has several thousand clerical employees under one roof may be examined as illustrative. The proportion of employees engaged in each of the different levels and classes of clerical work in the office of the Aetna Life Insurance Company, of Hartford, Connecticut, in August, 1935, is shown in Table XIII.

TABLE XIII. DISTRIBUTION OF OFFICE WORKERS IN ONE COMPANY

Showing the proportion of clerical employees in each category and level of the clerical classification, from office boy to actuary

(Officers of the company and building employees are not included)

I. *Clerks*		II. *Typists, Stenographers, Secretaries*		III. *Supervisors*			
Class	Per cent of total	Class	Per cent of total	Class	Per cent of total	Per cent of total on each level	Per cent in lower, middle, and upper brackets
A.	1.5					1.5	
B1.	11.4	S1.	3.2			14.6	
B2.	15.4	S2.	4.8			20.2	
							36.3
				BB.	1.2	1.2	
C1.	10.4	S3.	4.7			15.1	
C2.	14.2	S4.	3.5			17.7	
							34.0
				D.	2.4	2.4	
E1.	8.6	S5.	.1			8.7	
E2.	9.9	S6.	.6			10.5	
				F.	2.2	2.2	
G1.	2.5					2.5	
G2.	1.7					1.7	
				H.	1.4	1.4	
I.	.3					.3	
							29.7
Total	75.9		16.9		7.2	100.0	100.0

This table strikingly illustrates the relatively small proportion of typists, stenographers, and other operators of office machines in comparison with the large number of other clerks. The S classification accounts for only 16.9 per cent of the office force. There are more than four times as many clerks who do not belong in this S classification as there are those who do.

Class S 1, which includes typists doing direct transcribing, constitutes a fifth of those in the S classification or 3.2 per cent of the total force. Classes S 2 and S 3, which together account for more than half of the employees in the S classification, consist mainly of operators of dictating, bookkeeping, or calculating machines.

The secretaries and the stenographers doing some secretarial work (S 6 and S 5) constitute about 4 per cent of the S classification and only seven-tenths of 1 per cent of the office force. The E clerks, who have responsibilities and salaries comparable with this secretarial-stenographic class, are *twenty-six times* as numerous.

About one office employee in fourteen is a supervisor.

Most significant for the counselor and the student of clerical aptitudes is the number of clerks needed in the more responsible positions. There has been in some quarters a mistaken tendency to conceive of clerical occupations as providing opportunities chiefly for workers on the lowest levels, and to judge of the validity of tests of clerical aptitudes mainly by reference to the performance of routine workers. And yet clerical employees in the top brackets, E, S 5, S 6, G, and I—those who are relied upon to apply general principles and to use their own judgment in meeting situations not definitely covered by specific rules or formulations of standard practice—comprise a very substantial group. The entire office force may be classified into three main levels—a lower, an intermediate, and a higher. On the intermediate level the large majority of the employees are the C 1 and C 2 clerks, but here are included also the first-line supervisors (BB), the operators of dictating machines and comptometers (S 3 and S 3a), and the stenographers (S 4). These middle-level groups together make up one-third of the total force. Below them in rank and pay are, to be sure, somewhat more than a third of the office workers, but above them are almost as many—29.7 per cent in this company. Is this large proportion of high-level clerical workers exceptional? Not in the insurance business. In other lines the proportion is usually nearer 25 per cent than 30 per cent of the total. It is, however, not at all the very small fraction which some have supposed. Good heads are needed in an office no less than speedy operators.

Most clerks begin their employment on the B 1 level, including college graduates who are hired with the expectation that they will advance into the middle and upper ranks.

3

When examining the available means of measuring aptitudes for clerical occupations, it is necessary to keep in mind the responsibilities and duties indicated in the foregoing classification. At the same time we should have an eye on such typical activities as are common to the various kinds and levels of clerical work. When fulfilling their functions of planning, communication, and record-keeping, just what do clerical employees do?

Much of a clerk's work has to do with papers: memoranda, correspondence, records. On the papers are words, symbols, numbers. These he reads, compares, classifies, transcribes, or passes judgment upon, and in the course of so doing makes decisions which, except in the more routine operations, may require a high order of technical knowledge and good sense. The tools of his trade include the pencil and the pen, and sometimes the slide rule, the typewriter, the duplicator, the bookkeeping or calculating machine, the filing cabinet, the card index, and similar aids in classifying, cataloging, finding, rearranging, identifying, copying, computing, or otherwise manipulating for a purpose the papers and symbols used in recording and communication. It must be remembered, however, that a clerical worker's speed and accuracy in the mechanics of using these tools, essential though they are, rank lower in value than the correctness of his thinking about the problems which the papers present. A clerk may be called upon to do other kinds of work also, such as to use the telephone, receive visitors, make purchases, organize and supervise the work of others in the office. But as a clerical worker, the abilities indispensable to the effective performance of his duties are those which enable him to handle the problems arising in connection with his paper work judiciously as well as rapidly.

Here, then, is one clue to the selection of aids in appraising clerical aptitudes. The counselor, like the employer, wants reliable tests and other good indicators of a person's ability to read, quickly and accurately, printed and written symbols; to grasp their significance; to decide wisely what to do about them; and to perform the operations required as a consequence of these decisions.

Aptitudes for clerical occupations, then, are evidenced in part at least, by four different kinds of abilities. The first and simplest of these is strictly perceptual: ability to observe words and numbers, to see instantly and correctly what is on the paper. The second is intellectual: ability to grasp the meanings of the words and other symbols and to make correct decisions regarding the questions they raise. Although relatively less important on the level of purely routine and closely supervised clerical work, this intellectual ability becomes increasingly indispensable as the grades of employment above the lowest rung of the ladder are ascended. Clerical workers do not progress very far unless they are intelligent in what they do. The third group of clerical abilities consists of various mental skills peculiarly susceptible to improvement through special training. The most elementary of these skills include the ability to add and multiply, to spell correctly, to punctuate, and to use a wide variety of English words and expressions correctly; while the most advanced may require a technical knowledge of some learned profession. The fourth kind of ability is motor. With agile fingers and hands, the various papers, cards, pencil, typewriter, comptometer, and other office tools are adroitly manipulated. The person who, in doing paper work, is quick to see, skillful with the English language and with arithmetic, well educated in the subject-matter with which he is to deal, bright, and dextrous, has, then, the advantage in competition with anyone who is handicapped in visual perception, or incompetent in the use of language and numbers, or untrained, or dull, or clumsy.

4

With this analysis of clerical work in mind, it is not surprising that the ordinary paper-and-pencil tests designed to measure mental alertness, abstract intelligence, or scholastic aptitude have proved to be of use in estimating the probabilities that candidates for employment in clerical occupations will make good. Such intelligence examinations do not sample all the abilities indicative of the desired clerical aptitudes. They do, however, furnish a rough measure of both the perceptual and the intellectual abilities without which a clerical worker is bound to be at a disadvantage. The correlations between intelligence-test scores and clerical progress are not remarkably high, but are consistently positive and real.

For example, among a group of 130 clerical employees hired in 1925 and still with the firm seven years later, Bills reports that of those who scored 80 or less on the mental-alertness test known as Bureau Test VI, 64 per cent were still in the lowest grade jobs (A and B) while only 12 per cent had advanced to the upper-level positions (Class E and above). But of those who scored above 100, which corresponds roughly to 133 on Army Alpha, only 15 per cent were still working in Class A or B jobs, while 55 per cent had progressed to Class E positions or better. Similar studies by Pond in the Scovill Manufacturing Company confirm these findings. Brightness, of the sort measured directly by intelligence tests and indirectly by tests of English usage and vocabulary and by records of school progress, is certainly an important component of aptitude for clerical occupations.

This conclusion is supported by extensive experiments and studies carried forward during the past fourteen years by the Research Division of the U. S. Civil Service Commission under the direction of L. J. O'Rourke. A serious student of this subject will relish reading the annual reports of this Division, and will examine in detail some of the tests which have been developed, notably the Clerk-Carrier Examination used in sifting thousands of candidates for positions in the Post Office and the Railway Mail Service, and the Typist and Stenographer Examinations of which one set has recently been adapted and released for guidance use in schools and for employment in industry. (See page 327.)

A counselor helping a person to appraise his aptitudes for clerical work, then, looks not only for measures of his intelligence, but, more specifically, for evidences of his capacity to learn to do rapidly and accurately a variety of tasks quite similar to those performed by clerical workers. These tasks are illustrated in the standard examinations of clerical proficiency. And so, before examining in detail various prognostic tests which have been devised for the explicit purpose of measuring clerical aptitudes, it is well to review one of these proficiency examinations, used in measuring the ability of experienced employees. For example, the Examination in Clerical Proficiency developed by L. L. Thurstone at the University of Chicago was used in 1933 in a survey of the abilities of the clerical employees of the institution. It is a twenty-four page blank which required about three hours to administer. The twelve parts, together with the time limit for each part, are as follows:

Part I—Comparing (10 minutes)—consists of two pages of typed tabular matter, the first page an original and the other a copy. The copy is to be compared with the original and the errors noted.

Part II—Computation (30 minutes)—is made up of problems in addition, subtraction, multiplication, and division.

Part III—Alphabetical Filing (10 minutes)—lists in alphabetical order 79 proper names, all beginning with F, and 27 other names to be located in their proper alphabetical places in this list.

Part IV—Completion (10 minutes)—is a table of numerical data in which five items, left blank, can be computed after reference to the context. The missing figures are to be inserted in the table.

Part V—Business Information (10 minutes)—consists of fifty items in multiple choice form.

Part VI—Spelling (10 minutes)—lists 100 words to be examined and marked as correct or incorrect.

Part VII—Tabulation (10 minutes)—supplies statistical data to be classified.

Part VIII—Vocabulary (15 minutes)—is a test of 88 items in multiple-choice form.

Part IX—Arithmetical Reasoning (20 minutes)—consists of ten problems.

Part X—Reading (10 minutes)—requires the matching of proverbs similar in meaning.

Part XI—Estimating (20 minutes)—consists of questions like this: "Estimate the number of inhabitants per square mile in the most sparsely populated state of the United States in 1930 . . . 1( ) 10( ) 100( ) 1000( )."

Part XII—English Usage (20 minutes)—gives, in each of a hundred sentences, alternative expressions the better of which is to be selected.

This examination, consisting of tasks chosen as typical of those dealt with by clerical workers, is obviously in large part a test of verbal and mathematical intelligence. Although prepared for use in appraising the proficiency of experienced employees, it has here been described as illustrating the kinds of problems that may be used in order to estimate, not proficiency, but aptitude—the probability that a person without clerical training would find it easy to learn to follow a clerical occupation. This particular test, to be sure, is too long to be widely serviceable in either counseling or employment; and in any event its author has not published it for general use, or provided norms. Some of the available tests which have been specially designed to measure clerical aptitudes will be reviewed in the following chapter.

Chapter XIII

CLERICAL APTITUDES AND THEIR MEASUREMENT

1

THIS chapter is devoted to tests of clerical aptitudes. Representative tests are described in a way to help a counselor or an employer in interpreting such scores as he finds on a person's cumulative record, or in choosing for use in special situations the tests most appropriate to the particular problem faced. The fact will at no time be forgotten that aptitudes for clerical work cannot be appraised mechanically, by reference to test scores alone. Indeed, in considering so large and varied a field of occupation, it is peculiarly necessary to bear in mind that a person's performance on a standardized examination has significance only when it is viewed in relation to his educational assets, occupational experience, and preferences; with due regard also to differences in the nature of the work to be done in the various kinds and levels of clerical employment, as described in the preceding chapter.

Tests to measure aptitudes for clerical occupations are of two sorts: general and specific. The general tests strikingly resemble the common verbal intelligence tests. Specific tests, on the other hand, measure particular abilities deemed symptomatic of capacity to learn to do one or more kinds of clerical work such as filing, stenography, proof-reading, or accounting. Some tests bring together in a single examination tasks to measure abilities both general and specific.

The simplest form of specific test imposes a single task, such as comparison of numbers, and measures the time required to complete it or the amount completed within a specified time, together with the number of errors made. Illustrative of such tests are the O'Connor Number Checking Test and Word Checking Test, Worksamples 1 and 43, which use the amount-limit method especially adapted for individual examining (see page 327). The Minnesota Vocational Test for Clerical Workers (page 322), adapted for either group or individual administration, is also a number-comparison and name-comparison test. Developed on a foundation of intensive research, it has proved to be one of the more sensitive indicators of lack of clerical aptitude. The abilities it measures are known to be indicative of certain of the aptitudes needed in a wide range of clerical occupations such as routine card sorting, straight typing, stenography, filing, cashiering, computing, bookkeeping, and accountancy. Nearly all of the clerical workers examined have been found to surpass the average of the working population in this test. Its reliability is satisfactory. It may be used at any educational level from grammar school to university. It requires little over half an hour to administer and is readily scored. When a counselor is pressed for time and only a rough measure is possible, he may give the first half of the test only. A person's performance is but little affected by his previous training and experience; neither is it closely related to his academic intelligence. Consequently, when this test is given, together with a suitable test of intelligence, the scores furnish the counselor with two of the most useful items of information he can readily secure with which to estimate a person's chances of failure or success in the clerical field. It should, however, be noted that superiority in the abilities measured by the Minnesota test is relatively more important in the lower levels of routine work; and that in the most difficult and technical clerical occupations where sound judgment and specialized knowledge are indispensable, competent experts have been found who do not do exceptionally well in these number-comparison and name-comparison tasks.

2

Some tests of clerical aptitudes are constructed, like the clerical proficiency test described in the previous chapter, in such a way as to yield measures of several different abilities indicative of probable success. Benge's Clerical Test K, one of the early examinations used in employment offices, presents four sorts of tasks: *checking*, that is, comparing two numbers and indicating whether they are the same or different; *verifying* the answers to arithmetical computations; *extending*, that is, finding the answers to problems in arithmetic; and *classifying* correspondence according to the nature of the letter and according to the method of payment and shipment. The Scott Company File Clerk's Test, a fifteen-minute examination which has been used for years as a general clerical test as well as for its original purpose, consists of six sub-tests: number-checking, name-checking, alphabetical filing, numerical filing, topical filing, and paragraph comprehension. O'Rourke's Clerical Aptitude Test, Junior Grade, sets a greater variety of tasks, all obviously related to the sorts of work done by clerical employees. This examination is in two parts, called Reasoning Test, and Clerical Problems. The first part includes five kinds of items so designed as to sample the candidate's ability to read and follow directions, to indicate the best answers to information questions, to note verbal relations and the congruity or incongruity of words in sentences, to spell, and to think through short problems. The second part of the test sets problems in alphabetical filing, comparison of names and addresses and numbers, classification of data, and simple arithmetical computation. The Clerical Test of the British National Institute of Industrial Psychology, revised for use in this country by Herbert Moore, furnishes another example of an examination designed to sample a person's abilities in each of several typical kinds of tasks. It is in seven parts, appropriately called Oral Instructions, Classification, Arithmetic, Copying, Checking, Filing, and Problems. The twenty problems in this last part are such as often appear in an intelligence examination.

The Typist and Stenographer Examinations prepared by the Research Division of the U. S. Civil Service Commission under the direction of O'Rourke, include a seventy-five minute General Test,[1] as well as tests in typing from plain copy, typing from rough draft, and taking and transcribing dictation. The three tests of proficiency in typing and stenography, with the accompanying tables of norms, enable a teacher to ascertain which ones of his students have reached the standards of performance required in business firms and in government offices; while the General Test serves to measure a student's aptitude for clerical work and indicates in a general way the level of clerical employment to which he is best suited. Among

[1] Described, with norms, on page 327. Not to be confused with the shorter O'Rourke Clerical Aptitude Test, Junior Grade, previously mentioned.

the five varieties of items used in this General Test there are no arithmetical problems, but there are many which call for a correct understanding of the meaning of a paragraph of text. This test has been given by the Civil Service Commission to both stenographers and typists. The proportion making high scores is naturally greater among the stenographers than among the typists. Thus, in 1934, a civil-service rating of 90 on the General Test was reached by the best 20 per cent of the junior-typist eligibles and by 36 per cent of the junior-stenographer eligibles.

Intelligence scores have been widely used in schools and in employment offices as indicators of clerical aptitude. Among the many group examinations employed for this purpose are: Pressey Classification Test and Verification Test, Bureau Test VI, Otis Advanced Examination, Otis Self-Administering Higher Examination, Army Alpha as revised by Bregman and subsequently by Wells, and Terman Group Test of Mental Ability. Of these, a test which has had wide use in business employment is Bureau Test VI.[2] This is a spiral omnibus test consisting of items from Army Alpha, adapted for convenient administration within a fifteen-minute limit; but a number of the items taken from Army Alpha are out of date, so that the original forms should be abandoned. Fortunately, a revision has now been made. The nearest equivalent in length and in simplicity of administration is the Pressey examination. It is quite inexpensive, and fairly reliable for so short a test, although less reliable than Bureau Test VI. It is rather poorly printed on cheap stock, but since this is the form in which it has been standardized, a reprinting with clearer type on better stock would make it unsafe to use available norms without recalibrating the test. The Otis Self-Administering Higher Examination is not open to these criticisms and is equally convenient to administer, but like many intelligence tests, it is likely to impress older people as somewhat childish and schoolish in content. (The National Intelligence Test was for a time widely used in the upper grammar grades but is not suitable for high-school students.) The Terman Group Test of Mental Ability is well adapted for grammar- and high-school pupils, and like Army Alpha and the Otis Advanced Examination, provides not only a total score, but separate scores in the several parts, such as Arithmetic Information, Word Meaning, Sentence Meaning, etc. The Kuhlman-Anderson Intelligence Tests are growing in favor. The Psychological Examination issued annually by the American Council on Education is a one-hour

[2] So called by the Bureau of Personnel Research at Carnegie Institute of Technology, where it was first used by C. S. Yoakum in 1920.

test for high-school seniors and college freshmen. The Thorndike Intelligence Examination for High-school Graduates, which requires three and a half hours to administer, is made available annually, in three forms. Whenever a counselor finds on a student's record his mark on one of these examinations or on the Scholastic Aptitude Test of the College Entrance Examination Board, it should by all means be taken into consideration in appraising his aptitudes for clerical employment at any level from the most routine to the most responsible.

Intelligence test scores are definitely useful when a counselor is conferring, for example, with ninth- or tenth-grade students who are considering the election of special courses of training for any of the clerical occupations. The counselor should ascertain the critical minimum scores on the intelligence scale below which, in his school, a pupil's chances of mastering these particular vocational courses are slight.

Some components of a person's clerical aptitudes may be roughly appraised by reference to his scholastic achievement as represented by his marks in school. More valuable are the records of his performance in standard achievement tests, notably in English usage, arithmetic, spelling, vocabulary and reading comprehension. Tables of probability, based on these achievement test scores and on academic grades earned in junior high school, may be prepared in a way to indicate the chances a student has of creditably passing the different commercial courses if his previous accomplishments have been above certain specified levels.

Our analysis of clerical work suggested that at least a minimum of motor dexterity, of finger agility in manipulating papers, cards, pencil, or typewriter keys, may be a component of clerical aptitudes. No standard tests for measuring these motor abilities are, however, here suggested. With the possible exception of the motor-dexterity factor in aptitude for learning to operate a typewriter, it has been difficult to find suitable tests of hand or finger dexterity for which clerical norms or valid critical scores have been established. Perhaps a person's various manual abilities are so numerous, so specific, or so greatly subject to improvement by training that it is futile to attempt to differentiate by tests those students who will be seriously handicapped in clerical work by inability to acquire the motor skills. Champion typists, to be sure, excelled in tapping tests and in motor skills as measured with Robert H. Seashore's apparatus; but with the exception of these rare instances of superlative ability, no very significant relationship between motor dexterity scores and ability in typing was demonstrated. One motor test, developed by E. Stiles, shows promise of usefulness in measuring aptitude for typing in persons who are not at all familiar with a typewriter. This test consists in doing as fast as possible some extremely simple exercises on one row of the typewriter keyboard. Both speed and accuracy affect the score, which, in one experiment carried out at the Employment Stabilization Research Institute in Minneapolis, correlated +.49 with the measure of highest typing speed attained after several months of practice.[3] In other studies at the Institute,[4] dexterity, as measured by the finger-, tweezer- and manual-dexterity tests, was found to be no more characteristic of typists than of other women workers. Although stenographers and typists on the average exceeded somewhat the average of the standard sample of the working population, many of them fell considerably below. The minimum endowments of hand and finger agility needed in learning to type seem to be a common possession of nearly everyone who would seriously consider undertaking training for such an occupation. In so far as this is not the case, the counselor will ordinarily infer it in each individual instance from such observations as he may make regarding clumsiness of fingers or extreme lack of motor coordination, or else leave the discovery of the candidate's ineptitude for acquiring the desired skills until the slowness of his progress during early practice makes evident his limitations in this regard.

Specific aptitudes for stenography have proved difficult to isolate. The Hoke Prognostic Test for Stenographic Ability, issued in 1922, still lacks adequate norms and validation. It is a battery of very short tests yielding scores in Motor Reaction (speed in making pencil marks), Speed of Writing, Quality of Writing, Speed of Reading, Immediate Memory (for spoken sentences), Spelling, and Symbols (substitution of letters for digits). Some of these sub-tests are too short to yield very reliable measures, even if it were definitely known that the abilities tested were necessary for learning stenography.

Completion tests, consisting of passages in which certain missing words are to be supplied by reference to the context, seem to call for the use of mental processes very like some of those exercised by stenographers and dictating-machine operators. Substitution tests also measure abilities somewhat similar to those used in learning stenography. But the precise value of such tests in estimating the prob-

[3] *Cf.* E. G. Eriksen, "A Demonstration of Individualized Training Methods for Modern Office Workers," pp. 31, 32. *Employment Stabilization Research Institute Bulletin*, 3: No. 2, July, 1934.

[4] D. M. Andrew and D. G. Paterson, "Measured Characteristics of Clerical Workers." *E. S. R. I. Bulletin*, 3: No. 1, July, 1934.

ability that a candidate for stenographic training will learn rapidly and make progress in his occupation, is still a problem of research. There is need for intensive study of stenographic aptitudes and their measurement. This is equally true of aptitudes for operating office machines such as the comptometer, the Hollerith, and the bookkeeping machines now widely used in offices.

3

Employers who make use of intelligence tests as one means of selecting employees for clerical work have found that it is ordinarily advisable to place their lower critical score at a mark which corresponds more or less closely to the Minnesota Standard Score of 5.0, a score which represents the average performance of a standard population sample. This average, obtained by testing men and women representative of the entire range of occupations, is somewhat below the average of the high-school population, but is a little above the average of the adult population of the entire country and of the army norms. Employment standards vary; but in reviewing published and unpublished sources of information, a consensus of practice has been found which, reduced to tabular form, should be of aid in estimating the significance of a person's score in terms of the likelihood that he will be able to meet commercial requirements. Some of the critical scores that have been used by employers are given in Table XIV.

No two of the examinations in this list measure precisely the same abilities. Indeed, points on the scales for quite similar tests can be considered to correspond only roughly. Each test must stand on its own merits as a measure of symptoms of clerical aptitude.

When comparing an individual's score on any of these tests with the data in Table XIV, attention should go first of all to the line labeled $\sigma_{(M)}$ (the Standard Error of Measurement). No test is perfectly reliable. The likelihood that a person's true score in a test is close to the one he actually obtained varies with the reliability of the test as an instrument of measurement. The chances are 68 in 100 (about 2 in 3) that an obtained score does not vary from the true score by more than plus or minus the Standard Error of Measurement. The Pressey Classification Test—Column 7—for example, has a reliability of .91 and a Standard Error of Measurement of .3 σ, about 9 points. If a young woman has obtained a score of 57 in this test, the possibility must not be overlooked that her true score in the ability measured may be definitely higher or lower than this. Her true

TABLE XIV. SCORES USED BY EMPLOYERS AS AIDS IN SELECTION OF CLERICAL WORKERS

Showing standards as measured by various examinations[5]

	1 Civil Service General Test (O'Rourke)	2 Minn. Clerical (Women) Numbers	Names	3 Scovill Classi-fication	4 Bureau VI 15 m.	5 Army Alpha	6 Otis Higher 20 m.	7 Pressey Classi-fication	8 Binet M A Yr.-Mo.
$\sigma_{(M)}$	±2.7	±10.5	±9	±7	±11	±10	±4	±9	±0–7
I.	60			180	125	160	50	85	19–0
II.	55			170	110	145	42	73	18–4
III.	50	140	150	165	100	133	37	64	17–9
IV.	45	130	138	160	90	123	33	56	17–4
V.	40	120	125	150	80	110	29	50	16–8
VI.	35	110	112	140	70	95	25	42	16–1
VII.	30	100	100	130	60	85	22	37	15–6

$\sigma_{(M)}$ Standard Error of Measurement expressed in raw score units.

I. Interpreted to mean that chances are better than even for eventual advancement to intermediate and upper levels of clerical employment.

II. Construed as a lower critical score for preferred applicants for the more responsible clerical positions.

III. Satisfactory for secretarial and intermediate clerical positions. Sometimes regarded as a minimum for college-graduate applicants who are expected to advance to positions of at least intermediate level; below this score, the chances of eventual promotion to a position in the top brackets are slight.

IV. Below the average of clerical employees. Construed by a few discriminating employers as a minimum for clerical positions on the intermediate levels. For all new appointments in the government service as junior typist, stenographer, or clerk on the lowest level, a score of 45 on the Civil Service General Test is at present required.

V. Minimum expected of high-school graduates by a majority of discriminating employers. Above this score, the chances for eventual promotion from the simplest routine jobs are about even.

VI. Usual minimum for applicants who are expected to continue in simple routine work.

VII. Minimum acceptable to less discriminating employers of routine workers.

score would be, theoretically, her average score in an indefinitely large number of strictly equivalent forms of the test, if only it were possible to administer them all under the same conditions—that is, without previous familiarity with the test. This cannot be done; so we take note of the score she obtained in the single form we administered, remembering the limitations of the somewhat crude measuring instrument used. We think of her score of 57 not as a precise measure, but as the midpoint of a band of values, 57 ± 9, a *zone of approximation* which extends all the way from score 48 to score 66. There is about one chance in six that her true score might even turn out to be above the upper limit of this zone; and one in six that it

[5] While this table represents, to the best of the author's knowledge, a consensus of business practice, it is not a conversion table for ascertaining equivalent scores. In columns 3 to 8, to be sure, the corresponding scores do approximate the same percentiles of the distribution in the general population; but the examinations do not by any means all measure identical abilities. Quite the contrary. For example, the correlation between the Minnesota Clerical and the Pressey Classification tests is far from close.

might be below.[6] If we were to take as our estimate of her ability in this test her average score in two equivalent forms, the reliability would be higher than .91 and the zone of approximation would be substantially narrower. However, it is ordinarily good practice to devote whatever time is available for testing, not to the giving of equivalent forms of the same examination, but to the administering of several different tests. Other things being equal, the larger the number of separate measures of clerical aptitude we have, the surer becomes the verdict as to the probabilities of clerical success.

Neither employers nor counselors can lean very heavily on the evidence from any single test when estimating a person's potentialities for progress in a clerical occupation. His true score, as we have just seen, may be either higher or lower than his obtained score. Indeed, the Standard Error of Measurement on the particular test used should always be kept in mind. Then, too, a person's chances of future growth and accomplishment vary with factors additional to those measured by the test. When these other factors are known to be distinctly favorable, a low test score may be proportionately discounted. Any single test is of value chiefly either to confirm such evidences of clerical aptitude as may have been gleaned from other sources, or to raise a precautionary signal, meaning that clerical work should not be undertaken unless records of previous employment, school progress, or performance in more searching tests give clear indications that the individual really has the abilities which, from his initial test performance, he seems to lack.

4

Regarding temperamental characteristics which distinguish clerical workers from others, little that is authoritative can be said. It has been alleged that persons who do not like to be closely supervised or to take directions from others are apt to be unhappy in clerical occupations. Some supervisors are said to give such workers ratings lower than their output warrants. If this were known to be quite generally the case, then those who score "extremely dominant" on a scale of dominance-submission, should hesitate before embarking on a course of clerical training. There are, however, employers who prefer to include among their clerical workers some who do not hesitate to raise objection and to suggest ways of improving what has been standard practice. In such situations, a bright person who is skill-

[6] For a fuller treatment of the Standard Error of Measurement and the zone of approximation, see pages 245 ff.

ful and accurate in his paper work and who has a marked tendency to dominate in social situations may find himself in the line of advancement toward office supervision and executive responsibilities. In the present stage of knowledge regarding the vocational interpretation of scores on tests of temperament and personality, no recommendations are here offered regarding their use in counseling with reference to aptitudes for clerical occupations.

5

Suggestions growing out of our review of what is known about clerical aptitudes may now be summarized.

Counselors in search of aids in estimating a person's aptitudes for clerical occupations do wisely to review all available data regarding his standing in number- and word-checking tests, intelligence tests, tests of achievement in English usage, vocabulary, spelling, and arithmetic, and school marks.

If no test scores are found on the cumulative record, and only a limited time is available for examining, a good intelligence test appropriate to the person's age and schooling will at least furnish an indication of the general level of clerical employment toward which vocational plans might be focused. Not only the total score should be weighed; the errors and omissions, and the sub-scores, if any, should be scrutinized for suggestions of specific weaknesses or strong points. These may then be explored in the interview. Confirmations regarding these abilities can be sought in the available facts about school progress and grades, and about jobs held to the satisfaction or dissatisfaction of employers. Meanwhile the counselor will be building up a picture of his client's aptitudes, a picture which may more or less clearly correspond to the vocational requirements of clerical ability at a certain level, or which may, on the other hand, indicate unsuitability for clerical work of any kind.

The Minnesota test is suggested as the most useful single supplement to the general test. It consists of two forms, each made up of a number-comparison and a name-comparison part. If a high score is made on the first form (time limits: for number-comparison, 8 minutes, for name-comparison, 7 minutes), it is not necessary to give the second form; but if the score is disappointingly low it is advisable to administer also the second form, using time limits of 7 minutes and 6 minutes. The initial raw score may be translated into a Standard Score by reference to the table of norms on page 325. From these norms it will be clear that on this test, a Standard Score of only 5.0, meaning Average for the general population of workers examined, should be construed as a danger signal. On this test, few clerical workers make scores as low as this.

Other tests above mentioned may be resorted to as needed. They may be used to confirm indications of superior aptitudes for clerical work, or of specific weaknesses needing correction.

When appraising aptitudes for any of the higher-level clerical occupations such as secretary, proof-reader, editorial assistant, foreign correspondent, cataloger, computer, accountant, auditor, actuary, or statistician, the minimum standards of acceptable test performance are stepped up, particularly on the intelligence examinations; and attention is given to evidences of special aptitudes—linguistic, literary, mathematical, scientific or artistic—needed in the particular clerical occupation under consideration. Previous educational achievements and other relevant accomplishments are reviewed. An effort is also made to ascertain the strength of the person's informed interest in doing the kind of work most characteristic of the occupation, and his tolerance for the drudgery which goes with it.

In conclusion, if a person really wants to prepare for a clerical occupation, data regarding his mental alertness, as measured by tests of academic intelligence or scholastic aptitude and by general clerical tests, will aid a counselor in suggesting the most appropriate level of clerical employment for which to undertake training. His scores in specific tests of clerical aptitude such as have been here described should also be canvassed in comparison with available norms. Measures of his achievement in English usage, vocabulary, spelling, handwriting, reading comprehension, arithmetical computation and problem-solving, will reveal any deficiencies in these skills which need to be remedied. Counseling which takes into account such measures of present abilities and indications of aptitudes, as well as the facts with reference to relative supply and demand for clerical workers of various levels of ability and kinds of specialization, will greatly help to minimize the present wastes in clerical training, and will increase, among the millions who follow clerical occupations, the proportion of well-equipped, competent, and satisfied workers.

Chapter XIV

APTITUDES FOR THE PROFESSIONS

1. Reasons for the exceptional interest in this topic. 2. Personal selection and vocational guidance are not opposed, but mutually supplementary activities, apparent in the process of appraising aptitude for a profession. Steps in this process. 3. Aptitudes for engineering, and tests for appraising them. Measurement of engineering interests. Personality of engineers. Summary. 4. Law: the nature of legal work. Tests of aptitude for legal training. Interests and personality of lawyers. Conclusion. 5. Aptitude for medicine, surgery and dentistry. Methods of selection used by medical schools. Occupations related to the medical field.

1

Is IT possible to identify symptoms of aptitude for the various professions? If so, which of these symptoms can be measured by tests?

Interest in these questions is out of all proportion to the relatively small number of people who enter professional careers. This is but natural. The professions are held in high regard. The social status accorded to lawyers, journalists, librarians, preachers, engineers, scientists, teachers, and doctors, for example, more than compensates for the fact that the annual earnings of many of them are smaller than they might have been in business or in a skilled trade. The majority of boys at some time or other pass through a period of thinking that they want to become professional engineers, or possibly lawyers or doctors, while a great many girls think of teaching or of going on the stage. No wonder that parents and counselors, as well as the young people themselves, want to know, as definitely as can be, the requirements for successfully undertaking professional training and the symptoms indicative of probable achievement in a field toward which ambition points.

The institutions which provide the best training for the professions also are seriously concerned. Their facilities are limited. Their charges for tuition rarely cover more than a third or a half of its cost. They must choose from among more applicants than can be accommodated, restricting admission to those who seem to show the greatest promise. And so schools of nursing, librarianship, pharmacy, dentistry, accountancy and teaching, as well as of medicine, law, and engineering, have in recent years energetically attacked this problem of finding improved ways of estimating the likelihood that an applicant can profitably undertake the training offered. They have freshly examined the nature of the work to be done and formulated descriptions of the abilities it requires. These descriptions have then been checked against the findings of inquiries in which students who have dropped by the wayside have been compared with those who have continued to the end. Graduates who have drifted into work unrelated to the profession for which they were trained have also been compared with those who continued to follow their profession. These institutions have then experimented with ways of measuring the special aptitudes of candidates for entrance, as well as their general academic aptitudes and previous educational achievements. The experiments have not all been scientifically controlled; nor have the numbers been large enough, the period of time long enough, and the criteria of success precise enough to yield conclusions as clear cut as we should like. Nevertheless, it has generally been possible, by putting into effect the more rigorous processes of selection suggested by these studies, to raise the standards of admission in ways which have cut down somewhat the disconcertingly large proportion of students who fail or who change their minds and drop out, turning to other fields after having invested, during one or more years of intensive preparation, their own resources as well as those of the institutions they attend.

Our emphasis is on the individual, the person who is uncertain about his aptitudes, rather than on the financial and administrative problems of the professional schools. But we welcome investigations into the best methods of selecting candidates for entrance because they yield many suggestions useful in counseling. Ater all, the process of ascertaining an applicant's fitness to undertake a course of professional training is much the same in general outline, whether carried on for purposes of selection or of individual guidance.

The following sections outline this process, illustrate it in the fields of engineering, law, medicine, nursing, and teaching, and in conclusion touch upon the nature of artistic talent and ways used to detect special aptitudes for professional careers in music and the arts.

2

While personnel selection and vocational guidance may be contrasted in theory, in practice they often go hand in hand. Increasingly, during recent years, university officers whose task it is to choose the best from among the candidates for admission to professional schools have felt also a responsibility toward those whose applications they reject. Like typical employment managers in factories and offices, they deem it an obligation and a privilege to devote a good deal of time to conference with applicants who are not chosen, helping them to realize their best aptitudes and offering such practical suggestions as they can. When interviewing a satisfactory applicant also, it is no rarity to find an employer reviewing with him the possibility that he might be even more successful in a different field, with another firm; or to find the admissions officer of a professional school writing to a candidate for entrance in this vein: "We have examined your record in much detail and corresponded with your instructors. Your credentials are all in shape. You meet our requirements fully and are hereby admitted. However, I notice indications that you seem to have a good deal of ability and exceptional interest in shipping and navigation; also in construction and design. Have you looked into the opportunities in naval architecture, open to graduates of such-and-such a school? Possibly you would find in that institution a type of training even better suited to your capacities than our curriculum provides." The question may be tactfully raised as to whether the candidate has not made application because of the insistence of parents or the urging of fellow students, without full consideration of his own aptitudes. In education, as in industry, personnel practice has its ethics as well as its techniques. The social consequences, the good of the community and of the individual, must be weighed—not merely the convenience of the institution for which selections are being made. This is why officers of admission not infrequently ask, "Is this the best profession for this particular candidate?" instead of simply, "Is this the best of the candidates for this particular profession?" Selection and guidance as actually carried on are not two opposed, competing activities.

Whether the purpose is primarily one of guidance, or of selection from among applicants for entrance to a professional school, the process is in many respects the same. In either instance it is desirable as a first step to appraise the individual's record of accomplishments in the subjects he has studied and his performance in tests of scholastic aptitude, and from these data to estimate the probability that he is capable of mastering courses of study on the professional level. Next, the symptoms of special aptitude for a particular profession are canvassed. These symptoms, in the main, are of three sorts: abilities, interests, and personality traits. When all the evidence pro and con has been assembled and duly weighed—when the various indications of aptitude and of ineptitude for the profession have been considered separately and in combination, leading to an estimate of the probabilities of success—one more step must be taken. It still remains to inquire whether the chances of satisfactory adjustment may not be greater in some direction other than the one in question.

It is this third step which is likely to receive more serious attention by vocational counselors than by educational administrators engaged in making selection from among candidates, although, as we have seen, it is relevant whichever side of the shield one may be looking at. From the point of view of the individual most deeply concerned, it is obviously the most important step of all; and frequently the most baffling. He may want a professional career and yet not be drawn toward any of the fields with which he is familiar. What he chiefly needs is to have his horizon broadened. But perhaps he is hesitating between two professions or is attracted by several, feeling himself endowed with mind and personality apparently indicative of aptitude for each of them. In the latter instance he runs the grave danger of drifting, of arriving nowhere unless he more or less arbitrarily chooses a port and holds to one course. When neither personal preference nor outstanding special aptitude points the way, decision may rest heavily on considerations quite remote from those of aptitude, such as relative keenness of competition in the various professions, the financial rewards they offer, or the time required to complete the courses of training.

In general, it may be said that a majority of those who are capable of mastering one profession have a choice among many; and for two reasons. The first is that aptitudes are often not narrowly specialized, so that the chances are about equally good in any one of a number of careers. The other reason lies in the nature of the professions themselves; for the kinds of work to be done in any one of them are so varied that there are opportunities for practitioners of widely differing talents and inclinations. A priest, for example, who demonstrates exceptional financial acumen, managerial ability, and personal leadership may become an executive of a mission board, or a bishop;

while a professional nurse whose outstanding talent is in educational work may herself engage in the training of nurses. The range of opportunities within a recognized profession is broad indeed. The atypical man—the man whose interests and abilities are quite different from those of most of his associates—may even become the exceptionally successful specialist, as when a student with a flair for physics and engineering takes up medicine, becomes a Roentgenologist and invents new means of x-ray photography and diagnosis. An individual who once qualifies and attains professional status can generally find his place.

This fact may serve to explain in part why aptitude for a profession is frequently defined in terms of aptitude for successful completion of the training offered in the professional school. In any event, the school is the first hurdle; and so, young people want to know the probabilities of their being able to gain entrance to, and later to graduate from, the courses of training for the professions they contemplate. Such estimates of probability may be based on various kinds of data including school marks, test scores, interest schedules, and personality inventories, as will be seen in the following section which treats of engineering aptitudes.

3

ENGINEERING

A young man who is considering a career in one of the engineering professions may well take the time to review the evidences as to his aptitudes. Of students entering colleges of engineering, the proportion who fail to complete their courses of study is notably high. About 62 per cent of them drop by the wayside. Some leave for financial or other extraneous reasons; many, because they cannot make the grade, or because they discover that their interests and abilities fit them better for other pursuits. The standards of scholarship maintained by most engineering faculties demand of the students superior endowment of intellectual ability or scholastic aptitude. Moreover, certain subjects in the curriculum place a premium on special aptitudes: aptitude for learning higher mathematics, aptitude for the physical sciences, aptitudes for manipulating ideas of space relations and for understanding the construction and operation of mechanisms. Ways of ascertaining the degree to which a person possesses these aptitudes are described in the following pages.

But first, what is the engineering profession?

Engineering is at once a science and an art. Its purpose is to control the forces and utilize the materials of nature for the benefit of man. To do this calls for skill in organizing and directing human activities, as well as understanding of the natural forces and materials to be controlled. Engineering is indeed a broad field. There are really a dozen engineering professions, and within each there are many different kinds of work to be done. Nevertheless these professions have a great deal in common. Basic aptitudes characteristic of the majority of civil engineers are equally desirable in the mining, mechanical, automotive, aeronautical, electrical, metallurgical and chemical engineering professions.

The kinds of work which these engineers are called upon to do and the courses of training which prepare them to undertake their professional responsibilities are alike in requiring a high order of ability to think clearly in quantitative terms. Engineers deal with precise measurements, mathematical computations, formulas, statistics. They must know the properties of materials. The scientific laws and principles which explain these properties must be studied and understood. Then, too, an engineer is expected to exercise practical judgment regarding money values, and sound sense as to the feasibility and worth of whatever he undertakes. Finally, as we have seen, he is often expected to be able to organize and direct the work of others. These abilities, characteristic of engineers, suggest the aptitudes desired in students of engineering.

To anyone familiar with the content of an engineering curriculum it is not surprising that a young man's probability of success in such a course of study is rather closely related to his aptitude for higher mathematics. Indeed, a good reliable measure of his mathematical ability is by all odds the most significant single indicator of his aptitude for pursuing engineering studies. Consequently, his school marks in algebra and geometry should be scrutinized, and supplemented by his scores in objective tests of achievement and of aptitude in mathematics, such as the Iowa Placement Tests or those prepared by the Cooperative Test Service of the American Council on Education. The score in the mathematical part of the Scholastic Aptitude Test given annually in June by the College Entrance Examination Board is one of the most dependable measures; and so if a youth is really in doubt as to his mathematical aptitude he may well be encouraged to invest the time and the $10 required to enable his counselor to secure the evidence which this test yields.[1] A young man who, though ingenious

[1] Arrangements should be made early in May by corresponding with the College Entrance Examination Board at 431 W. 117th Street, New York.

with machines, is likely to find the sledding hard in his study of analytics, differential and integral calculus, advanced mechanics and descriptive geometry, may be encouraged to consider a mechanical trade, or a course in technical school preparatory to supervisory work in a factory, or a more general college training with a view to eventual employment in selling machinery or in managing an enterprise concerned with mechanisms. But if he is not endowed with more than average aptitude for learning mathematics it is fairly certain that he lacks one component of aptitude for a professional engineering course.

Ability to perceive the sizes, shapes, and relations of objects in space and to think quickly and clearly about these relations is another distinct asset for a student of engineering. He must be able to see how the parts of a mechanism fit together, and to infer what happens to one part when another part moves. Many engineers, although not all, are facile visualizers. But all, whether excelling in their powers of visual imagination or not, must somehow learn to read diagrams and prepare blue prints, to make and read topographical maps and profiles, to translate two-dimensional sketches into three-dimensional models and *vice versa.* Aptitudes for thinking about shapes, sizes, and space relations are particularly valuable in the study of drafting, descriptive geometry and mechanics. These aptitudes may be estimated by reference to a student's performance in such manipulative tests as the Minnesota Spatial Relations Test and the Kent-Shakow Form Board and in such paper-and-pencil tests as the Yale Spatial Relations Test and Likert and Quasha's revision of the Minnesota Paper Form Board. Anyone who has difficulty with tests such as these, or with the O'Connor Wiggly Block and Pyramid, and the Healy Puzzle Box, is likely to be deficient in aptitude for visualizing three-dimensional structure, and to be baffled by the distinctly engineering subjects above mentioned.

Aptitude for dealing with spatial relations may be thought of as one factor in mechanical intelligence, the kind of intelligence which characterizes the activities of a person who is ingenious in finding what is wrong with a machine, or in putting together the parts of a disassembled mechanism as in the Stenquist Assembling Test (or its more reliable revision, the Minnesota Mechanical Assembly Test). These tests, designed to measure ability to see the relationships between the parts of more or less complicated mechanisms, seem to be somewhat more suitable for predicting ability to learn a mechanic's trade than in estimating aptitudes for professional engineering.

Nevertheless, a below-average score in such assembly tests should be construed as a contra-indication.

Another type of information indicative of probable success or failure in the engineering college is furnished by the candidate's school grades and achievement test scores in physics and chemistry. Marks earned in Regents' or College Board Examinations should be noted. The Cooperative Test Service tests and the Iowa Placement Examinations in these subjects may well be given. In the event that a student's preparatory work to date has not included instruction in physics and chemistry, the Iowa Placement Tests of Physics Aptitude and Chemistry Aptitude are especially useful. Each of these tests is designed to measure abilities which are deemed to be indicators of aptitude for learning the subject, such as the ability to read a sample passage and to answer questions about it; the ability to utilize information so supplied in solving problems which, though simple, are typical of the kind of thinking required; and the ability to do arithmetical and algebraic computations of a sort frequently called for in the routine of such problem-solving. A more searching examination adapted for use in college as well as in senior high school is the Stanford Scientific Aptitude Test developed by Zyve.

Incidentally, a student's performance in the separate parts of some of these science tests is frequently helpful in identifying specific remediable weaknesses in reading ability, in arithmetical computation, and in algebra.

When appraising a student's aptitudes for engineering, evidences of his ability in English are of more than passing interest. Engineers must be lucid and logical in the writing of reports and specifications, and in the oral presentation of their arguments. A good vocabulary and a better than average score in English usage are distinct assets, although by no means so indispensable to a prospective engineer as are the aptitudes for mathematics and science. Cumulative indications of distinctly poor ability in English should, however, be construed as warnings against choice of engineering as a profession. This is partly because persons with very restricted vocabularies and poor command of correct English usage seldom have the mental alertness or scholastic aptitude required for passing the courses of study in a college of engineering.

The closeness with which a young man's interests resemble those of professional engineers is best measured by means of Strong's Vocational Interest Blank. The interests sampled by this questionnaire mature rapidly during later adolescence; consequently, when counseling a boy in senior high school, a score of B (meaning uncertainty as to whether his interests do or do not resemble those of men in the profession) need not be interpreted as a warning. The question remains an open one as to whether he will probably like the sorts of things engineers like, and will find the work and the personal associations of the profession congenial. An A score in engineering interest, or a B+ score if the youth is not yet eighteen years old, indicates with considerable certainty that his interests are similar to those of professional engineers. On the other hand, a score of C indicates that his interests do not resemble those of engineers any more closely than do those of men in general.

If any serious doubt exists as to the genuineness or depth of the young man's liking for engineering work, he should by all means seek an opportunity to get a taste of it, by working with engineers in an office or as a rodman on a construction job. Even two weeks of surveying and drafting, such as the preparatory-school boys get who attend the Stevens Institute Junior Camp, have been sufficient in some instances to confirm a boy's ambition, and in others to convince him that he has been mistaken, confusing his youthful fondness for mechanical devices with an interest in engineering.

There is no one type of personality essential to success in the engineering profession. Granted that a somewhat larger proportion of engineers than of salesmen and business executives are lone workers, meditative, retiring, thoughtful, subjective, introvert, solitary, scholarly, individualistic, preferring to work with mechanisms or with books and numerical symbols rather than to supervise people or to sell commodities to them, it does not necessarily follow that a person who does not exhibit these introvertive traits would do well to avoid the study of engineering. Many engineers are called upon to manage manufacturing or construction enterprises, to supervise groups of technicians, to sell complicated engineering products. Indeed, the most remunerative posts with the heaviest responsibilities generally go to engineers who are not only technically proficient, but who are also facile in human contacts, keen in their appreciation of people's motives, good persuaders, socially-minded—natural leaders of men.

Considerations of personality are therefore less apt to have weight at the time of deciding whether to study engineering than when choice of a particular type of work within an engineering profession is being made. During the course of his engineering training, when options of specialization are being chosen, it is of distinct value to a young man to have a well-informed understanding of his total personality, and of those particular traits which are deemed to be most characteristic of engineers engaged in selling, supervising and managing, in contrast to those who specialize in designing, development work and basic research. At such a time a counselor is glad to find on a man's cumulative record his scores on tests such as Allport's Ascendancy-Submission Test, Thurstone's Personality Inventory, and the Word Association Test administered as O'Connor prescribes and scored to yield a measure of objectivity or "group contact." Such data, while not decisive, do serve as points of reference in the interview. The same may be said of personality ratings made by instructors, self-ratings, and behavior data indicative of marked individual differences in aptitude for making social adjustments and impressing people favorably.

During an interview and also during the administration of individual performance tests, there is opportunity to note indications of significant traits of character, temperament, and methods of work. Herein lies one of the marked advantages of individual testing as contrasted with the more economical group method. An individually administered examination such as the Kent-Shakow Form Board or the Minnesota Spatial Relations Test presents a standard situation well adapted for observing a person's behavior. The experienced examiner, while noting whether his subject goes about his task in a systematic or a haphazard way, also seizes the opportunity to look for any responses which yield clues as to his persistence, his output of energy and his emotional control. Extremes of temperamental imbalance and nervous instability sometimes come to light during the progress of a series of performance tests even more clearly than they do in an intimate personal interview.

By way of summary: A counselor engaged in helping a young man to decide whether to undertake a course of training for any of the engineering professions brings together for appraisal the evidence as to his interests and ambitions, and as to his aptitudes, particularly his general scholastic aptitude and his special aptitudes for learning mathematics, for thinking about space relations, for understanding mechanisms, and for mastering the physical sciences. Superiority of performance in those school subjects and tests known to be indicative of these five kinds of aptitude furnishes evidence of capacity to succeed in the study of engineering, and when coupled with a liking for engineering work and the necessary health, energy, drive and constancy of purpose, indicates a high probability of success in the practice of an engineering profession.

Low scores in any of these measures of aptitude should be construed, not as definitely barring from further consideration the possibility of a career in engineering, but as warning signals, red flags of caution on a road which is still open but which is entered at the traveler's own risk, after he knows just what the hazards are.

Mention has been made of yet another danger signal: poor ability in English. A lack of equipment in the verbal tools of thought, revealed by low scores in tests of vocabulary and of English usage, may signify either insufficient training in the clear and precise use of language, or a shortage of verbal intelligence without which it is difficult to master college subjects.

A very superior performance in verbal intelligence tests and in literary subjects may also be regarded with some suspicion if the person's linguistic talents are seen to be definitely more outstanding than his mathematical and scientific abilities. Students whose scores in tests of vocabulary and verbal intelligence are even higher than their very good scores in mathematical reasoning and scientific aptitude, are prone to become restive in a college of engineering, to drift off into more liberal curricula, and eventually to choose a career in some profession like journalism, law, or teaching. A student whose superior verbal and mathematical aptitudes are coupled with marked capacity for spatial thinking and a flair for artistic design, not infrequently abandons engineering for architecture.

Here, as in all good counseling, the prime consideration is given, not to the separate measures of aptitude, but to the total pattern of the personality which these measures help to define.

Points stressed in the immediately preceding section—which dealt with aptitudes for engineering and ways of appraising them—are pertinent also when aptitudes for other professions are in question. Law, medicine and the ministry; teaching and librarianship; accountancy, journalism, and architecture, all resemble engineering in that they presuppose mental capacity of a relatively high order. Then, too, each profession opens the door to many different kinds of work, so varied, indeed, that people of differing temperaments may feel at home in it. But each has also its distinctive characteristics, so that a candidate, before deciding to prepare for a profession toward which he is inclined, should know about it well enough to be certain that his interests definitely focus in that direction—that it is a field he really wants to enter. Moreover, he should, if possible, make sure that he is not lacking in the special abilities ordinarily found to characterize those who make progress in it.

The candidate's previous school achievements and his performance in scholastic aptitude tests furnish evidence regarding his general mental ability. His interests, if they are in doubt, may be measured by means of such an inventory as Strong's and verified by a summer's tryout during which he has opportunity to work in close association with members of the profession. Such an experience ordinarily has the further advantage that it throws into relief not only his interests, but his special abilities as well.

These elementary principles are widely applicable. They need not be repeated as other fields of professional activity are passed in review. Our treatment is necessarily brief. Aptitudes for the professions is so broad a subject that it requires a book in itself. But the following sections will at least bring out the distinctive features of a few professions—law, medicine, nursing, teaching and the fine arts—and suggest ways of ascertaining the relative strength of specific aptitudes for them.

4

LAW

Colleges of law, like those of medicine, have for years been gradually stiffening their standards. State examinations for admission to the bar and to medical practice have likewise been made more thorough and severe. Even so, the average level of mental ability found among students admitted to the professional schools is little, if any, higher than among college students. But the proportion of failures in these schools has been significantly greater among those who had previously ranked in scholarship below the average of their associates—so much so that college marks and intelligence test scores which do not surpass this average serve as warning signals when entrance to a profession is contemplated.

This consideration fails to deter a great many mediocre students from attempting to study law. They have heard it said that even if they are not able to graduate, a year or two in law school is a fine preliminary to journalism, business, or politics. "It teaches you to think." "Every business man should know something about the law of contracts." "If you *can* get admitted to the bar," not mentioning, however, the number of law graduates who fail even after long attendance at coaching schools and repeated annual attempts, "you will have a status in your community, though you never practice but turn instead to selling real estate and insurance." Such is the talk. No wonder that the mortality rate in the first year of the Harvard Law School has far exceeded that in any other professional school of the University—not because the standards of accomplishment maintained by the law faculty have been more severe, but because somehow a seriously large proportion of those who have crowded its classrooms have lacked the requisite aptitudes for mastering law. If only those students who failed had been able first to ascertain where their aptitudes pointed and had undertaken graduate work, "learning to think," in a school of business administration, of accountancy, of technology, of architecture, or of forestry, as the case might be, many of them might have escaped the chagrin of scholastic failure.*

What, then, are the symptoms of aptitude for studying law and for successfully practicing the legal profession?

To sharpen thinking about this question we may look at the activities in which lawyers are called upon to engage, and then at the procedures now used in sifting candidates for entrance to law schools and for admission to the bar.

Pleading cases in courts of justice and prosecuting offenders against the law are often thought to be typical activities, most characteristic of legal practice. This is a misleading picture. Some lawyers are indeed "attorneys-at-law," appearing frequently in court. But most of a lawyer's work is done not in court-rooms but in his office. If there is any single activity typical of his varied profession, it is that of giving guidance to a client, advising him about the conduct of his affairs. What most people want when they retain a lawyer's services is prudent advice—advice based on technical knowledge and sound judgment—which will help them to get on smoothly with business competitors, government agencies, relatives and neighbors, in ways which insure amicable relations and essential justice without resort to courts of law.

It is necessary, to be sure, from time to time to invoke the courts, to have recourse to the formal machinery the state provides for interpreting the law and administering justice. The lawyer is then his client's attorney, his representative before the court. But even in these instances the bulk of the work is done in the lawyer's office preparing the case—assembling and analyzing the facts, ascertaining the relevant principles, mapping the entire plan of procedure, marshaling precedents and citations, preparing arguments and briefs, anticipating so far as possible the actions of opponents, and then very often effecting a settlement of the issues out of court. A lawyer works much behind the scenes, and only occasionally in the spot light.

Indeed, many lawyers never plead in court. This is particularly

* Changes in admission requirements announced January 14, 1937, are designed to exclude from the Law School a larger proportion of bad risks among the applicants.

true in city practice. A country lawyer has relatively more occasions to appear as an advocate at the bar. In small communities there can be no such specialization of function as exists in metropolitan law offices, where one may be required to devote his whole time to a single phase of practice such as the examination of real estate titles and mortgages; preparation of income-tax reports; settlement of estates; legal aspects of corporation financing; collections; domestic relations; labor relations; transportation. A practitioner may become expert in contracts, or patent law, or admiralty law, or corporation law, or criminal law, but not in all. As such an expert he is his client's "counselor." Only a small minority engage extensively in the special work of the trial lawyer.

It follows that an aptitude for public speaking is not, as boys imagine, the primary requisite for undertaking the practice of law. An ability to address judge and jury with clearness, force, and facility is indeed no handicap; but much more essential to a lawyer's professional success is the type of mind and personality which commands the well-merited confidence of his clients. Many who seek his guidance are themselves able business men, shrewd and well informed, but in need of professional counsel. The lawyer, then, keen to analyze a complicated problem so that he can put his finger on the crucial point, and well informed as to the intricacies of the law in their relation to this problem, must recommend a definite course of action under the circumstances. Upon the outcome depends the probability that his services will again be retained when a technical question of grave practical consequence arises. As one client put it, "I'm not looking for a glib tongue in my attorney, but for brains and backbone." Brains, in this instance, means breadth of grasp and soundness of judgment in practical affairs, as well as accuracy of technical information about statutes and the common law. A vocational counselor appraising a person's aptitudes for law looks first for evidence of brains, for indications that the young man or woman is much more than ordinarily intelligent, alert, analytical, sensible, able to learn quickly and to assimilate and marshal what he learns.

The reader may complain that brains are needed in other professions, too, and that the conclusion just reached regarding aptitude for the law applies equally to engineering or to medicine. Granted. Only by looking more closely at the work of the lawyer and the student of law, and by finding traits in which students who succeed tend to excel those who fail, can the differential abilities symptomatic of special aptitude for this profession be defined.

By means such as these it has been found that the specific abilities indicative of aptitude for legal training include not only the verbal facility and the relatively large vocabulary which popular opinion ascribes to lawyers, but also superior ability to grasp a mass of details, to comprehend their relationships, and to reason logically about them. Accurate and tenacious memory for the kinds of data with which lawyers deal is an asset; also a peculiarly fertile imagination which quickly pictures the possible implications from a fragment of evidence or of testimony, and which thinks of even the remotest contingencies when a contract is being drawn.

When Ferson and Stoddard constructed their Law Aptitude Examination[2] they selected the following abilities as in some degree representative of aptitude for law: capacity for accurate recall, comprehension of passages read, ability to reason by analogy, ability to reason analytically, and skill in pure logic. This examination can be given in about sixty-five minutes. Used in a number of universities to forecast the ability of law students to pass the first year's work, it has proved to be a valid instrument. Of the school grades subsequently earned by those students who ranked in the highest quarter in the test, more than half were either A or B. The median is a critical score. Among the students who ranked below this point in the aptitude test, the proportion of subsequent failures was so large that such scores may properly be interpreted as indications of lack of aptitude for legal training.

Examinations similar in purpose but much longer than this have been developed at Columbia, Yale, and other institutions to aid in selecting from among candidates for admission. In constructing these tests, the aim has been to set problems which do not presuppose legal knowledge, but which require exercise of the kinds of mental process involved in cogent legal thinking. The Yale examinations have been designed in part with an even more specific purpose: to sample the candidate's aptitude for inductive reasoning of the type which that faculty aims to cultivate by means of the seminar method of teaching the principles of law.

When constructing tests of aptitude, it is a safe practice, more generally followed in this country than in Europe, to use content obviously pertinent to the specific field. Examinations made in this way are less likely to seem queer and inappropriate to the candidates. Their best efforts are called out. In the Ferson and Stoddard examina-

[2] M. L. Ferson and G. D. Stoddard, "Law Aptitude Examination—Preliminary Report," *American Law School Review*, 1927, 6:78-81. This examination, requiring about sixty-five minutes to administer, is issued with manual of directions and scoring key, by the West Publishing Co., St. Paul, Minn., and furnished to cooperating colleges without charge.

tion, for example, only one of the parts, namely, the sub-test designed to sample the candidate's accuracy in judging the logical correctness of inferences, uses materials which might not strike the reader instantly as savoring of the law. All the passages used for testing memory for details, ability to analyze, ability to reason by analogy, and comprehension of difficult reading, are from legal documents or have a legalistic content. Even when the purpose is to measure such traits as abstract intelligence or accuracy in perception of details, something is gained by wording the problems in terms germane to the field of interest of the examinees. Moreover, traits like intelligence, observation, and memory are, in part at least, specific to the materials on which they are exercised.

Some officers of admission, to be sure, have been content to use without modification one of the longer and more difficult tests of scholastic aptitude, giving consideration to the applicant's performance in the test only when his scholarship grades and other available data left doubt as to the advisability of accepting his application. Some have set a minimum standard—a lower critical score in the test—at a point which their experience has shown them to be indicative of probable failure, and have rejected all applicants who do not attain this score. Still others have taken a further step. Recognizing that the significant data available about each candidate (such as age, rank in class, scholarship grades in prerequisite courses, scholastic-aptitude test scores and legal-aptitude test scores) are more or less interrelated, they have ascertained, by resort to the statistical methods of partial and multiple correlation, the particular combination and weighting of these several data which give the best prediction of success or failure in the professional school. This is the most scientific approach. It is also the most practical when large numbers of students are involved.

The interests characteristic of lawyers, the likes and dislikes which differentiate the great majority of them from physicians, engineers, and men in general, have been reliably ascertained and are measurable with a degree of precision which is a boon to vocational counselors. Strong's Vocational Interest Blank, to which reference has frequently been made in previous chapters, is unquestionably one of the implements which should be at hand when a person is in serious doubt as to his aptitude for the law. It presupposes, however, that he wants the facts as to his aptitudes, or at least is sincere at the moment of recording his feelings toward each of the 420 items listed. A candidate for admission can, if he so chooses, simulate a liking for the things which lawyers—or the members of any other designated profession—like. And so this measure of interests is unsuitable for inclusion in a battery of tests used to select from among applicants for entrance to schools of law. Its place is in the office of the vocational counselor.

Now, as to an attorney's "backbone," his courage, determination, and sense of responsibility both to his client and to the ethical standards of his profession. Such aspects of personality and character are frequently described, but are difficult to measure. Neither the personal traits which attract and inspire a client's confidence nor the stamina and integrity which hold that confidence can be adequately sampled by means of tests. Applicants for admission to law schools are often interviewed by officers who also undertake to get information about their traits by correspondence with instructors, employers, and associates. Authorities responsible for admission to the bar have to rely on similar procedures when ascertaining whether a candidate meets the minimum specifications as to "character." These authorities have had the help of distinguished practitioners who have given generously of their time in examining credentials and in interviewing. Even so, the results have been far from satisfactory. Bar associations bitterly complain that the state examinations too frequently grant professional status to clever but unprincipled or otherwise objectionable persons who soon become shysters, preying on the public and bringing disrepute to their profession. Psychologists have as yet offered little assistance in this situation. Those who have been interested in measuring character traits have developed tests useful in comparing groups; but the reliability of these tests is too low to warrant reliance upon them when dealing with individuals.

There are, however, a few personality tests which have proved to be of some use in individual counseling. It is well known that lawyers, more frequently than physicians, engineers, and scientists, tend to be socially inclined. Retiring personalities are not the rule in this profession. No wonder, then, that on tests of extraversion-introversion, ascendancy-submission, and objectivity-subjectivity, the scores of lawyers and law students are on the average significantly different from the general population tendency, leaning more toward the extraverted, ascendant, objective side of the personality scales. A majority of business executives and a large majority of salesmen also exhibit these traits. They are not peculiar to lawyers, nor indispensable to successful practice. But when a person is hesitating as between law and medicine or law and engineering (if other things are equal), the facts regarding his characteristics of personality as brought out during interview and by means of these personality tests may clear away some of the uncertainty.

Our conclusion must be that the symptoms of aptitude for law are to be sought partly in the behavior characteristic of outgoing personalities, socially inclined; partly in definite signs of interest in the work lawyers do; but chiefly in the realm of intellect, since keenness of mind as measured by previous academic achievements and by tests of intelligence correlates well with subsequent success both in law school and in legal practice. Specific tests of legal aptitude, as we have seen, undertake to sample a candidate's intellectual keenness in dealing with the very sorts of questions with which he as a law student must wrestle. Provided with the necessary information, he is required to comprehend it, to analyze it, to reason about it, to draw inferences that are logically sound. The most valid estimates regarding the probabilities of success in a school of law are based, however, not on any single measure of intellectual capacity, but on a combination of data, including previous achievements in college courses as well as scores in tests of aptitude.

5

MEDICINE, SURGERY AND DENTISTRY

Aptitudes for the medical professions are possibly less difficult to identify than those for law. Medical schools have been much more rigorous than law schools in prescribing the particular subjects of study which all who apply must have taken. They know that a marked interest in pre-medical sciences such as zoology, comparative anatomy, bacteriology, and organic chemistry, coupled with superior ability in them, bodes well for subsequent success in medical school. College students have opportunity to try out their abilities and interests in these directions before finally deciding to enter the long hard road—a costly one to travel—that leads toward a medical degree. Many a student who thought he wanted to follow in the footsteps of his family physician has found, while working in these laboratories, sufficient reason for changing his mind. He has recognized his profound distaste for the exacting detail involved, his lack of patience and carefulness, his difficulty in learning and retaining a large new vocabulary of Greek and Latin polysyllables, or his unconquerable revulsion toward odors of formaldehyde and carrion. When such inabilities and aversions exist, they should be frankly faced. If they cannot be overcome, plans to study human anatomy had better be abandoned.

Surgeons and dentists are craftsmen in addition to being medically trained. Clearness of eye, delicacy of tactile discrimination, steadiness and strength of hand, dexterity of fingers, are obvious necessities. Quite as indispensable is aptitude for visualizing vividly in three dimensions; for it is necessary to see in their true positions and to manipulate the forms observed in a dentist's little mirror or in a laryngoscope; also to picture correctly the highly complicated unseen structures beneath the body surface—arteries, nerves, muscles, tendons, joints, glands, vital organs—perhaps at the end of a probe. Add to these abilities the grit and steadiness of nerve as well as of hand, without which surgeon, oculist, or dentist is prone to disastrous slips at critical junctures, and we have the aptitudes most commonly mentioned as more essential for surgery than for general medical practice. It is, however, hard to imagine how any practicing physician can do his work without frequent resort to the exercise of these same abilities in at least some degree, if he ever has to remove a child's adenoids, drain a suppurating fester, re-set a dislocated shoulder joint, deliver a baby, or take a sliver from an eyelid.

So far as the professional schools are concerned, it is, to be sure, in the dental school rather than in the medical that a seriously large number of failures are directly traceable to lack of manual and mechanical aptitudes. Students who successfully pass the first two years of basic biological, physiological, and anatomical courses, not infrequently have to be dropped in the third year because they cannot master both the mechanical intricacies and the manual techniques of dental practice. This is why a battery of tests designed to ascertain aptitudes for dentistry must include several which sample a candidate's manual and mechanical aptitudes. Tests of manual dexterity and versatility described in Chapter X, and tests of mechanical ingenuity and ability to deal mentally with relations in space, described in Chapter XI, are pertinent here.

Although dental instruments are usually made for use with the right hand, left-handedness is not necessarily a bar to dentistry as has sometimes been alleged. An instance from the writer's experience may not be out of place. A bright young junior in college, with his heart set on dentistry as a career, had been warned by his father and his uncle, who were both dental practitioners, to change his plans because of his left-handedness. He asked whether I could help him resolve his dilemma. This was twenty-odd years ago, before vocational psychology had amassed much of a background. However, I gave him all the aiming, tapping, tracing, and steadiness tests in Whipple's Manual. As it happened, his performance in each test with his right (non-preferred) hand surpassed the median right-hand performance of his fellow students at Dartmouth. Fortified by this information, he dismissed the anxieties that had been aroused and went on with his pre-dental schooling. Fifteen years later I met a Harvard professor of dentistry, a member of the committee on admissions. He was that left-handed student.

An anecdote proves nothing. But this one strikingly illustrates how tests may sometimes function usefully. In the instance described, Whipple's tests of manual dexterity and motor control were not used to discover an unsuspected aptitude for dentistry. This bent had already revealed itself clearly. The student wanted this profession. He knew about it intimately enough to be certain that he would enjoy the work. He knew also, from the progress he had already made in college, that he had the mental acumen, the scientific aptitude, which would enable him to master the laboratory and lecture courses of instruction. Only the possible manual handicap remained as a source of concern. The tests helped to banish his anxiety. In other instances the manual aptitudes may be obvious enough, while uncertainty remains as to the mechanical aptitudes, or the scientific. The vocational psychologist then resorts to the appropriate tests, those known to yield reliable measures of the aptitudes in question.

On the other hand, a situation often arises in which only the general field—let us say the broad field of the medical and biological sciences—has been decided upon, while the specific profession remains to be selected. Then it is most desirable, by resort to tests, personality inventories, inspection of previous school records, or any other means, to identify so far as possible all the aptitudes in which the individual markedly excels, and then to look for that branch of the profession which is most likely to furnish some scope for the exercise of each and all of these aptitudes, be they manual, mechanical, clerical, mathematical, linguistic, scientific or social. The professions of medicine, surgery, and dentistry with their many subdivisions and auxiliary sciences—orthopedics, psychiatry, ophthalmology, pediatrics, Roentgenology, bacteriology, public health, sanitation and industrial medicine, to mention a few among many—offer choices suited to different temperaments and types of interest, calling indeed for quite varied talents: aptitude for laboratory research, for statistical research or for invention; aptitude for dealing with people in a peculiarly intimate and confidential relationship; aptitude for the type of reasoning required in making a diagnosis; aptitude for teaching. It is not easy to think of an important aptitude which might not somehow be capitalized in one of the many kinds of posts which doctors of medicine are asked to fill. A student should shape a course that will exercise as many of his different aptitudes as possible.

But the chance to develop one's abilities in any corner of the vast medical field presupposes that one has precisely those aptitudes requisite for completing a course of medical training. The door is barred to anyone who cannot gain entrance to a medical school or who, once admitted, is unable to graduate. The following pages describe the procedure now followed by the majority of medical schools in an effort to place their facilities at the disposal of only those who have the necessary aptitudes.

The Association of American Medical Colleges has had for nearly ten years a Committee on Aptitude Tests for Medical Students.[3] After preliminary experiments, a battery of tests was developed which correlated so well with success in medical school that in 1930 the Association voted to recommend their use as one of the aids in selecting medical students. New forms of the examination have been prepared annually. They are administered at the same time in upwards of 600 colleges giving pre-medical courses. Last year they were taken by about 10,000 candidates. The papers are scored at headquarters in Washington, after which the scores of each student in each of six sub-tests, as well as his total score and percentile rank, are reported back to his college and also to the dean of the medical school to which he is applying for admission. The sub-tests are called (1) Comprehension and Retention, (2) Visual Memory, (3) Memory for Content, (4) Logical Reasoning, (5) Scientific Vocabulary, and (6) Understanding of Printed Material. Some of the earlier forms had included a test of Pre-medical Information and a test called Ability to Follow Directions. The former of these was discontinued because it duplicated other measures to some degree and involved practical difficulties of interpretation when scores of students with different amounts of pre-medical instruction had to be compared. The Directions test was dropped after it was found not to increase significantly the validity of the test as a measure of medical aptitude.

How closely scores in this test of medical aptitude will correlate with criteria of relative success in the practice of the profession cannot yet be ascertained. It is known, however, that they bear a positive and significant relationship not only to success in medical school,

[3] See the annual reports of F. A. Moss, the secretary of the committee, in the *Journal of the Association of American Medical Colleges*, September, 1931; May, 1932; January, 1933; March, 1934; January, 1935.

but to ratings of ability as internes five years after the test had been taken.

Success in medical school is conditioned by many factors of which the student's aptitude for learning the subject-matter is but one. His health and vigor is doubtless another determiner, although attempts to measure this factor quantitatively or even to estimate its relative importance, are lacking. Similarly, social adaptability—defined by Moss as ability to fit in with fellow students and to not antagonize instructors—conditions a student's progress in his medical education to an extent not definitely known. His previous preparation, however, is a factor that can be at least roughly measured in terms of college credits, and grades earned in pre-medical subjects. In one study of a thousand students, a critical score in pre-medical scholarship was found to predict 44 per cent of the failures, but to exclude 25 per cent of those who actually attained high average marks in medical school. The medical-aptitude test scores of the same students predicted 53 per cent of the failures while excluding 5 per cent of the high scholarship students. A combination of pre-medical scholarship and test data predicted 69 per cent of failures while excluding 4 per cent of those who made high average grades.

When a school has more applicants than can be accommodated, it is not an unusual practice to admit first those who are high both in aptitude and in pre-medical scholarship; to reject those who are low in both; and to consider individually from every angle those who are below the critical score in one of these indices, but above in the other. In dealing with these border-line cases, an officer of admission wants all the information he can secure about their personal traits, the impressions they have made on their teachers, and the standards of instruction in the colleges they have attended. Some schools go to great pains in securing information from the teachers of each applicant. They ask not only for expression of opinion as to his fitness for medicine, but also for a comparison of his abilities and promise with those of students who have previously come from that same college to the medical school. Where such care has been exercised in the choice of students, the proportion of failures has been gratifyingly low.

We may, in conclusion, look at this subject from the other point of view, that of the student himself. His judgment regarding his aptitude for medicine, surgery, or dentistry ordinarily ripens gradually. Beginning with an interest in doctors and their work, or perhaps in the biological sciences, he picks up, from reading and conversation as well as from first-hand observation, some understanding of the requirements in this field and some facts on which to base an estimate of his liking for it. If he not only talks with practitioners but helps one of them in his office or his laboratory, so much the better. At this stage, three types of test may be of some assistance: a scholastic aptitude examination, to ascertain the probability that he can successfully carry academic subjects on the pre-professional and professional levels; a test of scientific aptitude; and a vocational interest schedule, to help in ascertaining whether his tastes and inclinations resemble those of medical men more certainly than they resemble those of men in other professions. If these indications are favorable, he will probably elect to study pre-medical subjects. Thereafter, his relative success in the chemistry laboratory and in biological science and his liking for such courses will furnish further evidence as to his aptitude for medical training.

As partial evidence of fitness, about 90 per cent of the medical schools now make some use of the Aptitude Test for Medical Students above described. This test is available, however, only to accredited representatives of the Association of American Medical Colleges.[4] There is a possibility that one of the earlier forms may be released for general use. In any event, counselors helping students to make wise decisions about their aptitudes will give consideration not only to school marks, interest schedules, and scores in tests of intelligence and of scientific aptitude. They will take into account all other available data, including records of performance in tests of vocabulary, memory, reading comprehension, and inductive reasoning; nor will they neglect the manual and mechanical tests, especially if dentistry or surgery is contemplated.

Students with a leaning toward the medical field who show some but not all of the essential aptitudes have a choice among many alternatives, such as bacteriological or biochemical research and teaching, or the occupations of laboratory technician, veterinarian, pharmacist, pharmaceutical salesman demonstrating new remedies to practicing physicians, optician, dental mechanic, oral hygienist, physician's secretary, psychiatric social worker, registered nurse, hospital attendant. (There are numerous openings as attendant in mental hospitals.)

Traits advantageous in one or the other of the many occupations related to medicine will occur to anyone familiar with the nature of the occupation. The embalmer-undertaker, for instance, whose work begins where the physician leaves off, should, in addition to being a

[4] Counselors in colleges not as yet represented in this program may write to F. A. Moss, George Washington University, Washington, D. C.

good business man, have at least some of the attributes of dignity, sympathy, and tact which one wants in his physician, and also some of the surgeon's and sculptor's plastic artistry. The social worker needs the intelligence and good sense of a doctor and his ability sympathetically to understand and deal with persons; and if she is to be attached to the out-patient department of a hospital, should have some aptitude for those phases of a medical education which will constitute part of her training. Relatively few women with medical inclinations have ever entered the practice of medicine, and their number seems to be growing even smaller. Instead, they follow one of these related callings, particularly that of registered nurse. Aptitudes for this occupation have been investigated in some detail and form the topic of the following pages.

Chapter XV

APTITUDES FOR THE PROFESSIONS (*Concluded*)

1. Aptitudes for nursing. Intelligence and other characteristics of student nurses. Qualifications of a good nurse. 2. Teaching. 3. Music and Art.

1

NURSING

APTITUDES indicative of capacity to profit by courses of training given to student nurses, and of probable success in the occupation of Registered Nurse, resemble, in certain respects, the aptitudes characteristic of the physicians with whom these workers collaborate. Nurse and doctor work in the same environment. They deal with the same patients. Their duties are in part identical. Both undertake in the first instance to make the sufferer as free from pain and discomfort as possible. They both have to observe and record pulse, temperature and other symptoms with precision; administer remedies without mistake; skillfully prepare and apply dressings; look after essential matters of cleanliness and diet; and bring into sick-rooms the tactful understanding and personal presence which create, even in trying situations, an atmosphere conducive to hope and to recovery.

Both doctor and nurse need more than ordinary grit, stamina and physical endurance. A nurse has heavy loads to lift, and occasionally long hours of fatiguing labor of which it was once supposed only men were capable. Indeed, there were very few women following this ancient occupation before the middle of the nineteenth century. But women tend to excel in the distinctly feminine impulses of intuitive sympathy and desire to relieve distress, and have now largely crowded men out of this occupation. Fortunately, that day has passed when the chief qualification for entrance to certain nurses' training-schools was a willingness to spend a year or two scrubbing the hospital floors and doing other necessary menial work for which the impoverished institution thought that it could not afford to hire a scrubwoman. Even today, however, a nurse without a strong physical constitution is under a handicap.

A nurse is ordinarily an assistant. She takes orders from a superior, carrying out meticulously the directions the physician prescribes. While she shoulders serious responsibilities, it is the physician who has to make most of the crucial decisions. The nurse must learn and understand a good deal about physiology, materia medica and sanitation, but she is not expected to know all about the scientific foundations and multifarious details of medical science, nor to exercise the high order of inductive reasoning needed in making a difficult diagnosis. An exceptionally keen mind is no handicap; quite the contrary. But it seems to be relatively less essential in nursing than are the aptitudes for building a well-balanced personality and for learning the required skills.

As a matter of fact, the intelligence scores of nurses in training have been found to average much lower than those of medical students; somewhat lower, indeed, than college freshmen, although a little higher than seniors in high school. Bregman,[1] in an extensive survey, ascertained that the distribution of mental ability among student nurses resembles that among students in normal schools. "Every level of ability found among college students," she says, "is to be found among students of nursing, but there are relatively fewer nurses at the higher levels, and the average college student surpasses the average nurse-in-training in the qualities measured by an intelligence test." Counselors may be interested in Table XV, prepared from Bregman's data, which shows the lower quartile, median, and upper quartile scores of first-year student nurses in training-schools requiring four years of high-school preparation for entrance.

TABLE XV. INTELLIGENCE SCORES OF STUDENT NURSES

Test	*Number tested*	Q_1	M	Q_3
Army Alpha	930	115	132	148
Otis Higher (30 minutes)	1629	40	47	54
Otis Advanced	274	140	158	172
Terman Group	2084	131	152	170
Miller Mental Ability	500	62	77	87
Am. Council (Thurstone)	551	92	122	158

Scores in a group test of intelligence do not correlate at all closely with ratings used as criteria of success in the practical work of a train-

[1] Elsie O. Bregman, "The Performance of Student Nurses on Tests of Intelligence," *Nursing Education Bulletin*, New Series, II. March, 1933.

ing course. They correlate somewhat better with grades in the theoretical subjects. Jones and Iffert[2] recommend their use as one of several aids in selecting from among candidates, together with high school achievement tests and a special test of aptitude for nursing. They urge that information should be available regarding subjects studied, school grades, class standing, and records of activities from which traits of personality may be inferred; also age, family circumstances, and indications of interests. They describe the typical nurse-in-training, in the Pittsburgh area, as between 20 and 22 years of age; she had taken an academic course in high school, where she definitely liked her courses in English and disliked mathematics; liked the physical sciences and modern languages moderately, but had a dislike, though slight, for Latin and social sciences. Her extra-curricular activities were athletic or dramatic rather than academic. She had a strong predilection for her chosen occupation of nursing.

This description may be compared with one given by Mrs. Miles[3] who studied in much detail a group of 78 student nurses in a school with standards of selection apparently higher than those which prevailed in the Pittsburgh area. Comparing those students with other young women, she says,

> With reference to occupational interests and activity drive we find that the nurses in training are active, they seek the more interesting and more varied types of work, they usually like vigorous play; creative adventure attracts them and they are willing to take risks in order to gain goals. The intelligence of the group is definitely above the average; the young nurses have fairly wide general interests, are rather immune to popular prejudices, think in terms of real rather than fallacious values. And these young women are balanced emotionally; they have reasonable fears and disgusts, they have typical social recreational attitudes for their age. Their special divergence from others in their age group, of equal intelligence, equal education, and comparable social experience is in their sense of awareness of suffering—they show the social emotion of pity. While being like other young girls in the primary emotions, *fear*, *anger*, and *disgust*, they rate at a point on the *pity*-scale which means that this emotion is for them not a theoretical one, but a basic starting-point for their life interest.
>
> The nurses described here were chosen as representatives of the entering and graduating classes in a standard Western nursing-school. They were high-school graduates, their intelligence was equal to that of the average college sophomore (IQ about 118); they resembled the more active outgoing college students in their interests; their fields of knowledge combined the scientific with the domestic. With slightly less general culture than the college sophomores

[2] W. B. Jones and R. E. Iffert, *Fitness for Nursing: A Study in Student Selection.* Pittsburgh, Bureau of Educational Records and Research, 1933.

[3] Catharine Cox Miles, "The Personality Development of Student Nurses." *American Journal of Nursing*, 1934, 34: No. 2.

they had slightly more scientific knowledge. They were somewhat more conservative in evaluation of types of wickedness and in this as in their "pity" they diverged from the young college group to resemble a more mature, more socially responsible group; in fact, they actually duplicate in these attitudes the "mothers of gifted children." This protective, idealistic, maternal attitude and urge tends in the profile which they themselves have unwittingly drawn, by their responses to many series of test questions, to differentiate them most clearly from other groups.

In this same article is a consensus of expert nursing opinion regarding the qualifications possessed by able nurses—a list of ten composite traits which can in part be developed but for acquiring which a candidate should have superior aptitude. These are said to be the qualifications for a good nurse:

1. Genuine liking for people and ability tactfully to work with and for them.
2. High grade of intelligence and understanding, with good general education and broad interests.
3. Emotional maturity, stability, and self-control seasoned with patience and a sense of humor.
4. Good physical health and cheerful personal outlook.
5. Integrity of character, exemplary ideals and morals; refined tastes; tolerance.
6. Sense of responsibility coupled with personal reliability and loyalty.
7. Attention to details, good observation with scientific attitude, and open-mindedness.
8. Resourcefulness and adaptability.
9. Cleanliness and attractiveness in appearance.
10. Ability to teach.

Aptitudes for acquiring these qualifications are for the most part not susceptible to precise measurement, but must be appraised mainly by recourse to judgments of teachers and associates, personal interview, observation of behavior, and scrutiny of the cumulative record.

Strong's Vocational Interest Blank for Women, previously described, yields a useful measure of the certainty with which a woman's interests resemble or do not resemble those of professional nurses.

A battery like Moss and Hunt's Aptitude Test for Nursing[4] does not attempt to measure interest or to assess the total personality, but concentrates on measuring abilities indicative of aptitude for learning what a nurse must learn. This examination, which requires less than an hour to give, consists of seven tests to measure scientific vocabulary, general information, understanding of printed material, visual mem-

[4] Published in 1931, with directions for giving and scoring, by the Center for Psychological Service, Washington, D. C. $12 a hundred. Obtainable also from the Psychological Corporation.

ory, memory for content, comprehension and retention of facts in a passage studied, and ability to understand and follow directions. In purpose and method, if not in length and difficulty, it resembles the test of medical aptitude described in the preceding section. It also resembles a group intelligence test and in part samples the same abilities, but has an advantage in that it makes use of content germane to the occupation.

Nursing, teaching, clerical work of many kinds, all give scope to about the same range of general mental ability. Granted the intellectual aptitudes requisite for profiting by the instruction offered in the training-schools, choice from among these callings is largely a matter of interests, temperament, and personality. "Have I a liking for the kinds of work nurses do, rather than for teaching or for working in an office? If so, have I the emotional stability, the cheerful disposition, the willingness to accept responsibility, the robust health, the carefulness in details, the patience, and the exceptionally strong desire to minister to all sorts of suffering persons, which characterize others who have made progress in the occupation of nurse?" The young woman who asks these questions of a counselor may be helped in many ways to clarify her thinking; but the most important answers only she herself can give.

2

TEACHING

We come now to the teaching profession, unique in that everyone has had years of opportunity to observe it intimately, at close range. Everyone has known personally a number of teachers and has observed day after day—while attending elementary school at least, if not also in high school and in college—what these teachers do when in the presence of their pupils. To be sure, the precise nature of their work as they give instruction may not be understood, while the professional duties which occupy them outside the class-room are grasped only vaguely, if at all. A favorite quip among students takes the form of a complaint that while they do all the work, the teachers get all the pay. But these young people know better. They recognize poor work—and good work—when they see it, as Hart[5] has convincingly shown. They appreciate—if they stop to think about it—that those who have taught them the most, those who have left the deepest impression, have certain characteristics in common: not only a knowl-

[5] F. W. Hart, *Teachers and Teaching*. New York: The Macmillan Company, 1934.

edge of their subject, but an infectious enthusiasm for it; not only a real liking for the young people or children in their classes, but also a wise understanding of how to awaken their minds and win their cooperation and respect. So, although there may be frequent misconceptions as to precisely what is required of a teacher—planning and preparing daily exercises, correcting papers, keeping records, administering achievement tests, maintaining discipline, counseling with individuals on all sorts of educational and personal matters, participating, as a teacher often must, in activities of school and community, keeping abreast of progress in his subject and fitting himself for professional advancement—it is doubtful, nevertheless, whether there is any other occupation with which people in general are as well acquainted.

As to prestige, teaching ranks high, particularly in the estimation of the great numbers of people who follow pursuits with lower rankings than this on the scale of social desirability. For example, the respect and admiration accorded to the occupation of college professor, as Hartmann[6] found, places it near the top of the hierarchy, close to the professions of medicine and law. No less highly regarded than the occupation of clergyman is that of school superintendent. Both principal and high-school teacher rank above merchant and factory superintendent; while the elementary-school teacher's calling, a few points lower on the scale of prestige, is nevertheless more highly esteemed than, for instance, the occupations of nurse, salesman, actor, electrician, bookkeeper, farmer, grocery-store owner, stenographer, or chef. The great majority of people look up to their teachers.

Teaching is also a populous occupation. There are not nearly so many engineers, nurses, doctors, lawyers, ministers, artists, or librarians as there are teachers, of whom the census enumerated more than a million in 1930. Little wonder that it is one of the first occupations to be thought of when a young person begins to turn over in his mind the various careers he might follow, for it offers many opportunities, is generally respected, and is one he already knows a good deal about.

Counselors, too, usually know this profession better than any other. They are ordinarily teachers themselves, or have been. They work in close cooperation with those engaged in teaching. They understand that it is at once a personal service occupation, a social occupation, and an intellectual occupation, and that aptitude for it—whether in college class-room, or in nursery school—implies the ability and the

[6] G. W. Hartmann, "The Prestige of Occupations: A Comparison of Educational Occupations with Others," *Personnel Journal*, 1934, 13:144-152.

desire to be helpful to immature but developing personalities, as well as ability to master the subjects taught.

It might seem superfluous, then, in a book of this kind to say anything more about the work that teachers do, or about the aptitudes which prospective teachers should have. We shall, nevertheless, ask what qualifications are sought by those who engage the services of teachers, and by institutions which select students for courses of professional training.

A university president[7] with responsibility for choosing able instructors has said, "The great teacher brings to his business accurate and wide knowledge, an informed technique, intelligence, energy, initiative, adaptability, common sense, high standards of personal character and professional achievement, singleness of purpose, sympathy, a rich social background, and a convincing sincerity of personality." An impressive picture! But would it not serve equally well as the portrait of a great business executive, political leader, preacher, social worker, physician, or lawyer? Perhaps these, too, are teachers. Teaching is not, however, their profession. The lineaments must be more sharply drawn if we are to recognize the essential qualities which characterize teachers in contrast to those who, in other professional relations, have the responsibility of dealing helpfully with people.

A more specific description of the ideal teacher was given long ago by George Herbert Palmer in his volume, *The Teacher*.[8] He puts his finger on four traits without which a teacher is handicapped. He places first a sympathetic imagination—a limberness of mind which enables one to think in terms of the other person's limitations, interests and needs, an aptitude for what he calls "altruistic vicariousness." Next is the necessity for a broad background of knowledge, an accumulated wealth extending beyond the bounds of what is actually taught. The third requisite he describes as the power to kindle interest, to invigorate the productive activity of pupils as only a stimulating person can do. Such a person is the very opposite of the grind. Finally, he stresses the capacity for disinterestedness—indifference to praise and recognition—a trait which he picturesquely de-

[7] Glenn Frank, quoted in *Teaching as a Career*. Bulletin of the University of Wisconsin (Series 2076, 1935), published by the Bureau of Guidance and Records of the university. This forty-eight-page pamphlet is addressed to students in high school and college. The question, "Should I choose teaching as a career?" is raised. The advantages and disadvantages of teaching are compared. Ways of ascertaining whether one has the requisite qualifications are suggested. Separate sections are then devoted to the fields of nursery-school teaching, elementary-school teaching, secondary-school teaching, college and university teaching, supervisory and executive positions, salaries, opportunities, and ways of securing the necessary preparation.

[8] Boston: Houghton Mifflin Company, 1908, pp. 3-30.

fines as "readiness to be forgotten"; for, he says, "the teacher must keep himself entirely out of the way, fixing young attention on the proffered knowledge, and not on anything so small as the one who brings it." An ideal teacher, then, is imaginative, intellectually wealthy, stimulating, disinterested.

Is this specific enough? If a young person is drawn toward teaching, how is he to find out whether he possesses the golden qualifications listed by Professor Palmer, or the capacity to acquire them? In facing this question, the qualities actually exhibited by promising candidates will be more clearly defined.

The necessary intellectual talents are the least difficult to appraise. Past performance in studies already pursued tells whether one has a bent for learning. The person who in his elementary and junior high school has not excelled the majority of his classmates in ease and accuracy of acquisition need not trouble to inquire further as to his aptitude for teaching. The college student who would like to follow in the footsteps of a favorite professor should make A grades, at least in the subject of his choice. A gentleman's C average will not do. Anyone who is to become a teacher needs an intellect capable of grasping not only the subject-matter and its place in the curriculum, but also the aims and processes of education. But assuming that the candidate is bright, that he learns readily and assimilates thoroughly what he studies, the question still remains as to the likelihood that he can also teach others. This aptitude sometimes reveals itself when classmates come to him for help. If he enjoys explaining difficult points, if he succeeds in finding ways of clarifying obscurities so that his fellows increasingly turn to him, that fact alone suggests that he probably has some aptitude for teaching.

The personal and social abilities—particularly sympathetic imagination and absorption in his pupils, without which a teacher fails to stimulate, counsel and instruct—are sometimes contrasted with the intellectual abilities which he exhibits in his own learning and productive thinking. Aptitude for teaching is set over against aptitude for scholarship, and it is asserted that the former, peculiarly necessary in elementary and secondary schools, is in college and professional schools of only incidental importance in comparison with intellectual grasp of the subject to be taught. It is indeed true that as the educational ladder is ascended, intellectual power becomes increasingly essential. In the postgraduate seminar, the specialist who really knows is sought out by students who covet the chance to collaborate in his investigations, even though he is personally uninspiring, socially inarticulate, completely absorbed in his own research. Fortunately, however, the two aptitudes are not mutually exclusive. On the contrary, the most profound scholars are frequently also the most skillful and stimulating teachers.

As in other callings, certainty regarding one's interest in and aptitude for teaching is enhanced by even a modest opportunity to participate in it. Instructors and counselors help those students who are seriously thinking of fitting themselves to teach, not only by telling them more about the things teachers do, but also by giving them a chance to share in some of them—helping a backward classmate; taking charge when the instructor is called from the room; marking papers; preparing a laboratory demonstration; organizing a nature-study trip. Opportunities like these should, of course, have come to every promising student not infrequently throughout his schooling. An interview with him regarding these teaching experiences may remove some of the uncertainty as to his aptitudes.

Preliminary to the counseling interview, a student's attention may be directed toward essential points by a series of questions such as the following:[9]

1. Are you genuinely interested in young people or children of the age you would be teaching?
2. Do you enjoy working with and for others?
3. Can you adapt and adjust yourself easily to new situations?
4. Do you control your temper when things go wrong?
5. Are you enthusiastic about the work teachers do?
6. Do you ordinarily succeed in securing the cooperation of others?
7. Are you above the average of your class in scholarship?
8. Do you have a high sense of honesty and fairness in your dealings?
9. Are you patient and sympathetic under trying conditions?
10. Do your friends comment favorably upon your appearance?
11. Are you sought by others both at school and outside?
12. Can you express yourself clearly and forcefully?
13. Can you plan and think things through for yourself?
14. Are you free from serious defects in voice and body?
15. Do others react favorably to your ideas and plans?
16. Do you try to be courteous and considerate with others?
17. Do you have plenty of reserve energy and vitality?
18. Are you careful, thorough, and accurate in your studies?
19. Do you like to know and use new methods and ideas?
20. Do you ordinarily look on the bright side of things?
21. Are you able to direct and discipline others?

These questions bring into relief desirable personal qualifications—

[9] This self-inventory for prospective teachers is adapted from page 8 of the Wisconsin Bulletin cited above.

most of them, that is, but not all. There is another characteristic—intangible and all too rare—eagerly sought by heads of schools and colleges in the teachers whose services they engage. Realizing that a teacher's every word and act is a pattern which students consciously or unconsciously copy, they ask about a candidate, "Is he a cultivated person?" This trait was not specifically mentioned in the self-inventory above because it is neither easy to define nor readily recognizable by a young person who happens to be deficient in it. Cultivation is the embodiment in a person of what is best in a culture. It is a highly complex trait. Usually acquired in the atmosphere of a cultivated home with fine traditions and standards of speech, diction, manner, social behavior, and taste in reading and in the arts, it can, nevertheless, be achieved also by those who are sensitive to cultural values, even if they have not had these early advantages. The language and voice of a cultivated person, the correctness of his every act and gesture, are natural, ingrained, automatic, never ostentatious or affected. Fortunate indeed are the pupils of a teacher who not only understands them and likes to work with them, not only knows his subject and how to impart it, but also in his own person exemplifies the best traditions and ideals of taste and conduct.

The professional schools for training teachers have as yet found no sure means of ascertaining in advance whether a candidate has or can acquire the traits described in the foregoing paragraphs, although marked defects and shortcomings are usually recognizable during an interview with an applicant for admission. His intellectual grasp and mental alertness can be fairly well estimated by reference to his previous school record and his performance in tests of scholastic aptitude, vocabulary, English usage, mathematics, and other academic subjects, supplemented when necessary by such specially devised tests of intelligence as the one known as the Coxe-Orleans Prognosis Test of Teaching Ability (see page 346), or the psychological examination prepared annually by the Teachers College Personnel Association.[10] The Stanford Educational Aptitudes Test, by M. B. Jensen, furnishes advanced students with some indication of the comparative strength of their aptitudes for teaching, for administration, and for research.

Furthermore, the resemblance of a young man's interests to those of men engaged in teaching can be measured by means of Strong's Vocational Interest Blank, Form A or B. For Women, Form WA or WB may be scored for the occupation of high-school teacher

[10] Officers of admission may secure full information about this test from J. D. Heilman, State College of Education, Greeley, Colorado.

(general) and for high-school teacher of English, high-school teacher of mathematics, and high-school teacher of social science.

Final decision as to an applicant's suitability must often be deferred until a period of supervised apprentice-teaching—an interneship—has made it evident whether or not he has it in him to become that valuable asset to any community—a good teacher.

3
MUSIC AND ART

It happens that a great many artists and musicians are also teachers. Players, singers, and composers usually have private pupils, even though they receive a salary from an orchestra or choir. Just as poets and professional writers occasionally engage in training those intent upon gaining literary proficiency, so sculptors, engravers, decorators, designers of stage settings, painters of portraits and landscapes, often conduct classes for those who want to learn their specialty. In addition to those whose teaching is secondary to the practice of their art are thousands whose main occupation it is to teach or to supervise instruction in schools and colleges; and since the number of artists who depend for a livelihood exclusively upon income from professional performance or creative invention is relatively small in comparison with the number who teach, aptitude for teaching is evidently an asset for one who thinks of embarking on an artistic career.

The teaching of music or any other art is distinctive, however, in emphasizing the acquisition of skills and of æsthetic judgment or taste, rather than of mere facts regarding the art, its history and its masters. Ability to impart knowledge, valuable though it may be, is, after all, secondary to the capacity to instil a discriminating appreciation of the beautiful and to train in the execution of artistic objects and effects. This implies æsthetic discrimination and a degree of proficiency on the part of the teacher. He must be something of an artist himself; which brings us face to face with our main question—basic when counseling anyone with ambition to become a composer, a creative artist, a performer, a commercial designer, or a teacher of art—the question as to the nature of artistic talent and how it can be disclosed.

Talent, as we saw in Chapter II, is a relatively high order of aptitude, and implies special capacity for taking a high degree of training. Artistic talent—given appropriate opportunity for development—

eventually shows itself either in the excellence of work executed or in superior taste when appraising or interpreting the works of others. It is customary to distinguish, then, between talent for artistic production and talent for appreciation. A critic, an art dealer, or a concert violinist may exhibit talent of this latter kind without having either the inventiveness or the proficiency which creative work demands. But some form of æsthetic sensitivity—of ability to distinguish between degrees of beauty or artistic excellence—is at the root of every form of artistic ability. It is needed by the musical performer as well as by the composer; by the skilled workman who executes a charming pattern as well as by the artist who designs it; and also by hosts of people in related occupations—architects, museum curators, buyers of dresses and furniture, salesmen of jewelry and lace, window-dressers, designers of type, craftsmen of every sort. Fortunately, aptitude for developing at least some æsthetic sensitivity is rather widely distributed throughout the population. Otherwise capacity to find enjoyment in numerous things of beauty would be rare instead of general, most efforts toward widespread art education would be futile, and opportunities to train for occupations similar to those just mentioned would be closed to all but a small number of the elect.

Aptitude for learning to distinguish the beautiful from the commonplace or the ugly, widespread though it is, nevertheless varies greatly from person to person. It varies in kind as well as in degree; for this aptitude is not a simple unitary trait, either present or absent, nor has it only one dimension. Instead, it is highly complex, being conditioned partly by the individual's sensory and motor equipment and partly by his several intellectual powers, as well as by his temperament and emotional make-up. Capacity to appreciate nuances of shade in an etching or apt metaphors in a poem does not necessarily imply responsiveness to the beauty of a tragic play or of a neat mathematical demonstration. The tonally deficient, like the color-blind, are by virtue of their sensory limitations cut off from certain kinds of æsthetic experience, no matter how keen their appreciation of visual and temporal patterns; while poor muscular coordination is a bar to many an artistic pursuit. Only rarely is anyone equally responsive to beauty in all its forms. There are, to be sure, poets who are gifted also in sculpture and in music; etchers who can write good drama; portrait-painters who sing well. Between different sorts of artistic aptitude there is a positive correlation; but these relationships are far from close. Talent, indeed, is in large measure specific to the particular medium in which it is to be exercised, to the special demands put upon it. It follows that the varieties of artistic talent are as numerous as the arts to be practiced.

Musical talent is a case in point. The separate components of this complex hierarchy of aptitudes are many, as Seashore's thorough analysis demonstrated.[11] The relative importance of these specific aptitudes varies with the type of musical activity to be undertaken. Thus the future pianist does not need the sharp ear for slight differ-

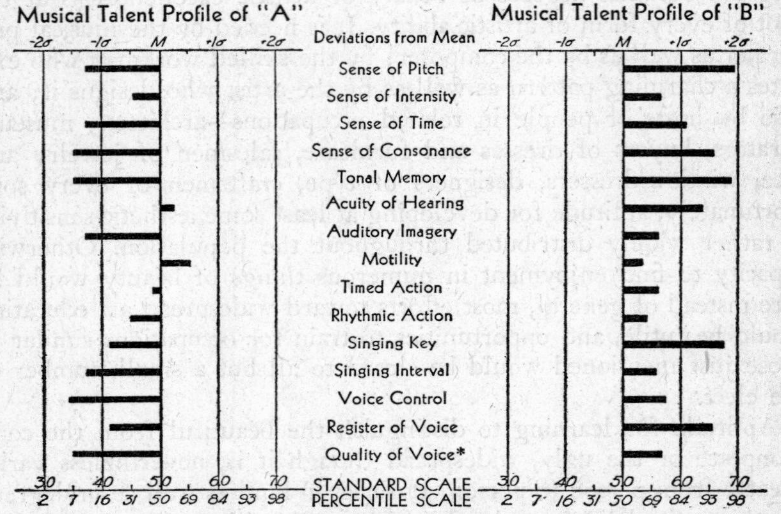

* "Quality of Voice" is estimated. All the other components of musical aptitude are objectively measured.

FIG. 11. MUSICAL TALENT PROFILES

Showing how the aptitudes of an unmusical man "A" and of a musically talented man "B" differ from those of the average person. Data from C. E. Seashore, *The Psychology of Musical Talent*, pages 23 and 25. Boston: Silver, Burdette and Co., 1919.

ences of pitch and timbre required in a student of the violin, nor vocal organs such as a good singer inherits. He should, however, excel in certain capacities—sensory, motor, intellectual, and emotional —including perception of minute differences of loudness, of consonance, and of time, sense of rhythm, agility and strength of fingers and hands, delicacy as well as firmness of touch, memory for tonal and dynamic configurations, and sensitivity to the beauty of the combinations and patterns of sound which his instrument permits him

[11] See, for example, the musical aptitude profiles of two individuals in Fig. 11, and the descriptions of these individuals in C. E. Seashore's *The Psychology of Musical Talent*, pages 22 ff. Boston: Silver, Burdette & Co., 1919.

to produce. The psychological profile of abilities symptomatic of aptitude for becoming a pianist resembles in many details, but not in all, the profile of promising candidates for training as organist, concert singer, flute-player, orchestral director, or composer. The embouchure—the "lip"—of the trumpeter is not identical with that of the oboist. A delicate sense of absolute pitch, said to be common among tympanists who must change the tuning of their kettledrums while the music is in progress, may be for players of other instruments only a painful handicap. Each medium of expression makes its unique demands; each type of musical activity presupposes distinctive aptitudes.

A battery of tests and ratings such as Seashore[12] and others[13] have developed for measuring musical talent is useful, then, not merely for distinguishing the musically endowed from those who are not, thus helping toward a decision as to the amount of musical instruction in which it is wise to invest. These tests have even greater usefulness in revealing, while musical education proceeds, those kinds of achievement toward which the individual's pattern of aptitudes points with greatest promise.

Several of Seashore's tests, available on phonographic discs for group administration, have served in school surveys to identify pupils with talents which neither they nor their parents had suspected, and to draw attention to others clearly unsuited to musical training already entered upon. In the hands of specially qualified music psychologists, these same tests, together with others which help to round out the inventory of an individual's musical aptitudes, are undoubtedly valuable aids in counseling. In conservatories of music they are useful both when selecting from among applicants for admission and when advising more advanced students with reference to their courses of training.[14]

It should go without saying that diagnosis of musical talent does not rest exclusively on the results of tests. Quite the contrary. As in all counseling, a picture of the student's aptitudes is first obtained from an appraisal of his accomplishments to date, his developmental history, his interests and ambitions, his temperament—indeed, all the

[12] C. E. Seashore, "The Discovery and Guidance of Musical Talent." Chapter XXI in the *Thirty-Fourth Yearbook of the National Society for the Study of Education.* Bloomington, Ill.: Public School Publishing Co., 1934.

[13] *Cf.* P. Farnsworth, "An Historical, Critical, and Experimental Study of the Seashore-Kwalwasser Test Battery," *Genetic Psychology Monographs*, 1931, 9, No. 5.

[14] Hazel M. Stanton, *Measurement of Musical Talent: The Eastman Experiment.* University of Iowa Studies in the Psychology of Music, Vol. II. Published by the University, 1935.

significant traits of his personality in so far as they can be ascertained by interview and by scrutiny of records. Psychological test data may then supplement or correct this picture in important details; but they never replace it.

It follows that a music counselor must be a good judge of the merit of what the incipient musician does when asked to play, or sing, or submit a sample of his compositions. The adviser must be able to recognize—or have the collaboration of a musical expert who can recognize—symptoms of promise in relatively untaught performance. The quality of this performance, when judged in the light of the character and extent of such musical education as the candidate may already have received, furnishes the safest ground on which to form a preliminary estimate of his capacity to benefit from more instruction. From this point of departure, detailed analysis of his specific aptitudes proceeds. The result of this analysis in turn should be checked from time to time against such improvement in musical performance as is observable after further training. At each stage, what the learner can do furnishes the best index of what he probably can learn to do.

Procedures in appraising aptitudes for sculpture, drawing, painting, and related arts resemble, in practice and in theory, those used in judging musical talent. "Show me a sketch you have made," says the instructor to an applicant for a course in design, and the would-be artist unties his portfolio as the interview proceeds. "When did you begin to draw?" "How much have you done?" "Where have you studied?" "Who taught you?" "Now let me see you sketch this urn, or that cast beside the easel." Such judgments as the instructor forms while he looks at the contents of the portfolio, listens to the narrative of early interests and experiences, and watches the way in which the sample sketch takes shape, are usually tentative. Before hazarding an opinion as to a candidate's promise he may prefer to watch his rate of progress during a course of instruction; for evidences of talent not at first observable are likely to be disclosed as training proceeds.

Meanwhile, it is possible by means of tests to measure certain components of artistic talent. The Meier-Seashore Art Judgment Test (see page 350) furnishes a measure of one important trait—æsthetic sensitivity to differences of merit when two pictures identical except in one respect are compared. The task consists of making 125 such comparisons, and the proportion of correct judgments seems to bear a significant relation to capacity for artistic development. The

McAdory Art Test (see page 352) requires exercise of artistic judgment in comparing the merit of pictures of familiar objects—furniture and utensils, textiles and clothing—also of architecture, shape and line arrangement, massing of dark and light, and color. Its use is advocated as a means of measuring growth in artistic sensitivity and analyzing the effects of art-training. Other tests, of which a number are described in Kinter's monograph,[15] require the actual performance of tasks deemed representative of what an artist does. Ideally, one likes to measure separately such traits as color sensitivity and color memory; sensitivity to nuances of light and shade—value, chiaroscuro, notan; sense of balance, stability, and symmetry; sense of proportion; sense of visual rhythm; sense of perspective and other aspects of spatial perception; richness of imagery and inventiveness; interest in detail; empathy; feeling for the medium; also essential aspects of motor coordination and control. Then, in so far as we know the relative contribution of each of these aptitudes to the more complex patterns indicative of aptitude for each of the main types of artistic activity, a scientific foundation for counseling with reference to art education is laid. As Seashore says,[16] "Just as there can be no single adequate measure of musicality there is no possibility of a single measure of artistic talent. Each is a hierarchy of natural capacities or resources which functions as a whole, but the description of the talent and the measure of the talent must always take into account the kinds of talent—*i.e.*, the forces at work. Let us, therefore, abandon the search for a single art quotient, just as we are gradually discarding the single intelligence quotient, and substitute therefor a progressive objective analysis in terms of which we may construct talent profiles indicating both kind and degree of special aptitudes."

The day is approaching when this can be done with confidence, thanks to many studies now in progress.[17] Already these investigations have clarified our understanding of the nature of artistic aptitudes. It is evident that talent of many kinds is more widely distributed and the possibilities of art education greater than has been commonly supposed. Counselors and artists who are in a position to help students in correctly identifying these talents can increase the likelihood that such endowments as each possesses will be capitalized at full value, either in the enrichment of his individual satisfactions or in the productivity of an artistic career.

[15] Madaline Kinter, *The Measurement of Artistic Abilities*, New York: Psychological Corporation, 1933.

[16] In Kinter's monograph, p. 73.

[17] See, for example, the volume of *Studies in the Psychology of Art*, edited by N. C. Meier. *Psychological Monographs*, No. 213. Princeton, N. J., 1936.

PART THREE

THE PRACTICE OF TESTING

Selection, Administration and Interpretation of Tests

Chapter XVI

SELECTION OF TESTS

1. Need for a grasp of general principles of aptitude-testing. 2. Basic concepts: aptitude, trait, test, score, scale, norm, correlation, validity, reliability. 3. Choice of a criterion of success precedes selection of tests. Possible criteria. 4. How validity of an aptitude test is ascertained. Why it is usually low. Ways of increasing it. 5. Considerations, theoretical and practical, to be weighed when selecting tests.

1

"What tests shall I use?"

This question takes many forms. Counselors who want to leave no stone unturned in their quest for information helpful to the persons coming to them for educational and vocational guidance, frequently ask, "Which are the most reliable and valid tests of scholastic aptitude?" "What battery of examinations is well adapted for high-school students who are about to choose between technical, commercial, agricultural, and academic curricula?" "Can you name a dependable test of mechanical ingenuity?" "Does the Minnesota Vocational Test for Clerical Workers furnish the best available means of estimating the likelihood that a person can learn to do filing within a reasonable time?" "For making a school survey of musical talent is there any means more suitable than the well-known battery of tests developed by Dean Seashore?"

These and a hundred similar queries are familiar to every vocational psychologist. They are fair enough. They deserve straightforward replies. But they can rarely be answered categorically. Instead, the psychologist is prone, like the typical Yankee, to put some questions himself: "Tell me first," he asks, "how much information you already have about the scholastic abilities, the mechanical ingenuity, the interest patterns, the musical talents, of the persons who want your suggestions regarding their aptitudes. In what detail have their cumulative records been maintained? Does not this information, together with what you can gather from teachers, employers, and associates, and in personal conference with the individuals themselves, give you about all that you and they will need in deciding on next steps?

"Furthermore," the psychologist continues, "I should like to know who is to administer the tests, if any are to be used. Has he finished his apprenticeship in giving individual performance tests, or has his experience been limited to administering the Binet, and to giving paper-and-pencil examinations? The answer will make quite a difference in the suggestions offered. Also, who will interpret the meaning of the scores? Has he mastered the subject of individual differences and the theory of probability? Does he thoroughly appreciate the limitations of test data? Can he, for instance, estimate the range of probable error in inferring a person's true score from his obtained score in each test used, and in addition make appropriate allowance for possible future changes in the trait measured?"

Vividly aware of inadequacies in many widely heralded tests, and realizing the pitfalls into which it is all too easy to stumble when giving them and when weighing the significance of individual scores, the practical psychologist is reluctant to commit himself as advocating any tests whatever, with the possible exception of some paper-and-pencil examinations such as the more searching standardized tests of school achievement and of academic aptitude. His first service to responsible officials and counselors in schools, social institutions, and public agencies is to tell them about the nature, meaning, and limitations of vocational tests and test results; for only after general principles have been firmly grasped are suggestions in order regarding the choice of tests.

The present chapter on the selection of tests first summarizes the principles of aptitude-testing, and then, in the light of these principles and of the uses to which test data are put, lists the main considerations to be kept in mind when choosing tests. The following chapters deal with test administration and with the interpretation of test data. Finally, in an Appendix which contains descriptions of representative tests, illustrations are given of the principles in accordance with which decisions should be made as to whether recourse to certain tests will be advisable in specific situations.

The pages which immediately follow will serve to recall certain vital points to readers already well acquainted with technical publications on psychological examining; while those who are less familiar with the general theory and the statistical aspects of mental measurement will, it is hoped, be encouraged to explore these subjects in detail.

2

Aptitude, as we saw in Chapter II, is a condition, a set of characteristics or combination of traits, symptomatic of capacity to acquire specified proficiencies or modes of behavior.

A *trait* is any attribute of an individual.[1]

Traits significant of aptitudes may be of three sorts:

1. Traits descriptive of the individual as he appears to others—handsome face, hesitant manner, impressive size, or raucous voice, for example.
2. Traits definable in terms of the things that he can do; his abilities.
3. Traits descriptive of what he ordinarily does under specified conditions: his characteristic modes of action, feeling, and thought; in other words, his behavioral tendencies.

What a person customarily does and what he is able to do may exemplify two very different traits, as in the case of the manager who is quite able to deal with his subordinates tactfully, but who rarely shows tact because his dispositional tendency is to be intentionally rude. Likewise, a trait term descriptive of the way in which an individual impresses others may be far from descriptive of either his abilities or his dispositions; as when conceited behavior cloaks a feeling of inferiority. Any or all of these three kinds of traits—appearances, abilities, and behavioral tendencies—may conceivably be symptomatic of vocational aptitude.

"There are as many abilities as there are enumerable things that individuals can do," as Thurstone points out.[2] "Each ability is therefore objectively defined in terms of a specified task and of a specified method of appraising it." He then defines a test, and a score, as follows:

"The task, together with the method of appraising it, which defines an ability is called a *test*.

"The linear evaluation of a test performance is called a *score*."

We shall use the term "test" to cover not only a specified task by means of which an ability may be defined and measured, but also a task which yields a measure of a behavioral *tendency*, a trait of our

[1] L. L. Thurstone, *The Vectors of Mind*, p. 48. Chicago: University of Chicago Press, 1935.

[2] *Loc. cit.*

Type 3. The well-known Kent-Rosanoff word association test, for example, may be scored to yield a measure of a person's tendency to give egocentric responses, a trait more often characteristic of scholars and poets than of salesmen. A vocational interest schedule becomes a test of affective tendencies when scored to show the degree of resemblance between the person's expressed likes and dislikes and those of the typical accountant or musician.

A *rating* is an opinion or judgment regarding a trait, recorded as an estimated score.

A *scale* is a series of numerical values for use as standards in measurement.

A *standard scale* is a scale the unit of which is sigma, the Standard Deviation from the mean of the population tested.[3]

A *percentile scale* is one which specifies the level of achievement which each per cent of the population failed to attain, while a *decile scale* lists only the tenth percentile, the twentieth, the thirtieth, etc.

The process of ascertaining the test performances to which points on a scale correspond is called *calibration* of the test.

A *table of norms* for a test shows the distribution of scores which has been found to obtain for a representative sample of the adult population, or for specified ages, educational levels, or occupational groups.

The *correlation* between two variables is their tendency to vary concomitantly. When such a relationship is found to exist between two sets of measures—such as the scores in a test of executive aptitude and subsequent rate of advancement in executive positions—knowledge of a person's score in the first measure makes possible an estimate of his probable score in the correlated measure. This estimate is subject to more or less error, depending on the closeness of the correlation between the two variables. Knowing the diameter of a circle, we can estimate without error what its circumference is; for

[3] The Standard Deviation from the Mean is a measure of dispersion or index of variability which expresses more reliably than other indices the extent to which the scores obtained in testing a certain population tend to scatter over a wide range or to cluster closely about the average. The Standard Deviation is sometimes called the root-mean-square deviation. Its symbol, σ, is the Greek letter sigma. The sigma of a distribution of scores is computed by first ascertaining the deviation of each score from the mean score, squaring it, averaging these squares, and extracting the square root of this average. So the formula for the Standard Deviation is

$$\sigma = \sqrt{\frac{\Sigma x^2}{N}}$$

where x is the deviation of a score from the mean; and N is the number of measures. Since the Standard Deviation is ordinarily the most reliable measure of dispersion, it has often been adopted as the unit of measurement in constructing scales.

the correlation between the diameters of circles and their circumferences is perfect. But no two human abilities that can be measured are correlated to any such degree as that. If we were to measure the strength of grip of a hundred men—or the time it takes them to run fifty yards, or their ability in a test of clerical aptitude—we could not even estimate without error, from their records of performance, precisely how well each one would be able to do in the same task when tested a second time. How much greater, then, is the margin of uncertainty when, from a person's score in a test of clerical aptitude, we venture to estimate what he would be able to do in a clerical occupation! Indeed, in such a case we would ask, not how nearly perfect our prediction is apt to be, but rather, how much better it is than a random guess.

To express in numerical terms the degree of correlation between two variables, the Pearson product-moment coefficient of correlation, r, is ordinarily used when the relationship is rectilinear; and the correlation ratio, η, when it is curvilinear. Except at the limiting value which represents perfect correspondence between the two variables, these coefficients or ratios are always less than one, diminishing to zero when there is entire absence of correlation. Coefficients of correlation between tests of aptitude and measures of subsequent educational or vocational achievement are apt to be nearer zero than one, and the zone of possible error in prediction is correspondingly wide. It is a wholesome, although at first disconcerting, exercise to note the wide margin of error for which allowance must be made in estimating criterion scores from aptitude test scores when the coefficient of correlation is, say, only .45. (See Table XVIII.) But some reassurance is found in the fact that even here the prediction is 10 per cent better than a guess; and that is about as well as one would do if he undertook to predict the scholarship marks of students in college from the grades they had earned in high school.

Add to this consideration the fact that in actual practice no counselor would venture a prediction based on a single symptom of aptitude, a lone test score. If he were merely to use the pooled results of two tests, his estimate would be a little more dependable than if he were to rely on but one. Actually he would take into account all the valid measurements available, and every other relevant item of information about the person whose occupational preparation he is helping to plan. Then his estimate of the probabilities, still far from infallible, should nevertheless be appreciably better than his client's unaided opinion. *In a field as vitally important as this, it is an achieve-*

ment to increase the likelihood of satisfactory vocational adjustment by even a few per cent over what it would otherwise be.

The *validity* of a test is the closeness of agreement between the scores and some other objective measure of that which the test is used to measure. This other measure is called the *criterion.* The coefficient of validity of a test is the coefficient of correlation between test scores and criterion scores. For example, tests of scholastic aptitude such as that of the College Entrance Examination Board or the Ohio Examination when given to high-school seniors may be construed as measures of ability to do college work. Grades subsequently earned in college courses furnish another objective, although not entirely reliable, measure of this same ability. When college grades earned in freshman year are used as the criterion, a scholastic aptitude test which correlates .60 with these grades is said to have a coefficient of validity of .60. The coefficient would, of course, be different if some other measure, such as the average of the grades attained throughout the four years of college, were used as the criterion. Or, if this same test were used as a measure of clerical aptitude, that is, of capacity to learn to do clerical work, and annual earnings three years after entering clerical employment were chosen as a criterion—a second objective measure of this ability—the coefficient of validity of the test as a measure of clerical aptitude would certainly be much lower than .60. This is only partly because the test is an imperfect measure of clerical aptitude, but partly because the criterion selected is not a very good measure of the ability in question. The fact that tests of vocational aptitude so frequently have low coefficients of validity is not alone due to the difficulty of devising reliable tests of the aptitudes it is desired to measure. Adequate and reliable criteria of success against which to validate the tests are no less difficult to define and to measure.

The *reliability* of a measure is its self-consistency. In this technical meaning of the word, a highly reliable test is one which yields approximately the same scores when given a second time, or when alternative forms of the test are administered to the same persons. One of the best statistical indices for use in comparing the reliability of two tests is known as the standard error of estimate of a true score. Another good index is a measure of the amount of variable error called the standard error of measurement. The smaller the standard error of measurement (in comparison with the standard deviation of the distribution of the ability in question throughout the general population) the more reliable is the test. These measures of reliability are more fully described on pages 255ff.

The coefficient of correlation between scores obtained on testing and re-testing a group, the familiar *coefficient* of reliability, and the square root of this coefficient which is called the *index* of reliability, are so dependent on the variability of the sample population tested that, valuable as they are in other connections, they are misleading when used to compare the relative reliabilities of two or more tests, unless the facts regarding the variabilities of the groups tested are at the same time taken into consideration. Here, for instance, are two tests of mechanical aptitude, with published coefficients of reliability of .50 and .87. If this were all that were known about them one might be prone to guess that the second of these tests is really the more reliable of the two. But it happens that the group tested and re-tested in order to ascertain the reliability of the first test was a highly selected, homogeneous group of machinist apprentices; while the larger coefficient for the other test was obtained by testing and re-testing a heterogeneous high-school population. The dispersion—the spread of abilities represented in this latter group—was twice as great as in the apprentice group. Taking this fact into consideration, the statistical probabilities are that if the first test were given to a population as heterogeneous in mechanical aptitude as was the high-school population mentioned, the resulting coefficient of reliability would also be .87, instead of .50. In other words, the two tests are, after all, equally reliable.[4] To compare the coefficients of reliability of two tests when comparable measures of dispersion of the groups tested are not available, is quite unwarranted. And yet, into this pitfall many a person has inadvertently stumbled without even realizing his predicament, when looking for the most reliable of several similar tests. Before accepting published coefficients of reliability at face value, it is advisable to ask whether the population samples used in computing them are equally representative of the range of abilities found in the general population.

3

When selecting tests for use in ascertaining aptitudes, it is necessary to know not only how much unreliability to expect and to allow for. It is even more essential to know whether the scores are in any

[4] The relation between standard deviations and reliability coefficients obtained from a small and a large range, when a measure is equally reliable throughout its range, is as follows:

$$\frac{\sigma_s}{\sigma_l} = \sqrt{\frac{1 - r_l}{1 - r_s}}$$

useful sense predictive of subsequent success in the occupation. Aptitude-testing is possible only because of the relationships which hold between (a) abilities and other traits as measured before entrance on training for the occupation or activity, and (b) abilities measurable after training and experience. When such relationships are known to exist, *a* is regarded as a symptom of capacity to acquire *b*. Our thinking starts with *b*, the achievements for which we have selected a criterion or standard of occupational success, the likelihood of attaining which we would like to be able to predict; and works back toward *a*, the aptitudes to be appraised in advance of training. Indeed, our choice of a standard of success may be determinative of the kind of tests we shall select. It is known, for example, that aptitude for engineering includes ability to learn higher mathematics, to master courses in physical science, and to think clearly about spatial relations of objects. A battery of examinations to measure a young man's aptitude for engineering is pretty certain to include tests designed to measure these abilities. Measuring aptitude for executive work is quite another matter. No single ability or trait has been found clearly to differentiate executives from other people in responsible business posts; but the executives usually show at least some superiority in a wider variety of abilities—linguistic, mathematical, clerical, scientific, social—and often exhibit a wider range of interests, than non-executives; and so a battery to measure aptitude for executive work naturally includes a number of quite different tests, in no one of which is outstanding excellence expected, but only better than average performance in all or nearly all; while an interest inventory and measures of such personality traits as dominance, independence, and extraversion furnish additional symptoms of possible executive talent.[5]

[5] A recent Vocational Aptitude Examination for Sales, Technical and Executive Ability Groups, has been prepared by Glen U. Cleeton and Charles W. Mason after several years of research, and may be recommended for experimental use. It is obtainable from the Psychological Corporation at the price of $4 for 25 booklets, instruction manual, scoring keys and tentative norms for workers in executive, sales, and research activities. The examination is in twelve parts, as follows:

General Information Test	10 minutes
Arithmetical Reasoning Test	15 minutes
Judgment in Estimating Test	10 minutes
Symbolic Relationships Test	15 minutes
Reading Comprehension Test	6 minutes
Vocabulary Test	5 minutes
Interest Inventory	No time limit
Dominance-Submission	No time limit
Independence-Dependence	No time limit
Extraversion-Introversion	No time limit
Sociability	No time limit
Judgment of Human Nature	No time limit

The condition or pattern of characteristics symptomatic of ability in a kind of work may be quite general, or highly specific, or a combination of general and specific traits.

The way in which success in a vocation is defined makes a good deal of difference in the traits we shall select to test. Shall we call a person successful if, after training, he has at least the minimum proficiency needed in order to hold his position? Or shall we count him a failure if he shortly finds the work so distasteful that he abandons it, even though he may have attained high proficiency in it? In the latter instance, length of service in the occupation as well as level of proficiency reached must be included in our criterion, our standard of success; and traits deemed symptomatic of a liking for that kind of work will be in the list of those to be tested, along with traits or abilities indicative of capacity to learn to do the work.

Consider the occupation of stenographer. Some commercial schools have defined success as the ability to take dictation at a rate of at least 120 words a minute. Employers rarely demand such speed, but do value a higher level of proficiency in English usage than many schools insist upon. Accepting the criterion of success established by employers rather than by such schools, it is at once evident that in testing aptitude for stenography, among the traits to be measured is the ability to learn with precision the essentials of correct usage in grammar, punctuation, syllabication, spelling, and above all, word meanings. Our selection of criteria precedes and in part determines our choice of aptitude tests.

Before choosing a test or a battery of tests, one makes sure that he knows the characteristics symptomatic of a person's capacity to learn the trade, the profession, or the school subject, aptitude for which is to be tested. A general acquaintance with the nature of the work to be done and the difficulties to be mastered in learning to do it well, is not always sufficient. Even a systematic job analysis[6] may still leave some doubt as to the precise abilities or other traits most indicative of fitness to undertake training for the work. Evidence is then sought as to the relationships between these traits and the criteria of subsequent success in acquiring a satisfactory level of proficiency. The traits which are found best to predict these criteria are the traits we are looking for.

A criterion of success may be expressed in terms of the length of

[6] See Chapter II, "Job Analysis," in *Procedures in Employment Psychology*, by W. V. Bingham and Max Freyd. New York: McGraw-Hill Book Company, 1926. Also Chapter IX in *Industrial Psychology*, by M. S. Viteles. New York: W. W. Norton & Company, Inc., 1932.

time required to gain a specified level of proficiency in the occupation; or in terms of the level of proficiency ultimately reached; or in other objectively definable standards. Scholastic success, for instance, may be defined as completion of the specified course of study within the usual period of training; or it may be expressed in terms of school marks attained, honors and distinctions won, etc. Success in industrial employment is sometimes directly measurable in terms of quantity and quality of output. When piece rates have been scientifically set, average weekly earnings have been used as the criterion of relative success. Other commonly used indices of success in an occupation include rate of advancement and degree of responsibility exercised. In addition to such criteria, success in trades like those of crane operator, aviator, motorman, taxi-driver or still operator in an oil refinery must be measured in terms of avoidance of accidents. Leather cutters in the shoe industry differ greatly in their ability to avoid spoilage and waste; indeed, one large element of expense, while a cutter is being taught his trade is the cost of the leather he uses which may mount to as high a figure as $500. In this instance the cost of the materials used during training furnishes one criterion of failure or success.[7]

4

Having chosen our criteria of success and tentatively selected the aptitudes which seem most likely to be predictive of those criteria, it is necessary to find out how closely the measures of aptitude (the test scores) are actually related to the measures of ultimate success (the criteria). The process of ascertaining the relationship between test performance and subsequent achievement of successful adjustment within the occupation is called *validation* of the test.

A test is said to have no validity whatever if it predicts the criterion no better than chance: its coefficient of validity is zero. If the prediction were perfect, the coefficient of validity would be 1.00; but this never happens, because there are always factors other than those measured by a test of aptitude which in considerable part determine the level of success. When predicting college grades from scores on a scholastic aptitude test, the coefficient of validity may in rare instances be as high as .80, but is oftener not much above .50. Most vocational aptitude tests have lower validities. This is to be

[7] Bingham and Freyd describe thirteen kinds of criteria of vocational success, in *op. cit.*, Chapter III.

expected. A person's occupational achievement is due to a great variety of causes in addition to his aptitudes. Moreover, any quantitative measure of the degree of that achievement is at best a rough one and subject to error. In other words the criteria are not always adequate or highly reliable.

In the nature of the case, a coefficient of validity cannot be expected to be greater than the coefficient of reliability of the criterion; nor of the test itself, for that matter. The main explanation, however, of the fact that most of the apparently good tests of aptitude have relatively low coefficients of validity is not that the test is unreliable, nor the criterion used as a measure of success against which the test is validated. The trouble is more often to be found in the narrowness, inadequacy or impurity of this criterion. We need to validate a medical aptitude test, for instance, before using it as a means of estimating the likelihood that a student will be able to master his medical courses. Scholarship grades obtained in medical school furnish a possible criterion of success. But here are three students of equal ability. One has to earn his expenses, while the others do not. Another crams industriously before each examination; while the third prefers instead to put in extra time in the clinics. Are the marks these students receive—no matter how reliable the examinations—perfect measures of their relative ability to do the work of the medical curriculum? Obviously not. Are the annual earnings of two lawyers—even though these earnings are reliably ascertained—adequate measures of their relative legal ability when one of them chooses to accept only the most profitable clients, while the other prefers to devote half of his time to the problems of neighbors in trouble who can afford to pay only modest fees?

Good objective criteria of occupational success are extremely difficult to define and to measure. This phase of the problem of test validation has not yet received the searching scrutiny that its importance demands. Until vocational psychologists have developed adequate ways of measuring levels of achievement and satisfactory adjustment in the various vocations, coefficients of validity of the best tests of aptitude will necessarily continue to be smaller than their true merit warrants.

Validity of prediction can be increased (1) by improving the adequacy and reliability of the measures of success used as criteria; (2) by choosing those traits for testing which are most indicative of aptitude for achieving the success specified; (3) by choosing the tests which most accurately measure those traits; and (4) by ascertaining the proper weight to be assigned to the scores in each test in order most closely to predict the criterion.[8]

5

In selecting tests to be included in a battery, it is advisable to include those which correlate most closely with the criterion, and least closely with each other. By avoiding duplication in this way, each test used contributes maximally to the forecast.

Tests which may look promising but which are far from reliable because they are too short, or not well graded in difficulty, or for other reasons are uncertain instruments of measurement, will be passed over. If a test has a Standard Error of Measurement of more than .3 sigma, the scores are too unreliable for use in individual counseling, unless they are to be supplemented by the scores on a second form of the same test or on other tests which measure much the same ability.

Judicious selection among available tests, then, takes into consideration the nature, adequacy, and reliability of the criteria the authors have used, quite as much as the numerical size of the reported coefficients of validity and reliability of the tests themselves.

Other considerations pertinent to the choice of tests are: the length of time they require, in relation to the time available for testing; simplicity and convenience of administration; ease and objectivity of scoring; and cost. To be sure, in so important a matter, tests admittedly less reliable or otherwise not so well suited to the purpose would scarcely be chosen merely because they are cheaper or easier to score; but among equally good tests, some are less costly of both time and money than others. The Ohio State University Psychological Test, for instance, is not only one of the most reliable and valid of the longer mental tests for use with large groups of high-school or college students, but is also relatively inexpensive and conveniently scored.

Scores near either the upper or the lower limit of a test's range are generally less reliable than those nearer the middle of the distribution; and so it is advisable to select a test which will probably

[8] The procedures followed in computing the optimal weighting of each test in a battery are described in detail in the standard statistical texts. See the chapters dealing with multiple regression equations in H. E. Garrett, *Statistics in Psychology and Education.* New York: Longmans, Green and Co., 1926. (Now being revised.) Also Bingham and Freyd, *Procedures in Employment Psychology*, Chapter XVII, and C. L. Hull, *Aptitude Testing*, Chapters VIII, XIII, and XIV.

be neither extremely easy nor too difficult for the person to be examined.

A test should be suited to a person's age, as well as to his educational and mental level. With mature people, for example, it is inappropriate to use tests which, from the wording or the pictures, are obviously designed to interest school children. Tests containing items which might appear ridiculous or absurd, should also be avoided. Not all compilers of tests have remembered that sensitive people, if asked to do problems that look childish, are inclined to imagine that the examiner is poking fun at them. Common sense in the wording of directions and test items avoids even the appearance of being facetious. It is well, then, to be certain that the test is suited to the age, ability, education, and status of the persons to be examined.

Be sure that adequate norms, applicable to such persons, are available.

Avoid resort to individual tests requiring expertness on the part of the examiner unless he is known to be thoroughly experienced in their administration.

Consider most carefully the evidence that the test is valid *for the purpose in hand*. A test can be "good" only in relation to the specific purpose to which it is put. It may be used

(1) to help in estimating the probabilities that a person can achieve the educational status appropriate for entry on an occupation he is considering, and that his mental powers will be equal to the demands made upon him while training for the occupation, and after;

(2) to find out the relative strength of his special aptitudes for undertaking different kinds of activity; and in particular, to reveal any exceptional talents;

(3) to indicate whether his interests are such that he will probably enjoy the work and its associations;

(4) to help in ascertaining any limitations or specific disabilities which should be corrected before undertaking the occupation or beginning a special course of training for it.

These are obvious uses. In addition, tests may be given in order to stimulate a person to think seriously about his plans so that he will make decisions only after due consideration of the facts as to his aptitudes; and also to help him to get an objective attitude toward himself and his abilities.

Parents, too, are aided to subordinate personal predilections and to think objectively about the best interests of their sons and daughters when a discussion of plans is prefaced by a review of test performances. School principals have used test data to good effect when conferring with parents who insist that a student should undertake a certain curriculum in which the probabilities of success are much less than in some more suitable course of study. "Agnes could do very well in her English and stenography, I am sure," the mother says, "if only she would apply herself. Can't you induce her to work?" But when the principal points out that her English achievement-test records for several semesters have been uniformly poor and her verbalistic intelligence scores low, while students with such records have practically always failed or dropped out before finishing the secretarial course, mother, as well as daughter, is more ready to listen to the principal's suggestions.

From the counselor's point of view, as well as the principal's, tests may be used not only to help in resolving doubts in his own mind as to the aptitudes of the person examined; but also to supply a factual point of departure when discussing with him in a subsequent interview matters vital to judicious planning.

The choice of tests will vary with the needs of the situation. Are they to be employed in a preliminary exploratory way in order to bring to light possible aptitudes which the interview and the review of previous accomplishments may not have suggested, or to resolve a specific doubt with respect to the person's general level of ability, or to ascertain the strength of some one talent or trait? In the first instance, a good interest schedule may serve the purpose for the time being at least; after which use of a wide variety of tests would be appropriate. In the second instance, suitable tests of intelligence or scholastic aptitude will help; while in the third instance, selection of appropriate tests is limited to those which would have a bearing on the particular trait in doubt.

The urgency of a person's problem has also to be considered. How near is he to the fork in the road? Must he decide this week whether to elect agriculture instead of engineering, or will there be ample time for him to go into the matter thoroughly, even to the point of sampling both kinds of work before arriving at a choice? The point cannot be over-stressed that a cumulative record of tests taken over a period of years throws light on a person's developmental history, and tells more about him than even a comprehensive battery of tests all taken at one time can show. In this respect it is like the physician's record of annual medical examinations. But when there is no such cumulative record, the counselor, like the medical specialist called in an emergency, selects the tests for immediate use which bear most closely on the problem which presses for solution at the moment.

For the vast majority of occupations, no special tests of specific aptitude have been developed. Here the problem takes the form of choosing tests which will help in ascertaining whether the person has (1) the general level of intelligence deemed essential for progress in the occupation; (2) such special capacities as a careful scrutiny of the occupation suggests as indispensable; and (3) a real interest in doing the kind of work characteristic of the occupation.

In general, the best tests to use in connection with a program of educational and vocational guidance are those which have already proved their value in the counseling situation, rather than in research projects only, or in school surveys. A test may be of little help to a counselor face to face with a single individual, even though it is exactly what is needed when measuring the differences between *groups* of people or in analyzing general characteristics of human behavior. On the other hand, an aptitude test may be of some worth in helping to explore a student's talents, even though it falls short of meeting the specifications for an ideal instrument of research.

Of all the considerations we have enumerated relevant to the comparison and selection of the best tests for use in a given situation, the question as to which are the most valid is usually the hardest to answer. This is even more emphatically the case when selecting tests to measure interests, personality traits or specific aptitudes than when choosing among tests of intelligence. The guiding principle is simple enough. Other things being equal, choose the test known to correlate most closely with a good criterion of that which we wish to measure. The trouble arises from the fact, emphasized throughout this chapter, that really good objective criteria are so rare. When the best objective criterion that has been available is obviously a less adequate and precise measure of the ability in question than is the test itself, the resulting coefficient of validity is apt to mislead. The psychologist either has to let his client wait for months or years while he resorts to new experiments and elaborate statistical analyses in order to compare the merits of similar tests, or else he has to lean heavily, as a physician does, on his informed common sense. He weighs the adequacy and reliability of the criteria that have been used, as well as the numerical size of the coefficients of validity.

This chapter has dealt both with technical matters regarding the nature of reliable and valid tests of aptitude, and with practical considerations to be weighed when choosing between alternative tests offered as suitable for various uses. We shall now inquire how tests must be administered, if the scores they yield are to be of greatest value in helping persons to find their way toward satisfactory educational and vocational adjustment.

Chapter XVII

ADMINISTRATION OF TESTS

1. Arrangements and conduct of testing when individuals are examined singly. Precautions taken by seasoned examiners. 2. Detailed observations and interpretations of behavior supplement the numerical scores. What to look for. 3. Examiner's check list. 4. Necessity for practice in sharply separating interpretations from the record of what is seen, and in securing data for qualitative as well as quantitative evaluation of performance.

1

An aptitude-testing program, no matter how ingeniously conceived, yields disappointing results unless the tests that have been chosen are well administered.

The accuracy of any measure is quite as much a function of the way the instrument is applied as it is of the instrument itself. Like a surveyor's chain, a machinist's micrometer, or a chemist's balance, a psychologist's test gives variable readings in unpracticed hands. To insure that test scores are as accurate as the tests themselves allow, an examiner must be fully aware of possible sources of error and see that they are ruled out of his procedure. There are perhaps a few tests so simple and straightforward that little need be said about the proper way of giving them; but most tests—even those which have been painstakingly built to be fool-proof—yield the most reliable results and the most illuminating insights into aptitudes when administered by seasoned examiners who keep in mind the principles of good test administration.

Suggestions are here offered regarding precautions to be taken when testing in order that the resulting scores may be as accurate as possible. Attention is also drawn to kinds of valuable information—over and above the numerical scores—which tests, properly administered, will help to secure. A wise examiner or psychometrist who knows what to look for as well as how to follow specified procedures, can furnish counselors with useful quantitative data, and much besides. That this holds true of group testing, we shall see in the following chapter. Our present concern is to ascertain the best ways of administering tests to individuals singly; for in this situation, where examiner and examined are face to face, alone, the perils as well as the possibilities of aptitude-testing stand out in clearest relief. After the principles of good test administration have been grasped as they apply in this field, the special problems that arise when testing people in groups will not be hard to master.

Individual testing certainly has its difficulties as well as its unique merits. The following suggestions regarding arrangements and the conduct of the testing[1] will indicate to less experienced examiners how some of these difficulties may be met.

When tests are to be given to one person he should be alone with the examiner. Spectators, companions, and relatives—particularly parents—are out of place. The examining-room should be arranged to insure quiet and freedom from interruption, as well as privacy. It should be well lighted. To lessen possible distractions it should preferably be furnished more like a comfortable office than a laboratory. Formidable apparatus, charts, and other strange objects should be in closets or in an adjoining room. A compartment in the examiner's desk or a small screen on his table is convenient for keeping equipment and blanks out of view until needed. The screen helps also in recording scores and observations without distracting the examinee. There should be suitable writing or working space in addition to the examiner's desk. When the test calls for writing, the pencil, provided by the examiner, should be sharpened at both ends to prevent loss of time during the test by erasing, pausing to sharpen a broken point, or asking for another pencil.

If a stop-watch is required, it is advisable to have one of the cumulative stop-watches with a sliding lever near the stem which operates noiselessly and allows the examiner to measure both partial and total times, or to take time out for unforeseen interruptions. A watch which must be sprung back to zero after each timing is not adapted for recording cumulative times.

When the examinee arrives, it is usual for the tester to introduce himself, and to use the person's name when speaking to him. To relieve possible tension and secure a cooperative attitude, it is not

[1] Adapted in part from Chapter XII on "Test Administration" in Bingham and Freyd's *Procedures in Employment Psychology.*

necessary that an informal courteous bearing should be tinged with familiarity. Without too many preliminaries, the examiner gives a frank and brief account of the purpose of the tests, unless this has already been taken care of in a general announcement. This opening statement need not be standardized. Rather, it should be flexible and adaptable to any attitude on the part of the one examined. Adults in particular appreciate a clear, straightforward explanation.

The introductory talk should not be so long as to put the examinee on edge or make him nervous. As soon as he takes his eyes off the examiner's and looks around for the tests, it is time to begin the examination.

A rather easy test may be given first; or a short series of simple questions asked in a casual manner may be introduced as a shock-absorber. (Some tests make provision for a standard fore-exercise which serves the double purpose of shock-absorber and of means to make certain that the subject understands what he is to do.)

"The function of the examiner," as Wells reminds us, "is to draw out the subject, not to impress him."[2] To this end his manner is one of confidence and encouragement, making it clear that he really wants and expects the examinee to make the best possible showing he can. Some people come to the examination with a lurking suspicion, not unnatural, that the tester is trying to catch them in error, to disclose their weaknesses. This lurking embarrassment interferes with their performance. The examiner should scrutinize his own interest in the testing and make certain that, in his practice at least, there exists no ground for such suspicion; and then should word his directions in a way that implies the examinee's ability to do the task set. He tells him, "Now, do so and so," instead of saying, "I want to see whether you can do this," or asking him if he can. Indeed, his whole attitude as well as his words should convey the well-founded impression that he is sincerely interested, not at all in showing up the examinee, but in seeing him succeed.

The examiner should know the directions for the various tests so well that he can give them without hesitation, and without any unintentional deviations from standard practice. At the same time he must not be wooden or machine-like in his utterance, but, like the actor, speak his familiar lines with a convincing naturalness.

The examinee should not be prompted except when this is part of the specified procedure. On completing a task he may be commended for his performance; but this cannot be done indiscriminately with-

[2] F. L. Wells, *Mental Tests in Clinical Practice*. World Book Company, 1927.

out arousing suspicion. If the examinee is doing poorly, nothing need be said about the fact. If he expresses disappointment at not being able to complete a test during the time allowed, he may be told that the test is so made that even the most rapid workers are not expected to finish it (which is the case), or that relative standing is what counts.

While the examinee is at work, the tester should be observing him inconspicuously; not staring at him, confronting him with a stop-watch, or doing anything else which might distract, embarrass, or irritate him. The watch should be out of sight; also the protocol on which scores and observations are jotted down.

No matter what happens, the examiner should preserve his composure, avoiding any expression of surprise, amusement, or annoyance.

The kinds of observations to be noted will be dwelt upon at length later in this chapter. The skill with which significant acts, attitudes, and expressions are observed, and the insight with which they are interpreted, are evidences of the examiner's competence no less than the ease with which he secures the full collaboration and confidence of the person he is examining, or, for that matter, the precision with which he follows the procedures laid down for giving each test.

The protocol on which these observations are noted, along with the test scores, should be in a form convenient for filing in the examinee's folder. It should contain notations of any interruptions or disturbances, as well as any evidences of nervousness or over-anxiety on the part of the examinee which might have affected his performance. Later on, some of the examiner's observations may be brought forward in the counseling interview if they have an obvious bearing on the questions at issue regarding the individual's aptitudes in relation to his educational and vocational plans.

When examiner and counselor are the same person, the significance of the test results can be discussed with the client at once. This has undoubted advantages. When the examiner is a psychometrist who does the testing at the counselor's request, it is usual to leave discussion of the meaning of the test results to the counselor, although there is something to be said in favor of encouraging the psychometrist also to talk with the client about his performance. This holds particularly in those instances in which psychometrist and counselor may be in some disagreement regarding the vocational significance of the scores; for in that event the person most concerned, the subject himself, is stimulated to think through his own problem rather than to lean too heavily on advice of counsel.

2

A psychological test is too often thought of simply as a measuring device. It is this, and more. It is a standard situation in which to observe behavior. The psychometrist wants to find out all that he can about the girl or boy, the woman or man, whose adjustment is at stake. What this person does in a standardized test situation is revealing of his temperament and personality as well as of his ability to do the assigned task. His attentive or inattentive attitude while the directions are being given, his interest in the enterprise, his manner of responding to the examiner's directions, his facial expression as well as what he says, writes, or does with his hands, his way of doing the task, his composure or irritation when difficulties are encountered, his persistence or his readiness to give up, his attitude toward his own performance as well as toward the examiner, all furnish clues as to the kind of person he is. The measured product of his performance—in other words, his test score—may be all that is subsequently entered on his cumulative record. It may be all that his counselor asks the examiner to report about. But if so, the nature, the purpose, and the possibilities of psychological testing have been only partially realized. The score is important; so, too, are the detailed observations and interpretations made by the examiner under the conditions imposed by the test situation.

Among the thousands of unemployed adults who came to the Adjustment Service in New York for counsel in 1933 and 1934, a number were found to be in need of psychiatric assistance; but these distraught persons who really required professional psychiatric service were less often identified as such by the counselors who talked with them intimately about their problems than by the examiners who administered the individual performance tests and so had a chance to observe them under exceptionally revealing circumstances. Evidences of valuable character traits were also noted from time to time during the performance tests, as well as emotional characteristics and trends of interest. The great superiority of individual testing over group testing lies chiefly in the opportunity it provides to make just such observations of behavior under standard conditions. Numerical scores tell but half the story.

What should be looked for when administering a test to an individual? His methods of attack, his output of energy, his industry and tenacity, his relative interest in the several tests, his personal reaction to the difficulties imposed, his awkwardness or skill, his emotional control, all may be observed to advantage. Any marked individual differences in these regards are suggestive of vocationally significant traits.

3

Details of behavior to be observed during the test period and certain interpretations which the examiner may be able to place on this behavior are seen in the accompanying Examiner's Check List.[3]

EXAMINER'S CHECK LIST

FOR USE IN NOTING AND INTERPRETING BEHAVIOR DURING THE TEST PERIOD

BEHAVIOR	INTERPRETATION
I. DURING THE PRELIMINARY INSTRUCTIONS	
a. Looks steadily at the examiner, listening attentively	1. Is really attentive 2. Can look at a person without listening
b. Gazes around the room	1. Can give effective divided attention 2. Is not able to concentrate 3. Is not interested
a'. Asks questions	1. Has heard imperfectly, due to i. poor hearing ii. lack of concentration 2. Has not understood 3. Has been particularly interested 4. Wishes to gain time and not be compelled to do the task immediately (evident from the type of question)
b'. Asks no questions	1. Is stupid 2. Has understood everything well 3. Is in a hurry to do the task
c. Approaches the test	
a. quickly	1. Is sprightly 2. Has an active nature 3. Is interested in the test 4. Comprehends quickly 5. Lacks foresight
b. slowly	1. Is apathetic 2. Lacks interest in the task 3. Is both apathetic and uninterested
c. hesitatingly	1. Does not grasp the instructions 2. Is cautious 3. Is indecisive 4. Is shy 5. Is unwilling to take the test

[3] Adapted from "Die Tastmethode," by Franziska Baumgarten, in *Handbuch der biologischen Arbeitsmethoden*, edited by E. Abderhalden, pp. 1089-1095. Vienna: 1934. (A translation by F. J. Keller appeared in *Occupations*, 1935, 14: 115-122.)

EXAMINER'S CHECK LIST (*Continued*)

BEHAVIOR	INTERPRETATION
d. Shows toward the task an attitude which is	
a. serious	1. Is of a serious nature 2. Is impressed at the moment with the importance of the task 3. Is anxious
b. playful	1. Happens to be in a good humor 2. The task seems like play 3. Is of a carefree nature
c. zealous	1. Is greatly interested 2. Wants to have the task over with quickly
e. Anticipatory expressions with reference to his own capacity for accomplishment	
a. Talks as if the task were easy	1. The task is easy for him 2. He does not see the difficulties 3. He tends to boastfulness and conceit
b. Expresses enthusiasm	1. Is interested 2. Is uncritically enthusiastic
c. Says he cannot do it	1. Is conscious of his limitations 2. Has an inferiority complex 3. Does not properly understand the task 4. As a defense mechanism (in view of his lack of interest)
f. Judgment upon or criticism of the task	
a. Aloud	1. Wants to cooperate 2. Tends to find fault 3. Wants to assert himself
b. Through gestures	1. Indicating interest 2. Indicating dislike 3. Indicating disdain
II. DURING EXECUTION OF THE TASK	
1. *At the start*	
a. Deliberates	1. Finds the task difficult 2. Is of a cautious disposition 3. Has a tendency to reflect
b. Does not deliberate	1. Comprehends at once 2. Cannot reflect 3. Resents the task
c. Makes repeated starts	
a. always in the same way	1. Due to mental inertia (or persistence) 2. Cannot reflect 3. Resents the task
b. always in a new way	1. Has a wealth of ideas as to possibilities 2. Feels that he ought to be able to do it somehow 3. Exercises sheer will power ("I must!")

EXAMINER'S CHECK LIST (*Continued*)

BEHAVIOR	INTERPRETATION
2. *While at work*	
A. Direction of attention	
a. Is attentive to the task	1. From a desire to achieve 2. In order to be done with it
b. Attention wanders	1. Lacks interest 2. Lacks power of concentration
A′. Degree of concentration	
a. Attention highly concentrated (during the whole time does not avert his gaze from the task)	1. Is interested in the task 2. Is overawed by the presence of the examiner 3. Has perseverance and determination
b. Distracted	1. By interest in the new surroundings 2. Lacks interest in the task 3. Lacks power of attention 4. Is apathetic
B. Expression of Feelings and Emotions (Pleasure, Displeasure, Surprise)	
a. Gives expression to feelings	
a. during the entire test, in a way to indicate that	1. He has confidence in the examiner 2. He is cooperative and cheerful 3. He lacks respect or is ill-bred
b. during single phases, in a way to indicate	1. Satisfaction in his progress toward a solution 2. (See also 1, 2, 3, of preceding item)
b. Expresses no feelings	1. Because he experiences none 2. Because he knows how to control them as a result of i. training ii. habit iii. his own will power
C. Bodily Movements	
a. are well coordinated with the task	1. Is able and clever 2. Has had good physical training 3. Is animated with the purpose of finishing as quickly as possible
b. are not coordinated	1. Has poor control over movements 2. Does not readily see what to do (lacks mental agility)
D. Work Tempo	
a. Quick	1. Has a lively disposition 2. Wants to finish a burdensome task
b. Slow	1. Has a phlegmatic nature 2. Is lazy 3. Is indifferent to the task

EXAMINER'S CHECK LIST (*Continued*)

BEHAVIOR	INTERPRETATION
E. Movements of the Hands	
a. Skillful, appropriate	1. Has had practice 2. Has a natural aptitude
b. Sure, steady	1. Has natural aptitude 2. Has a strong will
c. Quick, nervous	1. Has a natural aptitude 2. Is ambitious 3. Wants to finish as soon as possible
F. Manner of Work	
A′. As to Order	
a. Works systematically	1. As a result of reflection 2. Loves order
b. Works unsystematically, darting from one thing to another	1. Is very active, vivacious 2. Is nervous 3. Is scatterbrained 4. Is continually searching for something more interesting
c. Works regularly	1. Possesses poise and foresight 2. Has a firm purpose
d. Works irregularly	
a. at first slowly, then more and more quickly	1. Because his persistent attack succeeds 2. Because the task gradually becomes clearer and seems easier 3. Interest progressively mounts
b. at first quickly, then more slowly	1. Loss of interest 2. Weak concentration 3. Quick fatigue
c. alternating, now slowly, now quickly, at intervals	1. Unstable way of thinking 2. Fluctuating attention 3. Renewed attempts to reinforce waning powers
B′. As to Kind of Performance	
a. Careful, neat	1. Possesses aptitude for correctness and exactness 2. Has a natural interest in the task
b. Careless, sloppy	1. Is naturally careless 2. Lacks interest 3. Has a bad temper
G. Handling of his Tools During the working period, does he put the necessary tools in the same place?	
a. Yes	1. Has a good memory 2. Loves order 3. Has a flair for organization
b. No	1. Is forgetful 2. Is careless 3. Is not orderly 4. Lacks mind for organization

EXAMINER'S CHECK LIST (*Continued*)

BEHAVIOR	INTERPRETATION
3. *As difficulties emerge*	
A. Asks no help	
a. Maintains indifferent attitude	1. Lacks interest 2. Is apathetic 3. Is negligent
b. Immediately throws up the sponge	1. Has a passive nature 2. Is convinced that effort is useless because he knows his own meager abilities 3. Has an unjustified feeling of inferiority or of discouragement
c. Overcomes incidental difficulties	
a. immediately	1. Has the knowledge and ability
b. gradually	1. Thinks very slowly (racks his brain) 2. Feels pressure ("I *must* do this thing!") 3. Takes satisfaction in overcoming difficulties
d. Overcomes inherent difficulties	
a. through correct methods	1. By accident 2. By ability 3. By efforts at reasoning
b. through a trick	1. By a clever vagary 2. By cheating
B. Asks help	
a. several times	1. Has a correct appreciation of his own limited powers 2. Has a feeling of inferiority 3. Has developed bad habits (burdening people with questions)
b. once	1. Difficulty due to an oversight possibly caused by a distraction 2. Difficulty arises from ignorance
C. Conduct while being helped Receives help	
a. indifferently	1. From apathy 2. From a conviction that help must be given to him (that it is due to him)
b. happily	1. Satisfaction at being able to pick up the task again and in not being left in the lurch 2. An interest in the thing itself 3. The task is lightened for him and he no longer has to take such pains
c. with a thankful glance	1. The same motives listed under "b" 2. Good will

EXAMINER'S CHECK LIST (*Continued*)

BEHAVIOR	INTERPRETATION
d. skeptically and critically	1. He doubts its authoritative nature 2. Is proud 3. Has real ability 4. Has a tendency to reject 5. Is cautious
e. trustfully and credulously	1. Lacks any critical sense 2. Is well-disposed 3. Has been trained to obedience or docility 4. Is suggestible
f. showing offense	1. Self-reliance is injured 2. Feels loss of standing among his mates
4. *Carries out the instructions*	
A. Exactly	1. Possesses the knowledge and traits demanded of him
B. With deviations	
a. of a positive kind	1. By chance 2. Has a clever imagination 3. Has superior knowledge 4. Has special interest
b. of a negative kind	1. Weak attention 2. Weak memory 3. Lack of interest 4. Lack of persistence 5. Lack of knowledge
III. ATTITUDE TOWARD HIS PERFORMANCE	
A. Notices his mistakes	
a. occasionally	1. By accident 2. Is a casual person
b. at the end, when he checks his work for the first time	1. Is careful but not systematic 2. Has been absorbed in the task
c. during the work, always proving his results before he proceeds	1. Is naturally systematic and cautious 2. Has been trained to be critical of his work
B. Does not perceive his mistakes or check his results	1. Has a deep conviction of his own ability 2. Is concentrated on the end result 3. Is not critical 4. Is indifferent 5. Is apathetic
C. Shows mild feeling	1. Indicating that he is pleased 2. Indicating that he is vexed
IV. CONDUCT AT THE END OF THE TEST	
A. Remains silent and watches quietly	1. Is shy 2. Is well trained 3. Lacks decision 4. Does not know what to do

EXAMINER'S CHECK LIST (*Continued*)

BEHAVIOR	INTERPRETATION
B. Announces the result himself	1. Is overjoyed at having solved the problem 2. Is loud-mouthed and obstreperous 3. Supposes he is expected to do it
C. Asks questions, such as: "Isn't that good?"	1. Feels urge to communicate 2. Feels uncertain, wants confirmation 3. Wants to hear himself praised
D. Expresses emotions of	
a. satisfaction	1. Is pleased at having finished 2. Is pleased at having solved the problem (confirming his awareness of his own ability) 3. Is relieved from fear of being taunted by his comrades
b. vexation	1. His aspiration has been thwarted 2. He is disappointed 3. He expects to be punished or reproved
V. AFTER THE TESTING	
A. Leaves his tools	
a. in order	1. Has a love of order 2. Is considerate of others 3. Has been well trained
b. in disorder	1. Is disorderly 2. Is restless 3. Is inconsiderate 4. Has no time
B. Disposes of the materials in ways which indicate that he	1. Is economical 2. Is wasteful
C. Leaves his place of work	
a. quickly	1. Is brisk 2. Is eager to get away to something else
b. slowly	1. Is sluggish 2. Is reluctant to leave

4

Veteran psychometrists may use a list like Baumgarten's as a reminder of points to be noted, and as an aid in training less experienced examiners to conserve these by-products of testing. When recording notes suggested by this or any similar check list, it is imperative to keep distinct and separate the notations of behavior actually seen and the *interpretations* which the examiner places on this behavior. The former are observations; the latter, inferences. Both may have value. Both can be greatly improved through practice and training in the administration of individual tests.

The examiner supplies the counselor (if the two are not the same person) not only with the test scores, but also with his notes on the behavior observed, and with his impressions as to what this behavior signified; in other words, with his interpretations made at the time, while the test was being taken. But the form in which these interpretations are recorded should make it perfectly clear what they are, namely, inferences. The wiser and more experienced the examiner is, the more accurate his inferences will be; and the counselor who receives his reports will value them proportionately.

The examiner's final interpretations are based partly on the scores attained, partly on the other observations. For example, in giving the Healy Puzzle Box, a notation as to how the examinee starts to solve it (Item II., 1. in the Check List) is indispensable to a correct evaluation of his score; for if he begins by deliberately examining the box from every angle and makes no move until he sees exactly what things must be done and in what order, he may take as long as some one who instantly starts trying one hole after another indiscriminately until he hits upon the first correct move in the solution. This does not mean that the test is a poor one. As a matter of fact it is a useful test, as one measure of mechanical aptitude. But the examiner should follow Healy's injunction to "note method of attack and procedure."[4] The counselor should insist on having this information as well as the score.

Qualitative as well as quantitative evaluations of performance may furnish useful clues to aptitudes. The word-association test is an instance in point. It may be scored to yield several quantitative measures, including average association reaction time; commonality of responses; proportion of individual reactions; number of delayed reactions; difference between average association time and the time taken to respond to critical, emotionally charged stimulus words. Any or all of these measures may conceivably aid in appraising a personality or indicating fitness for a selling occupation, an executive post, a teaching position, a nurse's profession, or, in general, a career that presupposes a degree of social understanding and self-control. But no clinical psychologist or experienced counselor is content with only such statistical analyses of the data. He notices also the trend of ideas and the kinds of preoccupations indicated by the words spoken in response to the common stimulus words; for these, too, are revealing. To uncover by means of the word-association test, suggestions regarding intellectual

[4] In *A Manual of Individual Tests and Testing*, p. 103. Augusta F. Bronner, William Healy, Gladys M. Lowe, and Myra E. Shimberg. Boston: Little, Brown & Company, 1929.

and emotional make-up, does not require that the examiner be versed in Freudian speculation or psychoanalytic symbolisms; nor is more than a general knowledge of the psychological processes of association and mental habit presupposed, at least when this knowledge is supplemented with personal insight and that wholesome antidote to far-fetched inferences, common sense.

5

We have emphasized the value of *observing* as well as *measuring* a person's behavior; of recording inferences from these observations at the time of testing, as well as the facts on which these interpretations are based; and of making qualitative as well as quantitative analyses of the test results. It must not, however, be inferred that we are inclined to minimize the quantitative aspect or to condone any neglect of attention to details essential to maximum accuracy in testing. We shall next describe those procedures which help to insure the accuracy of data when tests are administered to groups.

Chapter XVIII

GIVING GROUP TESTS

1. Maintaining prescribed conditions. The external setting. Uniformity of motivation. 2. Common errors, avoidable by careful preparation on the part of the examiner. 3. Minimizing temptations to copy, and effects of coaching. 4. Strict observance of time limits. 5. Procedures in scoring group tests. 6. Summary.

1

GROUP tests are ordinarily the simplest to give; and yet even administering a paper-and-pencil examination to a group has its pitfalls. Mistakes may be made in arranging for the examination, in giving the oral instructions, in timing, and in recording what transpires.

The first rule in test administration is to secure and to maintain the conditions prescribed for each test. These conditions lie partly within the persons examined, and partly without. The attitude with which an examination is approached may affect the score much more than the illumination and ventilation of the room or the arrangement of the desks. An examiner will not, however, fail to look carefully to the external conditions. He will secure suitable quarters, free from disturbances and interruptions. He will have comfortable seating arrangements, distributed in a way to minimize the opportunities for copying. Desks near the front will be given to any who may be short-sighted or hard of hearing. Blanks, timer, and other supplies will be conveniently at hand, the forms counted and assorted for prompt distribution, the ample supply of pencils freshly and uniformly sharpened at both ends, the timepiece newly compared with a reliable chronometer for correctness throughout the range of the time-intervals to be observed. All will be in readiness.

The experienced examiner takes the steps necessary to secure complete cooperation, and uniform motivation. When introducing the test he says what needs to be said in the way it should be said in order that all the members of the group will be on their toes, set to do their best work. Even when the standard directions specify the wording of the introductory statement, it remains for the examiner to deliver this message in a manner to insure that everyone is interested in putting forth his best abilities and in being entirely straightforward about it.

An examiner does well to put himself in the position of the persons he is to test and think how he himself would feel. He might wonder what this was all about, how it was going to benefit him, and whether a high or a low score might later be used by teachers or employers to cause him annoyance. Such apprehensions should be put at rest by a brief but clear explanation of the nature and purpose of the testing. In making this explanation, a misplaced pleasantry or a lack of frankness may cost the examiner the cooperation of his group. To keep a steady hand on the helm is not easy unless all necessary details have been well provided for in advance and the actual conduct of the examination carefully rehearsed.

2

It is a wise precaution first to take the test onself, and then to administer it individually to several persons, including two or three who are likely to be as slow to grasp verbal instructions as the dullest in the groups to be tested. In this way the examiner becomes familiar with the specified procedure, learns what to expect, and is less apt to be caught unawares.

The examiner should know in advance just how much to say and in what words to say it when a person asks a question. Some tests, to be sure, specify that no questions are to be answered. Others permit the examiner to re-read, in the same words, those passages in the instructions which cover the point raised. Still others specifically invite "Any questions?" after the directions have been read or after the fore-exercise has been corrected, and leave a good deal of latitude to the discretion of the examiner in answering. An inexperienced examiner is prone to meet these inquiries hesitantly or obscurely unless he has already prepared the precise answers to be made to all sorts of questions, whether well considered or trivial, shrewd or stupid. He may even cause confusion in the minds of certain members of the group, or, by being too helpful in his answers, unintentionally furnish a clue which makes the test for them an easier task than the prescribed one.

For example, in the MacQuarrie Test for Mechanical Ability, after the group has completed the fore-exercise to Sub-test Four—copying geometric figures—and the correct and incorrect solutions have been identified, the writer has heard a bright boy ask, "Don't you have to use the line of dots at the right in copying *any* of the figures?" The examiner might have said: "That is for you to decide. Be sure that each line you draw has the same direction and the same length as the line you are copying." Instead, his immediate answer, a true one, was "No," and forthwith the nature of the task to be done was simplified, and all who happened to be listening were given an advantage over the members of groups in which this clever question is not raised, or when asked, not answered categorically. Similar instances might be cited from many kinds of examinations.

A temperamentally sympathetic or easy examiner tends to err by being helpful in ways that are not in strict conformity with standard procedure; while an examiner with the disposition of a martinet may be abrupt or sarcastic, and so sacrifice the necessary morale. Indeed, most examiners need both training and practice in administering group tests if they are to be surefooted and objective, never over-anxious, hesitant or misleading. Readings and lectures on the subject, valuable as they are in calling attention to general principles and to details of procedure, cannot entirely take the place of supervised experience and participation in the actual administration of tests.

The optimal rate of speaking when addressing the group or reading aloud the directions to be followed is, for example, not ordinarily stated in the manuals. This rate is partly a function of the examiner's clarity and crispness of enunciation, and of the rate of comprehension of the dullest listeners. While a rate of ninety to one hundred words a minute is usually suitable, I have observed one examiner who made himself entirely clear at nearly twice that speed, while another, who talked very much as though he had hot oatmeal in his mouth, could be understood only when he slowed down to sixty or seventy words a minute. When training military psychologists to give Army Alpha, it was frequently necessary to get them to alter their natural rate of speaking and to increase their loudness and distinctness of enunciation. The general rule is obvious enough—to address the person in the farthest seat, enunciating clearly in an unhurried tempo, no faster than the rate at which everyone can readily hear and follow. This rate is more easily ascertained by a listener than by the examiner himself.

3

One responsibility of the examiner is to minimize the temptation to copy another's work. Even when an opportunity to see a neighbor's paper is not seized, the fact of being able to do so may be distracting. Ample spacing of desks is the commonest device to meet this problem. When two equivalent forms of the test are available, they may be distributed to alternate desks.

One proctor for each twenty persons is ample. A proctor's duties are not to answer questions, but to help in distributing forms, supplying fresh pencils if called for, and collecting the papers promptly at the close of the test. After the work begins, his inconspicuous presence is an aid to concentration.

The complicating effects of previous coaching cannot always be forestalled, particularly when widely known tests are given. Coaching students to take various tests of scholastic aptitude, vocabulary, English usage, mathematical aptitude, and achievement in school subjects has become fashionable in a number of preparatory schools. Only recently the writer was called upon to confer with two students soon to leave an Eastern university. They were vague about their vocational plans. They took a battery of examinations, and both did strikingly well only in the O'Connor Vocabulary Test. On inquiry it came out that at the preparatory school they had attended together, their English instructor, intent on developing his students' mastery of words, had required his classes to study all of the Inglis vocabulary tests, of which O'Connor's are a revision. The pedagogical value of using standard tests as drill exercises is not here in question, but only the test administrator's problem of how to ascertain and make suitable allowances for the effects of such drill.

There are, fortunately, measures of aptitude—for example, some of Seashore's tests of musical talent—in which a person's performance is bettered little if any by familiarity or practice. But scores on most group tests are raised 5 or 10 per cent merely as a result of having taken them before. And so an increasing number of psychologists and educators no longer make use of any group test of mental alertness, educational achievement, or vocational aptitudes in a form which has previously been on the market. This extreme position may be warranted when the abilities to be measured are subject to substantial improvement through practice and the incentive to coaching is strong, as in tests which have a bearing on college entrance.

Even when an examiner has reason to believe that no members of his group are familiar with the examinations he is to give, he will nevertheless keep an eye to windward. Familiarity with a test or one closely resembling it can occasionally be ascertained at the close of the examination by saying, "Turn back to page one. If you have taken this test before, put a check mark in the upper right-hand corner of the page. If you have taken one like it, write the name of the test and the date, as nearly as you can recall it." When discussing at a later time with any member of the group his relative performance in the test and its bearing on his plans, the facts as to previous experience in taking this or similar tests are easily drawn out; for the one examined appreciates that just such facts are relevant to his decisions.

4

When observance of time limits is an essential feature of the test, an error in calling time is devastating. In giving the Minnesota Vocational Test for Clerical Workers, to take a convenient instance, the specified limits on Part One are eight minutes for the number checking and seven minutes for the name checking; and on Part Two, seven minutes for the number checking and six minutes for the name checking. Adherence to such limits is a simple matter; and yet one examiner has been known to misread his timer; another, to confuse the specified times; a third, to allow an extra fifteen seconds, "just to be quite fair"; a fourth, to go wool-gathering and wake up forty seconds too late; while a fifth neglected to write down the precise moment of starting, and, finding himself in doubt, called time exactly a minute too soon.

It is safe practice to draw up in advance a schedule of the anticipated times of starting and stopping; to check off or record the actual times as they occur; and then to save as part of the permanent record the rough protocol on which this has been done. On this protocol should also be noted any interruptions, distractions, or deviations from the prescribed conditions and procedure. A common precaution is for the examiner to have assistance in keeping track of these details. The time taken for a horse to run a mile is deemed to be in doubt unless it is clocked independently by several experienced judges with similar results. If a test is such that the timing has an appreciable effect on the score, surely similar precautions should be taken to guard against errors.

The selection of a suitable timepiece should be made with reference to the length of the intervals to be measured as well as the degree of accuracy desired. For timing intervals of one minute or longer, a sturdy clock with a second hand, known to be keeping accurate time, or even an ordinary watch, is preferable to most stop-watches. Stop-watches differ in accuracy and dependability just as people do. Even the expensive split-second chronometers, most satisfactory for measuring intervals of a few minutes or less, cannot always be depended upon to keep uniformly accurate time for a quarter of an hour or longer while the sweep-second hand is engaged. A well-adjusted stop-watch which has once stood a thorough test for accuracy should nevertheless be retested often, throughout the range of intervals to be measured.

In a psychological laboratory an examiner may measure to a hundredth of a second his personal equation, and also find out the possibly disappointing range of his variability in starting and stopping a timer and in reading times from the second hand of a clock. Practice in taking times, both with a stop-watch and with a second hand, increases his precision and enables him to ascertain the procedure which is for him the more accurate under different conditions. For most testing in which it is unnecessary to measure fractions of a second, he may find that it is best to place reliance on his own good watch, saying, "Begin!" or "Stop!" just as the second hand arrives at the indicated point, and noting on the protocol the hour, minute and second.

Finally, when collecting the blanks at the close of the examination, make certain that all are accounted for.

5

The scoring of tests, whether given individually or to a group, though often tedious, is not wholly a routine matter. That it must be done painstakingly goes without saying. It is safe precaution to have the work checked by a second scorer.

When the examiner himself can take the time to do at least a part of the scoring, he not infrequently notices points of interest which would escape the attention of a clerk. He may observe, for instance, unusual superiority in some aspect of the task, obvious misunderstanding of a point in the instructions, or undue frequency of a particular kind of error. It is a prodigal waste to administer a battery of tests and then to take cognizance only of the quantitative measures of performance while tossing into the waste-basket those qualitative data which close inspection would reveal.

To return to the purely clerical task. Most paper-and-pencil tests are constructed with attention to the matter of convenience in scoring. With the aid of suitable stencils, the strictly routine work can ordinarily be completed in a surprisingly short time. It is well to select for this task clerks who excel in accuracy as well as speed in a number-checking and name-checking test.

If the number of papers to be done is large, it is an economy to complete the scoring of one page or sub-test on all the papers before beginning with the next page. The same point applies to the work of totaling partial scores, and transmuting the raw scores into percentile ranks, standard scores or letter grades. The general rule is to subdivide the work and complete the several parts in succession. Each step should be checked before the next is begun.

When the scoring of a performance test is not entirely objective—when, for example, the quality of the work completed has to be given a rating for excellence in comparison with a scale made up of graded samples of the work—the examiner should make the necessary comparisons himself or entrust them only to an assistant with equal ability in appraising the several items to be judged.

6

What has been said about giving group tests may now be briefly summarized. It is clear that familiarity with the details of the prescribed procedures and skill in following them meticulously add to the accuracy of the resulting scores. To insure that a test is properly administered to a group, the preliminary arrangements, the working conditions, the motivation, the oral instructions, the answering of questions, the timing, the recording of what actually transpires, all in turn need attention; also possible opportunities for cheating, which should be inconspicuously eliminated. If there is reason to suspect that any in the group may have been coached or have had previous experience with the examination, the facts should, if possible, be ascertained. Ways of dealing with these varied problems have been described, and the value of securing experience under the critical supervision of a seasoned administrator of group tests has been emphasized.

In scoring tests, as well as in giving them, the greater the care exercised in seeing that the specified procedures are strictly observed, the greater the likelihood that the scores may be of real use in counseling.

Chapter XIX

INTERPRETING TEST PERFORMANCE

1. Steps in appraising the significance of a score. 2. Norms. Critical scores. Percentile scales and standard scales compared. 3. A score represents, not a point, but a band or zone of values. The zone of approximation. Functions of coefficients of reliability and of validity. Standard error of an estimated true score. Standard error of measurement. Standard error in predicting a criterion score. 4. Extraneous sources of error and their elimination. 5. The fact of regression toward the mean. A prediction table. 6. Narrowing the zone of uncertainty. Cumulative value of small differences. 7. Final precautions.

I

THE most difficult phase of aptitude-testing is interpretation of results. After the tests have been carefully administered and painstakingly scored, the findings must be appraised and translated into information helpful to the individual examined. Here are data, both quantitative and qualitative—the scores, the observations, the examiner's inferences and impressions as to what the individual's behavior in the test situation probably signifies. These must be brought together and fitted into the framework of whatever is known about the person. His developmental history, his experience, his circumstances, his health, his interests and aspirations, all form part of the picture. For a counselor to understand correctly what the test data add to this picture and to appreciate their bearing on the person's plans for the future, calls for not a little technical knowledge, sagacity, and human insight. Interpretation of test performance is no routine mechanical process.

The present chapter deals with the meanings which can properly be attached to test scores as symptoms of aptitudes. It describes ways of ascertaining whether a particular score represents a deviation.

favorable or unfavorable, from the average of a group with which the individual's performance is compared, and the probabilities that this deviation is large enough to be significant. To this end, scales and tables of norms with which to compare an individual measurement will be described. It will be emphasized that a person's test score represents not simply a point on a scale of aptitude but a zone of values about that point, within which a true measure of his aptitude probably lies; also, that inferences as to the vocational significance of scores, whether high or low, are necessarily in terms of probabilities. Both the accuracy of the individual measures and the degree to which they are indicative of future possible accomplishment must be scrutinized. The fact will be stressed that several similar indicators of a person's aptitude, any one of which taken alone might be but a feeble clue, may nevertheless cumulatively have real significance. The conclusions toward which these indicators point must, finally, be translated into statements of probabilities which the client can grasp, statements which he will not construe as oracular pronouncements, but as aids to his own self-understanding. Such are the tasks which psychometrist and counselor face in interpreting test performance.

Two steps are involved in appraising a test score regarded as a symptom of aptitude. The first step is to compare the person's performance with what others have done in the same test situation in order to decide whether his score shows a deviation, large or small, from the average of a group with which his performance may appropriately be compared, and from the general average of his own aptitudes. To do this, it is necessary to ask how accurately the score represents the individual's real ability in the task set by the test. How reliable is it? Does it measure a satisfactory sample of his performance? Then, having decided within what range of possible error allowance should be made for inadequacies of the test as an instrument of measurement, keeping in mind also the possibility of errors in administration, and the chance that the person may not have been at his best, the second step is, to consider the evidence that deviations of this magnitude are symptomatic of later performance in the line of activity under consideration, and from this evidence to estimate the probabilities of failure or success.

2

We need a yardstick with which to measure the magnitude of the deviation of a person's score from the general population average, or from the average of his group. A table of norms shows the range of the scores others have made and the way these scores are distributed. A norm is a standard of reference; so a table of norms serves as our yardstick.

By reference to a table of norms it is seen that a person's score—obtained, let us say, in a certain vocabulary test—corresponds to the average score among twelve-year-old pupils; or to the average for college juniors. However, when using such age or grade norms, the distribution of abilities at each level should be borne in mind, and not merely the average for that level. Mr. Hennessey was appalled at Mr. Dooley's observation that "half the people are below average." Some teachers, too, apparently forgetful of what an average is, are disconcerted when any of their students are found to be below the "norm" for their grade or age, and think that something ought to be done about it. A table of norms giving for each level not only the average but the distribution about this average, relieves this unwarranted anxiety.

A person's scores should be referred to norms obtained from a population with which he may properly be compared; for only then does the comparison have meaning. Also, when talking with him about his score, he is more likely to appreciate its significance if the comparison can be stated in terms of the norms of a group to which he belongs. If he has graduated from high school, it is better to say, "You did better than 30 per cent of high-school graduates," rather than, "Your score is the same as the average for high-school juniors." When conferring with a college freshman who has done exceptionally well, it is preferable to say, "Only 20 per cent of freshmen made scores higher than yours," rather than, "Your performance equals that of the average senior." Similarly with Mental Ages and Intelligence Quotients: if a fourteen-year-old girl makes a Binet Mental Age score of 13, why not compare her with others of her own age, and note that she did as well as 35 per cent of them? Status in comparison with one's own group is readily understood.

When norms are available for occupational groups, it is advisable to compare the person's score with these as well as with the norms for the general population or for the age or school grade to which he belongs. If the trait measured is of importance in the occupation, it may be that an individual will be found to stand well in comparison with his own group, but be outside of the preferred range for those entering the occupation.

A preferred range is ascertained by comparing the scores made by two groups; for example, those entering a certain occupation and those not entering it; those succeeding in it and those who fail; those who learn it quickly and those who take a longer time to acquire the necessary vocational skill. "A test score above which or below which the members of one group are represented in conspicuously greater proportion than the members of the other group, is called a *critical score*. The range marked off by a critical score is called a *preferred range* or a critical section."[1]

It has been possible, in connection with some kinds of work, to locate upper as well as lower critical scores. Thus, for clerical or sales work of a highly routine sort, employers have found it inadvisable to engage persons testing above a certain upper critical score, because they are likely to become dissatisfied and leave before they have made good.

Some tables of norms show only the average score for each age or each school grade; others go into more detail. Certain authors report for each group the middle or median score and the upper and lower quartiles. Reference of a person's score to such a table shows whether he ranks in the top quarter, the second quarter, the third quarter, or the lowest quarter of the population reported upon. The most common way is to give the score equaled or exceeded by only the top 10 per cent of the persons in the group tested, the score equaled or exceeded by the next 10 per cent, and so on down to the score equaled or exceeded by 90 per cent of the group. This is called a table of deciles.[2]

A decile scale is suitable for many purposes; but when measuring aptitudes it is of great interest to know whether a person did better than 99 per cent of the population, or better than only 91 per cent. If the test differentiates reliably near the extremes, and if the norms have been obtained by giving it to a large group, such a difference is very significant. Indeed, it is more important to know a fact like this than to know whether a person scored in the sixth or only in the fourth decile.

Since differences in performance near either extreme of the scale mean so much more in counseling than those near the middle, it is not unusual to add to a decile table of norms the percentile scores

[1] Bingham and Freyd, *Procedures in Employment Psychology*, p. 190. Methods of ascertaining and interpreting critical scores are treated in *op. cit.*, Chapters XV and XVI.

[2] Rigorously defined, a median is the midpoint in a series of values. If the scores made by a hundred persons are arranged in order of size, the median score is midway between the scores made by the fiftieth and the fifty-first persons. Of course, if they happen to make the same score, that is the median. The ninth decile lies between the scores made by the ninetieth and the ninety-first individuals in the series. Similarly, the upper quartile lies between the seventy-fifth and the seventy-sixth scores.

within the highest and lowest deciles. Some tables go into still more detail and show each percentile score throughout the entire range. Such norms, in terms of "centiles," as they are sometimes called, make it possible to see at a glance what percentage of the population reported upon did no better than the person whose score is to be interpreted.

A percentile scale may be prepared by arranging in order of magnitude the scores of all the persons tested and then ascertaining what

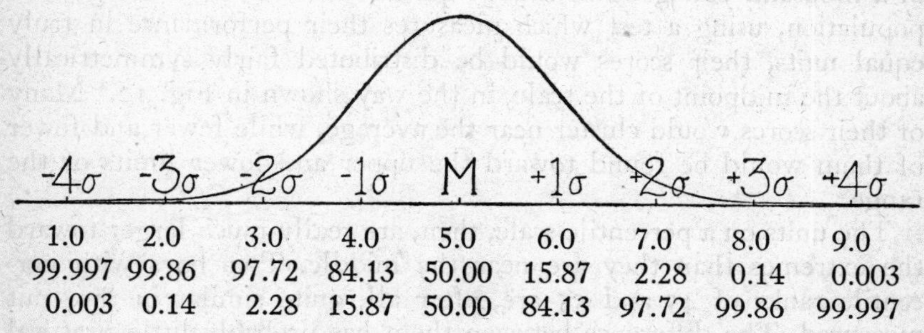

FIG. 12. NORMAL DISTRIBUTION, STANDARD SCALE, AND PERCENTILE RANKS

Showing a bell-shaped frequency surface or normal surface of distribution of measures of an aptitude, such as might be found in a large representative sample of the general population. In the first scale, score values are expressed in terms of deviations from the mean (Standard Deviations or sigmas); in the second, in terms of a Standard Scale on which 5.0 is taken as the mean and the unit is one sigma. The third row of figures shows the corresponding centiles or percentile ranks; and the fourth row, the per cent of the population not exceeding each Standard Score. When the distribution of scores in a test takes this form, the mean (M) and the median (the fiftieth percentile) coincide. About 16 per cent of the population make scores better than +1 sigma, a Standard Score of 6.0. A score of +4 sigma, corresponding to a Standard Score of 9.0, would be expected of only about three people in a hundred thousand.

percentage of the group failed to attain each score. The zero point on such a scale is obviously some score lower than that of any in the group, no matter how large the group may be. The fiftieth percentile is that point on the continuous scale above and below which exactly half of the measures are found. At the sixty-third percentile, for instance, is the score which 63 per cent of the group failed to attain, and which 27 per cent exceeded.

The simplicity and convenience of percentile scales tends to blind the user to one defect: inequality of the scale units. Percentile differences are smallest at the middle of a scale, and grow larger toward either extreme, as is seen in Fig. 12 and in Table XVI. Near either end of the scale a difference of five centiles represents a much greater difference in ability than it does in the middle range. In fact, if one person scores at the second percentile from the bottom and another at the seventh, the difference between their performances is about as great as it would be if one of them had scored at the fortieth percentile and the other at the sixtieth. This peculiarity follows from the fact, noted in Chapter III, that people with "average" abilities are numerous, while wide deviations from the central tendency are relatively rare. Thus, if we were to test the clerical aptitudes of a thousand young women taken quite at random from the general population, using a test which measures their performance in truly equal units, their scores would be distributed fairly symmetrically about the midpoint of the scale, in the way shown in Fig. 12.[3] Many of their scores would cluster near the average, while fewer and fewer of them would be found toward the upper and lower limits of the range.

The units on a percentile scale, then, are really much larger toward the extremes than they are near the middle. Two boys with percentile ranks of 45 and 55 are, after all, quite similar in the trait measured. The difference between them has probably little practical significance, whereas the difference between two whose percentile ranks are 85 and 95 is large, and apt to be of importance. Although these facts are familiar enough to everyone who has looked into the subject, there is an inveterate tendency to forget them when making use of decile or percentile scales. For this reason it is better to use a scale on which the units of difference in ability are more nearly equal throughout the range. It is usually impossible to employ for this purpose the units in terms of which the raw scores are first obtained—time required to do the task, number of errors, or whatever it may be. The difference between the ability of a champion

[3] See page 249. Such a bell-shaped figure, a normal frequency surface, illustrates the way that differences in many kinds of abilities are found to be distributed throughout the population. Indeed, this is how we would expect the differences of performance in any aptitude test to be distributed, provided that it is a good test which differentiates clearly through the entire range of the group tested; provided that this group is a large representative unselected sample of the population; and provided that the ability measured is the product of several independent factors and not due merely to the presence or absence of a single specific determiner of ability. When the scores tend to cluster toward the lower or the upper end of the scale instead of in the middle—because the test is too hard or too easy, or because the units of measurement in which it is scored do not all represent really equal units of ability, or because the group tested is not representative of the general population, but is selected—the curve of distribution is not symmetrical, but skewed. It does not follow that because the scores on a test are distributed normally it is therefore a good test; for if it is sufficiently shot through with purely random errors, a normal (chance) distribution of scores is certain to be obtained.

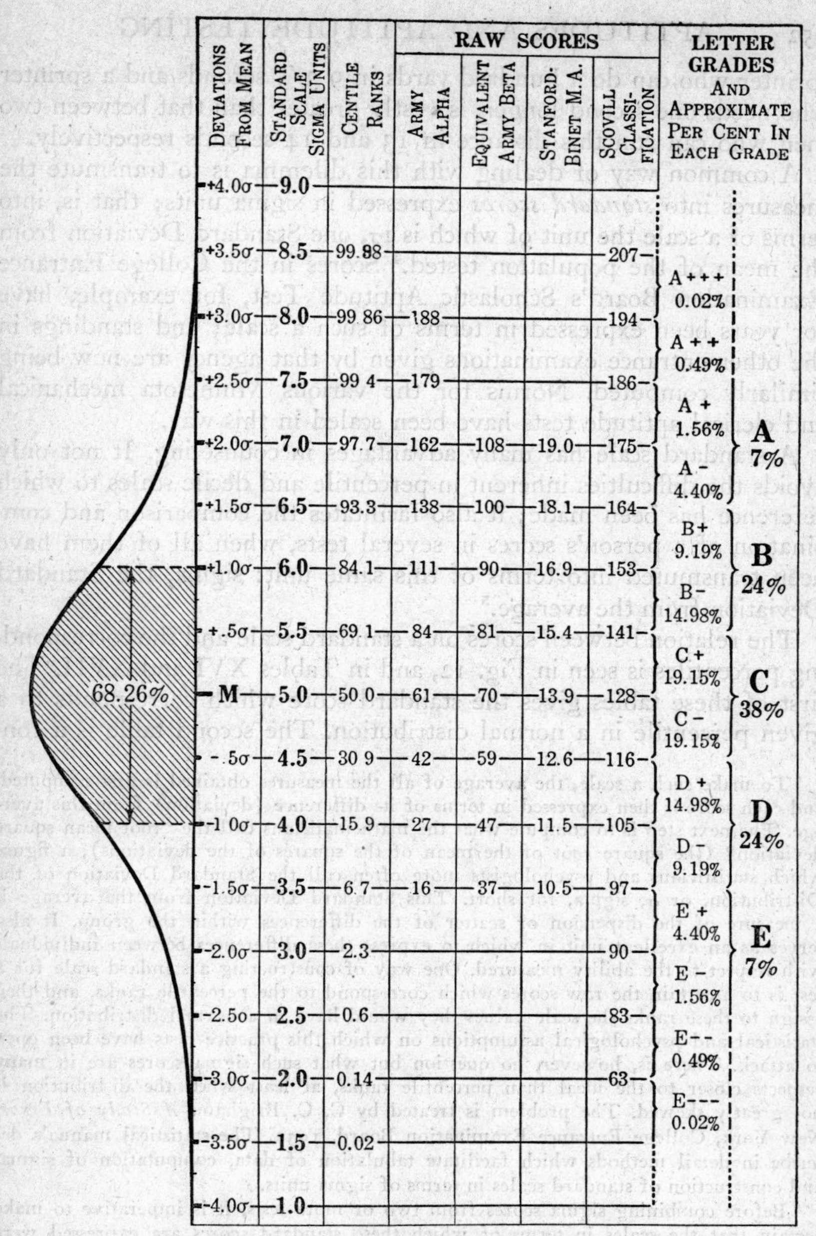

FIG. 13. RAW SCORES, STANDARD SCORES AND LETTER GRADES

Showing the relations between a frequency surface representing a normal distribution of measures about their Mean (M), a scale in terms of deviations from this Mean, and the Standard Scores, Percentile Ranks, Raw Scores and Letter Grades* in four tests: Army Alpha, Army Beta, Stanford-Binet, and Scovill Classification.

* These letter grades are not the same as the letter ratings used in the army which, for Alpha, were defined as follows: A, 135 and above; B, 105 — 134; C+, 75 — 104; C, 45 — 74; C−, 25 — 44; D, 15 — 24; D−, 0 — 14.

sprinter who can do a hundred yards in 9 3/5 seconds and a sprinter who needs one second longer, is vastly greater than that between two men who can run this distance in 13 and 14 seconds respectively.

A common way of dealing with this dilemma is to transmute the measures into *standard scores* expressed in sigma units; that is, into terms of a scale the unit of which is 1σ, one Standard Deviation from the mean of the population tested.[4] Scores in the College Entrance Examination Board's Scholastic Aptitude Test, for example, have for years been expressed in terms of such a scale; and standings in the other entrance examinations given by that agency are now being similarly computed. Norms for the various Minnesota mechanical and clerical aptitude tests have been scaled in this way.

A standard scale has many advantages in counseling. It not only avoids the difficulties inherent in percentile and decile scales to which reference has been made; it also facilitates the comparison and combination of a person's scores in several tests, when all of them have been transmuted into terms of this same unit: sigma, the Standard Deviation from the average.[5]

The relation between scores on a standard scale and the corresponding percentiles is seen in Fig. 12, and in Tables XVI and XVII. The first of these tables gives the standard score which corresponds to a given percentile in a normal distribution. The second table is a con-

[4] To make such a scale, the average of all the measures obtained is first computed, and each score is then expressed in terms of its difference (deviation) from this average. The next step is to compute what the mathematicians call the "root mean square deviation" (the square root of the mean of the squares of the deviations), a figure which statisticians and psychologists more often call the Standard Deviation of the Distribution, or σ, sigma, for short. This Standard Deviation from the average is a measure of the dispersion or scatter of the differences within the group. It also serves as an excellent unit in which to express these differences between individuals with respect to the ability measured. One way of constructing a standard scale for a test is to ascertain the raw scores which correspond to the percentile ranks, and then assign to these ranks the scale values they would have in a normal distribution. The statistical and psychological assumptions on which this practice rests have been open to attack. There is, however, no question but what such sigma scores are in many respects closer to the ideal than percentile ranks, at least when the distribution is not greatly skewed. The problem is treated by C. C. Brigham, *A Study of Error*, New York, College Entrance Examination Board, 1932. The statistical manuals describe in detail methods which facilitate tabulation of data, computation of sigma, and construction of standard scales in terms of sigma units.

[5] Before combining sigma scores from two or more tests, it is imperative to make certain that the scales in terms of which these standard scores are expressed were constructed from measures of one and the same population, or equivalent samples of the total population. If one clerical test, for example, has been calibrated after testing a population of commercial-high-school students, while the norms and scale for another test have been obtained from a population of employed adults, the two averages would not be identical, nor the two sigmas equivalent, as they would be if the tests had been calibrated on the same group.

venience when it is desired to find the percentile which corresponds to a given standard score.

Table XVI. Deviations from the Mean and Scores on a Standard Scale Corresponding to Percentiles of a Normal Distribution

Percentiles	Deviations in σ Units	Standard Scores[1]
99.99767	+3.5	8.50
99.95166	+3.3	8.30
99.9	+3.09	8.09
99.8	+2.88	7.88
99.7	+2.75	7.75
99.4	+2.51	7.51
99.2	+2.408	7.41
99.1	+2.367	7.37
99.0	+2.327	7.33
98	+2.053	7.05
97	+1.882	6.88
96	+1.751	6.75
95	+1.646	6.65
94	+1.555	6.56
93	+1.477	6.48
92	+1.403	6.40
91	+1.342	6.34
90	+1.282	6.28
89	+1.228	6.23
88	+1.174	6.17
87	+1.126	6.13
86	+1.079	6.08
85	+1.039	6.04
84	+ .993	5.99
83	+ .954	5.95
82	+ .917	5.92
81	+ .877	5.88
80	+ .843	5.84
79	+ .806	5.81
78	+ .772	5.77
77	+ .739	5.74
76	+ .708	5.71
75	+ .674	5.67
74	+ .641	5.64
73	+ .614	5.61
72	+ .583	5.58
71	+ .553	5.55
70	+ .526	5.53
69	+ .496	5.50
68	+ .465	5.47
67	+ .438	5.44
66	+ .411	5.41
65	+ .384	5.38
64	+ .357	5.36
63	+ .330	5.33
62	+ .304	5.30
61	+ .279	5.28
60	+ .253	5.25
59	+ .229	5.23
58	+ .202	5.20
57	+ .175	5.18
56	+ .148	5.15
55	+ .128	5.13
54	+ .101	5.10
53	+ .074	5.07
52	+ .050	5.05
51	+ .027	5.03
50	.000	5.00
49	− .027	4.97
48	− .050	4.95
47	− .074	4.93
46	− .101	4.90
45	− .128	4.87
44	− .148	4.85
43	− .175	4.83
42	− .202	4.80
41	− .229	4.77
40	− .253	4.75
39	− .279	4.72
38	− .304	4.70
37	− .330	4.67
36	− .357	4.64
35	− .384	4.62
34	− .411	4.59
33	− .438	4.56
32	− .465	4.54
31	− .496	4.50
30	− .526	4.47
29	− .553	4.45
28	− .583	4.42
27	− .614	4.39
26	− .641	4.36
25	− .674	4.33
24	− .708	4.29
23	− .739	4.26
22	− .772	4.23
21	− .806	4.19
20	− .843	4.16
19	− .877	4.12
18	− .917	4.08
17	− .954	4.05
16	− .993	4.01
15	−1.039	3.96
14	−1.079	3.92
13	−1.126	3.87
12	−1.174	3.83
11	−1.228	3.77
10	−1.282	3.72
9	−1.342	3.66
8	−1.403	3.60
7	−1.477	3.52
6	−1.555	3.45
5	−1.646	3.35
4	−1.751	3.25
3	−1.882	3.12
2	−2.053	2.95
1.0	−2.327	2.67
.9	−2.367	2.63
.8	−2.408	2.59
.6	−2.51	2.49
.3	−2.75	2.25
.2	−2.88	2.12
.1	−3.09	1.91
.04834	−3.3	1.70
.00233	−3.5	1.50

[1] To second decimal.

3

When interpreting a person's performance, his obtained score should not be thought of as a point on the scale, but rather as a band

TABLE XVII. PERCENTILES CORRESPONDING TO SCORES ON A STANDARD SCALE

	Standard scale	*Percentiles*		*Standard scale*	*Percentiles*
+3.5 σ	8.5	99.98	Mean	5.0	50.00
	8.4	99.97		4.9	46.02
	8.3	99.95		4.8	42.07
	8.2	99.93		4.7	38.21
	8.1	99.90		4.6	34.46
+3 σ	8.0	99.86	−0.5 σ	4.5	30.85
	7.9	99.81		4.4	27.43
	7.8	99.74		4.3	24.20
	7.7	99.65		4.2	21.19
	7.6	99.53		4.1	18.41
+2.5 σ	7.5	99.38	−1 σ	4.0	15.87
	7.4	99.18		3.9	13.57
	7.3	98.93		3.8	11.51
	7.2	98.61		3.7	9.68
	7.1	98.21		3.6	8.08
+2 σ	7.0	97.72	−1.5 σ	3.5	6.68
	6.9	97.13		3.4	5.48
	6.8	96.41		3.3	4.46
	6.7	95.54		3.2	3.59
	6.6	94.52		3.1	2.87
+1.5 σ	6.5	93.32	−2 σ	3.0	2.28
	6.4	91.92		2.9	1.79
	6.3	90.32		2.8	1.39
	6.2	88.49		2.7	1.07
	6.1	86.43		2.6	.82
+1 σ	6.0	84.13	−2.5 σ	2.5	.62
	5.9	81.59		2.4	.47
	5.8	78.81		2.3	.35
	5.7	75.80		2.2	.26
	5.6	72.57		2.1	.19
+0.5 σ	5.5	69.15	−3 σ	2.0	.14
	5.4	65.54		1.9	.10
	5.3	61.79		1.8	.07
	5.2	57.93		1.7	.05
	5.1	53.98		1.6	.03
Mean	5.0	50.00	−3.5 σ	1.5	.02

or zone about that point; and for several reasons. The first of these lies in the very nature of measurement. Whether measuring the mechanical aptitude of a trade apprentice, the weight of a truckload of grain, the speed of an airplane, or the length of a timber, the recorded figure represents a band of values rather than a precise point. This band can be no narrower than the smallest unit used in making and recording the measure. When a machinist says that he has trued a one-inch bearing to an accuracy of a thousandth of an inch, what he means is, not that the bearing now has a diameter of one inch, but that it is not less than 999-thousandths of an inch nor more than one and one-thousandth inches. A boy solves twelve out of twenty problems in a spatial-relations test. His score of twelve then means, "at least twelve, but less than thirteen." It stands, not for the point twelve on the continuous scale, but for a band of values, a band one problem in width, as it were.

Next, the band of values of which a score stands as a numerical symbol is further widened by any unreliability inherent in the instrument of measurement; and widened still further by chance errors of administration or of scoring. Just as the chemist or the astronomer undertakes to ascertain the limits of reliability of his instrument and the probable error of his observations when using it, so the psychologist computes the probable error or the standard error of his scores.[6] An obtained score may appropriately be thought of as representing a band bounded by "plus and minus the standard error of measurement."

When thinking about a person's ability as expressed by a single score on a particular test, his adviser then notes not only the point where the obtained score is located on a scale or in a table of norms. He thinks of the *zone*, the band or penumbra of values about that point, within which the person's true score probably lies. No examination, no test, no instrument of precision, yields a perfectly reliable measure of a person's ability to do just such tasks as those set by the test. His true ability in such tasks, to be sure, approximates the ability he demonstrated when he took the test. The more reliable the test, the narrower is this zone of approximation. With a highly reliable test, the chances are good that an estimated true score approximates an obtained score fairly closely. But even here it is safer to think of the zone or band of values within which his true score probably lies, rather than to think only of his reported score or of his estimated true score.[7]

[6] The probable error of a measure indicates the limits of the band of values within which the chances are even that the measure would lie, if it could be made repeatedly. The standard error (the root-mean-square deviation of a series of measures from their average) indicates the boundaries of a wider band, within which the measure should fall about sixty-eight per cent of the time if the measuring could be repeated indefinitely.

[7] An estimated true score is defined as the most probable score if all variable errors of measurement were eliminated. It is sometimes described as the average score the person would make if it were possible to give him a great many strictly equivalent forms of the test under identical conditions. The symbol for a true score as so defined is x_∞, and the formula for estimating a true score from a single obtained score is

$$\bar{x}_\infty = r_{11}x_1$$

where the scores are expressed as deviations from the mean, and r_{11} is the coefficient of reliability.

The relation between the width of this zone of approximation and the reliability of the test may be illustrated by a comparison of three tests. Test A has a high coefficient of retest reliability, .96; Test B has a reliability of .90; and Test C, .80. Suppose that a person has taken these three tests and in each instance has, as it happens, obtained a score which is exactly at the middle of the scale. His obtained scores are precisely "average." His estimated true scores, in these instances, are also just average. But this estimate is less likely to be in error in Test A than in Tests B and C. In Test A, with a coefficient of reliability of .96, the chances are 68 in 100 (about two out of three) that his true score lies within a zone of plus or minus the "Standard Error of Estimate of a True Score" (σ_{∞}), which in this instance is .196 σ (practically two-tenths of a sigma unit).[8] In other words, there is a zone, extending from $+.2\sigma$ to $-.2\sigma$ on the Standard Scale, within which there is a good deal of likelihood that the true score lies. There are only 16 chances in 100 (about one in six) that it is higher than $+.2\sigma$; and the same probability that it is not lower than $-.2\sigma$. On Test B, with a reliability of .90, the Standard Error of Estimate of a True Score is $\pm.3\sigma$. On Test C, with a reliability of .80, this Standard Error is $\pm.4\sigma$, so that the zone within which the chances are two out of three that the true score lies is twice as wide as in the case of Test A.

The Standard Error of Estimate of a true score inferred from a single score on a test of which the coefficient of reliability is specified, is shown in the fourth column of Table XVIII.

The Standard Error of Measurement ($\sigma_{(M)}$) is another function of the coefficient of reliability (r) which furnishes a clue to the width of the zone of approximation. When the distribution of scores is normal, 68 per cent of obtained scores do not diverge from their corresponding estimated true scores by more than this amount, $\pm\sigma_{(M)}$. It will be noted in Table XVIII that, for coefficients of reliability of .90 or above, $\sigma_{(M)}$ is nearly equal to $\sigma_{\infty \cdot I}$. Either function serves as an aid in judging the width of the zone of error when esti-

[8] The standard error of estimate of a true score by means of a single score of the same function is computed by the formula

$$\sigma_{\infty \cdot I} = \sigma_I \sqrt{r_{II} - r_{II}^2}$$

in which σ_I is the standard deviation of the distribution of scores when the test has been administered to a representative sampling of the population and r_{II} is the coefficient of self-correlation of the test. If the coefficient of reliability, r_{II}, has been computed on a more homogeneous population sample than that used in making the Standard Scale, r_{II} will be too small and the corresponding standard error of estimate too large.

mating a true from an obtained score. But in dealing with data from less reliable tests, it is well to keep in mind the size and meaning of both functions, the standard error of a true score (σ_∞) and the standard error of measurement ($\sigma_{(M)}$).

Explanation of Table XVIII. Values of Functions of r

This table shows for decreasing values of the coefficient of correlation, the corresponding values of related functions. *E.g.*, if a coefficient of reliability is .90 (in the first column headed r) the index of reliability ($\sqrt{r}$ in the second column) is nearly .95; the standard error of estimate of a true score by means of a single obtained score ($r_{\infty.1}$ in the fourth column) is .300 σ; and the Standard Error of Measurement—a measure of the probable divergence of an obtained score from its corresponding true score ($\sigma_{(M)}$, fifth column) is .316 σ. In the seventh column is found the coefficient of alienation, k, which is the standard deviation of errors of estimate when inferring scores in a criterion from scores in the test. Thus if the correlation, r, between a test and a criterion is .90, the corresponding coefficient of alienation is .436 sigma units on the criterion scale. The efficiency of predictions made with such a test is seen in the adjoining column to be 56 per cent better than chance.

Table XVIII giving the values of functions of r, has other uses also. Knowing the coefficient of correlation between two variables, such as scores in a test and scores in a criterion, one may read the standard error of estimate when predicting scores in the criterion from scores in the test. This standard error of estimate is shown in the column headed k. (It is sometimes called the coefficient of alienation.) The adjoining column tells how much better than a random guess such estimates are. A perfect test—if there ever were a test which correlated 1.00 with a criterion—would be 100 per cent efficient in predicting that criterion; but note that if the correlation is .99, a little less than perfect, the per cent efficiency in prediction is not 99 per cent better than chance, but only 86 per cent better. This column warrants thoughtful scrutiny by any user of test data who may not previously have looked into the mathematical laws of probability in this connection.

4

The interpreter of test scores will bear in mind another precaution. These mathematical aids for use in ascertaining standard errors of measurement indicate only the allowances that should be made for unreliability inherent in the test, due to the limited sampling of the ability in question. They do not take into account any other sources of possible error such as mistakes made by the examiner in administering the test, carelessness in scoring, the possibility that the examinee did not put forth his best efforts, that he was ill or otherwise incapacitated, or that he had been coached. If there is reason to sus-

TABLE XVIII. VALUES OF FUNCTIONS OF r

r	$\sqrt{r}$	r^2	$\sqrt{r-r^2}$	$\sqrt{1-r}$	$1-r^2$	$\sqrt{1-r^2}$	$100(1-k)$	r
			$\sigma_{\infty \cdot 1}$	$\sigma_{(M)}$		k	% Eff.	
1.00	1.0000	1.0000	0.0000	0.0000	0.0000	0.0000	100.00	1.00
.99	.9950	.9801	.0995	.1000	.0199	.1411	85.89	.99
.98	.9899	.9604	.1400	.1414	.0396	.1990	80.10	.98
.97	.9849	.9409	.1706	.1732	.0591	.2431	75.69	.97
.96	.9798	.9216	.1960	.2000	.0784	.2800	72.00	.96
.95	.9747	.9025	.2179	.2236	.0975	.3122	68.78	.95
.94	.9695	.8836	.2375	.2449	.1164	.3412	65.88	.94
.93	.9644	.8649	.2551	.2646	.1351	.3676	63.24	.93
.92	.9592	.8464	.2713	.2828	.1536	.3919	60.81	.92
.91	.9539	.8281	.2862	.3000	.1719	.4146	58.54	.91
.90	.9487	.8100	.3000	.3162	.1900	.4359	56.41	.90
.89	.9434	.7921	.3129	.3317	.2079	.4560	54.40	.89
.88	.9381	.7744	.3250	.3464	.2256	.4750	52.50	.88
.87	.9327	.7569	.3363	.3606	.2431	.4931	50.69	.87
.86	.9274	.7396	.3470	.3742	.2604	.5103	48.97	.86
.85	.9220	.7225	.3571	.3873	.2775	.5268	47.32	.85
.84	.9165	.7056	.3666	.4000	.2944	.5426	45.74	.84
.83	.9110	.6889	.3756	.4123	.3111	.5578	44.22	.83
.82	.9055	.6724	.3842	.4243	.3276	.5724	42.76	.82
.81	.9000	.6561	.3923	.4359	.3439	.5864	41.36	.81
.80	.8944	.6400	.4000	.4472	.3600	.6000	40.00	.80
.79	.8888	.6241	.4073	.4583	.3759	.6131	38.69	.79
.78	.8832	.6084	.4142	.4690	.3916	.6258	37.42	.78
.77	.8775	.5929	.4208	.4796	.4071	.6380	36.20	.77
.76	.8718	.5776	.4271	.4899	.4224	.6499	35.01	.76
.75	.8660	.5625	.4330	.5000	.4375	.6614	33.86	.75
.74	.8602	.5476	.4386	.5099	.4524	.6726	32.74	.74
.73	.8544	.5329	.4440	.5196	.4671	.6834	31.66	.73
.72	.8485	.5184	.4490	.5292	.4816	.6940	30.60	.72
.71	.8426	.5041	.4538	.5385	.4959	.7042	29.58	.71
.70	.8367	.4900	.4583	.5477	.5100	.7141	28.59	.70
.69	.8307	.4761	.4625	.5568	.5239	.7238	27.62	.69
.68	.8246	.4624	.4665	.5657	.5376	.7332	26.68	.68
.67	.8185	.4489	.4702	.5745	.5511	.7424	25.76	.67
.66	.8124	.4356	.4737	.5831	.5644	.7513	24.87	.66
.65	.8062	.4225	.4770	.5916	.5775	.7599	24.01	.65
.64	.8000	.4096	.4800	.6000	.5904	.7684	23.16	.64
.63	.7937	.3969	.4828	.6083	.6031	.7766	22.34	.63
.62	.7874	.3844	.4854	.6164	.6156	.7846	21.54	.62
.61	.7810	.3721	.4877	.6245	.6279	.7924	20.76	.61
.60	.7746	.3600	.4899	.6325	.6400	.8000	20.00	.60
.59	.7681	.3481	.4918	.6403	.6519	.8074	19.26	.59
.58	.7616	.3364	.4936	.6481	.6636	.8146	18.54	.58
.57	.7550	.3249	.4951	.6557	.6751	.8216	17.84	.57
.56	.7483	.3136	.4964	.6633	.6864	.8285	17.15	.56
.55	.7416	.3025	.4975	.6708	.6975	.8352	16.48	.55
.54	.7348	.2916	.4984	.6782	.7084	.8417	15.83	.54
.53	.7280	.2809	.4991	.6856	.7191	.8480	15.20	.53
.52	.7211	.2704	.4996	.6928	.7296	.8542	14.58	.52
.51	.7141	.2601	.4999	.7000	.7399	.8602	13.98	.51
.50	.7071	.2500	.5000	.7071	.7500	.8660	13.40	.50

TABLE XVIII. VALUES OF FUNCTIONS OF r (continued)

r	$\sqrt{r}$	r^2	$\sqrt{r - r^2}$	$\sqrt{1 - r}$	$1 - r^2$	$\sqrt{1 - r^2}$	$100(1 - k)$	r
			$\sigma_{\infty \cdot 1}$	$\sigma_{(M)}$		k	% Eff.	
.50	.7071	.2500	.5000	.7071	.7500	.8660	13.40	.50
.49	.7000	.2401	.4999	.7141	.7599	.8717	12.83	.49
.48	.6928	.2304	.4996	.7211	.7696	.8773	12.27	.48
.47	.6856	.2209	.4991	.7280	.7791	.8827	11.73	.47
.46	.6782	.2116	.4984	.7348	.7884	.8879	11.21	.46
.45	.6708	.2025	.4975	.7416	.7975	.8930	10.70	.45
.44	.6633	.1936	.4964	.7483	.8064	.8980	10.20	.44
.43	.6557	.1849	.4951	.7550	.8151	.9028	9.72	.43
.42	.6481	.1764	.4936	.7616	.8236	.9075	9.25	.42
.41	.6403	.1681	.4918	.7681	.8319	.9121	8.79	.41
.40	.6325	.1600	.4899	.7746	.8400	.9165	8.35	.40
.39	.6245	.1521	.4877	.7810	.8479	.9208	7.92	.39
.38	.6164	.1444	.4854	.7874	.8556	.9250	7.50	.38
.37	.6083	.1369	.4828	.7937	.8631	.9290	7.10	.37
.36	.6000	.1296	.4800	.8000	.8704	.9330	6.70	.36
.35	.5916	.1225	.4770	.8062	.8775	.9367	6.33	.35
.34	.5831	.1156	.4737	.8124	.8844	.9404	5.96	.34
.33	.5745	.1089	.4702	.8185	.8911	.9440	5.60	.33
.32	.5657	.1024	.4665	.8246	.8976	.9474	5.25	.32
.31	.5568	.0961	.4625	.8307	.9039	.9507	4.93	.31
.30	.5477	.0900	.4583	.8367	.9100	.9539	4.61	.30
.29	.5385	.0841	.4538	.8426	.9159	.9570	4.30	.29
.28	.5292	.0784	.4490	.8485	.9216	.9600	4.00	.28
.27	.5196	.0729	.4440	.8544	.9271	.9629	3.71	.27
.26	.5099	.0676	.4386	.8602	.9324	.9656	3.44	.26
.25	.5000	.0625	.4330	.8660	.9375	.9682	3.18	.25
.24	.4899	.0576	.4271	.8718	.9424	.9708	2.92	.24
.23	.4796	.0529	.4208	.8775	.9471	.9732	2.68	.23
.22	.4690	.0484	.4142	.8832	.9516	.9755	2.45	.22
.21	.4583	.0441	.4073	.8888	.9559	.9777	2.23	.21
.20	.4472	.0400	.4000	.8944	.9600	.9798	2.02	.20
.19	.4359	.0361	.3923	.9000	.9639	.9818	1.82	.19
.18	.4243	.0324	.3842	.9055	.9676	.9837	1.63	.18
.17	.4123	.0289	.3756	.9110	.9711	.9854	1.46	.17
.16	.4000	.0256	.3666	.9165	.9744	.9871	1.29	.16
.15	.3873	.0225	.3571	.9220	.9775	.9887	1.13	.15
.14	.3742	.0196	.3470	.9274	.9804	.9902	.98	.14
.13	.3606	.0169	.3363	.9327	.9831	.9915	.85	.13
.12	.3464	.0144	.3250	.9381	.9856	.9928	.72	.12
.11	.3317	.0121	.3129	.9434	.9879	.9939	.61	.11
.10	.3162	.0100	.3000	.9487	.9900	.9950	.50	.10
.09	.3000	.0081	.2862	.9539	.9919	.9959	.41	.09
.08	.2828	.0064	.2713	.9592	.9936	.9968	.32	.08
.07	.2646	.0049	.2551	.9644	.9951	.9975	.25	.07
.06	.2449	.0036	.2375	.9695	.9964	.9982	.18	.06
.05	.2236	.0025	.2179	.9747	.9975	.9987	.13	.05
.04	.2000	.0016	.1960	.9798	.9984	.9992	.08	.04
.03	.1732	.0009	.1706	.9849	.9991	.9995	.05	.03
.02	.1414	.0004	.1400	.9899	.9996	.9998	.02	.02
.01	.1000	.0001	.0995	.9950	.9999	.9999	.01	.01
.00	.0000	.0000	.0000	1.0000	1.0000	1.0000	.00	.00

pect that any of these extraneous sources of error has affected the performance, the remedy is not to juggle with the score, but to repeat the test in an alternative form when conditions are more favorable to accuracy.

Some of these extraneous sources of error operate to lower a person's score; others tend to raise it. When it is known that there has been no coaching or cribbing and that errors of giving and scoring the test have been eliminated by competent administration, the chances are that the score more nearly represents the *lower* rather than the upper limit of the person's ability; for there still remains the possibility that he may not have been physically up to par, or for other reasons may not have done himself full justice.

Examiners should be especially painstaking to note any disabilities extraneous to the aptitude being measured which nevertheless might hamper performance: poor eyesight, for example, or lack of facility in reading instructions. When such disabilities are suspected they may be tested for separately.

5

Skilled examiners can to a large degree eliminate extrinsic sources of error. But we must consider further certain characteristics intrinsic to test scores which, by their very nature, represent only samplings of what is measured. There is, for example, the familiar fact of regression, to which Sir Francis Galton drew attention half a century ago. He showed that, for any given value of an independent variable, the most probable value of the dependent variable *regresses* toward the mean of that variable. Thus, an estimated true score is always *nearer the mean* of the standard scale than is the obtained score from which the estimate is computed. If the reliability of the test is high, this regression toward the mean is slight; but as reliability diminishes, the tendency increases for true scores to approach the mean. At the lower limit—that is, in the case of a hypothetical test with no reliability whatsoever—everyone's "true" score would be precisely at the middle of the scale, whether estimated from a high obtained score or a low one; and the chances would be zero that any other score would more correctly represent a person's performance in the task set by such a perfectly unreliable test.

This relationship between the coefficient of reliability and the standard error of estimate of a true score is seen at the bottom of the first and fourth columns in Table XVIII. In the fifth column the corresponding Standard Error of Measurement is seen to be

1.00; which is the same as saying that in such a test the obtained scores would tend to diverge from their corresponding estimated true scores as much as they would if one were to obtain them by guessing blindly instead of by administering the test. Most tests which have value in estimating an individual's aptitudes have reliabilities within the range from .85 to .97. Corresponding to these reliabilities, the standard errors of estimate when inferring true scores from obtained scores are seen in the table to be less than thirty-six hundredths but more than seventeen-hundredths of a sigma unit on the standard scale.

The tendency of true scores to be nearer the mean than the obtained scores from which they are estimated, is pictured in Table XIX. This table shows the most probable standard score in any measure, estimated from a standard score in another measure, when the coefficient of correlation between the two measures is known. At the top of the table is a Standard Scale on which 5.0 represents the average or mean score of the population measured, and the unit is one sigma, one Standard Deviation from the Mean.[9] Suppose now that a person's score is 3.5 on the Standard Scale. What is his true score, the score he would most probably have if all variable errors were eliminated? If the reliability of the test is .95, his estimated true score, as seen in the second line of the body of the table, is 3.58; while if the reliability is only .80, his estimated true score is 3.80, which is still nearer the average.

Again, suppose that the correlation between a test of clerical aptitude and average annual earnings is .45, and that both test scores and earnings are expressed in scores on a standard scale. We want to know the most probable annual earnings of a person who has done very well indeed on the test, scoring at point 7.0 on the Standard Scale, which means that he has done better than 97.7 per cent of the population tested. Should we infer that his salary will probably be better than that of 97.7 per cent of this group? Not at all. The prediction table shows—in the .45 row and the 7.0 column—that his most probable Standard Score in the criterion is only 5.90. So far as this test is indicative of his probable earnings, the likelihood is that they will exceed the earnings of only 82 per cent of the group. Such comparisons serve to emphasize the fact that scores which deviate most widely from the average—the extremely high or low scores in which a counselor is certain to be most interested—are the very ones which have to be discounted the most. So far as the statis-

[9] The percentage of the population failing to attain each standard score may be read from Table XVII.

TABLE XIX. PREDICTION TABLE

Showing a person's most probable standard score in one measure, estimated from his standard score in another measure, when the coefficient of correlation between the two measures is known.

		-3σ		-2σ		-1σ		M		$+1\sigma$		$+2\sigma$		$+3\sigma$		
r	*k*	2.0	2.5	3.0	3.5	4.0	4.5	5.0	5.5	6.0	6.5	7.0	7.5	8.0	σ_∞	*r*
1.00	.00	2.00	2.50	3.00	3.50	4.00	4.50	5.00	5.50	6.00	6.50	7.00	7.50	8.00	.00	1.00
.95	.31	2.15	2.63	3.10	3.58	4.05	4.53	5.00	5.48	5.95	6.43	6.90	7.38	7.85	.22	.95
.90	.44	2.30	2.75	3.20	3.65	4.10	4.55	5.00	5.45	5.90	6.35	6.80	7.25	7.70	.30	.90
.85	.53	2.45	2.88	3.30	3.73	4.15	4.58	5.00	5.43	5.85	6.28	6.70	7.13	7.55	.36	.85
.80	.60	2.60	3.00	3.40	3.80	4.20	4.60	5.00	5.40	5.80	6.20	6.60	7.00	7.40	.40	.80
.75	.66	2.75	3.13	3.50	3.88	4.25	4.63	5.00	5.38	5.75	6.13	6.50	6.88	7.25	.43	.75
.70	.71	2.90	3.25	3.60	3.95	4.30	4.65	5.00	5.35	5.70	6.05	6.40	6.75	7.10	.46	.70
.65	.76	3.05	3.38	3.70	4.03	4.35	4.68	5.00	5.33	5.65	5.98	6.30	6.63	6.95	.48	.65
.60	.80	3.20	3.50	3.80	4.10	4.40	4.70	5.00	5.30	5.60	5.90	6.20	6.50	6.80	.49	.60
.55	.84	3.35	3.63	3.90	4.18	4.45	4.73	5.00	5.28	5.55	5.83	6.10	6.38	6.65	.50	.55
.50	.87	3.50	3.75	4.00	4.25	4.50	4.75	5.00	5.25	5.50	5.75	6.00	6.25	6.50	.50	.50
.45	.89	3.65	3.88	4.10	4.33	4.55	4.78	5.00	5.23	5.45	5.68	5.90	6.13	6.35	.50	.45
.40	.92	3.80	4.00	4.20	4.40	4.60	4.80	5.00	5.20	5.40	5.60	5.80	6.00	6.20	.49	.40
.35	.94	3.95	4.13	4.30	4.48	4.65	4.83	5.00	5.18	5.35	5.53	5.70	5.88	6.05	.48	.35
.30	.95	4.10	4.25	4.40	4.55	4.70	4.85	5.00	5.15	5.30	5.45	5.60	5.75	5.90	.46	.30
.25	.97	4.25	4.38	4.50	4.63	4.75	4.88	5.00	5.13	5.25	5.38	5.50	5.63	5.75	.43	.25
.20	.98	4.40	4.50	4.60	4.70	4.80	4.90	5.00	5.10	5.20	5.30	5.40	5.50	5.60	.40	.20
.15	.99	4.55	4.63	4.70	4.78	4.85	4.93	5.00	5.08	5.15	5.23	5.30	5.38	5.45	.36	.15
.10		4.70	4.75	4.80	4.85	4.90	4.95	5.00	5.05	5.10	5.15	5.20	5.25	5.30	.30	.10
.05		4.85	4.88	4.90	4.93	4.95	4.98	5.00	5.03	5.05	5.08	5.10	5.13	5.15	.22	.05
.00	1.00	5.00	5.00	5.00	5.00	5.00	5.00	5.00	5.00	5.00	5.00	5.00	5.00	5.00	.00	.00

Locate the known Standard Score, S_1 in the top row, and the coefficient of correlation, *r*, in the left column. Corresponding to these two points in the body of the table is the most probable value of the correlated measure, S_2, in terms of its Standard Scale. Thus, if Smith's score on a test puts him one sigma above the mean (Standard Score = 6.0) and the correlation of this test with a criterion is .70, Smith's most probable score in the criterion is seen to be 5.70. Corresponding to a correlation of .70, the Standard Error of Estimate, *k*, is $.71\sigma$. So we might say that Smith's estimated score in the criterion is 5.70 ± .71. In other words, the chances are 68 in 100 that Smith's ability in the criterion lies within the zone between the points 4.99 and 6.41. Those two points on the standard scale mark the boundaries of what we have called the zone of approximation, in predicting Smith's ability in the criterion from his original test score.

Or, if Smith's obtained score is 6.0 in a test which has a reliability of .95, and it is desired merely to find his probable true score in the test, we read off the figure corresponding to these two entries, which is 5.95. We note also at the right of the table that when a coefficient of reliability is .95, the standard error of estimate of a true score from a single obtained score is .22. So in this instance the zone of approximation within which the chances are about two out of three that his true score lies is 5.95 ± .22; or between the points 5.73 and 6.17 on the standard scale.

tical probabilities are concerned, the chances are that the person's true abilities do not deviate from the average quite so much as these extreme scores would at first indicate.

To judge what a score means, it is of importance to know within what range of accuracy it is possible to estimate a person's score in a criterion of subsequent accomplishment, knowing only his score in an aptitude test and the coefficient of correlation between test scores and criterion. The Prediction Table already described will serve to bring home to the reader the possibilities and the limits of such statistical predictions.

This Table XIX shows a person's most probable standard score in the criterion, estimated from his standard score in a test. If the coefficient of correlation between test and criterion were 1.00—which it never is—the standard score in the criterion would always be the same as in the aptitude test. Predictions would be without error. This relation is seen in the first row of the body of the table.

At the opposite extreme is the situation in which there is no correlation whatever between test and criterion. In that event, if nothing were known about the person but his test score, the best estimate of his probable performance in the criterion would have to be 5.00—just average—no matter what his score in the test. This is seen at the foot of the table. If, however, the test scores, though by no means perfect indicators of later accomplishments, are known to bear some relation to them, discriminating estimates are possible. The closeness of the relation is indicated by the size of the coefficient of correlation between test and criterion. Suppose, for example, that a person's standard score in a test is 6.5 and that the test correlates .60 with the criterion. The table shows that his most probable performance in the criterion is 5.90. Note that it is somewhat nearer the average than is his score in the test.

Referring now to the second column of the table, it is seen that when a coefficient of correlation is .60, the standard error of estimate, *k*, is eight-tenths of a sigma unit. This makes it possible to estimate the width of the zone of approximation within which the person's ability in the criterion probably lies; for the chances are 68 in 100 that his criterion score will actually be somewhere within a range of ±.80 on either side of his most probable score, which in this instance was 5.90. In other words, the chances are about two out of three that his score on the criterion will be not less than 5.10 nor more than 6.70. Such are the probabilities. Certainties are not to be expected.

6

It is, however, quite within the power of counselors and examiners to narrow somewhat the broader zones of uncertainty. A single straw tells which way the wind blows; but an anxious farmer looks to his weather vane, and a meteorologist uses an instrument which records velocity as well as direction. The psychometrist likewise spares no pains to get the most reliable measures of aptitude he can, and as many as he can. He realizes how wide the zone of approximation is whenever an estimate of capacity for future accomplishment is based on a single test score. If the test is repeated and the average of the two performances is computed, with due allowance for practice effect, the combined score yields an estimate not twice as good, but nevertheless better than that from a single measure. And when a whole battery of pertinent tests is brought to bear, the properly weighted contribution of each to the total score makes further inroads against the zone of uncertainty. Bring into the picture the developmental history from the cumulative record. Ascertain whether other pertinent facts tend to conflict with or to confirm the test indications. If most of the data harmonize, if they point even with uncertain fingers in the same direction, the counselor is warranted in offering suggestions which he should hesitate to make in the absence of such cumulative indications of aptitude.

7

A final word. Understanding of the vocational significance of test scores does not rest on mathematics alone; nor on general psychology. Close familiarity with the occupations and their requirements is also indispensable. It is, to be sure, not always safe to assume from one's observations of workers and one's familiarity with certain tests that an aptitude measured by a test and an aptitude apparently demanded by an occupation are really identical. They may be similar in name only. There is, with reference to a great majority of the occupations, a deplorable lack of data regarding the measured characteristics and minimal abilities of people successfully pursuing them, and a correspondingly strong temptation to make assumptions regarding essential aptitudes which later experience may not justify. Even when measurements are available, there is a further danger in assuming uncritically that any one ability or aptitude is really essential in an occupation, since it is possible that the lack of it can be compensated for by exceptional excellence in other aptitudes. When interpreting test results, ingenuity and fertility of insight as well as an understanding of psychological statistics is indeed to be desired, and richly informed common sense must hold the reins.

The author parts with his reader reluctantly. In the areas we have been exploring together, a great deal remains to be examined and discussed. Many kinds of work have not even been mentioned. Many aids in ascertaining individual differences of aptitude have not been described. But the covers of one volume cannot contain an encyclopedia of vocations, a handbook of guidance practice, or a comprehensive manual of tests—much less, all three. We have undertaken, rather, to see in correct perspective the relations between these allied subjects.

The glass through which a person surveys his educational and occupational progress to date, and peers at his plans for future adjustment, rests on a tripod: one leg, his own knowledge about the world of work; another, his self-knowledge; the third, such knowledge as his counselors and the organized agencies of education supply. Is the tripod a little sturdier, the field of vision clearer, when self-knowledge is buttressed by psychological measurement?

This question the author now leaves his reader to answer, venturing only the opinion that no one who has come with him through all the chapters of this book can take an extreme position, maintaining either that a psychological test is a marvel of clairvoyance or that every attempt to measure symptoms of aptitude is folly.

THE END

APPENDIX

Representative Tests and Interest Schedules

APPENDIX

THE tests and inventories described in the following pages have been chosen as representative of various aids available for use in psychological examining.

Others, equally desirable for counselors to know about, might have been included. But this is not an encyclopedia. Whipple's *Manual of Tests*, revised in 1915, filled two quarto volumes. A current edition of such a work—greatly needed—would be still more voluminous. It would, to be sure, describe only a fraction of the three thousand tests and rating scales classified in Hildreth's Bibliography[1] and the 500 additional tests, new within the past three years, which Buros[2] has listed; for these compilers have not winnowed the wheat from the chaff. Three-fourths of these tests would be blown onto the straw pile by a single blast of criticism; but the grist remaining would far excel, in quality as in quantity, all that had been garnered two decades ago.

For present purposes the aim has been to choose for description, tests which educational and vocational psychologists have found to be helpful when counseling. Wherever possible, preference has been accorded to tests for which both general adult norms and vocational norms are available, as well as to those of which the statistical reliability is known to be at least fairly satisfactory. Selection from among these and from the many other tests classified in the Hildreth and Buros bibliographies, should, however, be made in the light of the considerations set forth in Chapter XVI and in earlier chapters of this volume where these and other tests have been briefly described and compared.[3]

The headings under which the titles have been grouped are general—for convenience of reference only. Some of the tests might have been placed under other captions. The General Clerical Test of the U. S. Civil Service Commission, for example, is essentially a test of verbal intelligence; while several of the intelligence tests have been useful chiefly as tests of clerical aptitudes. Anyone familiar with the Coxe-Orleans Prognosis Test of Teaching Ability will recognize that it is not inappropriately listed with tests of intelligence. The aptitudes sampled by the I. E. R. Assembly Test for Girls, although in part

[1] Gertrude H. Hildreth, *Bibliography of Mental Tests and Rating Scales.* New York: Psychological Corporation, 1933.

[2] Oscar K. Buros, *Educational, Psychological and Personality Tests of 1933, 1934, and 1935.* New Brunswick, N. J.: Studies in Education, No. 9. School of Education, Rutgers University, 1936. An annual supplement to this bibliography is promised.

[3] C. A. Oakley and A. Macrae, *Handbook of Vocational Guidance (Secondary and Public Schools)*, London: University of London Press, Ltd., 1937, contains in Chapter III, a description of psychological tests with special reference to those current in Great Britain.

mechanical, are in the author's opinion chiefly manual, and the test is so classified.

One omission—the Stanford-Binet Scale—must instantly be explained. This examination, after many years of usefulness, has now been radically revised and extended. As this paragraph is being written, a book by Terman[4] descriptive of these revisions, is on the verge of publication, providing an authoritative source which psychometrists and counselors will wish to consult directly.

The Seashore Measures of Musical Talent,[5] long recognized as perhaps the most scientifically grounded and carefully developed of aptitude tests, have also not been here described in detail. Users of these aids will in any event wish to be familiar with the full descriptions of the tests and their various uses contained in the references cited on pages 202-203.

Indeed, one of the main purposes of this book will have been fulfilled if its readers develop the habit of turning to original sources and then exercising their own judgment, both in the choice of tests and in the interpretation of results. Just as an individual with whom a counselor confers is helped most, not by being told what it is advisable for him to do, but by being assisted to think through his situation so that he can make up his own mind; so a user of tests is better off in the long run when he learns to stand on his own feet instead of leaning heavily on the advice of specialists, no matter with what authority they may speak.

[4] Lewis M. Terman and Maud Merrill, *Measuring Intelligence*. Boston: Houghton Mifflin, 1937. This Stanford-Binet manual describes two closely equivalent scales —Form L and Form M, each extending from the second year mental level to the very superior adult level—and provides examiners with a manual for administering the tests and interpreting the scores. Record booklets, printed card materials and boxes of testing equipment (one for each scale) are obtainable from the same publishing-house. These scales have been standardized on representative American-born white children, 3,000 in number. Unevennesses of standardization of the earlier scale have been ironed out. The standard deviation of the I Q distribution at each age is close to 16 points, so that the I Q scores are much the same as sigma scores. The probable error of an I Q score for subjects below 70 I Q is 1.5 points; for subjects of 100 I Q, about 3 points; for subjects above 130 I Q, nearly 5 points. Either scale requires on the average an hour to administer. An abbreviated scale which can be given in about forty minutes is also described.

[5] The phonographic records used for measuring tonal memory and sensitivity to differences of pitch, intensity, time, consonance, and rhythm are obtainable from the C. H. Stoelting Company, Chicago. It is understood that additional records are in preparation.

CONTENTS

I

TESTS FOR COLOR BLINDNESS, VISUAL ACUITY AND ASTIGMATISM

ABILITY to distinguish colors, desirable in certain occupations, is essential in others. Normal color vision is needed by chemists, ironworkers and airplane pilots, as well as by locomotive engineers, buyers and salesmen of silks and clothing, and inspectors and sorters of colored materials. From 5 to 8 per cent of men and a much smaller proportion of women—less than half of one per cent—have some defect of color vision. This condition, curiously, characterizes many who are unaware of their handicap; and so an examiner's kit is certain to include a set of Holmgren yarns, Ishihara color plates, or some similar means of identifying color blindness, as well as a Snellen chart or an equally convenient device for estimating visual acuity.

We shall here describe M. B. Jensen's test for color blindness. Similar in principle to the Ishihara test, it is a small wall chart on which are four circular groups of colored dots, designated Plates A, B, C and D. The colors and intensities of the dots are such that people with normal color vision see clearly certain bars radiating from the centers of the circles. In giving the test it is convenient to refer to these bars as hands on the face of a clock. When looking at Plate D, for example, a person with normal color vision sees two hands, a green one pointing to 5:00 and a red one to 10:00. A red-blind eye sees only the hand pointing to 5:00; a green-blind eye sees only the other hand; and the totally color-blind sees neither, but only the circular field irregularly filled with dots. To guard against memorizing the position of the hands, the chart may be changed in position and hung from any of its four sides.

Precise instructions for giving the test are contained in the Manual of Directions accompanying the chart. Numerical scores are not used; a person either has one of the three more common forms of color blindness, is "border line," or is "normal."

This test has advantages when testing little children, but is not superior to the Ishihara for adults. While either test detects color blindness, it does not measure ability to discriminate fine differences in color. When precise measures of ability in color perception are necessary, see the tests described by Pierce (5).[1]

Jensen's chart provides also for a rough measure of astigmatism, and of the ratio between a person's visual acuity and that of the normal eye. When this or the Snellen chart reveals visual deficiency, examination by an oculist and

[1] Numbers in parentheses refer to the references listed at the end of the section.

prescription of proper glasses should be made before any decision is reached regarding the seriousness and the vocational implications of the handicap.

At least 20 per cent of people have keen eyes which are decidedly better than normal. Their superior acuity may be thought of as one indicator of aptitude for employments in which exceptionally good eyesight is an advantage, such as instrument-maker, dental mechanic, monotype operator, lithographer, engraver, map-maker, pharmacist, architect, surgeon. Bonnardel's monograph (4) lists some 500 occupations and classifies them according to the minimal visual acuity required. It also describes more than 200 occupations suitable for the blind, who clearly are not restricted to such familiar callings as basketry, upholstering, marble-polishing, piano-tuning, and vending newspapers.

DISTRIBUTORS:

Jensen Chart and Manual of Directions, Psychological Corporation. $3.

Ishihara Color Perception Test, C. H. Stoelting. $7.50.

Snellen Chart, Lowell Modification, for measuring visual acuity, C. H. Stoelting. 50 cents.

REFERENCES:

1. W. R. Miles and Homer Craig, "Color Blindness in Dry Goods Salesmen." *Personnel Journal*, 1931, 9: 437-449.

2. W. R. Miles, "One Hundred Cases of Color-Blindness Selected with the Ishihara Test." *Journal of General Psychology*, 1929, 2: 535-543.

3. I. A. Haupt, "Tests for Color-Blindness: A Survey of the Literature." *Journal of General Psychology*, 1930, 3: 222-267.

4. R. Bonnardel, *Vision et Professions.* Paris: Conservatoire National des Arts et Métiers, 1936.

5. W. O'D. Pierce, *The Selection of Colour Workers.* New York and London: Pitman, 1934.

II

TESTS OF AUDITORY ACUITY

BECAUSE normal ability to hear is necessary in many occupations, a test of auditory acuity is often indicated. Several kinds of tests are available. The simplest procedure is to ascertain the distance at which the subject can barely hear the ticking of the examiner's watch or the click of an acoumeter; but this method is not very reliable. Moreover, it does not measure ability to hear the most important of sounds—the consonants and vowels of human speech—as does the Andrews Whispered Speech Test, for example, or the Western Electric Audiometer, Type 4A or 4B. Pending the time when each school system and counseling service has access to a reliable speech audiometer, the Andrews test will continue to be useful both in individual examining and in school surveys.

A person found to have defective hearing may be referred to a physician for thorough examination and possible remedial treatment. Meanwhile his counselor reviews with him vocational opportunities in relation to his sensory defect. Such a person is often anxious to know of occupations in which people with auditory acuity no better than his have nevertheless succeeded. Reference to lists of occupations in which deafened soldiers and civilians have been rehabilitated and satisfactorily placed by bureaus for the hard of hearing, shows that suitable callings are both numerous and varied. In these lists are authors, automobile assemblers, auditors, bookkeepers, building contractors and cooks; cabinetmakers, cobblers, dental mechanics, and domestic servants; farmers and file clerks; inspectors of castings, of textiles, and of clothing; janitors and jewelers; lawyers; manicurists, masseurs and maintenance mechanics; operators of lathes, punch presses, and screw machines; paper-box-makers, porters and poultrymen; press-feeders and typesetters; restaurant proprietors, stonecutters, and x-ray technicians. The range of occupations in which success has been achieved in spite of serious auditory deficiency permits a selection to be made in accordance with the client's general abilities, tastes, and special aptitudes.

ANDREWS' WHISPERED SPEECH TEST

Administration.—The procedures are minutely described in Whipple's Manual (1). He recommends the use, if possible, of an oblong room of average proportions and a length of about 100 feet. In this room, establish by rough preliminary tests a range such that not over 90 of 100 test words can be correctly heard by a normal ear. If space will not permit this range to be established otherwise, place screens between examiner and client, or use adjoining rooms. Whatever may be the arrangement that affords a suitable range, make careful note of all acoustical conditions—*e.g.*, distance of range from walls, dimensions of rooms, exact position of examiner and client, disposition of large carpets or rugs and pieces of furniture, number of doors or windows open or closed, etc. Be sure always to work under precisely these conditions. Have at hand a snapper for signaling, small rubber stoppers for ear plugs, and a standard list of stimulus numbers such as those in the accompanying table:

TABLE XX. TEST-NUMBERS FOR AUDITORY ACUITY

I	II	III	IV	V	VI	VII	VIII	IX	X
6	84	19	90	25	14	8	52	73	24
29	69	53	7	13	31	93	35	41	95
42	17	34	39	46	9	27	64	16	62
87	92	28	62	7	65	60	81	95	49
53	33	97	84	54	98	15	6	57	80
94	26	45	21	70	76	74	19	38	71
70	50	72	56	91	40	36	78	20	16
35	75	60	75	83	23	49	40	89	3
18	48	3	43	68	52	82	23	64	58
61	1	86	18	92	87	51	97	2	37

Seat the client at the end of the range selected, with his right ear toward the examiner. Carefully close his left ear by means of a stopper. Then tell him to close his mouth and his eyes. Under no circumstances permit him to watch your lips. Give him a short practice series, and then proceed with the test.

Pronounce the numbers in the following manner: as you finish exhaling a breath, snap the sounder once as a ready signal; at the end of the next expiration, pronounce the first test-number in whispered speech with the residual air in the lungs; then snap the sounder twice to indicate that the word has been pronounced, and let the client either speak or write down the number he has heard (using a dash if nothing is heard). Meanwhile breathe three times, then give the warning signal, then whisper the next test-number after the fourth breath, and so on until ten test-numbers are given. Allow a brief rest and then proceed as before. Whipple recommends that 100 numbers be pronounced, but experienced examiners get reliable results with 30.

Test the left ear in the same manner, after reversing position and changing the ear plug to the right ear.

Finally, remove ear plug, have the client face you and test his ability to hear with both ears. See that he keeps his eyes closed, and his mouth also, since hearing may be more acute with the mouth open.

If time is limited, give only this last test because, after all, it samples the kind of hearing used in daily life.

Scoring.—Compute the percentage of test-numbers correctly heard, and divide by the percentage normally heard under the same conditions.

Norms.—Since acoustical conditions vary from place to place, each examiner must develop his own norm, by averaging the percentages of many persons tested by him in the room he uses. Each client's acuity is then expressed in relation to this normal percentage. Thus, if his per cent correct is 80 while the normal per cent is 70, his acuity is 8/7; that is, better than normal. In other words, the measure of his acuity is a ratio in which the numerator is his percentage and the denominator is the average percentage.

REFERENCES:

1. G. M. Whipple, *Manual of Mental and Physical Tests, Part 1: Simpler Processes.* Baltimore: Warwick and York, 1914, 200-213.

2. H. A. Peterson and J. G. Kuderna, "Reliability of School Tests of Auditory Acuity," *Journal of Educational Psychology*, 1924, 15: 145-156.

WESTERN ELECTRIC AUDIOMETER

Obvious shortcomings of the whispered speech test are eliminated when an instrument such as the Western Electric 4A or 4B audiometer can be used. The 4A audiometer, pictured on page 124, has for ten years been used in school surveys and in individual testing of auditory acuity, but is no longer obtainable and is about to be replaced by an improved model, 4B. The instrument consists of a phonograph with a magnetic reproducer which provides auditory stimuli of measured intensity—spoken numbers of two digits or three digits each. The listener, wearing a headphone, writes down what he hears. The instructions read, "You will hear numbers spoken by a person who is moving away from you. The voice will get weaker and weaker. Listen carefully and write as many numbers as you can." During the course of a test, the intensity of the successive stimuli decreases in small uniform steps to a minimum scarcely audible to a normal ear, then returns abruptly to a maximum and gradually decreases again. This process is repeated four times. The headphone is then adjusted to the other ear, the phonograph disc is turned over and the test proceeds as before. Four of the eight series of numbers are spoken in a woman's voice, four in a man's. In all eight series the same rate of diminution of loudness is maintained, so that when the numbers written on the data sheet are compared with those on a master sheet, the errors and omissions show the point of diminishing intensity at which the sounds are so faint that they are no longer intelligible. The degree of hearing loss, if any, in each ear, is then read directly from the data sheet. As many as forty listeners can be tested at once.

DISTRIBUTOR:

Graybar Electric Company, Graybar Building, New York, with branches in most large cities. Price of the new model with all accessories including forty headphones, two phonograph discs, two master sheets, and 500 data sheets, all in two carrying cases, $430.

REFERENCES:

1. H. Fletcher, *Speech and Hearing*, New York: D. Van Nostrand Company, 1929.

2. H. Newhart, "Audiometer," in *The Cyclopedia of Medicine* (Piersol), 4: 863-868. Philadelphia: F. A. Davis Company, 1932.

III

TESTS OF MANUAL APTITUDES

THERE are many kinds of dexterity. The simplest dextrous movements, such as those made in packing cartons, require control of only the larger muscles of hand and arm in picking up objects and placing them quickly in position. Other movements call for greater delicacy of adjustment, involving control of the smaller muscles. Still others, like throwing a ball, can be dextrously made only when the muscles of eyes, fingers, hands and arms are well coordinated with the action of the skeletal muscles of back and legs which maintain bodily posture. It is no wonder that, for measuring various kinds of dexterity, numerous forms of tests have been developed.

Four of these tests, briefly described in Chapter X, are selected for detailed description here. One—the Minnesota Manual Dexterity Test—measures speed of gross movements of hand and arm in picking up objects and placing them in position. Another—O'Connor's Finger Dexterity Test—is a pin-placing test which requires control of smaller muscles. A third—O'Connor's Tweezer Dexterity Test—places a premium on a still higher level of manual coordination. The fourth—Frazier's Card-dropping Test—while similar in certain respects to each of the other three, has had its chief usefulness as one measure of manual versatility. All must be administered individually.

MINNESOTA MANUAL DEXTERITY TEST

W. A. ZIEGLER'S RATE OF MANIPULATION TEST (PLACING)

This test measures the speed with which a person picks up and places cylindrical blocks, all of the same size, in holes in a board.

Detailed specifications should be followed to the letter. There are 58 round blocks 1 11/16 inches in diameter and 7/8 inch thick. The board is 9/16 inch thick, 10 1/4 inches wide, and 39 1/2 inches long, with 58 round holes 1 3/4 inches in diameter bored through. The holes are arranged 4 in a column except in the first and last columns, where there are 3. See illustration in reference (1).

Performance in this simple task depends neither on judgment of differences in size or shape, nor on precision in eye-hand coordination, but on speed of gross hand and arm movements. It has been useful chiefly in ascertaining aptitude for semi-skilled factory operations which place a premium on manual dexterity of this particular sort. Food wrappers and packers, for instance, do well on the test. This kind of manual dexterity is occasionally found to characterize workers in occupations not primarily manual—for example, that of bank teller.

This aptitude matures early. The Standard Norms for adults are applicable to children as young as thirteen.

Administration.—The board is placed on a work table before the person to be tested, with the blocks arranged just beyond the board. The proper arrangement is most easily obtained by first placing the board directly beyond where it is to be, putting the blocks into it and then picking it up, leaving the blocks in position. The board is then placed on the table between the blocks and the client. Say:

> "Stand facing the board. This is a speed test; go as fast as you can. Use one hand. Put all the blocks in the board. Put the nearest block in the left-hand column into the hole nearest it, the next block into the next nearest hole in the same column, etc., until you have filled each column. Watch the way I do it." (Demonstrate on the left-hand column.) "Do you understand? As fast as you can!"

When the board has been filled once, pull it back and lift it up, leaving the blocks in their original position. Then replace the board where it was, ready for the next trial. Allow four trials, timing each with a stop watch.

The test can be administered in from six to eight minutes.

Scoring.—The most reliable method is to treat the first trial as a practice exercise and to use as the score the sum of the number of seconds taken to complete the last three trials. The following norms are in these terms. Those published in the references cited (1), (2), are in terms of time required to complete all four trials.

Interpretation of Performance.—Standard norms are based on samples of men and women representative of occupational and age distributions of workers in an urban area. These norms may be used in interpreting the scores of persons 13 years of age and over.

Speed of hand movement as measured by this test is one factor in a person's performance with form-boards. It has been administered in connection with such tests of aptitude for dealing with spatial relations in order to ascertain the extent to which the form-board measures mechanical aptitude apart from manual dexterity. The test is also of value as an indication of aptitude for semi-skilled factory occupations which require little expertness but only rapid movements of hand and arm. Many people who are unable to climb the educational ladder find a place in such manual occupations for there is scarcely any relation between this trait and verbal intelligence; but it must not be assumed that because a person lacks verbal facility he therefore probably has manual facility. It is safer to give a test such as this.

When interpreting the vocational significance of a score, reference may be made to the following data for eight occupations, which show in Column I

TABLE XXI

STANDARD NORMS

Raw Score (in seconds) Men	Women	*Standard Score*	*Percentile Rank*	*Letter Grade*
138	...	7·5	99·4	
				A+
145	144	7·0	97·7	
				A–
152	150	6·5	93·3	
				B+
159	156	6.0	84.1	
				B–
167	162	5·5	69.1	
				C+
175	168	5.0	50.0	
				C–
184	174	4·5	30.9	
				D+
197	181	4.0	15.9	
				D–
213	190	3·5	6.7	
				E+
222	198	3.0	2.3	
				E–

The Standard Error of a man's score is ±.22 of a unit on the Standard Scale. In terms of raw scores, the Standard Error near the center of the distribution is ±3.8 seconds. The corresponding figures for women are ±.28 of a Standard unit and ± 3.4 seconds.

the average Standard Score of people in each occupation; and in Column II, the percentage of people in the general population who fall below this.

	I	II
Butter-packers	6.6	94
Butter-wrappers (1 lb. block)	6.4	92
Food-packers	6.2	88
Bank tellers	6.05	85
Semi-skilled workers	5.38	64
Skilled manual workers	5.25	60
Stenographers and typists	5.13	55
Garage mechanics	5.13	55

Although many manual occupations demand a good deal of dexterity of the sort sampled by this test, some do not. It seems, for example, that neither the work of the garage mechanic nor the operation of a typewriter calls for more than a moderate amount of the ability which this test measures.

DISTRIBUTOR:

Mechanical Engineering Department, University of Minnesota, Minneapolis. Complete equipment, $6.50.

A slightly modified form with additional items is sold by the Educational Test Bureau, Fifteenth and University Avenues S.E., Minneapolis. The manual supplied by this distributor contains norms for this test and also for the Ziegler Turning Test for which the same board is used. The norms given above are for the original board.

REFERENCES:

1. Helen J. Green, Isabel R. Berman, D. G. Paterson and M. R. Trabue, *A Manual of Selected Occupational Tests.* Minneapolis: University of Minnesota Press, 1933.

2. D. G. Paterson, R. M. Elliott, L. D. Anderson, H. A. Toops and E. Heidbreder, *Minnesota Mechanical Ability Tests,* pp. 314-327. Minneapolis: University of Minnesota Press, 1930.

FINGER DEXTERITY TEST

JOHNSON O'CONNOR'S WORKSAMPLE NO. 16

Finger dexterity tests are used as indicators of aptitude for those kinds of bench work which involve rapid manipulation of objects; particularly the picking up and placing of small parts, as in the assembling of clocks, meters, and similar instruments.

The equipment for giving the Finger Dexterity Test consists of 310 cylindrical brass pins one inch in length and 0.072 inches in diameter, in a shallow metal tray about 5 x 6 inches with gently sloping sides; and a metal plate in which 100 holes have been sunk to a depth of ¾ inch with a No. 9 drill. The diameter of the holes is 0.196 inch; they are spaced one-half inch apart, forming ten rows of ten holes each. Picking up three pins at a time, the client puts them in the holes as fast as he can.

The test is suitable for use with adults and with young people over thirteen years old.

Administration.—Seat the client comfortably at a table thirty inches in height. Place the pin-board before him about a foot from the edge of the table, with the tray at the right if the right hand is to be used, and at the left if the left hand is preferred. Suggest that he draw the chair close to the table in order that he may rest his arms on its surface. The tray should contain 310 pins. The board should be at an angle of about 90 degrees to the client's working hand, but the client may change this position if he desires.[1] Say:

"Here is a board with room for three pins in each hole. Pick up three

[1] Wells has pointed out that some of the unreliability of this test is directly traceable to differences in length of the finger nails. It is suggested that before the test is given, the nails be freshly and uniformly clipped.

at a time and fill the holes, placing three pins in each as fast as you can. Use only one hand." Illustrate with three holes. "Start in the farthest corner and work toward you, like this [gesturing]. If you start in this corner [nearest], your sleeve [or fingers] may catch the pins." Show, by gesturing, that the holes are to be filled from left to right, for a right-handed examinee, and each row completed before the next is started. "Fill each row completely before you start the next. Do not skip around. There are extra pins in this tray so that if you drop one or two on the floor you will still have enough left. Do not stop to pick them up." Explain that the elbow may rest on the table, but do not give this or any other of the suggestions in a mandatory form; say, for example, "Some people like to . . ." etc. Have the client place thirty pins, thus filling the top line of ten holes, for practice.

Allow neither more nor less than the prescribed practice, because this practice affects performance on the test.

Tip the pins out, allow a moment's rest, and then time accurately with a stop-watch the number of seconds required to fill the board. Note the time separately for filling the first fifty holes, and the second fifty.

Total administration time varies, according to a person's speed, from about eight to sixteen minutes.

Scoring.—Multiply the number of seconds taken to fill the second half of the board by 1.1; add this to the time taken to do the first half. The score is one-half of this sum.

Interpretation of Performance.—The Standard Norms are based on the performance of samples of men and women representative of occupational and age distributions of workers in an urban area (4).[2] Since this ability matures early, it is possible to use the adult norms in interpreting scores of pupils as young as 14.

The vocational significance of various scores is indicated by the following data, which show, in Column I, the average Standard Scores of people in each of six occupations; and in Column II, the percentages of people in the general population who do not attain these scores.

	I	II
Women engaged in meter and instrument assembly	5.7	76
Bank tellers	5.86	80
Garage mechanics	5.03	50
Skilled workers	4.9	46
Semi-skilled workers	4.9	46
Butter-wrappers (1 lb. blocks)	4.57	36

The women who were successfully employed at meter and instrument assembling scored distinctly higher, on the average, than the general population. Moreover, all the women in this group who made a Standard Score of 5.1

[2] Figures in parentheses correspond to references at ends of sections.

or better were successful; whereas only a third of those scoring below 5.1 were able to do the work. This and other evidence indicates that the chances of satisfactory adjustment to factory occupations involving rapid manipulation of small objects are not very good if a person scores below average on this test; while if he scores as high as 5.5, it is quite probable that he has the requisite manual aptitude. Neither skilled nor semi-skilled workers, by and large, score on the average higher than the average of the general population, which indicates that the ability measured by this test is a specialized one, and that there are many manual occupations which do not require it to any great extent. Indeed, the fact should be kept in mind that there are several apparently similar but distinct kinds of dexterity. The butter-wrappers, for example, did not, on the

TABLE XXII. STANDARD NORMS

Raw score (in seconds) Men	Women	*Standard score*	*Centile rank*	*Letter Grade*
183	166	8.0	99.86	
				(A++)
194	175	7.5	99.4	
				A+
207	186	7.0	97.7	
				A−
221	197	6.5	93.3	
				B+
238	211	6.0	84.1	
				B−
257	226	5.5	69.1	
				C+
280	244	5.0	50.0	
				C−
307	265	4.5	30.9	
				D+
340	290	4.0	15.9	
				D−
382	319	3.5	6.7	
				E+
434	356	3.0	2.3	
				E−
503	402	2.5	.6	
				(E−−)
598	462	2.0	.14	

The Standard Error of Measurement for men, is ±.26 of a unit on the Standard Scale. In terms of raw scores this Standard Error near the center of the distribution is ± 13 seconds. The corresponding figures for women are ±.31 of a Standard unit, and ± 12 seconds.

average, excel in the kind of dexterity measured by this test, but almost all of them did better than the average person on the Minnesota Manual Dexterity Test.

Distributor:

Address Human Engineering Laboratory, Stevens Institute of Technology, Hoboken, New Jersey.

References:

1. Mildred Hines and Johnson O'Connor, "A Measure of Finger Dexterity," *Personnel Journal*, 1926, 4: 379-382.

2. Johnson O'Connor, *Born that Way*. Baltimore: Williams and Wilkins, 1928.

3. E. G. Hayes, "Selecting Women for Shop Work," *Personnel Journal*, 1932, 11: 69-85.

4. Helen J. Green and others, *Manual of Selected Occupational Tests*. Minneapolis: University of Minnesota Press, 1933.

5. D. G. Paterson, Editor, *Research Studies in Individual Diagnosis*. Minneapolis: University of Minnesota Press, 1934.

Tweezer Dexterity Test

johnson o'connor's worksample no. 17

The Tweezer Dexterity Test measures the speed with which a worker using tweezers can pick up pins one at a time and place them in the holes of a board or metal plate.

Although the apparatus somewhat resembles that used in the Finger Dexterity Test, the task is essentially different. People who make good scores in finger dexterity do not always possess the higher order of steadiness and fineness of eye-hand coordination which the Tweezer Dexterity Test measures.

A high score indicates aptitude for work requiring precision in the use of small hand tools, such as the forceps of the anatomist, surgeon, or biological laboratory worker, or the tweezers of the watch-repairer.

The test is adapted for use with people above 13 years of age.

The necessary equipment consists of 105 cylindrical brass pins 0.072 inch in diameter and one inch long; a pair of tweezers, size 00; and a metal plate 7/8 inch in thickness, 5¾ inches wide, by 12 inches long. In one half of the plate are drilled one hundred holes, arranged in ten lines of ten each, ½ inch apart both ways; depth of holes, ¾ inch; diameter of holes, 0.082 inch (No. 45 drill). The other half of the plate consists of a shallow tray approximately 5 by 6 inches with gently sloping sides.

Administration.—Place the metal plate before the client with the tray to the right if the right hand is preferred, and to the left if the left hand is to be used. Be sure that the tray contains 105 pins. Say:

"Here is a board with room for one pin in each hole. Pick up with the tweezers and place one pin in each hole as fast as you can." (Illustrate.) "Pick up the pins by the end opposite or farthest away from you. Use only the hand in which you hold the tweezers." (Illustrate.) Continue giving such explanation as will give the examinee the fullest possible understanding of the best technique for placing the pins. Say, for example, "Pick up the pin rather lightly, so it will fall into vertical position by itself, all ready to drop into the hole,—so." (Place a pin in upper left-hand corner from examinee.) "That is the best way. You see, if you hold the pin tightly like this" (placing pin), "or pick it up by the middle, like this" (placing pin), "or by the wrong end, like this" (placing pin), "it takes an awkward twist of the wrist to get it in. But this way it goes naturally." Illustrate while you are talking, filling three more holes in the correct manner. "It is easiest to start in the farthest corner and work toward you like this" (gesturing). "If you start in this corner" (the nearest), "your sleeve [or fingers] will catch the pins. There are enough extra pins in the tray so that if you drop one or two on the floor you will still have enough left. Do not stop to pick them up."

Have examinee place ten pins for practice. Allow neither more nor less practice than this because practice affects test performance. Tip out the ten pins, allow a moment's rest, and then observe accurately with a stop-watch the number of seconds required to fill the board, from placing the first pin to placing the last.

The test can be given to the average person in about eight minutes, and to all but the slowest ten per cent in ten minutes.

Scoring.—The score is simply the number of seconds elapsing between placement of first and last pins.

Norms.—The accompanying table is based on the performance of standard population samples of men and women representative of occupational and age distributions of workers in an urban area. Since boys and girls as young as 14 are apt to do as well on the test as adults, their scores may be compared with these adult norms.

O'Connor's norms (from *Born That Way*, p. 217), are based largely on the performance of factory employees and applicants, and for the men he examined, are higher than the above, but much lower for the women:

	Male	*Female*
Upper quartile	300	324
Median	340	372
Lower quartile	372	438

Interpretation.—It has been suggested that a high degree of the kind of dexterity measured by this test may well be an asset to persons engaged in die-making, in watch-making and other delicate assembling, in glasswork, in fine

TABLE XXIII. STANDARD NORMS

Raw scores (in seconds) Men	Women	*Standard score*	*Centile rank*	*Letter Grade*
255	249	7.5	99.4	
				A+
271	263	7.0	97.7	
				A−
289	279	6.5	93.3	
				B+
309	297	6.0	84.1	
				B−
333	318	5.5	69.1	
				C+
360	342	5.0	50.0	
				C−
393	369	4.5	30.9	
				D+
432	401	4.0	15.9	
				D−
479	440	3.5	6.7	
				E+
539	487	3.0	2.3	
				E−
615	544	2.5	.6	

The Standard Error of Measurement is estimated to be about ±.32 of a unit on the Standard Scale.

inspection work, as of jewels, and in laboratory work, dentistry, surgery, and other occupations requiring delicate and rapid manipulation of small tools. But, with the exception of workers engaged in fine instrument assembly jobs, the actual test achievements of large numbers of people succeeding or failing in such occupations have not been published; and so a counselor has to rely largely on his good sense to guide him when considering what level of tweezer dexterity might be desirable in a specific occupation.

The majority of manual occupations do not require this kind of dexterity, for semi-skilled workers, and even skilled manual workers, as a group make an average Standard Score of about 5, the same as the average of the general population sample.

DISTRIBUTOR:

Address Human Engineering Laboratory, Stevens Institute of Technology, Hoboken, New Jersey.

REFERENCES:

See publications listed under Finger Dexterity Test, page 284.

Manual Versatility

L. R. FRAZIER'S CARD-DROPPING TESTS

Manual versatility, important in factory occupations in which the work to be done varies more or less from hour to hour or from week to week, is best estimated—as we saw in Chapter X—after the candidate has taken a battery of several manual tests. For inclusion in such a battery, Frazier's Card-dropping Tests have proved useful. (See pages 118ff.)

The average time for administering this series is sixteen minutes. It seldom requires more than twenty minutes.

Equipment.—An armless chair of usual height, a sturdy table, 31 inches high, with a top 36 by 15 inches, in the center of which, running lengthwise of the table and flush with the table top, is set a brass plate, 8 by 3 inches. In the plate are two slots, each exactly 2 9/16 by 1/16 inches, end to end, 1/2 inch apart. In line with these slots and 10 inches from the outer end of each slot is a card-rack (inner dimensions, 2 inches high, 3 7/8 inches long and 2 3/4 inches deep, open at the top and in front, toward the examinee). The floor of each of the two racks is 1 1/4 inches from the table top in front, sloping to 3/4 inch at the back. The racks are adjustable as to distance from the slots and as to the angle which they make with a line running through the slots, so that the examinee may easily take the cards from the racks. Frazier kept this angle at 30 degrees. Under the slots is a deep drawer which pulls out toward the examiner. It is divided into two bins, each 8 inches wide, 7 inches deep and 11 inches from front to back.

In each rack are placed, backs up, fifty playing-cards of good quality, linen finish, size 2 1/2 by 3 1/2 inches. Those in one rack have red backs, and in the other blue. Occasionally cards are warped and cannot be used. Any card which becomes bent or torn must be replaced. A new set is needed for each twenty-five or thirty tests.[1]

Administration.—The examinee is seated before the table in such a way that the open sides of the card-racks face him. Say: "Suppose you try dropping cards through these slots. Are you right or left handed?" If right, say, "Try a few with your right hand first, just for practice. Pick the cards up one at a time and drop them through the right-hand slot" (pointing). After examinee has done six or eight, say: "All right. Now try a few with the left hand, dropping them through this other slot."

When about the same number have been tried with the left hand, say: "All right; that's good for practice." Examiner pulls out the drawer and removes cards from bins, placing them, backs up, in the appropriate racks, making certain that they are lined up evenly. "Now do *all* of these," point-

[1] Frazier used cards with blank faces, to avoid possible distraction. These blank-faced cards are rarely stocked by dealers and are hard to secure; but it is improbable that rate of manipulation is appreciably affected by designs on the faces of the cards.

ing to the proper card-rack, "with your right [preferred] hand. Try to do them just as quickly as you can, one at a time. All ready? Go ahead!" The watch is started as the examinee touches the slot with the first card, and stopped as the last card drops through. Record the elapsed time.

Without removing these cards from the bin, say: "All right. Now try it with the other hand and see if you can do it just as fast." Record time as before.

Remove cards from bin, placing one set on the table. Examiner rearranges one set, and indicates that examinee may help by rearranging the other. When cards are again in position, examiner says: "Now we are going to do the same thing right over again. See if you can do it even faster than you did it the first time. Right hand first." Record the time. Repeat with the left hand.

Remove cards and rearrange them in position. Say: "This time we are going to try using both hands together, like this." Demonstrate the motion of picking up cards one in each hand, and dropping them through their respective slots simultaneously. Ask the examinee to try a few for practice. After he has tried six or eight cycles, remove cards from bin, arrange them, and say, "Now do them all just like that. Remember to do them as quickly as you can." Record time as before.

Replace cards in racks. Say: "Now here is the last thing that we do with these cards. This time we do it alternately. We pick up a card with *one* hand" (demonstrating the motion), "while we are dropping a card through the slot with the *other* hand, like this." Demonstrate three or four cycles. "Now try a few of them for practice; first right, then left, then right, then left, and so on." Permit practice with at least a dozen cards with each hand and as many as twenty if examinee seems to have special difficulty either in understanding what is wanted or in adapting himself to the alternating cycle. Replace cards in position and say: "Now do all of them in that same way, as quickly as you can." Record time taken.

Note on the test record any aspect of the performance which deviates markedly from the usual—especially with regard to unevenness of rhythm on the Alternating Test or any serious tendency to jam the cards through the slot.

Scoring.—Five scores are computed:

1. *Average Right:* Average time of two trials with *preferred* hand.
2. *Average Left:* Average time of two trials with *other* hand.
3. *Together:* Time.
4. *Alternating:* Time.
5. *Total:* Sum of the times on all six trials.

A sixth score—the difference between Average Right and Average Left —is sometimes noted, a small rather than a large difference having been found to be desirable; but the use of this score is not advocated because of its low reliability.

TABLE XXIV. NORMS

Based on Scores of 366 Young Women Applicants for Factory Work

Av. Right	*Av. Left*	*Together*	*Alternating*	*Total*	*Centile rank*
	Raw scores in seconds				
79	83	104	112	554	90
83	88	109	116	578	80
84	89	111	119	589	75
86	91	113	121	596	70
88	93	116	125	610	60
90	96	119	129	622	50
92	98	122	133	637	40
94	101	125	137	641	30
96	103	128	139	662	25
98	104	130	142	673	20
103	109	136	150	699	10

The Standard Error of Measurement is about three and a half seconds for Average Right and for Average Left; less than five seconds for both hands together and for the alternating test; and fourteen seconds for Total Score.

Interpretation.—A candidate who consistently scores above the fiftieth centile is more likely to show manual versatility in learning to do manipulative operations at the bench than one who does very well on one or two of the tests, but poorly on the others.

Of the five scores, the first (time with the preferred hand) and the fifth (total time) are the most nearly related to subsequent performance in an occupation requiring manual versatility. Even this relation, however, is not close, so that it is desirable to consider all five of the scores, and also the candidate's standing in other manual tests as suggested in Chapter X. When several of these tests have been given (*e.g.* card-dropping, card-wrapping, card-sorting and assembling, and pin-placing), the number of the tests in which the median score is exceeded furnishes a useful measure of manual versatility.[2]

[2] Frazier compared in this way the means of "satisfactory" and "below-satisfactory" employees in an experimental population of 115 young women operatives engaged in paper-box-making, and found a difference ratio 4.8 times its standard error. When the scores in the tests were weighted according to their several difference ratios and combined by addition, the difference between the means of the criterion groups was 5.3 times its standard error. The difference ratio for each of the five card-dropping tests, together with the mean score, Standard Deviation, reliability, and Standard Error of Measurement, are as follows:

	Av. Right	*Av. Left*	*Together*	*Alternating*	*Total*
Mean	88.8	94.3	116.5	130.0	612.3
Standard deviation	7.2	8.4	9.7	12.2	43.0
Reliability	.75	.83	.76	.85	.89
$\sigma_{(M)}$ (Raw scores)	3.60	3.46	4.75	4.73	14.26
Difference ratio	3.67	3.22	3.23	3.02	4.04

DISTRIBUTOR:

The table, with slots, card-racks, and bins, can be made to specifications in any shop. Slots and card-racks should be of the precise dimensions specified. Other dimensions may be less exactly approximated. Good linen-finish playing cards, size 2½ x 3½, can be readily obtained.

I. E. R. ASSEMBLY TEST FOR GIRLS (SHORTENED FORM)

H. A. TOOPS'S TEST, REVISED BY EMILY T. BURR AND ZAIDA M. METCALFE

As a measure of a girl's aptitude for working with her hands, Toops's battery of eleven manual tests known as the I. E. R. Mechanical Assembly Test for Girls has been used in schools and vocational bureaus since its publication by the Institute of Educational Research in 1923. Each of the tasks calls for reproducing a model. Most of them call for dexterity of fingers, manual versatility and appreciation of simple spatial relations of objects, rather than for much mechanical ingenuity; and so it is quite appropriate that common usage has dropped the term "Mechanical" from the name of the battery. It is more useful as a measure of manual than of mechanical aptitudes.

The test can be given individually or to a group. Individual administration, however, is strongly recommended because only so is it possible closely to observe a girl's ways of working, her clumsiness or deftness with different sorts of materials, and her personal attitudes toward the different kinds of tasks—information which may be even more valuable to a counselor than the numerical scores.

In its earlier form the test was given with a forty-five-minute time limit. Scoring and replacement of materials ready for the next examinee required about fifteen minutes more. When given individually without time limit, it took some girls nearly three hours. By eliminating four of the sub-tests which were found to contribute least to the total result or which were particularly time-consuming, difficult to score, not very reliable or otherwise unsatisfactory, Burr and Metcalfe (2) have shortened the test by half without loss of differentiating value.

Standard models and the materials for reproducing them, together with scoring sheets and instructions, are obtainable from the distributor.

The shortened scale includes these items:

1. The original sub-test B, insertion of tape; and C, making a rosette—both of which are operations similar to simple factory jobs in assembling.

2. Sub-test D, cross stitch; and G, the sewing of a piece of tape on a strip of unbleached muslin—tests giving an indication of a girl's facility with the needle.

3. Sub-test F, assembling a chain of clips; and I, which involves wrapping a piece of string about a section of cardboard in a prescribed manner—both tasks analogous to certain industrial processes in difficult assembling.

4. Sub-test K, paper cutting or trimming—an operation corresponding to several tasks frequently performed in factories.

This scale is not a substitute for a job-operation test on a specific task, but is useful in appraising a girl's ability to work with her hands at tasks more or less resembling these.

Administration.—When the test is given to a group, each girl should have a desk or three feet of space at a table upon which to work. Separate desks or benches are preferable, for then the girls are less tempted to watch their neighbors at work.

Distribute one test-box and one scoring-sheet to each girl. Have them fill out the information called for at the top of the scoring-sheet, and then fold it lengthwise through the middle and place beneath the box, out of the way.

Give the following instructions: "When you open your boxes (wait for the signal) you will find a pair of scissors and some envelopes. Open the first envelope which has a big letter B on it, and put together the parts you find there so that they will look just like the sample. Then take the parts in envelope C and put them together so that they will look just like the sample. Then do the other envelopes one after the other. Do not spend too long on any one package, but work as fast as you can and do your work neatly. Ready! Open your boxes, find your scissors, and begin on envelope B. Thread the tape so that it will look just like the sample."

At this point note the time to the second. Note the time at which each girl finishes. About half of them complete the seven sub-tests in less than thirty minutes. If conditions of administration require use of a time limit, allow exactly 30 minutes. Give the signal, "Stop! Put all your parts, together with the scraps, back into your box, and close it quickly."

Most examiners when giving the test to one girl at a time, will prefer to note how long it takes her to do each task, and will permit trial of all seven tasks.

Scoring.—When the finished pieces of work are compared with the models, scores for quality of performance are given according to the following schedule of credits:

Test B. *Inserting tape.*	Credits
Correct in all particulars	10
Correct except that one hole in end is not threaded	8
Correct except that one hole in body is skipped	8
Correct except that tape is twisted in not more than three spaces	8
Correct except that tape is twisted in more than three spaces	5
If more than one of these errors has been made, or any other combination used, or the test not attempted, score	0

(The only possible scores are 0, 5, 8, or 10.)

Test C. *Making rosette.*	
Correct in all particulars	10
Correct except for the hard knot	8
Correct except that one pair of threads is twisted	6
If both these errors are made, or if there is any other error	0

Test D. *Cross-stitch.*

If precisely like sample—cross-stitching begun at the right corner, corners turned correctly, all stitches in the corners of the squares, no puckering, no loose thread, fastened or knotted securely...... 10

Partial credits

For placing the 7 X's on the face of the cloth all on the darkest squares 2

On the reverse side of the cloth, for doing correctly the three squares at the corner 2

For doing correctly the other squares on the reverse side of the cloth 2

For fastening or knotting thread securely 1

For neatness .... 1, 2, or 3

(The maximum credits for neatness are reduced by 1, 2, or 3 points if the work is puckered; by 1, 2, or 3 points if stitches are not in corners of squares; by 1 or 2 points if thread is too loose.)

Test F. *Assembling chain of clips.*

All six clips properly joined (*i.e.*, single end of each clip linked through double end of next clip)........ 10

If not all connections are made in this way, allow for *each* connection properly made 2

If each connection is made through a single instead of a double strand 2

Test G. *Tape-sewing.*

Product like model in all respects 10

Partial credits

Tape doubled over evenly, both sides equal in amount........ 1

Tape holds at all points when pulled 4

Stitches in straight line and uniform in size .... 1 or 2

Stitches spaced uniformly 1

Stitches small, like model 1

Thread properly knotted or securely fastened 1

Test I. *Card-wrapping.*

Product like model in all respects 10

Partial credits

For crosses correctly made within the lines, one credit each up to a maximum of 7

For making both knots within the lines 1

For bows correctly made within the lines, one credit each; total 2

Test K. *Trimming paper.*

I. If the cutting has been done between the boundary lines, give one credit for each space between adjoining numbers in which neither line has been cut. Maximum score 10

II. If, instead of cutting *between* the boundary lines, a consistent ef-

fort has been made to cut *on* one of these lines, score 2
Also, in this instance, give partial credits for precise trimming of the several parts of the strip as follows:
For following closely the straight lines and curves .... 1 or 2
For each of the three sharp concave corners on left side correctly turned, one credit; total 3
For cutting concave curl and following line for one inch on each side of angle .... 1 or 2
For cutting both convex corners on right side and one inch each side of each corner 1
Maximum score 10

Maximum total score for all seven tests 70

Interpretation.—Burr and Metcalfe have tentatively adopted the following standards for use in the Vocational Adjustment Bureau as aids in interpreting scores:

Girls and women who score at least 50 per cent of the maximum on Tests B and C (inserting tape and making rosette) are deemed to be possible candidates for simple assembly jobs, or for training which prepares for such work.

Fifty per cent of the maximum on Tests F and I (Clip-chain and Card-wrapping) is the minimum score expected of candidates to be trained for more difficult assembly jobs.

Fifty per cent of the maximum on Tests D and G (Cross-stitch and Tape-sewing) is a critical score for candidates to be trained for sewing.

A score of less than 6 on Test K (Paper-trimming) indicates serious deficiency in eye-hand coordination. This test has proved to be one of the most useful in the battery. It not only requires motor control, good eyesight and ability to observe carefully, but also ability to concentrate on a manual task and to persist in it. This test is therefore construed as furnishing a measure of a girl's aptitude for manual employment, and, together with the other tests in the battery, gives clues as to the kind of manual work for which she should prepare.

If the score on Test K is low, performance on the other tests must be exceptionally good to compensate for this deficiency.

A total score below 38 on this revision of the Assembly Test for Girls has been found to indicate unsuitability for factory work of any sort.

Distributor:

C. H. Stoelting Company, Chicago.

References:

1. H. A. Toops, *Tests for Vocational Guidance of Children 13 to 16.* Teachers College Contributions to Education No. 136. New York: 1923.

2. Emily T. Burr and Zaida M. Metcalfe, "A Practical Form of the Girls' Mechanical Assembly Test." Unpublished manuscript, to appear in the *Journal of Applied Psychology*, Vol. 20, January, 1937.

IV

TESTS OF MECHANICAL APTITUDE

Minnesota Mechanical Assembly Test

Patterned after the well-known Stenquist Mechanical Assembling Test, the Minnesota Mechanical Assembly Test measures a person's ability to put together the parts of mechanical devices; for example, a bicycle bell, an expansion nut, a die-holder. Thirty-three disassembled mechanical contrivances are used, a larger number of items than Stenquist specified. The parts are conveniently placed in the compartments of trays called Boxes A, B, and C. A specified time is allowed for putting together each device. Each item correctly assembled within the time allotted receives a score of 10, and partial credit is given in proportion to the amount of work correctly done.

Facility in correctly assembling these devices is related to mechanical intelligence. It has been construed as one indication of aptitudes for such trades as woodworker, ironworker, machinist, toolmaker, sheet-metal worker, and auto mechanic. When given in combination with other tests in junior high school, it improves considerably the accuracy with which quality of work in shop courses can be predicted.

This test should not be used for individual diagnosis unless all three boxes are administered. This takes a little more than an hour. If the standard procedure is rigidly and skillfully followed, the test has a satisfactory reliability when taken by boys, but is less reliable with adults, since previous familiarity with mechanical contrivances affects the score to an appreciable extent. The test is really too easy for mechanically inclined men, and too difficult for many women.

Administration and scoring are more complicated than with many tests, and require a good deal of preliminary practice on the part of the examiner. The following detailed directions are taken from pages 11 to 17 of *A Manual of Selected Occupational Tests* (2).

Say: "In this box you will find some common mechanical things that have all been taken apart. Each compartment contains all the parts belonging to an object. Take the parts and put them together as you think they should be. In this position the cover forms a tray in which to work.

"You will be allowed a certain amount of time to work on each object. If you have not finished an object when time is called, leave it and go to the next one. If you finish an object before time is called, start to work on the next one. Work on them in the order in which they are placed in the box.

"Work as fast as you can, but do not break the parts. When you finish an object, or when you are instructed to do so, go to the next one in the box. Do you understand what you are to do?"

If questions are asked at this time, the examiner should re-read the directions, calling attention to the point in question. If anyone still fails to understand, the necessary explanations should again be made.

When all indicate that they understand the directions, the examiner says, "Ready, go!" At the same time he points to compartment number 1 in the box. As soon as the time is up for the first object, he points to number 2 and says, "Go on to number 2." When the time for number 2 is up, he points to number 3 and says, "Go on to number 3." This procedure is followed throughout the test. If anyone completes the box before time is called, he may be permitted to go back and change any of the work he has already done.

Table XXV shows how much time is to be allowed for assembling each article. In the first column the objects are numbered to correspond to their positions in their respective boxes, and in the second column the names of the objects are given. The third column shows the amount of time to be given to each object, and the fourth column shows how the total amount of time is distributed over the entire series. This column, the cumulative time record, is the one the examiner uses in timing the test. For example, if the subjects are working with Box A, the examiner says, when the stop-watch indicates 35 seconds, "Go on to number 2"; when the watch indicates 1 minute and 35 seconds, "Go on to number 3"; and so on throughout the test.

When the time is up, the examiner says, "Stop work. Close your box."

The boxes should be moved about as little as possible. Assembled objects may fall apart if the boxes are handled carelessly. There are no fixed time limits for the rest periods between work on Boxes A, B, and C. As a rule, the time required for removing the box that has just been used, and replacing it with the next one, constitutes a long enough rest period.

Directions for Scoring.—Before attempting to score the test, the examiner should be thoroughly familiar with the correct way of assembling each object. The best way to gain the necessary knowledge is to consult a skilled mechanic and, under his direction, to put the parts together and take them apart until complete familiarity with the material is attained. In the instructions for scoring the objects in the test the correct manner of assembling each object is described. This information, however, is not intended to take the place of the knowledge gained by actual experience in assembling and disassembling the objects.

Each object which is correctly assembled receives a score of 10. If the object is not completely assembled, but is correctly assembled in part, it is given credit in proportion to the amount of work correctly done. The correct assembling of each object requires a definite number of connections. (The word "connection" will be used to denote the putting together of

TABLE XXV

TIME LIMITS ON THE OBJECTS IN BOXES A, B, AND C OF THE MINNESOTA MECHANICAL ASSEMBLY TEST

Number of object	*Name of object*	*Time per object in seconds*	*Total Elapsed Time Minutes*	*Seconds*
	Box A (18 minutes)			
1	Expansion nut	35	..	35
2	Hose pinch clamp	60	1	35
3	Hunt paper clip	65	2	40
4	Wooden clothespin	70	3	50
5	Linked chain	110	5	40
6	Bottle-stopper	125	7	45
7	Push-button door bell	170	10	35
8	Bicycle bell	195	13	50
9	Corbin rim lock	250	18	0
10	Coin purse*	...	..	..
	Box B (21 minutes, 5 seconds)			
1	Safety razor	45	..	45
2	Monkey wrench	45	1	30
3	Ringstand clamp	65	2	35
4	Test-tube holder	100	4	15
5	Spark plug	100	5	55
6	Inside caliper	200	9	15
7	Electric plug and wire	210	12	45
8	Clover-leaf coin purse*	...	..	..
9	Handle for iron	500	21	5
10	Mouse trap*	...	..	..
	Box C (16 minutes)			
1	Haemostat	100	1	40
2	Die-holder	20	2	0
3	Pliers	45	2	45
4	Electric-light socket	45	3	30
5	Wing nut	25	3	55
6	Glass drawer-knob	25	4	20
7	Rope-coupler	45	5	5
8	Kettle-cover knob	45	5	50
9	Lock nut	50	6	40
10	Ford magneto-post	50	7	30
11	Petcock	50	8	20
12	Hose clamp	60	9	20
13	Radio switch	70	10	30
14	Pencil-sharpener	80	11	50
15	Air-gauge valve	115	13	45
16	Metal pencil	135	16	0

* Not included in the present series.

any two parts of an object.) The principle on which the scoring is based is as follows: the score of a partially assembled object is to 10 as the number of correct connections in the partially assembled object is to the number of connections in the completely assembled object. For example, if three correct connections are made in an object requiring five connections, the score is 6.

The following key shows how an object requiring a given number of connections is scored. The figures in the first column represent the number of connections required by the various objects in the test; the possible scores from 10 to 0 are arranged across the top of the table above the horizontal line; the other figures represent the possible numbers of correct connections in incompletely or incorrectly assembled objects. The score for an object is discovered by finding in the first column the number of connections required for the completely assembled object, reading across the table to the figures representing the number of connections actually made, and reading at the top of the column the score for the object. For instance, if two connections are made in an object requiring four connections, the score may be found by beginning with the figure 4 in the first column, reading across the indicated row to the figure 2, and reading the score 5 at the top of the column.

	Score										
Number of connections	10	9	8	7	6	5	4	3	2	1	0
6........	6		5	4		3	2		1		0
5........	5		4		3		2		1		0
4........	4			3		2			1		0
3........	3				2			1			0
2........	2					1					0
1........	1										0

This is the general principle upon which the scoring is based. Directions for scoring the particular objects are given below.

Box A

1. Expansion nut

Number of connections to be made 3

Possible scores 0, 3, 6, 10

The three connections to be made are: (1) placing the smaller washer on the bolt with its larger end near the head of the bolt; (2) putting on the larger washer so that it fits down over the sides of the smaller washer; (3) screwing the nut on the bolt below the second washer so that both washers are held on the bolt.

Points to be especially noted are: (1) that the objects are put on the bolt in the order indicated; (2) that neither washer is put on the bolt upside down; and (3) that both washers, though they fit together properly, are not placed on the bolt upside down.

2. Hose pinch clamp

Number of connections to be made..................1

Possible scores 0, 10

The one connection to be made is the insertion of the lever so that the free arm of the clamp is held down by the lever. No credit is given if the lever is upside down.

3. Hunt paper-clip
 Number of connections to be made 2
 Possible scores 0, 5, 10

The two connections to be made are inserting the two handles. Each handle must be pushed into the slot as far as it will go, so that the convex surfaces are on the outside and the concave surfaces face each other.

Points to be especially noted are: (1) that the handles are pushed into the slot so that the grooves on the jaws are completely inside the spring, and (2) that neither handle is wrong side out.

4. Wooden clothespin
 Number of connections to be made 2
 Possible scores 0, 5, 10

The two connections to be made are: (1) placing the two wooden parts so that they face each other correctly; and (2) inserting the spring so that the coil fits into the inside notches and so that the ends fit into the outside grooves. The spring must be inserted in exactly the manner indicated.

5. Linked chain
 Number of connections to be made 5
 Possible scores 0, 2, 4, 6, 8, 10

The five connections to be made are those involved in fastening the six links together so that they form a straight, continuous chain. The connection between any two adjacent links, A and B, is made by drawing one link, A, through the two loops of the other link, B, so that the band between the loops of link A curves around the ends of the two loops of link B.

Points to be especially noted are: (1) that all the links are placed end to end in the manner described; (2) that no fastening is made by passing one link through another so that the band between the loops of one passes around the band between the loops of another; and (3) that no fastening is made by clamping the curved band of one link between the loops of the adjacent link.

6. Bottle-stopper
 Number of connections to be made 3
 Possible scores 0, 3, 6, 10

The three connections to be made are: (1) passing the piece of wire containing no loop beneath the semicircular projection on the top of the stopper; (2) fastening this piece of wire to the one having a single loop at each side by passing the ends of the first piece through these loops; and (3) fastening the wire having the single loops to the piece having double loops by passing its ends through the double loops, so that the double loops face in the same direction as the single loops.

A point to be noted especially is that the third piece of wire is attached in the manner described, and does not face in the opposite direction.

7. Push-button door bell
 Number of connections to be made....................3
 Possible scores..............................0, 3, 6, 10

The three connections to be made are: (1) placing the button in the dome-shaped top so that its extended base is inside the top and the rest of the button protrudes through the hole; (2) placing the fiber base in the center of the metal base so that the contact will be inside; (3) inserting the metal base properly and fastening it to the top.

The points to be noted especially are: (1) that the button is not put in upside down; (2) that the metal base is not put in upside down; (3) that the metal base is not merely put in place without being fastened to the top; (4) that the fiber base is inserted so that the contact is inside.

8. Bicyle bell
 Number of connections to be made....................4
 Possible scores..............................0, 2, 5, 7, 10

The four connections to be made are: (1) fastening the lever to the part near the opening in the rim and attaching the spring to the hook in the base; (2) placing the cog on the post opposite the one to which the lever is attached, with the notched disc uppermost; (3) placing the double clapper on the center post so that the cogs are engaged; (4) screwing the cover to the center post.

The points to be noted especially are: (1) that the lever is not upside down; (2) that the spring is not unhooked or attached to the wrong post; (3) that the cog is not upside down; (4) that the double clapper is not upside down.

9. Corbin rim lock
 Number of connections to be made....................5
 Possible scores..............................0, 2, 4, 6, 8, 10

The five connections to be made are: (1) fitting in the smaller metal plate so that the perforation slips over the post in the base and the curved side fits around the center post; (2) placing the spring so that one end fits between the projections on the rim and the other catches the projection on the plate; (3) inserting the larger metal plate so that the slot slides over the center part and the projection makes the proper engagement with the projection on the smaller metal plate; (4) placing the cover so that the two sides of the keyhole match; (5) fastening the whole together by screwing the bolt through the cover and into the center post.

Points to be noted are: (1) that the spring is properly attached; (2)

that the cover is not upside down; (3) that the small parts, the spring and bolt, are not left out or are not merely placed inside without being properly attached.

10. Coin purse (not included in the present series)

Box B

1. Safety razor

Number of connections to be made....................3

Possible scores 0, 3, 6, 10

The three connections to be made are: (1) placing the blade on the top plate so that the center post of the plate passes through the slot; (2) placing the notched underplate so that the center post of the top plate passes through the middle hole and so that the two projections pass through the slot in the blade and the small slots in the top plate; (3) screwing the handle to the center post so that all the parts are held together firmly.

Points to be noted in scoring are: (1) that no departures are made from the order indicated; and (2) that the notched plate is not upside down.

2. Monkey wrench

Number of connections to be made...................2

Possible scores 0, 5, 10

The two connections to be made are: (1) inserting the head into the handle so that the jaws are properly matched and so that the screw fits the notches on the crosspieces of the handle; (2) placing the nut on the screw between the crosspieces.

Points to be noted in scoring are: (1) that the head is not reversed in position; (2) that the screw fits into the notches properly; (3) that the nut is between the crosspieces, not above or below them.

3. Ringstand clamp

Number of connections to be made...................2

Possible scores 0, 5, 10

The two connections to be made are: (1) putting the screw through the hole in the small end of the clamp; and (2) placing the rod in the angle of the trough so that it is held in place by the screw.

The points to be noted in scoring are: (1) that the screw is not put through the hole in the wrong end of the clamp; and (2) that the rod is not put through either of the holes or through both holes.

4. Test-tube holder

Number of connections to be made..................5

Possible scores 0, 2, 4, 6, 8, 10

The five connections to be made are: (1) placing the arms so that they face each other properly; (2) inserting the cotter pin so that it passes through the four small perforations (two in each arm); (3) placing the rod through the two larger holes in the arms; (4) placing the spring on the rod so that it is between the arms; (5) placing the thumbscrew on the projecting part of the rod so that the whole will be held together.

Points to be especially noted are: (1) that the spring is between two arms, not outside either of them; (2) that the rod passes through the perforations in both arms. No credit is subtracted if the cotter pin is not spread.

5. Spark plug
   Number of connections to be made 5
   Possible scores 0, 2, 4, 6, 8, 10

The five connections to be made are: (1) inserting the firing pin inside the porcelain casing properly; (2) screwing on the smaller nut so that the porcelain casing is held firmly; (3) screwing on the thumb nut so that its smaller disc is in contact with the thumb nut; (4) placing the smaller part of the metal casing so that the part containing the screw thread is caught by the projecting part of the porcelain casing; (5) screwing the larger metal casing on the smaller metal casing.

Points to be noted in scoring are: (1) that the thumb nut is not upside down; (2) that the positions of the two nuts are not interchanged; (3) that the porcelain case is not upside down; (4) that the firing pin is not upside down; (5) that the two parts of the metal casing are screwed together; (6) that the nuts are not placed inside the metal casing.

6. Inside caliper
   Number of connections to be made 5
   Possible scores 0, 2, 4, 6, 8, 10

The five connections to be made are: (1) placing the caliper arms so that they face each other properly and so that the rod terminating in a screw passes through the metal loop attached to the caliper arm; (2) placing the pivot washer between the two arms so that it fits into the notches which face each other; (3) placing the circular lock so that its ends fit into the outside notches on the caliper arms, holding the arms together; (4) placing the washer on the rod so that its rounded end is in contact with the metal loop; (5) screwing on the thumb nut so that the smaller end is in contact with the washer.

Points to be noted in scoring are: (1) that the washer is in the position described and not reversed; (2) that the thumb nut is in the position described and not reversed; (3) that the rod attached to one arm passes through the loop on the other arm and is not left dangling.

7. Electric plug and wire
   Number of connections to be made 4
   Possible scores 0, 2, 5, 7, 10

The four connections to be made are: (1) inserting the insulated wire through the hole in the dome-shaped part of the plug so that the two free ends are inside; (2) and (3) attaching each wire end to its appropriate screw, winding the wire around the screw and turning the screw down tightly; and (4) pushing the two parts of the plug together so that the metal projections on one go through the proper perforations in the other. A point to be especially noted is that the two wire ends are properly attached.

8. Clover-leaf coin purse (not included in the present series)

9. Handle for Iron

Number of connections to be made 5
Possible scores 0, 2, 4, 6, 8, 10

The connections to be made are: (1) placing the metal piece to which the wooden knob is attached in the metal base so that it is pivoted in the proper groove and so that the projecting part passes through the proper opening in the base: (2) placing the flat metal spring so that it holds down the pivoted end of the metal piece to which the knob is attached and so that its perforation matches the perforation in the metal base, permitting the screw to go through both holes; (3) placing the curved wooden handle so that the ends fit into the circular depressions in the metal base; (4) inserting the screw at one end so that it passes through the perforations in the metal base and in the flat spring and is screwed into the wooden handle; (5) inserting the other screw so that it passes through the perforation in the metal base and is screwed into the wooden handle.

Points to be noted in scoring are: (1) that the flat spring is not left out; (2) that one of the screws is not placed through the perforation in the projecting part of the metal piece attached to the wooden knob; and (3) that the flat spring is not screwed on below the metal base. If no correct connections are made except that the handle is correctly placed and is screwed at both ends, two correct connections are counted and a score of 4 is given, one connection for the proper placing of the handle and the other for the proper insertion of one screw. One screw is incorrectly inserted since it does not pass through the flat spring.

10. Mouse trap (not included in the present series)

Box C

1. Haemostat

Number of connections to be made 2
Possible scores 0, 5, 10

The two connections to be made are: (1) placing the bolt in the arm containing the larger perforation so that the head fills the depressed disc; and (2) attaching the other arm by driving the screw through the proper perforation.

A point to be noted in scoring is that the two arms face each other properly.

2. Die-holder

Number of connections to be made 1

Possible scores 0, 10

There is only one connection to be made, namely, screwing the unattached part to the only screw-thread on the instrument.

3. Pliers

Number of connections to be made 3

Possible scores 0, 3, 6, 10

The three connections are: (1) placing the bolt in the arm with the smaller perforation so that the head is on the outside surface of that arm; (2) placing the bolt through the perforation in the other arm so that the two arms face each other properly; and (3) screwing the nut to the end of the bolt so that the parts are held in place.

A point to be noted in scoring is that the bolt goes through from the side having the smaller hole.

4. Electric-light socket

Number of connections to be made 2

Possible scores 0, 5, 10

The two connections to be made are: (1) inserting the porcelain part so that the two plugs on its sides fit into the grooves in the fiber base; and (2) screwing on the dome-shaped top so that the wires project through the hole in its center.

A point to be noted in scoring is that the porcelain part is inserted properly with the plugs in the proper grooves, and not put in loosely so that the top cannot be screwed down tightly.

5. Wing nut

Number of connections to be made 2

Possible scores 0, 5, 10

The connections to be made are: (1) placing the circular disc on the rod terminating in a screw thread; and (2) screwing on the nut so that the handles turn away from the head of the rod.

A point to be noted in scoring is that the nut is not turned upside down so that the handles turn toward the head rather than away from it.

6. Glass drawer-knob

Number of connections to be made 2

Possible scores 0, 5, 10

The connections to be made are: (1) placing the knob on the bolt so that the larger part of the knob is next to the thread of the bolt; and (2) screwing the nut on the screw thread of the bolt.

A point to be noted is that the knob is not reversed—i.e., that the smaller end is not next to the head of the bolt.

7. Rope coupler

Number of connections to be made 3

Possible scores 0, 3, 6, 10

The connections to be made are: (1) inserting the U-shaped bolt so that the ends project from the flat side of the base; (2) and (3) screwing the two nuts on the two ends of the bolt.

Points to be noted in scoring are: (1) that the bolt is not inserted upside down; and (2) that the bolt goes through both holes, not merely through one.

8. Kettle-cover knob

Number of connections to be made 4
Possible scores 0, 2, 5, 7, 10

The connections to be made are: (1) placing the bolt through the wooden knob so that the larger end of the knob is next to the head of the bolt; (2) placing one of the tin discs on the bolt so that its convex surface touches the wooden knob; (3) placing the other tin disc on the bolt so that its concave surface faces the concave surface of the other disc; and (4) screwing the nut to the bolt so that it is in contact with the convex surface of the second disc and holds all the parts tightly together.

The points to be noted in scoring are: (1) that the wooden knob is not upside down; and (2) that the discs face each other properly.

9. Lock nut

Number of connections to be made 2
Possible scores 0, 5, 10

The connections to be made are: (1) screwing on the nut so that its smooth surface is toward the head of the bolt; and (2) pushing the cotter pin through the perforation near the end of the bolt. The nut must be screwed down just far enough so that when the cotter pin is inserted, the nut cannot be turned.

Points to be noted in scoring are: (1) that the nut is not turned upside down; (2) that the nut is not put on outside the cotter pin; and (3) that the nut is in contact with the cotter pin.

10. Ford magneto-post

Number of connections to be made 3
Possible scores 0, 3, 6, 10

The connections to be made are: (1) inserting the coil in the base so that the screw protrudes from the narrow end of the base; and (2) and (3) screwing on the two nuts so that their flat surfaces are in contact and so that all the parts are held together.

Points to be noted are: (1) that both nuts are screwed on and in proper positions; and (2) that the coil is not inserted upside down.

11. Petcock

Number of connections to be made 3
Possible scores 0, 3, 6, 10

The connections to be made are: (1) inserting the rod to which the handle is attached so that it fits down snugly in the perforation in the base; (2) placing the washer so that it is flat against the broad side in contact with the base; and (3) screwing the small bolt into the proper perforation so that all the parts are held together firmly.

Points to be noted especially are: (1) that the washer is not upside down; and (2) that the washer has not been left out.

12. Hose clamp

Number of connections to be made 3

Possible scores 0, 3, 6, 10

The connections to be made are: (1) attaching the curved strip containing a row of perforations to the projecting hook of the large circular metal piece; (2) placing the bolt through the two rounded perforations in the projecting ends; and (3) screwing the nut to the bolt so that the whole instrument is held together.

Points to be noted especially are: (1) that the two parts of the clamp are properly attached; and (2) that the bolt goes through the proper perforations.

13. Radio switch

Number of connections to be made 6

Possible scores 0, 2, 4, 5, 7, 8, 10

The order in which the connections are to be made is: (1) placing the metal pointer next to the rubber knob on the bolt; (2) placing the large burr next to the metal pointer; (3) placing the spring next; (4) placing the washer between the spring and the burr; (5) and (6) placing the two similar burrs next to one another, so that the one locks the other.

A point to be noted especially is that the turned flange on the metal pointer is not placed so that it points toward the rubber knob.

14. Pencil-sharpener

Number of connections to be made 2

Possible scores 0, 5, 10

The connections to be made are: (1) inserting the blade so that the rounded end of the metal fits into the rounded end of the groove in the base, thus leaving the cutting edge of the blade facing the remaining groove in the base; and (2) placing the bolt through the perforation in the blade and screwing it into the depression in the base. The blade must be placed exactly in the position described.

15. Air gauge valve

Number of connections to be made 3

Possible scores 0, 3, 6, 10

The connections to be made are: (1) placing the spring on the plunger so that it is in contact with the broader edge of the metal band near the middle; (2) inserting the plunger from the narrower end of the valve-case, so that the spring is toward the narrower end; and (3) screwing on the smaller end of the valve-case.

Points to be noted are: (1) that the spring is not on the wrong end of the plunger; and (2) that the plunger is not put in upside down.

16. Metal pencil
    Number of connections to be made.....................3
    Possible scores.............................0, 3, 6, 10

The connections to be made are: (1) inserting the wire so that one end is pushed into the wooden part of the pencil, the looped end pushed out through the perforation in the end of the metal case; (2) attaching the ring to the projecting loop; and (3) fitting the metal case tightly to the wooden pencil.

Points to be noted are: (1) that the wire is not completely inside the metal case; (2) that the ring is not inside the metal case; and (3) that the wire is not pushed through the perforation in the metal case from the outside, so that it can be pulled out by pulling the ring.

TABLE XXVI. STANDARD NORMS FOR MEN AND WOMEN

Raw score Men	*Raw score* Women	*Standard score*	*Percentile rank*	*Letter grade*
329	308	8.00	99.86	
				(A++)
323	302	7.50	99.4	
				A+
318	289	7.00	97.7	
				A−
311	270	6.50	93.3	
				B+
302	257	6.00	84.1	
				B−
293	240	5.50	69.1	
				C+
281	225	5.00	50.0	
				C−
262	208	4.50	30.9	
				D+
245	193	4.00	15.9	
				D−
224	178	3.50	6.7	
				E+
201	148	3.00	2.3	
				E−
177	126	2.50	.6	
				(E−−)
171	114	2.00	.14	

The Standard Error of Measurement in terms of units on the Standard Scale is, for men, ± .46; for women, ± .57; and in terms of points of raw score near the middle of the scale, for men, ± 14 points; for women, ± 18 points.

Norms.—Adult norms based on the scores made by population samples of men and women representative of occupational and age distributions of workers in an urban area are given in Table XXVI. Table XXVII shows the age norms for boys.

TABLE XXVII. AGE NORMS FOR BOYS

Age Group											Centile rank	Letter grade
11	12	13	14	15	16	17	18	19	20	21 and older		
314	329	329	329	329	329	329	329	329	329	329	99.4	A+
305	316	316	316	322	324	321	327	327	327	326	97.7	A–
291	296	295	298	311	315	309	321	321	324	321	93.3	B+
270	281	281	282	295	305	298	314	314	319	312	84.1	B–
251	257	271	272	278	293	288	302	310	311	303	69.1	C+
231	232	252	257	260	276	273	287	299	299	289	50.0	C–
211	209	225	234	242	255	254	274	285	284	267	30.9	D+
184	189	199	211	221	222	232	256	259	262	238	15.9	D–
160	168	177	186	190	192	207	231	219	241	208	6.7	E+
152	156	160	164	148	147	183	200	199	230	173	2.3	E–
149	149	149	149	119	119	164	179	189	224	149	0.6	

When the test is given to boys, the Standard Error of Measurement in terms of units on the Standard Scale is ± .24, and in terms of points of raw score near the middle of the scale, ± 9.

Suggestions regarding the vocational significance of a score are found in Table XXVIII which shows in Column I the Average Standard Scores of men in six occupations; in Column II, the nearest corresponding raw scores; and in Column III, the percentage of men in the general working-population sample whose scores did not exceed these averages.

TABLE XXVIII. OCCUPATIONAL NORMS

	I	II	III
1. Machinists	5.85	300	80
2. Manual-training teachers	5.49	293	68
3. Ornamental ironworkers	5.48	293	68
4. Auto mechanics	5.42	290	66
5. Skilled manual workers	5.05	282	52
6. Machine operators (lathe, drill press, etc.)	4.98	281	49

Interpretation.—In comparing the scores made by garage mechanics with those of office clerks it was found that 70 per cent of the mechanics did better on this test than the average office clerk, while only 11 per cent of the mechanics had the verbal intelligence of the average office clerk. These occupational differences are explainable as differences in endowment only in part. Differences in experience and schooling doubtless also affect the performances of adults on both mechanical and verbal tests.

A person's verbal intelligence seems to have little relation to his performance in mechanical assembly tests. Brightness in abstract school subjects does not imply mechanical aptitudes; neither does dullness. In the distribution of human endowments, the so-called law of compensation has not been found to hold. To make trade schools the dumping-ground for students whose only qualification for entrance is their inability to learn from books is nothing short of scandalous. The youths' mechanical aptitudes should first be ascertained, by reference to their achievements in pre-vocational tryout courses and their test records. Assembly tests have proved useful in such situations, as parts of a battery for ascertaining unsuspected mechanical talents and for estimating the probabilities of mastering vocational courses in which some aptness for handling mechanical contrivances is needed.

A person's score may be thought of as determined in part by his endowment of mechanical ingenuity, in part by his familiarity with mechanical devices more or less similar to these in principle. His score, then, cannot be taken as a pure measure of his mechanical intelligence, but must be appraised in the light of what is known about his previous background and opportunity for knowing about and manipulating a large variety of mechanisms. This precaution is particularly to be observed when interpreting the significance of an adult's score.

It is no less necessary to take into consideration the size of the Standard Error of Measurement—the figure which helps to estimate the chances that a person's true score may really be much larger or smaller than his obtained score. The chances are about 68 in 100 (roughly two in three) that a true score does not vary from an obtained score by more than this Standard Error. For the Minnesota Mechanical Assembly Test, the Standard Errors are as follows: for boys, ±.24; for men, ±.46; and for women, ±.57, in terms of the Standard Scale; or in terms of points of raw score near the middle of the scale, for boys, ± 9 points; for men, ± 14 points; and for women, ± 18 points.

For example, when a boy's score is 270, the chances are roughly two out of three that his true score lies between 261 and 279. But when a man makes this same score, the range of uncertainty is wider. The chances are two out of three that his true score lies somewhere between 256 and 284. The greater unreliability of the test when taken by an adult makes somewhat dubious the meaning of his score if it is neither exceptionally high nor exceptionally low.

Unless a person's performance on an assembly test of this sort is much below average and is also accompanied by other indications of lack of mechanical ability or interest, it need not discourage him from entering a mechanical occupation.

Distributor:

Marietta Apparatus Co., Marietta, Ohio. Boxes A, B, and C, $29.

References:

1. D. G. Paterson and others, *Minnesota Mechanical Ability Tests.* Minneapolis: University of Minnesota Press, 1930.

2. Helen J. Green and others, *A Manual of Selected Occupational Tests for Use in Public Employment Offices.* Minneapolis: University of Minnesota Press, 1933.

Minnesota Spatial Relations Test

The Minnesota Spatial Relations Test, patterned after H. C. Link's Form Board, uses a set of four standard form-boards (A, B, C, D), out of each of which have been cut 58 pieces of different forms and sizes. The task is to put each of these pieces in its proper space.

The test is used to measure speed and accuracy in discriminating sizes and shapes. It is suitable for testing adults, as well as pupils in the upper elementary grades and in secondary school.

A high score is taken as indicative of one of the aptitudes contributing to ability in the quick perception of sizes and forms such as is thought to be of value to sculptors, architects, designers, dressmakers, pattern-makers, sheet-metal workers, engineers, dentists, surgeons, layout men, sorters, auto mechanics, and others who manipulate objects and have to observe the spatial relations of these objects. Its use is indicated as an aid in ascertaining a person's aptitude for such an occupation; or his probability of success in a course of training or apprenticeship leading to such an occupation; or his likelihood of being able to carry a school subject such as descriptive geometry or machine design, in which ability to deal with shapes and sizes is known to be an asset. It is not known, however, how valid the test is, in making such specific vocational forecasts; and so, in interpreting the meaning of a very high or a very low score as an indication of the presence or absence of an aptitude important for a particular vocation, a counselor must rely on his own caution and good sense. He will attach little weight to a person's performance in this test in the absence of confirming evidence from other sources; but either a high or a low score is a strong hint to be on the lookout for any such confirmations.

Incidentally, this test, like other form-boards, furnishes an admirable standard situation within which to make observations regarding certain traits of personality and tendencies of behavior such as a person's systematic or unsystematic way of attack, and his energy, persistence, and self-control in such a situation.

The test is sufficiently reliable for purposes of individual diagnosis if all four form-boards are used. This takes fifteen to forty-five minutes.

Administration.—The test is administered to one person at a time. Form-board A must be given first, and the others in alphabetical order. The boards are so constructed that one set of 58 blocks is used for Boards A and B, and another set for Boards C and D. Board A is placed flush with the edge of the table, with the side labeled A farthest from the person taking the test. The blocks are placed just beyond the empty board in the positions they have in Board B. This is most easily done by placing Board B directly beyond A, putting the blocks into Board B, and then picking it up so as to leave the blocks on the table in standard position.

The following instructions are read to the examinee:

"Put these blocks in their proper places in the board. They fit easily; do not force any of them. Use one hand. You may have to turn some of the blocks around, but do not turn any of them over. Keep the black side of the blocks up. Go as fast as you can and get all of the blocks in the board. Ready? Go!"

Note the number of seconds it takes to fill the form-board.

After the examinee has finished putting the blocks in Board A, slide this board back away from him and remove it from the blocks in the manner described above. This leaves the blocks in standard position, and the test proceeds as before. A rest period of 30 seconds between trials is recommended.

Boards C and D are presented in the same manner as Boards A and B. One trial is given for each board.

Scoring.—The most reliable method is to treat the performance on Board A as a practice exercise and to use as the score the total number of seconds required to place the blocks in Boards B, C, and D. The accompanying Norms for Men and Women are in these terms. (The norms given in the references cited below, including age norms for boys in school, are, however, in terms of the number of seconds required to fill all four boards.)

Interpretation.—That this test measures one component of mechanical aptitude is indicated by the fact that 102 auto mechanics did better on the average than 82 per cent of people in general; and that the median score for 65 students of dentistry was even higher, at the ninetieth percentile of people in general.

The score is relatively independent of verbal intelligence. Performance is also largely free from the influence of past experience. Coefficients of reliability of .80 to .91 (Forms AB *vs.* CD) have been reported.

Vocational-school boys and industrial workers are not superior to academic groups in this test. This emphasizes the fact that selection for vocational training and industrial employment is based on many considerations in addition to a person's ability to discriminate shapes and sizes.

TABLE XXIX. STANDARD NORMS FOR MEN AND WOMEN

BASED ON POPULATION SAMPLES OF 498 MEN AND 232 WOMEN IN MINNEAPOLIS, ST. PAUL AND DULUTH

The standard samples are representative of the age and occupational distribution found in this area among the population reported in the 1930 Census as having gainful occupations.

Raw score (in seconds) Boards B, C, and D Men	Women	*Standard score*	*Centile rank*	*Letter grade*
				A+
608	605	7.0	97.7	
				A−
652	648	6.5	93.3	
				B+
726	758	6.0	84.1	
				B−
814	838	5.5	69.1	
				C+
916	933	5.0	50.0	
				C−
1047	1037	4.5	30.9	
				D+
1218	1156	4.0	15.9	
				D−
1442	1354	3.5	6.7	
				E+
1583	1571	3.0	2.3	
				E−

The Standard Error of Measurement in units of the Standard Scale is estimated to be, for men, ±.30; for women, ±.33.

DISTRIBUTOR:

Marietta Apparatus Co., Marietta, Ohio. Price: Boards A, B, C and D, $34.

REFERENCES:

1. Helen J. Green, Isabel R. Berman, Donald G. Paterson and M. R. Trabue, *A Manual of Selected Occupational Tests.* Minneapolis: University of Minnesota Press, 1933. (Bulletins of the Employment Stabilization Research Institute, Vol. 2, No. 3.)

2. Donald G. Paterson, Editor, *Research Studies in Individual Diagnosis.* Minneapolis: University of Minnesota Press, 1934. (Bul. E. S. R. I., Vol. 3, No. 4.)

3. D. G. Paterson, R. M. Elliott, L. D. Anderson, H. A. Toops and E. Heidbreder, *Minnesota Mechanical Ability Tests.* Minneapolis: University of Minnesota Press, 1930.

The Wiggly Blocks

JOHNSON O'CONNOR'S WORKSAMPLE NO. 5

This intriguing mechanical puzzle consists of nine wooden blocks of irregularly wavy contour. When properly assembled they fit together to make a solid rectangular block. The speed with which this is done is taken as a measure of ability to visualize structure in three dimensions, an ability indicative of aptitude for such occupations as machinist, tool and die maker, draftsman, engineer, and architect. Its originator discourages its general use, for it is difficult to administer correctly without special training; and even in experienced hands its reliability is not so high as is desired in tests for individual diagnosis.

For these reasons, the specifications,[1] directions for administering, reliabilities and norms given in the following references are not reproduced here.

The best usefulness of this test will probably be found eventually as one unit in a scale which would include similar tasks, easier and harder than this.

References:

1. Francis L. Keane and Johnson O'Connor. "A Measure of Mechanical Aptitude," *Personnel Journal*, 1927, 6: 15-24.

2. Johnson O'Connor. *Born That Way*. Baltimore: Williams and Wilkins, 1928.

3. Johnson O'Connor, *Psychometrics*. Cambridge: Harvard University Press, 1934.

4. H. H. Remmers and J. W. Schell. "Testing the O'Connor Wiggly Block Test," *Personnel Journal*, 1933, 12: 155-159.

Minnesota Paper Form-Board

REVISED BY R. LIKERT AND W. H. QUASHA

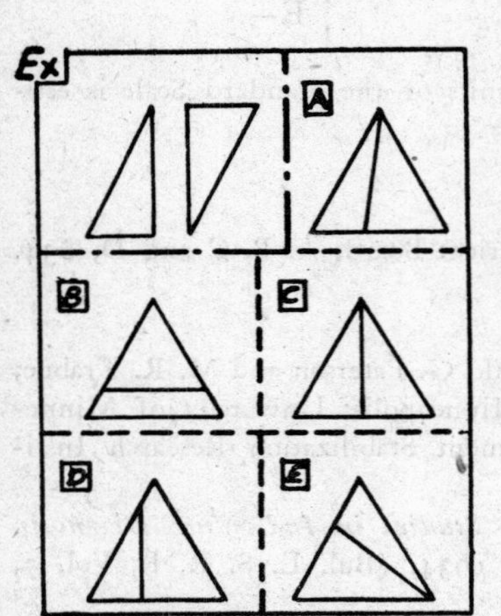

The paper form-board presents sixty-four problems similar to the one illustrated. In the upper left-hand corner of the diagram, at "Ex," are two geometrical forms. The task is to decide which one of the other five figures represents these forms placed together.

The test furnishes an indication of ability to discriminate geometrical patterns in two dimensions and mentally to manipulate such figures.

The Minnesota Paper Form-Board evolved from the Geometrical Construction Test in Army Beta and from a longer and more difficult paper form-board subsequently developed by O'Rourke. It measures, without the

[1] The exact shape of the blocks is not readily reproduced from printed specifications. Interested psychometrists and research psychologists should address Johnson O'Connor, Stevens Institute of Technology, Hoboken, N. J.

use of apparatus, somewhat the same abilities as are sampled by means of the Minnesota Spatial Relations boards and other form-boards. The Paper Form-Board does not permit manual manipulation, but it measures one component of mechanical aptitude. Of all the paper-and-pencil tests experimented with in the Minnesota investigation of mechanical abilities, the Paper Form-Board gave the most dependable data. No one test, however, is a highly valid measure of mechanical aptitude. A battery made up of the Minnesota Paper Form-Board, Spatial Relations, and Mechanical Assembly Tests was found to predict, with an efficiency 23 per cent better than chance, the quality of work done in school shop courses.

Consideration of performance on these tests and of information about interests, grades in various school subjects, and achievement outside of school, provides a fairly useful basis for judgment regarding mechanical aptitudes.

There are two forms, Series AA and Series BB. Reliability is considerably increased by administering both forms.

Administration.—Distribute the test blanks with the title page face up. When everyone has filled in the information called for on this page, say, while demonstrating how it is done:

"Turn the test over in this way without opening it. You should now have the page containing the directions and sample problems before you. Look at the directions while I read them." Then read the directions for the fore-exercise up to and including the statement, "Do these problems now." Allow about two minutes and then say: "Will those who wrote A in the box above 5 at the top of the page please raise their hands. . . . How many wrote B? . . . How many wrote D? . . . How many wrote E? . . . C is the correct answer; therefore you should have printed C in the box above 5."

If there were any who did not know that "C" was the correct answer, explain the problem more fully. Then say: "The answer to problem 6 is D, so you should have printed D above 6 at the top of the page. In problem 7, the answer is A. In problem 8, the answer is B. If your answers are not the same as I have read, raise your hands." Explain their errors to those who raise their hands, and tell them what they should have done. "Are there any questions? No questions will be answered after you have started."

Being sure that none of the examinees opens his booklet until told to do so, finish reading the directions, then show how the booklet opens and that to get to page 3 the entire booklet must be opened. Repeat: "Are there any questions?" . . . "Open your booklets and begin." Note the time. After precisely twenty minutes say: "Stop. Fold your booklet and turn it so that the page with your name is on top." Collect the booklets.

Scoring.—Key is supplied. The Score is the total number done correctly minus one-fifth the number done wrong. Omissions are counted as neither right nor wrong. After the score is totaled, count one-fifth or two-fifths as zero: count three-fifths or four-fifths as 1, etc.

TABLE XXX. TENTATIVE ADULT NORMS

Based on performance of 607 men and 449 women examined by the New York Guidance Service. From unpublished data supplied by J. E. Mayman, Supervisor.

Raw Score Men	Women	*Standard score*	*Centile rank*	*Letter grade*
56	54	7.5	99.4	
				A+
53	51	7.0	97.7	
				A−
49	46	6.5	94.3	
				B+
44	42	6.0	84.1	
				B−
40	38	5.5	69.1	
				C+
35	33	5.0	50.0	
				C−
29	27	4.5	30.9	
				D+
22	19	4.0	15.9	
				D−
16	11	3.5	6.7	
				E+
8	5	3.0	2.3	
				E−
4	3	2.5	0.6	

The Standard Error of Measurement is about ± 2.3 points, which is less than one-fourth of a unit on the Standard Scale.

Vocational and age norms are being accumulated by the authors and are supplied with the Manual of Directions. High school seniors applying for admission to a college of engineering make fewer low scores and average nearly one-half sigma higher than the above norms for men.

DISTRIBUTOR:

Psychological Corporation, 522 Fifth Avenue, New York. Series AA or BB, 100 copies, $4.

REFERENCES:

D. G. Paterson and others, *Minnesota Mechanical Ability Tests*. Minneapolis: University of Minnesota Press, 1930.

T. W. MACQUARRIE'S TEST FOR MECHANICAL ABILITY

The MacQuarrie Test for Mechanical Ability is intended to furnish a first rough indication of aptitudes for acquiring manipulative skills. It requires some ability to recognize space relations, speed of decision and of movement, hand

and eye coordination, muscular control, and visual acuity. It is a paper-and-pencil test which can be administered to an individual or to a group in about half an hour.

There are seven sub-tests, each preceded by a fore-exercise to familiarize the candidate with the tasks expected of him. These tasks are: to draw a pencil line as fast as possible through a pattern of irregularly spaced openings without touching them (thirty seconds); to put three pencil dots in each of a number of circles as fast as possible (thirty seconds); to put a dot in each of many smaller circles (thirty seconds); to copy patterns each of which consists of four connected straight lines (two and a half minutes); to identify the locations of dots in squares by reference to the corresponding positions of letters in a larger square (two minutes); to count the blocks which touch certain blocks in each of several pictured piles (two and a half minutes); and to follow with the eye, one after another, each of several numbered lines drawn irregularly through a maze-like pattern, and to identify by means of the appropriate number the end of each line (two and a half minutes).

These sub-tests, administered and scored as directed in the pamphlet of instructions which accompanies each packet of blanks, yield scores with maximum possible values as follows:

Tracing	80
Tapping	70
Dotting	33
Copying	80
Location	40
Blocks	30
Pursuit	40

The "total score" is the sum of the sub-scores divided by three.

Total score was found to correspond only very roughly with teachers' ratings of mechanical ability; but with better criteria of ability, as when pupils were required to do some mechanical work and this work was then carefully rated by judges who did not know the identity of the pupils, the correlation between test scores and ratings was much higher (.81).

Norms for each age from 10 to 20 years, as given in the pamphlet of instructions, are reproduced in Table XXXI.

TABLE XXXI. AGE NORMS

Showing the raw scores corresponding to three points on a Standard Scale, for different age groups in a large school population.

Age 10	11	12	13	14	15	16	17	18	19	20	Standard score
34	46	55	61	66	71	75	79	81	83	84	6.0
26	37	44	49	53	57	60	63	65	67	68	5.0
18	28	33	37	40	43	45	47	49	51	52	4.0

Counselors are, however, less likely to be interested in the total score than in the separate scores a person makes on each of the sub-tests. The total score masks striking individual differences in the more strictly visual and motor activities of the Tracing, Tapping, and Dotting tests, in the abilities required by the sub-tests in which visual perception of space relations is more obviously a factor, and in such verbal intelligence as is needed to grasp the instructions which, in spite of the excellent fore-exercises provided, are more likely to be only partly understood in some sub-tests, such as Copying, than in others. Certain of the sub-tests have found a place in other batteries, for instance in Viteles' Tests for the Selection of Substation Operators.

To facilitate inspection of a person's scores, a scale and table of norms for the sub-tests is given in Table XXXII. The data for this table—the scores made by 124 apprentice toolmakers, from 16 to 22 years old, in the employ of the Scovill Manufacturing Company—were supplied by Millicent Pond.

TABLE XXXII. VOCATIONAL NORMS FOR SUB-TESTS AND TOTAL SCORE

Based on performance of 124 toolmaker apprentices

Sub-tests									
1 Tracing	*2* Tapping	*3* Dotting	*4* Copying	*5* Location	*6* Blocks	*7* Pursuit	*Total score*	*Standard scale*	*Letter grades*
59	52	28	72	39	26	38	89	7.5	
									A+
55	49	26	65	37	24	34	83	7.0	
									A–
51	46	24	58	34	22	31	78	6.5	
									B+
47	43	22	51	30	19	27	72	6.0	
									B–
43	40	20	44	25	16	24	67	5.5	
									C+
39	37	18	37	21	13	20	61	5.0	
									C–
35	34	16	30	17	10	16	56	4.5	
									D+
31	31	14	23	12	7	13	50	4.0	
									D–
27	28	12	16	7	4	9	45	3.5	
									E+
23	25	10	13	3	1	6	39	3.0	
									E–
19	22	8	12	1	0	2	34	2.5	

The Standard Error of Measurement of a total score is not more than one-third of a unit on the Standard Scale—about 5 points. The sub-tests are less reliable, and a score in one of these may have a Standard Error of as much as half a unit on the Standard Scale.

It will be noted that the average total score made by this group of carefully selected learners corresponds closely to the MacQuarrie average for age 16, but that the apprentices made relatively fewer low or high scores than the school population on which MacQuarrie's norms were based. Since the toolmaker apprentice group is more homogeneous, it need not surprise a counselor to find individuals whose scores on some of the sub-tests are quite beyond the upper or lower limits shown in this table.

MacQuarrie aimed to prepare a test which would not measure intelligence. He found only negligibly low correlations (not exceeding .20) between his test scores and performances in intelligence tests. Others have since found somewhat higher correlations with intelligence. Pond, for example, has obtained for 83 of the Scovill toolmaker apprentices their scores in the Otis Higher Examination, and in several other verbal and non-verbal tests. The correlations among these tests are so interesting that they are reported in full.

Table XXXIII. Correlation Table

Showing inter-relationships between scores made by 83 toolmaker apprentices on the following:

(1) Scovill Apprentice Scale, a weighted combination of five non-verbal sub-tests in the Scovill Classification Test, plus accuracy in one test, and age.
(2) F-Score, a simple average of the four non-verbal and three verbal tests in the Scovill battery.
(3) Otis Higher Examination, Form A.
(4) Kent-Shakow Form Board.
(5) O'Connor Wiggly Block, average for three trials.
(6) MacQuarrie Test for Mechanical Ability.
(7) Schooling: years completed prior to hiring.

	Appr. Scale	*F-Score*	*Otis*	*Kent*	*O'Connor*	*MacQuarrie*	*Sch.*
1. Appr. Scale...	——	.629	.404	.219	.176	.293	
2. F-Score.......	.629	——	.793	.290	.333	.507	.635
3. Otis..........	.404	.793	——	.157	.270	.381	
4. Kent.........	.219	.290	.157	——	.501	.431	.039
5. O'Connor.....	.176	.333	.270	.501	——	.336	.050
6. MacQuarrie...	.293	.507	.381	.431	.336	——	.291
7. Schooling.....		.635		.039	.050	.291	——

P. E. ranges from .06 when r = .039 to .03 when r = .793

From Table XXXIII it will be seen that the MacQuarrie test correlates .291 with years of schooling, .293 with the Scovill Apprentice Scale, .336 with the O'Connor Wiggly Block, .381 with the Otis Higher Examination, .431 with the Kent-Shakow Form Board, and .507 with the Scovill F-Score. There are factors in common between the abilities measured by this test and those demanded by tests of both verbal and practical intelligence, and by tests like the Kent and the O'Connor, in which quick, accurate perception of relations of space and form, as well as some facility in manual manipulation, are called for.

It should be apparent that the MacQuarrie test provides only a rough indication of the degree to which a person has either manual or mechanical aptitudes. Before a counselor would venture to suggest that plans should be changed because of a high or a low score on this test, confirmatory evidence from other sources would be needed. He will, however, wish to examine the scores on the sub-tests, and also the frequency and nature of the errors in Tracing, Dotting, Copying, Location, and Blocks, for indications of possible abilities or disabilities which it would be desirable to measure more accurately or otherwise to inquire into as opportunity offers.

DISTRIBUTOR:

Southern California School Book Depository, 3636 Beverly Boulevard, Los Angeles, California. Price $1.50 a package, containing 25 copies of the test, directions, scoring key and age norms. Tryout set (5 copies, with directions), 50 cents.

REFERENCES:

1. T. W. MacQuarrie, "A Mechanical Ability Test." *Journal of Personnel Research*, 1927, 5:329-337.

2. S. D. Horning, "Testing Mechanical Abilities by the MacQuarrie Test." *Industrial Arts Magazine*, Oct., 1926.

L. J. O'Rourke's Mechanical Aptitude Tests

A wide range of familiarity with tools and their uses is generally traceable—as we saw in Chapter VI—to an interest in mechanical contrivances and an aptitude for learning to manipulate them. It follows that a well-selected sample of a person's stock of information in this field furnishes a useful indication of his mechanical aptitude.

A paper-and-pencil information test of this kind is O'Rourke's Mechanical Aptitude Test—Junior Grade. Part I is pictorial. The task is to indicate which of the pictured tools, such as a screwdriver, a wrench, and a brace, is used with each of the pictured objects, such as a nut, a bit, and a screw; also, to indicate which tools are used to do certain things, such as to thread a round hole in a piece of metal. Part II is entirely verbal. Sixty mechanical information questions are presented in multiple-choice form. This examination was originally standardized on the performances of 9,000 young men aged 15 to 24, a majority of whom had not gone beyond the elementary grades before leaving school. The percentile norms from this large group—together with directions for giving and scoring—are printed on each blank.

In selecting from among many thousands of applicants for work, laborers who were to be given opportunity to learn various trades and occupations, the Tennessee Valley Authority made use of three forms of this examination together with O'Rourke's non-language General Classification Test.

Administration.—Part I of the Mechanical Aptitudes Test has a 30-minute time limit, and Part II, a 25-minute limit; so that total administration requires about 65 minutes. Detailed directions appear on each blank.

Scoring.—Give one point for each correct answer. Final score is the number right in Part I plus four times the number right in Part II.

The maximum possible score is 342.

TABLE XXXIV. NORMS

Showing total scores corresponding to points on a Standard Scale, based on performance of 9,000 young men entering mechanical occupations.

Raw score	*Standard score*	*Centile rank*	*Letter grade*
			A+
317	7.0	97.7	
			A−
295	6.5	93.3	
			B+
265	6.0	84.1	
			B−
233	5.5	69.1	
			C+
198	5.0	50.0	
			C−
172	4.5	30.9	
			D+
145	4.0	15.9	
			D−
115	3.5	6.7	
			E

The Standard Error of Measurement has not been ascertained precisely, but is not more than ± 18 points of raw score.

Interpretation.—The distribution of scores among high-school students averages higher than the norms of Table XXXIV. Few candidates for engineering training fail to score 6.0 or better. In the TVA, on the other hand, mature workers averaged about 4.3, which is roughly one quartile lower than these norms.

A youth with a strong bent for things mechanical will have seized upon and profited by opportunities which one without such aptitudes would tend to ignore. He will know many items of which the average boy remains in ignorance. A young man's interest in and aptitude for work of an essentially mechanical sort is properly called in question if he scores below 5.0. His test performance should, however, be viewed in the light of his schooling and of the facts regarding his previous opportunities for observing and taking part in various kinds of work with tools.

Entrance standards vary widely among trade and technical schools, and employers; also, from occupation to occupation. Each counselor who makes use of this test is urged to ascertain the percentage of young men who attain any given score in the organization or the training courses for which he makes selections, or with reference to which he advises boys.

Distributor:

Educational and Personnel Publishing Co., Washington, D. C., and Psychological Corporation, 522 Fifth Ave., New York. Price, $1.50 for 30.

References:

1. Douglas Fryer, *Measurement of Interests*, Ch. VIII. New York: Henry Holt and Company, Inc., 1931.

Stenquist Mechanical Aptitude Tests I and II

J. L. Stenquist's two paper-and-pencil tests of mechanical aptitude resemble Part I of O'Rourke's Mechanical Aptitude Test in the use of pictorial materials. Test I consists of 95 problems. In each, the task is to find which of five pictures—of common tools, mechanical contrivances or parts—belongs with one of five other pictures. Test II consists partly of material similar to that of Test I and partly of questions about pictures and diagrams of machines and machine parts. These questions do not presuppose experience with the machines, but are of a general nature. They presumably call for keen perception of mechanical relations and ability to reason about them.

Many users have considered these tests helpful as indicators of interest in things mechanical; for such an interest tends to develop a fund of information on which a high score, particularly in Test I, depends. Stenquist found a median coefficient of correlation of .67 between scores and shop teachers' ratings of "general mechanical aptitude," and about the same correlation with scores in the Stenquist Assembling Test. It should, however, be noted that the authors of the *Minnesota Mechanical Ability Tests* (2) found these picture tests to be less reliable and valid than several others described in that volume.

There is a positive correlation between standing in these tests and in tests of verbal intelligence; more, indeed, than is the case with some mechanical tests. Such correlations mean that a verbally bright person is more likely than a dull one to possess marked ability of the kind here measured. There are, however, verbally stupid but mechanically clever people who can excel in tests such as these. When interpreting an individual's score, it should then be considered in relation to some measure of his verbal intelligence and scholastic aptitude, as well as to his age and his prior experience with things mechanical.

Administration.—The actual working time is 45 minutes for Test I and 50 minutes for Test II. The Manual of Directions contains full details regarding procedure in giving and scoring, together with age norms for boys from 12 to 15.

Distributor:

World Book Company, Yonkers, N. Y. Test I or II, package of 25, including scoring key, $1.30. Manual of Directions, 15 cents.

REFERENCES:

1. J. L. Stenquist, *Measurement of Mechanical Ability*. Teachers College Contributions to Education, No. 130, 1923.

2. Donald G. Paterson, Editor, *Research Studies in Individual Diagnosis*. Minneapolis: University of Minnesota Press, 1934. (Bul. E. S. R. I., Vol. 3, No. 4.)

3. D. G. Paterson, R. M. Elliott, L. D. Anderson, H. A. Toops and E. Heidbreder, *Minnesota Mechanical Ability Tests*. Minneapolis: University of Minnesota Press, 1930.

V

TESTS OF CLERICAL APTITUDES

APTITUDE for clerical work is not a simple trait; it is complex. An examiner looking for symptoms of capacity to learn a clerical occupation and successfully to carry a clerk's responsibilities, resorts to several kinds of tests.

In the first place, as we saw in Chapters XII and XIII, definite *lack* of clerical aptitude is indicated by less than average ability in number-checking and word-checking tests. Positive aptitude for clerical occupations other than the most routine, however, calls for much in addition to facility and accuracy in comparing and checking data. The examiner, therefore, next undertakes to measure abilities similar to those sampled by tests of verbal and arithmetical intelligence or scholastic aptitude. Finally, tests to measure mastery of correct English usage, vocabulary, spelling, handwriting and skill in arithmetical computation find a place in the battery, unless these abilities have already been assessed by means of standard achievement tests or by close observation of school progress in these subjects.

From among the tests mentioned in earlier chapters a selection has been made of those most likely to be of service in vocational bureaus and schools. This choice carries no implication that counselors should ignore data from other tests of intelligence, of school achievement, or of specific clerical aptitudes when such data are at hand, including norms indicative of the levels of attainment characterizing students and workers who succeed in mastering clerical skills and who have subsequently made progress in clerical occupations.

Of the current number- and word-comparison tests, we shall here describe the Minnesota Vocational Test for Clerical Workers and O'Connor's Worksamples No. 1 and No. 43; while one of the tests developed by the U. S. Civil Service Commission under the supervision of O'Rourke will illustrate the use of intelligence-test data in appraising general clerical aptitudes. Norms to aid in interpreting scores on other commonly used tests of mental alertness and scholastic aptitude are given in Chapter XIII.

MINNESOTA VOCATIONAL TEST FOR CLERICAL WORKERS

LONG FORM AND SHORT FORM, ARRANGED BY DOROTHY M. ANDREW

Performance in the number-comparison and word-comparison tasks set by the Minnesota Vocational Test for Clerical Workers furnishes one indication of aptitude for occupations which require speed and accuracy in noticing whether two numbers are the same or different, or whether two names are the same or different. Bank tellers, accountants, bookkeepers, stenographers, typists, and general office workers have done very well on this test. Accountants and bookkeepers, for example, have been found to make better scores on the average than 95 per cent of workers in a general population sample. The test differentiates not only between clerical workers and other people, but also to some degree between classes and grades of clerical workers. For instance, accountants on the average do better than stenographers; and stenographers than office machine operators. When predicting ability in clerical occupations the efficiency of this test alone has been found to be as high as 35 per cent better than chance. A significant relationship has also been found between scores and later progress in commercial high school.

The complete test—known as the Long Form—can be given to an individual or to a group in about thirty-five or forty minutes. The first half—known as the Short Form—takes about twenty minutes to give. Each half is in two parts. The first part consists of 200 pairs of numbers; and the second of 200 pairs of names. The instructions on the blank read, ". . . If the two names or the two numbers of a pair are *exactly the same*, make a check mark (√) on the line between them; if they are *different*, make no mark on that line." Samples of pairs of numbers done correctly follow:

79542———79524

5794367———√———5794367

Then are given samples of pairs of names done correctly:

John C. Linder———John C. Lender

Investors Syndicate———√———Investors Syndicate

A brief practice exercise is provided, to make certain that the instructions are understood.

The prescribed time limits for the Short Form are:

1. Number checking	8 minutes
2. Name checking	7 minutes
Total working time	15 minutes

For the Long Form the time limits are:

1. Number checking	8 minutes
2. Name checking	7 minutes
3. Number checking	7 minutes
4. Name checking	6 minutes
Total working time	28 minutes

Although the Long Form is a little more reliable than the Short Form and may well be used when there is room for uncertainty as to an examinee's status, the Short Form has a satisfactory reliability, the Standard Error of Measurement for combined number and name checking being not more than three-tenths of a Standard Scale unit. For this reason it is the practice of most examiners, especially when pressed for time, to give only the Short Form, in order that there may be opportunity to give other clerical tests also. Occasionally an individual makes a much lower score in the number checking than in the name checking part of the Short Form, in which event it is best to administer the remaining parts of the Long Form, or at least to repeat the number checking part of the Short Form, to ascertain whether the poor performance was due to lack of ability, or to a lack of appreciation of the need for speed.

Administration.—Pass out the folders, with a caution not to open them. Say:

> "Write your name on the first page. Now read the instructions and work the samples as directed on the lower half of the first page." Look over each examinee's work to make sure he has completed the samples and understands the directions; or, if the group is large, read the correct answers to the sample exercises and ask if there are any questions. Then say: "Be ready to open the folder, and when I give the signal to start, begin checking those that are the same; those that are different you leave blank. When I give the signal to stop, stop immediately and draw a line under the last one you are looking at. Now open your folder and start." Note the time to the second. At the end of exactly *eight* minutes, say, "Stop! and draw a line under the last one you are looking at." Then say: "Turn the page to test 2, and start." At the end of exactly *seven* minutes say, "Stop! Draw a line under the last one you were looking at and turn back to the front page."

If the long form is being used, continue with Tests 3 and 4, using the same directions as for Test 2. The time limits for these parts are shorter: seven minutes and six minutes, respectively.

Scoring.—Correct items are those in which the "*sames*" have been checked and the "*differents*" left blank. (A scoring key is supplied by the publisher.) The score for each test is the number of items correct minus the number wrong. Subtracting twice the number wrong from the number attempted gives the same result.

Norms.—For the Short Form, reference may be made to Table XXXV, which shows Standard Scores and letter grades corresponding to the raw scores made by a standard population sample of adults representative of the age and occupational distributions of workers in an urban area (1). Since women tend to excel men in both number checking and name checking—especially the latter—this table gives the norms for each sex and each of these tasks separately. These norms hold for girls as young as 17, and boys of 19. When the performance of younger persons is in question, however, it should be remembered that the traits measured may not have fully matured.

TABLE XXXV. STANDARD NORMS (SHORT FORM)

Raw score: Number checking Men	Number checking Women	Name checking Men	Name checking Women	*Standard score*	*Centile rank*	*Letter grade*
173	199	180		8.0	99.9	
						(A++)
163	193	163		7.5	99.4	
						A+
147	185	146	184	7.0	97.7	
						A−
131	165	129	166	6.5	93.3	
						B+
112	145	112	148	6.0	84.1	
						B−
96	125	95	130	5.5	69.1	
						C+
83	109	78	111	5.0	50.0	
						C−
67	97	60	93	4.5	39.9	
						D+
53	84	43	75	4.0	15.9	
						D−
41	70	26	57	3.5	6.7	
						E+
29	57	9	38	3.0	2.3	
						E−
21	44	0	20	2.5	0.6	

The Standard Error of Measurement in terms of the Standard Scale is less than ±.35 of a scale unit for Number Checking and less than ±.3 of a unit for Name Checking. In terms of raw score it is not far from ± 10 points, for numbers and for names, men or women.

In the manual of directions supplied by the publisher are norms for both short and long forms based on the performance of fairly large population samples of employed clerical workers. It is significant that of 284 women clerical workers reported upon, only the lowest 10 per cent failed to score above the median for women workers in general—that is, C+ or better. Of 120 men clerical workers, all but the lowest 10 per cent scored B− or better, in comparison with the Standard Norms for men. Tentative occupational norms based on the performance of smaller population samples are given for each of several different clerical occupations, including women office machine operators, women stenographers and typists, men bank tellers, men accountants and bookkeepers, women general clerical workers, men general clerical workers, women routine clerical workers, men routine clerical workers, and men shipping and stock clerks. For a full treatment of these norms and their significance, see Andrew and Paterson (2).

Some of the more striking differences are suggested in Table XXXVI. This table shows for nine clerical groups their median scores in comparison with the performance of the standard population sample of adult workers.

TABLE XXXVI. TENTATIVE OCCUPATIONAL NORMS

Showing for each of nine clerical groups the number tested (N), the median (M) in terms of Raw Score, the corresponding Standard Score (SS) and the percentage of the general population of male or female workers failing to attain this score.

Occupational Group		*Number checking*			*Name checking*		
Women	N	M	SS	%	M	SS	%
Typists and stenographers	181	147	6.04	85	158	6.28	90
Office machine operators	21	149	6.09	86	134	5.59	72
General clerical workers	60	139	6.10	86	147	5.97	84
Routine clerical workers	24	133	5.70	76	134	5.61	73
Men							
Accountants or bookkeepers	29	144	6.91	97	127	6.45	93
Bank tellers	17	137	6.69	95	134	6.64	95
General clerical workers	44	134	6.59	94	131	6.55	94
Routine clerical workers	30	124	6.35	91	118	6.19	88
Shipping clerks	23	104	5.75	77	102	5.72	76

Interpretation.—The vocational significance of this test is apparent from a comparison of the performance of clerical workers with the Standard Norms. For example, a man scoring 83 on number checking does as well as the average man; but most men clerical workers do better than this. Indeed, a man must excel about 95 per cent of the general male working population in order to score as high as the average clerk.

It seems plausible that the abilities which this test measures should contribute in varying degrees to aptitude for clerical occupations other than those listed above; for example, proof-reading, linotype operation, statistics, some forms of executive work, and other occupations requiring quick and accurate perception of words and numbers. Counselors should, however, bear in mind that such specific conjectures have in most instances not been scientifically validated; and so they will give little weight to scores as indicators of aptitude for these particular occupations without confirmatory evidence from other sources. On the other hand, a distinctly low level of performance may with confidence be construed as a warning against undertaking clerical work of any sort.

DISTRIBUTOR:

Psychological Corporation, 522 Fifth Avenue, New York. 100 copies and manual, $2.00; scoring key, 25 cents.

REFERENCES:

1. Helen J. Green, Isabel R. Berman, Donald G. Paterson and M. R. Trabue, *Manual of Selected Occupational Tests.* Minneapolis: University of Minnesota Press, 1933.

2. Dorothy M. Andrew and Donald G. Paterson, *Measured Characteristics of Clerical Workers.* Minneapolis: University of Minnesota Press, 1934.

Number Checking and Word Checking

JOHNSON O'CONNOR'S WORKSAMPLES NO. 1 AND NO. 43

The kind of aptitude indicated by superior ability to notice slight differences between pairs of numbers or pairs of words has been called by O'Connor "accounting aptitude." This term is not intended to suggest any restriction on the vocational implications of a person's performance; for this aptitude is obviously an asset in numerous callings besides that of accountant. Clerical workers of many kinds tend to excel in number-comparison and word-comparison tests. It is not surprising that executives, continually faced with the necessity of making decisions based on reports of production, sales data, and financial statements, also have been found quite generally to score above average in such tests as these. Although a high degree of this aptitude is not indispensable to lawyers, teachers, nurses, salesmen, scientists, and others a part of whose work requires the keeping of records or the examination of data, a serious deficiency in it may operate as a handicap to one who enters such a calling.

The tests (1) must be administered individually, with expertness. Since accuracy of measurement is more than ordinarily dependent on the examiner's skill, and since computation of a score is a rather complicated matter, the originator discourages use of these tests by any but specially trained psychological examiners. Scores are not quite so reliable as on the Minnesota Vocational Test for Clerical Workers (3); but some examiners prefer the O'Connor tests because of a predilection for the amount-limit method, and because age norms are available. (2, pp. 179-181.) Research workers may obtain the necessary blanks, together with instructions which differ in some details from those originally published, by addressing Johnson O'Connor at Stevens Institute of Technology, Hoboken, N. J.

References:

1. Johnson O'Connor, *Born That Way.* Baltimore: Williams and Wilkins, 1928.
2. Johnson O'Connor, *Psychometrics.* Cambridge: Harvard University Press, 1934.
3. Dorothy M. Andrew and Donald G. Paterson, *Measured Characteristics of Clerical Workers.* Minneapolis: University of Minnesota Press, 1934.

General Test for Stenographers and Typists

DEVELOPED BY THE RESEARCH DIVISION, U. S. CIVIL SERVICE COMMISSION

This General Test has much in common with tests of verbal intelligence. It is designed to measure the adaptability, mental alertness, and knowledge which typists and stenographers should have, aside from their specific skills. Prepared under the direction of L. J. O'Rourke for government use as part of a battery of examinations for selection of stenographers and typists, it proved so effective that it was released by the U. S. Civil Service Commission in 1935 for use in schools and industries. It is a seventy-five-minute test preceded by a ten-minute fore-exercise to acquaint the candidate with the kinds of questions he is to answer—questions involving practical judgment as well as vocabulary, English usage, spelling and reading comprehension: eighty items in all. Although there is a time limit, the carefully graded difficulty of the items makes it a test of power rather than of mere speed. It can be given in about an hour and a half.

Administration.—Distribute the preliminary sample test. Say:

"Fill in the place of examination, your name and the date. . . . Now look at the note 'To the Competitor' while I read it to you." After reading the paragraph aloud, say, at an even minute, "Ready? . . . Begin." Record the time. After exactly ten minutes, say "Stop!" Record the time, and collect the test samples.

Issue the test proper and say, "Fill in the headings. . . . Now look at the instructions while I read them to you. The questions contained in this sheet are similar to those in the sample on which you have just practiced. One hour and fifteen minutes will be allowed; since there are 80 items in the test, do not spend too much time on any one item. Your score will depend only upon the number you get right. If it seems to you that more than one answer could be given for any question, write the number of the *one* that you think is *most clearly* the answer. *Answer every question* even though you are not certain of the correct answer. No extra credit is given for finishing before time is called. Begin!" At the end of exactly 75 minutes, say, "Stop!" and record the time. Collect all papers at once.

Scoring.—Key is supplied by the publisher. Score is number of items correct; that is, 80 minus the number of omissions and errors (including double answers).

Interpretation.—A person's score may be compared with the percentile norms of Table XXXVII. If, for example, his score is 55 (first column), he has done better than 56 per cent of industrial stenographers who have taken the test, and better than 82 per cent of typists. He is superior to 71 per cent of civil-service applicants, but to only 46 per cent of those who achieve status as eligibles on the civil-service typist and stenographer registers. His score exceeds that of 63 per cent of seniors studying stenography in one commercial high school. Such comparisons help teachers and counselors as well as the students and workers who take the test to appreciate the requirements of commercial employment and the somewhat higher requirements which at present prevail in the government service with respect to the abilities which this test measures.

That the test samples those aptitudes which business executives have in mind when they speak of employees' "ability to use their heads," is shown by the relationship between test scores and efficiency ratings. In two industries where studies have been made, the coefficients of correlation were .71 and .76. Stenographers and typists in the latter industry who scored in the highest quarter on the test were almost without exception rated above average in efficiency; whereas almost all of those who scored in the lowest quarter were judged to be below average in efficiency.

A young woman who is intent upon becoming a stenographer but who does correctly less than 45 items, may be informed that her chances of making progress in stenographic employment are not very good. The requirements for typist are less exacting; but if she scores as low as 35, she is quite unlikely to be rated above average as a typist. As for the probability that she will become a competent secretary, the odds are in her favor only if she scores above 55. Other relevant inferences may be drawn after consulting the table on page 162. A counselor estimating the probabilities will, however, take into consideration all the other pertinent information available, in the manner described in Chapter XIII. School progress, particularly in English and mathematics, is relevant; also achievement test scores in English usage, arithmetical computation and problems, vocabulary, reading comprehension, spelling and handwriting, as well as scores in intelligence tests and in number-and-word-checking tests of clerical aptitude.

TABLE XXXVII. VOCATIONAL NORMS FOR STENOGRAPHERS AND TYPISTS

Showing raw scores and the corresponding percentile ranks in each of five groups: stenographers employed in industry, typists employed in industry, stenographers and typists securing a place on the eligible list for appointment to the Federal Civil Service, stenographers and typists applying for civil-service appointment, and seniors specializing in stenography in a commercial high school.

Score	*Employees of eight industries, Stenographers*	*Employees of eight industries, Typists*	*Civil-service eligibles, stenographers and typists*	*Civil-service applicants, stenographers and typists*	*High-school seniors, stenographers only*
80	100	100	100	100	100
75	99	100	99.5	100	100
70	96	98	94	98	97
65	83	97	81	93	94
60	69	93	65	85	72
55	56	82	46	71	63
50	38	76	25	57	25
45	30	60	6	42	19
40	19	48	0	25	12
35	8	32	0	12	3
30	3	22	0	8	3
25	3	12	0	2	0
20	1	4	0	1	0
15	0	2	0	0	0

The Standard Error of Measurement is less than ± 3 points.

DISTRIBUTOR:

Psychological Corporation, 522 Fifth Avenue, New York.

REFERENCES:

1. L. J. O'Rourke, "Scientific Personnel Selection," *Occupations*, Vol. XII, No. 8, April, 1934: 29-39.

VI

TESTS OF INTELLIGENCE

Army Alpha Examination

INCLUDING REVISIONS BY ELSIE O. BREGMAN AND BY F. L. WELLS AND C. R. ATWELL

THERE are newer, better group tests than Army Alpha for measuring scholastic aptitude and general intelligence; but for none are there available so many occupational data, or norms based on such large samples of the general adult population. For these reasons this epoch-making battery has been kept in use, both in certain of its original forms and in several revisions.

Like the original Army Alpha (1), the Bregman Revision (2) consists of eight sub-tests, namely, following directions, arithmetic problems, practical judgment, synonym-antonym, disarranged sentences, number-series completion, analogies, and information. It may be had in two forms. Form A is identical with Form 8 prepared by the army psychologists during the World War, except that military and outmoded items have been replaced with items of equivalent difficulty from other forms. Form B is an alternate to Form A. The scores correspond to the original Army Alpha scores, so that comparisons with the earlier data may be made directly. The examination is suitable for use with literate adults and with high-school and college students. Its best usefulness is in testing persons of superior mental ability. It is less satisfactory in the middle range; and when given to people of distinctly less than average mental endowment, the measures it yields should always be checked or supplemented by tests in which linguistic factors are less heavily weighted.

The Wells revision (3) is somewhat more drastic. It simplifies the administration and scoring and removes the cultural incongruities, making the examination more suitable for use in schools and in industries while preserving the irreplaceable norms. Scores which fall in the upper quartile of the distribution are directly comparable with the original Alpha scores. There are two forms: 5 and 7; also a Short Form 6, prepared jointly with C. R. Atwell (4), which consists of sub-tests 2, 4, 7 and 8 from the Wells revision of Alpha Form 6.

Administration.—Instructions for giving and scoring are found in the Manuals of Directions supplied by the publisher. Administration of The Bregman revision can be simplified by omitting the particularly troublesome Sub-test 1, "Following Directions." The total administration time is about 40 minutes for the full examination, while without Sub-test 1 it is 7 minutes less.

Norms.—The norms of Table XXXVIII were obtained with the original Army Alpha. They are based on scores made by literate native white soldiers drafted into the United States Army, plus the scores made by officers, in the proportion of 20 to 1. They therefore represent the performance of a cross-section of the literate adult male population. (See pages 44ff., and Fig. 13 on page 251.)

TABLE XXXVIII. ADULT NORMS FOR ARMY ALPHA AND BREGMAN REVISION

Raw scores			
Full test	*Omitting Sub-test 1*	*Standard score*	*Centile rank*
188	176	8.00	99.86
184	172	7.75	99.70
179	168	7.50	99.39
172	161	7.25	98.78
162	151	7.00	97.72
150	140	6.75	95.99
138	129	6.50	93.32
125	116	6.25	89.44
111	103	6.00	84.13
97	89	5.75	77.34
84	77	5.50	69.15
72	66	5.25	59.87
61	55	5.00	50.00
51	46	4.75	40.13
42	37	4.50	30.85
34	29	4.25	22.66
27	23	4.00	15.87
20	16	3.75	10.56

The Standard Error of Measurement is about ± .23 of a Standard Unit.

Interpretation.—Tests like Army Alpha are of use in vocational counseling chiefly as indicators of the general occupational level for which a person is able to prepare, and in which he is most likely to succeed and to find his working associates intellectually congenial. Vocational norms and suggestions regarding their use are found in earlier chapters of this volume—particularly Chapter V, beginning with page 45. The army occupational norms may advantageously be compared with those from the Scovill Classification Test on pages 51-55, since the occupational status of the employees studied with that examination is known more precisely than that of the soldiers and officers examined by the military psychologists.

DISTRIBUTOR:

Psychological Corporation, 522 Fifth Avenue, New York. Price for Bregman Revision, Form A or B, or for Wells Revision, Form 5 or 7, six cents a copy;

$5 a hundred; Manual, Key and Norms, 25 cents. Atwell and Wells' Short Form 6, 4 cents each; $3 a hundred.

REFERENCES:

1. R. M. Yerkes, Editor, "Psychological Examining in the U. S. Army," *Memoirs of the National Academy of Sciences*, 1921. Vol. 15.

2. E. O. Bregman, "On Converting Scores on Army Alpha Examination into Percentiles of the Total Population," *School and Society*, 1926, 23: 695-696.

3. F. L. Wells, "Army Alpha—Revised," *Personnel Journal*, 1932, 10: 411-417.

4. C. R. Atwell and F. L. Wells, "Army Alpha Revised—Short Form," *Personnel Journal*, 1933, 12: 160-165.

5. Douglas Fryer, "Occupational-Intelligence Standards," *School and Society*, 1922, 16: 273-277.

6. M. V. Cobb, "The Limits Set to Educational Achievement by Limited Intelligence," *Journal of Educational Psychology*, 1922, 13: 449-464, 546-555.

ARMY BETA

REVISED BY C. E. KELLOGG AND N. W. MORTON

The non-language group examination Beta, developed by the military psychologists (1) for use in making a first rough classification of illiterate and non-English-speaking recruits, necessitates use of a blackboard and pantomime in giving the instructions. The Kellogg and Morton Revision (2) uses instead a printed exercise preceding each of the six tests. The test items have been rearranged as to difficulty, the time limits altered, and some new material introduced. These changes have reduced the number of zero scores and made the distributions more nearly normal.

An examination of this type, given to workers and students who are not verbally inclined, not infrequently discloses highly significant differences of mental ability not clearly indicated by an exclusively verbal test. It is particularly useful with groups whose scores on Alpha would be apt to fall below the general population average.

The Manual supplied by the publisher gives explicit directions for administering and scoring, together with norms and letter grades comparable to those for Army Alpha, and tentative age and grade norms for children.

DISTRIBUTOR:

Psychological Corporation. Price eight cents; $7 a hundred, with Manual; Manual and Scoring Key, fifteen cents.

REFERENCES:

1. R. M. Yerkes, Editor, "Psychological Examining in the U. S. Army," *Memoirs of the National Academy of Sciences*, 1921, vol. 15.

2. C. E. Kellogg and N. W. Morton, "Revised Beta Examination," *Personnel Journal*, 1934, 13: 94-100.

Scovill Classification Test

The Scovill Classification Test, developed by John E. Anderson and Millicent Pond (1) for industrial use, unites in one examination the best features of both Army Alpha and Army Beta. This battery consists of three verbal and five non-verbal tests, as follows:

1. Picture Completion (non-verbal)
2. Number Checking (non-verbal)
3. Digit-Symbol Substitution (non-verbal)
4. Geometrical Construction (non-verbal)
5. Arithmetical Reasoning (verbal)
6. Synonym-Antonym (verbal)
7. Analogies (verbal)
8. Circle Crossing (non-verbal)

Except for Test 8, these are taken with slight modifications from the army series. By an ingenious but simple device of scoring, the illiterate and the non-English-speaking are not penalized for total failure on the verbal sub-tests. This feature explains in part the fact that the battery differentiates quite clearly and dependably within the lower and the upper as well as the intermediate ranges of adult mental ability.

Wall charts or blackboards are needed in addition to the blanks. The examination takes about forty minutes to give and is easily scored. There is but one form.

An outstanding merit is the availability of the industrial norms shown in Table XXXIX,[1] secured from a factory population of 9,075 men, together with the table reproduced on page 54, which provides information regarding the distribution of mental ability in forty-four occupational groups.

Attention may be drawn to the studies of toolmaker apprentices made with this battery, as described on pages 138-139; also to the norms for clerical workers (286 men and 244 women) and critical scores useful in estimating clerical aptitude and probability of subsequent advancement in office work as given on pages 161-162 of this volume and in Reference 4, pp. 51-53.

Distributor:

This test has not been released for general use. Upon application to the Scovill Manufacturing Company, Waterbury, Connecticut, psychologists affiliated with the Psychological Corporation and other research workers may secure copies of the blanks and detailed directions for administration and scoring.

[1] See also the graphic representation of these norms in Fig. 13, page 251.

TABLE XXXIX. ADULT NORMS

Based on the distribution of scores made by a factory population of 9,075 men.

Raw scores	*Standard scores*	*Centile rank*	*Letter grades*
207	8.5	99.997	
			(A+++)
194	8.0	99.9	
			(A++)
186	7.5	99.4	
			A+
175	7.0	97.7	
			A−
164	6.5	93.3	
			B+
153	6.0	84.1	
			B−
141	5.5	69.1	
			C+
128	5.0	50.0	
			C−
116	4.5	39.9	
			D+
105	4.0	15.9	
			D−
97	3.5	6.7	
			E+
90	3.0	2.3	
			E−
83	2.5	0.6	
			(E−−)
63	2.0	0.135	

The Standard Error of Measurement is estimated to be not more than ±.3 of a unit on the standard scale.

REFERENCES:

1. M. Pond, "Selective Placement of Metal Workers," *Journal of Personnel Research*, 1927, 5: 345-368; 405-417; 452-466.

2. M. Pond, "What is New in Employment Testing," *Personnel Journal*, 1932, 11: 10-16.

3. M. Pond, "Occupations, Intelligence, Age and Schooling," *Personnel Journal*, 1933, 11: 373-382.

4. M. Pond and M. A. Bills, "Intelligence and Clerical Jobs," *Personnel Journal*, 1933, 12: 41-56.

Bureau Test VI—Mental Alertness

Prepared in 1920 by C. S. Yoakum (1) as a self-administering adaptation of Army Alpha for use at the Bureau of Personnel Research, Carnegie Institute of Technology, this short convenient test of mental alertness has been extensively used by business organizations, chiefly in connection with the selection of clerical workers, salesmen, supervisors and minor executives. When administered with a fifteen-minute time limit, it can be given and scored in about twenty-five minutes. Its reliability is high for so brief an examination.

The test consists of the items in six of the eight sub-tests of Army Alpha, arranged in spiral-omnibus form, with a page of fore-exercises to make clear the kinds of tasks. The items used are the arithmetic problems, synonym-antonym, disarranged sentences, number series completion, analogies, and information. The following-directions items, which do not lend themselves to this type of test administration, and the practical-judgment items, which appear to measure speed of reading quite as much as practical judgment, are omitted.

Several of the information items are now out of date, so that the original forms should no longer be used. A recent revision is available in two forms, A and B.

Administration.—Simple instructions, scoring key and norms are supplied by the publisher. Time limit, 15 minutes or 20 minutes.

In Chapter XIII, the Table on page 162 shows the raw scores corresponding to Standard Scores, together with the interpretations given to them by employers of office workers. The publisher's norms for the original form are expressed in terms of deciles for each of various populations: executives, specialty salesmen, life insurance salesmen, clerical groups, high-school graduates, college students, and college graduates. It is, however, recommended that these norms be not used without first checking them with norms for larger populations, obtained with other, preferably longer, examinations. The references below may also be consulted.

One disadvantage of such an omnibus test is that sub-scores are not available. The experienced examiner, however, will note, by inspecting the blank after it has been scored, whether most of the errors are of one sort: arithmetic, information, analogies, or number-series-completion, for example.

Distributor:

Psychological Corporation, 522 Fifth Avenue, New York. $5 a hundred.

References:

1. H. G. Kenagy and C. S. Yoakum, *Selection and Training of Salesmen*, Chapters XII-XIII. New York: McGraw-Hill, 1925.

2. M. A. Bills, "Methods for the Selection of Comptometer Operators," *Journal of Applied Psychology*, 1921, 5: 275-283.

3. M. Pond and M. A. Bills, "Intelligence and Clerical Jobs," *Personnel Journal*, 1933, 12: 41-56.

Otis Group Intelligence Scale

PRIMARY EXAMINATION AND ADVANCED EXAMINATION

and

Otis Self-Administering Tests of Mental Ability

INTERMEDIATE EXAMINATION AND HIGHER EXAMINATION

The Otis Advanced Examination (1) embodies a successful pioneer venture in the construction of a scale of mental ability in terms of performance in a battery of group tests. Designed for use with examinees of any age, provided they can read, it found immediate application in high schools, and in elementary schools above the fourth grade. It requires an hour to administer, too long to give in an ordinary school period; but parts may be given on successive days. For many years this examination has been extensively used because it has a wide range of application, relatively high reliability, and norms based on large populations.

The Primary Examination, consisting of eight non-reading group tests, was subsequently issued, extending the applicability of the Otis Scale into the primary school and kindergarten.

Then followed the two Otis Self-Administering Tests: the Intermediate Examination designed for grades four to nine, and the Higher Examination for high-school students and adults. These are shorter examinations of the omnibus type, which can be given in about thirty-five minutes.

The ten tests in the Advanced Examination include: following directions, opposites, disarranged sentences, proverbs, arithmetic, geometric figures, analogies, similarities, narrative completion, and memory. There are two forms, A and B. Norms for ages 8 to 18 (adult) are given in the very complete *Manual of Directions*, together with instructions for administering the ten separately timed tests, scoring, and translating a point scale score into a mental age score, a percentile rank, an Index of Brightness and an I Q. Two precautions may be emphasized. Before giving the examination, the directions, particularly the selection to be read in connection with Test 10 (Memory), should be carefully rehearsed. In interpreting the scores, it should be borne in mind that I Q's from this point scale are not comparable with I Q's computed from Mental Ages obtained with a Binet test. Neither is Otis's Index of Brightness a precise equivalent of a Stanford Binet I Q.

The two Self-Administering Examinations, the Intermediate and the Higher, are each issued in four alternate forms, A, B, C, and D. A fore-exercise familiarizes the examinee with the way of recording answers and with the nature of the tasks. The test proper consists of 75 problems, informational, arithmetical, number series completion, recognition of opposites, analogies, understanding of proverbs, logical inferences, and practical judgment items, arranged in apparently chance sequence. None of the problems is difficult for a very bright person; and so the test is a better measure of mental speed or alertness than of power, at least in the higher ranges of mental ability. On a relatively short group test of this sort a low score serves first of all to suggest the advisability of securing a more adequate measure of the individual's mental ability, such as that provided by a Stanford Binet Examination or by one of the longer and more exacting group tests of scholastic aptitude.

Administration and Scoring of the Higher Examination.—Although the ease with which this test is given led the author to call it "self-administering," the usual care should be taken and the directions adhered to as prescribed in the *Manual.* Either a 30-minute or a 20-minute time limit may be used. The longer period ordinarily yields more reliable scores except when testing students or adults of superior ability. Here the 20-minute time is more satisfactory. Even with this shorter time limit, however, the test does not differentiate clearly near the upper end of the scale.

Scoring instructions, keys, and guides to interpretation are given in the *Manual.* Scoring time is less than one minute.

TABLE XL. NORMS FOR OTIS HIGHER EXAMINATION

Showing raw scores (with 30-minute and 20-minute time limit) and the corresponding scores on a Standard Scale, a Binet Mental Age Scale, and an Otis I Q Scale; and percentile ranks in a General Population (age 18), a population of high-school seniors and a population of college students.

Raw scores			*Binet*		*Centile Ranks*		
30 min.	*20 min.*	*Standard scores*	*MA Yr.—Mo.*	*Otis I Q*	*General (age 18)*	*H.-s. seniors*	*College students*
72	63	7.5	19—3	130	99.4	99	98
66	54	7.0	18—6	124	97.7	96	87
60	47	6.5	17—9	118	93.3	88	69
54	42	6.0	17—0	112	84.1	68	52
48	37	5.5	16—3	106	69.1	52	31
42	32	5.0	15—4	100	50.0	31	16
36	28	4.5	14—4	94	30.9	13	6
30	23	4.0	13—3	88	15.9	5	2
24	19	3.5	12—2	82	6.7	1	0.6
18	14	3.0	11—0	76	2.3	0.3	0
12	9	2.5	10—0	70	0.6	0	0

When the 30-minute time limit is used, the Standard Error of Measurement is ± 4 points.

Interpretation.—The *General Norms* for the Higher Examination given in Table XL are based on the performance of unselected adults and are used directly in interpreting scores of persons 18 years of age or older. To find a younger person's Standard Score or I Q, the proper age correction (Table XLI) is first added to his raw score to make it comparable to adult performance. The raw score thus corrected is referred to the table of norms. Charts in the *Manual* facilitate this step and permit the examiner to read off directly, for each point score on either examination, the corresponding percentile rank, Binet Mental Age, Intelligence Quotient and Index of Brightness.

TABLE XLI

Age	Age correction 30-min. limit	Age correction 20-min. limit
12.....	19	14
13.....	14	10
14.....	10	7
15.....	6	4
16.....	3	2
17.....	1	0

A short convenient test of this kind has been widely used to get a rough prediction of what an individual would be likely to do in a more difficult and searching examination. Knowing the correlation between two tests, together with the average scores and standard deviations of the group tested, a table can be prepared showing for each score in one test a person's most probable score in the other. The three-hour Scholastic Aptitude Test prepared under the direction of C. C. Brigham and given annually in many centers by the College Entrance Examination Board, is such an examination. Brigham (2, p. 336) ascertained that the correlation between the Otis Higher (Form A, 30 minutes) and the Scholastic Aptitude Test is .7931, and computed the prediction table here reproduced as Table XLII. In this table it is seen, for example, that if a student has an Otis score of 59, his most probable Scholastic Aptitude Test score is 502, which is at the median for these college-entrance candidates. Note that the maximum Otis score of 75 cuts off the upper end of the distribution of abilities in such a group. It is not possible with this test to ascertain the probability that a candidate might make a letter grade of A when he takes the College Board Test of Scholastic Aptitude.

The median score of Otis's college population is 53. By reference to Table XLII it is seen that if a student with such a score were to take the Scholastic Aptitude Test, his most probable score would be 447, which is far below the median of these candidates, corresponding to a percentile rank of only 29 and a letter grade of D+.

The likelihood that a student will remain in college at least two years varies with his Otis score, as seen in Table XLIII, from a study by Jordan (3).

The general trend is obvious; but a counselor will not overlook the fact that *some* of those who did poorly on this test nevertheless were able to make progress in college. Of the 562 entrants here reported upon, 54 tested below 95 I Q on the Otis Higher Examination; and of these, 20 remained in college at least two years. Estimates of educational potentialities should rest on firmer ground than is provided by a single score in such a relatively brief test.

The standards of the particular institution should also be taken into consideration, for there are colleges of all sorts. A student who would be outclassed in one institution might find himself one of the intellectually superior members of another student body. The median scores (30-minute limit) from 21 colleges and

TABLE XLII. PREDICTION OF S. A. T. SCORE FROM OTIS HIGHER EXAMINATION

Showing the most probable Scholastic Aptitude Test score, centile, and letter grade for each score in Otis Self-Administering Test (Higher, Form A, 30 minutes).

Otis score	*S. A. T. score*	*Centile rank*	*Letter grade*
75	647	92	B
74	638	91	B
73	628	90	B
72	619	88	B
71	610	86	B
70	601	84	B
69	592	82	B
68	583	79	B
67	574	77	B
66	565	74	B
65	556	71	B
64	547	68	C
63	538	64	C
62	529	61	C
61	520	58	C
60	511	54	C
59	502	50	C
58	492	46	C
57	483	43	C
56	474	39	C
55	465	36	C
54	456	32	C
53	447	29	D
52	438	26	D
51	429	24	D
50	420	21	D
49	411	18	D
48	402	16	D
47	393	14	D
46	384	12	D
45	375	10	D
44	366	8	D
43	356	7	D
42	347	6	E
41	338	5	E
40	329	4	E
39	320	3	E
38	311	2	E
37	302	2	E
36	293	1	E
35	284	1	E
34	275	1	E
33	266	.9	E
32	257	.7	E
31	248	.5	E
30	239	.4	E
29	230	.3	E
28	220	.2	E
27	211	.1	E
26	202	.1	E
25	193	.1	E

The Standard Error of S. A. T. scores estimated from Otis Higher scores is ± 59.

Table XLIII. Per Cent Remaining in College Two Years

Otis I Q	*Number entering*	*Number remaining*	*Per cent remaining*
115–124	158	114	72
105–114	247	153	62
95–104	103	59	57
85– 94	43	18	42
75– 84	11	2	18
Total	562	346	62

universities are given by Otis as follows: 37, 39, 45, 46, 51, 51, 52, 53, 53, 54, 55, 55, 56, 56, 57, 59, 61, 62, 62, 64, and 65. These medians vary from almost a half sigma below the general population average to almost two sigmas above. Strang (6) provides an exhaustive digest of the literature in this field.

In Chapters V, XI, and XIII we have treated the vocational significance of scores in mental-ability tests of this sort.

Distributor:

World Book Co., Yonkers, N. Y. Self Administering Tests, either examination, package of 25, including *Manual*, $.80. Group Intelligence Scale, Advanced Examination, package of 25, including *Manual*, $1.25.

References:

1. A. S. Otis, "An Absolute Point Scale for the Measurement of Intelligence," *Journal of Educational Psychology*, May and June, 1918. The *Manuals of Directions* contain full information about the construction and standardization of the tests, as well as norms and suggestions for use.

2. C. C. Brigham, *A Study of Error*. New York: College Entrance Examination Board, 1932.

3. A. M. Jordan, *Educational Psychology*, p. 372. New York: Holt, 1928.

4. L. V. Koos and G. N. Kefauver, *Guidance in Secondary Schools*, Ch. X. New York: The Macmillan Company, 1932.

5. G. M. Ruch and G. D. Stoddard, *Tests and Measurements in High School Instruction*, Ch. XII. Yonkers: World Book Co., 1927.

6. Ruth M. Strang, *Personal Development and Guidance in College and Secondary School*, pp. 72-92. New York: Harper & Brothers, 1934.

Senior Classification and Verification Tests

BY S. L. PRESSEY AND L. C. PRESSEY

The Senior Classification Test (1) and its alternative form, the Senior Verification Test, are short examinations for measuring ability to answer quickly and accurately four types of questions—opposites, information, practical arithmetic, and common sense. The abilities sampled by this test are known to be related both to past educational achievement and to scholastic aptitude; so, by taking into consideration a person's age and schooling, as well as his score, an opinion may be formed as to his aptitude for further formal education or for those occupations which require in part the same abilities that school work demands. Designed for pupils in grades 7 to 12, the test has been used successfully with adults also. It does not, however, supply an adequate measure of superior adult ability.

Although there are much more reliable and searching measures of academic aptitude, this test is described here because norms based on standard population samples of adult men and women are available; more is known about the vocational significance of its scores than is the case with most tests of verbal intelligence; it is brief (16 minutes) and reasonably reliable for so short a test; and two forms are available in case of doubt about the accuracy of the first score. Explicit directions for administering and scoring are supplied by the publisher. Total score is simply the number of items correctly answered.

TABLE XLIV. STANDARD NORMS

Raw score Men	*Raw score* Women	*Standard score*	*Centile rank*	*Letter grade*
95		8.00	99.86	
				(A++)
94	96	7.50	99.4	
				A+
90	91	7.00	97.7	
				A−
84	86	6.50	93.3	
				B+
71	74	6.00	84.1	
				B−
56	59	5.50	69.1	
				C+
41	44	5.00	50.0	
				C−
31	34	4.50	30.9	
				D+
21	25	4.00	15.9	
				D−
13	18	3.50	6.7	
				E+
8	10	3.00	2.3	
				E−
5	3	2.50	.6	
				(E−−)
1	1	2.00	.14	

The Standard Error of Measurement is ±.3 of a unit on the Standard Scale.

Interpretation.—An adult's performance should be compared with the scores of other adults. The Standard Norms of Table XLIV are based on population samples of men and women representative of occupational and age distributions of workers in an urban area (2). These norms are suitable for use in interpreting scores of people as young as 17.

TABLE XLV. EDUCATIONAL NORMS

Showing median raw score of pupils in each school grade.

School grade....	7B	7A	8B	8A	9B	9A	10B	10A	11B	11A	12B	12A
Median score...	23	27	30	34	38	42	46	50	54	58	62	68

Scores may also be interpreted in terms of educational level by reference to the norms in Table XLV which shows the typical performance of pupils in each school grade from the seventh to the twelfth. Comparison of an individual's score with these grade norms indicates the approximate scholastic acceleration or retardation of students in junior and senior high school, and also the status of adults. Some persons make progress educationally after leaving school, while others tend to drop back. The achievement of an adult who scores 23, for example, is equal to that of a typical pupil in grade 7B. When counseling, it is often useful to have even this rough measure of educational status, for it is fully as valid as "grade actually reached on leaving school."

The vocational significance of a score may be inferred from Table XLVI, which gives for each of thirteen population samples representative of occupa-

TABLE XLVI. VOCATIONAL NORMS

Showing Standard Score and Centile Rank corresponding to the average score in each of thirteen population samples.[1]

	Standard score	*Centile rank*
1. Professional and managerial occupations	6.08	86
2. Sub-professional, business and minor supervisory occupations	5.80	78
3. Accountants and bookkeepers	6.00	84
4. Insurance salesmen	5.86	80
5. General clerical workers	5.83	79
6. Draftsmen	5.82	79
7. Stenographers and typists	5.79	78
8. Trained nurses	5.68	75
9. Retail salesmen	5.02	50
10. Policemen	5.15	56
11. Semi-skilled workers	5.00	50
12. Garage mechanics	4.98	49
13. Casual laborers (literate)	3.70	10

[1] Adapted from a thesis by Beatrice J. Dvorak, *Differential Occupational Ability Patterns*, Bulletins of the Employment Stabilization Research Institute, Vol. III, No. 8. Minneapolis: University of Minnesota Press, 1935.

tional groups, the average Standard Score, and the percentage of people in the general working population whose scores do not exceed this score.

For fuller treatment of the vocational significance of scores on this and other tests of mental alertness, academic aptitude, or abstract intelligence, see Chapters V, XI, and XIII, especially p. 162.

DISTRIBUTOR:

Public School Publishing Co., Bloomington, Ill. $1.25 a hundred, for either test.

REFERENCES:

1. S. L. Pressey and G. S. Long, "A New Idea in Intelligence Testing, *Ohio State University Educational Research Bulletin*, 1924, 3: 365-368.

2. Helen J. Green, Isabel R. Berman, Donald G. Paterson, and M. R. Trabue, *A Manual of Selected Occupational Tests for Use in Public Employment Offices*. Minneapolis: University of Minnesota Press, 1933.

3. J. G. Darley, "The Reliability of the Tests in the Standard Battery," in *Research Studies in Individual Diagnosis*, edited by D. G. Paterson. Minneapolis: University of Minnesota Press, 1934.

4. D. M. Andrew and D. G. Paterson, *Measured Characteristics of Clerical Workers*. Minneapolis: University of Minnesota Press, 1934.

TERMAN GROUP TEST OF MENTAL ABILITY

The Terman Group Test of Mental Ability has long been considered one of the most satisfactory group examinations for use with pupils in grades 7 to 12. Other tests of scholastic aptitude are more suitable for high-school graduates and college freshmen. The examination consists of ten sub-tests: Information, Best Answer, Word Meaning, Logical Selection, Arithmetic, Sentence Meaning, Analogies, Mixed Sentences, Classification, and Number Series Completion. Two equivalent forms, A and B, are available.

Administration and Scoring.—The test can be given in about 35 minutes. General directions, with detailed instructions for administering the separately timed sub-tests, are given in the *Manual of Directions*. Scoring keys are supplied by the publisher. A pupil's raw score may be referred to the norms for his school grade as given in Table XLVII.

Interpretation.—Performance on this test is first of all a measure of aptitude for school work. An eighth- or ninth-grade pupil who scores below the average for his grade will probably find high-school courses, especially the more abstract ones, very difficult. The chances are that he will leave high school before graduation. A pupil whose score is not well above the ninth-grade average should seldom be encouraged to prepare for college. Nor unless his score is at least average, is he likely to profit greatly by either a commercial or a technical high-school course. Aptitude for trade or industrial courses, on the other hand, is not so clearly indicated; for, generally speaking, success in them depends to a greater extent upon mechanical and manual aptitudes than on verbal intelli-

TABLE XLVII. EDUCATIONAL NORMS

School grade*						Standard	Centile	Letter
7	8	9	10	11	12	scale	rank	grade
147	170	181	194	203	207	7.5	99.4	
								A+
134	159	172	185	196	200	7.0	97.7	
								A−
117	142	160	173	185	190	6.5	93.3	
								B+
99	125	141	158	173	178	6.0	84.1	
								B−
82	106	122	140	157	164	5.5	69.2	
								C+
68	89	104	122	138	147	5.0	50.0	
								C−
55	74	87	104	119	129	4.5	30.9	
								D+
44	59	72	87	100	110	4.0	15.9	
								D−
33	46	57	71	82	91	3.5	6.7	
								E+
25	36	44	58	66	74	3.0	2.3	
								E−
20	30	35	48	55	63	2.5	.6	

The Standard Error of Measurement of ninth-grade pupils' scores is ±.33 of a Standard Unit.

* Grade norms apply to February.

gence. It should, however, be remembered that some industrial subjects, such as electrical courses, make definite demands on conceptual as well as practical and mechanical intelligence.

Symonds (5) gives norms of achievement in different academic subjects for students with specified scores on this test.

A pupil's relative superiority in the different kinds of sub-tests, verbal and mathematical, has been construed as a clue to his relative aptitude for different kinds of courses—linguistic, technical, and commercial. Such clues may be investigated by means of tests of achievement and special aptitude.

DISTRIBUTOR:

World Book Company, Yonkers, N. Y. Form A or B, 25 for $1.20.

REFERENCES:

1. G. N. Kefauver, "Relationship of the Intelligence Quotient and Scores on Mechanical Tests with Success in Industrial Subjects," *Vocational Guidance Magazine*, 1929, 7: 198-203, 227.

2. A. M. Jordan, "The Validation of Intelligence Tests," *Journal of Educational Psychology*, 1923, 14: 348-366, 414-428.

3. C. W. Flemming, *A Detailed Analysis of Achievement in High School.* Teachers College Contributions to Education, No. 196, 1925.

4. B. F. White, "The Correlation and Comparison of Teachers' Marks and Scores Made in the Terman Group Intelligence Test," *Journal of Educational Research*, 1925, 12: 78-81.

5. P. M. Symonds, *Ability Standards.* New York: Teachers College, 1927.

6. L. V. Koos and G. N. Kefauver, *Guidance in Secondary Schools.* New York: The Macmillan Company, 1932.

I. E. R. Intelligence Scale C A V D

"C A V D" is one of the most scientifically constructed of the scales for measuring abstract intelligence, or aptitude for dealing with verbal and mathematical ideas. Developed by the Institute of Educational Research under the direction of E. L. Thorndike (1), its name is derived from the four types of task which it presents, namely, completion of sentences (C), arithmetic problems (A), vocabulary (V), and reading or following directions (D). A battery of tests is provided for each of seventeen levels so that the scale covers a very wide range of difficulty. The items on level A are such that children having a mental age of about three years get approximately half of them right. The subsequent levels increase in difficulty at a constant rate up to level Q, at which half of the items can be done by less than 10 per cent of college graduates. The tests for levels A to E, F to H (for elementary-school pupils), G to K (for junior-high-school grades), I to M (for high-school students), and M to Q (for college and graduate levels) are bound in separate booklets. Levels A to E must be administered individually with a technique somewhat similar to that used for the Stanford Binet. All levels beyond E may be administered either individually or to a group. Speed is not measured, as time is not limited at any level. The "altitude" score, representing the level of difficulty of the questions an individual can correctly answer, is the one in which counselors are most apt to be interested. It is positively correlated with other dimensions of intelligence, including area (the number of problems an individual can solve at a specified level of difficulty) and speed. Except for Levels M to Q there is only one form; available age and grade norms are not based on very large population samples; and the scoring at all levels requires special expertness, so that the use of these tests in educational and vocational counseling is restricted.

This scale has had and will continue to have its greatest usefulness as a research instrument when there is need for precise measurement of intellectual ability on a scale of equal units, in order accurately to ascertain the relative position of individuals within a group, rather than to provide comparisons with age and grade standards.

Distributor:

Test booklets, as well as information regarding administration and norms, may be procured from the Institute of Educational Research, Teachers College, New York. The Institute also can arrange to provide a scoring service.

REFERENCES:

1. E. L. Thorndike and others, *The Measurement of Intelligence.* New York: Bureau of Publications, Teachers College, 1927.

COXE-ORLEANS PROGNOSIS TEST OF TEACHING ABILITY

The Prognosis Test of Teaching Ability was designed by W. W. Coxe and J. S. Orleans to measure ability to learn the subject-matter taught in normal schools. The five parts test the candidate's general information, knowledge of teaching methods and practices as acquired from his observations as a student, ability to learn the type of material included in professional books used in teacher-training courses, ability to understand educational reading matter, and ability to study and work out educational problems. The total time for administering is approximately three hours. Detailed directions and scoring key are supplied by the publisher. There is but one form.

Tryout in ten normal schools proved the test to be fairly dependable, the coefficients of correlation between test scores and achievement at the end of the first school year ranging between .53 and .84. The Terman Group Test of Mental Ability was found to be equally dependable; but the content of the Teaching Ability Test appeals to prospective teachers as appropriate; and the

TABLE XLVIII. NORMS

Showing scores corresponding to the half-sigma points in the distribution, among 2,601 applicants for admission to New York State Teacher-Training Institutions in 1933.

Raw score	*Standard score*	*Centile rank*	*Letter grade*
337	7.5	99.4	
			A+
325	7.0	97.7	
			A−
309	6.5	93.3	
			B+
293	6.0	84.1	
			B−
275	5.5	69.1	
			C+
257	5.0	50.0	
			C−
239	4.5	30.9	
			D+
221	4.0	15.9	
			D−
201	3.5	6.7	
			E+
179	3.0	2.3	
			E−
156	2.5	0.6	

two kinds of test supplement each other. Although high-school grades are distinctly less prognostic than either of the tests, these data also should be considered in estimating probable success in normal school.

It may be noted that, although the authors have demonstrated the value of this test for predicting school achievement, the extent to which it is prognostic of actual teaching ability has not been ascertained.

Norms and Interpretation.—Table XLVIII shows the distribution of scores among 2,601 applicants for admission to New York State teacher-training institutions in 1933. A table in the *Manual* (p. 4) shows the expectation of success in teacher-training from relative standings in the test. These help in interpreting the significance of an individual's score; but since standards vary greatly from school to school, it is important for counselors to ascertain, if possible, the norms of the institutions in their vicinity.

DISTRIBUTOR:

World Book Co., Yonkers, N. Y. Price, for 25 copies with Manual and Key, $2.25.

VII

TESTS OF SCIENTIFIC APTITUDE

Stanford Scientific Aptitude Test

BY D. L. ZYVE

Conceiving scientific aptitude to be a compound of abilities, Zyve (1) developed exercises to measure eleven of these components including ability to suspend judgment, to detect fallacies and inconsistencies, to reason logically and originally, and to draw correct inductions and deductions.

This two-hour test for students in college and senior high school has been shown to reveal at least as much about the relative scientific aptitude of college students as science teachers discover after a semester or more of contact with them. It provides one indication of aptitude for the various branches of engineering, chemistry, physics, biology, and other work in which success depends in part upon the ability to profit by training in scientific method. Performance is relatively independent of acquired knowledge. Whatever specific information is needed is furnished in the test. Since it makes no attempt to ascertain whether a person actually knows enough about mathematics, for example, to enable him to profit by engineering studies, such information must be sought from the school record or from standard achievement tests.

Administration and Scoring.—Specific instructions and scoring key are supplied by the publisher. Speed is not important. While there is a two-hour time limit, most people finish within this time. A blank can be scored in about five minutes.

Interpretation.—The accompanying table of norms is based on the scores of 323 college students, predominantly freshmen. Since performance is affected little by schooling, these norms may be used in interpreting scores of students in the upper two years of high school, or in college.

The average Standard Score of one group of research students in physics, chemistry, and electrical engineering was 5.9; that of college teachers of science was 6.6. Only a small proportion of the research students scored as low as 5.0, and none of these were judged to have superior scientific aptitude. A Standard Score of 5.0 or less may be construed as symptomatic of lack of aptitude for engineering or other scientific subjects. Many students who score little better than average are able to succeed in engineering colleges; but those who contemplate a career as scientist or college teacher of science should hesitate if they score below 6.0. Assuming adequate preparatory training, the higher a person's score, the greater are his chances of scientific attainment.

TABLE XLIX. NORMS

Raw score	*Standard score*	*Centile rank*	*Letter grade*
165	7.5	99.4	
			A+
158	7.0	97.7	
			A−
151	6.5	93.3	
			B+
138	6.0	84.1	
			B−
121	5.5	69.1	
			C+
104	5.0	50.0	
			C−
89	4.5	30.9	
			D+
76	4.0	15.9	
			D−
63	3.5	6.7	
			E+
51	3.0	2.3	
			E−
41	2.5	.6	

The Standard Error of Measurement is ±.26 of a Standard Unit.

This test measures something other than general scholastic aptitude; for successful students in non-scientific courses frequently score below average in it.

DISTRIBUTOR:

Stanford University Press, Stanford University, California. Test blanks, 1 for 25 cents, 10 for $2, 100 for $14.50. Explanatory Booklet, 25 cents; Scoring Key, 25 cents.

REFERENCE:

The Explanatory Booklet contains detailed information. Stanford University Press, 1930.

VIII

ART JUDGMENT TESTS

Meier-Seashore Art Judgment Test

N. C. Meier and C. E. Seashore (1) have provided a test of æsthetic judgment or "the capacity for perceiving quality in æsthetic situations relatively apart from formal training." The task is to select from each of 125 pairs of pictures the one that is better—"more pleasing, more artistic, more satisfying." Each pair consists of a reproduction of a picture which is time-tested (*e.g.*, a Rembrandt composition exemplifying qualities which have survived centuries of critical examination) and the same picture altered so as to lower its artistic merit. The number of unaltered masterpieces considered "better" is taken as a measure of æsthetic judgment or insight.

This test undertakes to sample only a single part of that complex combination of abilities and aptitudes called artistic talent. It gives, for example, no indication of facility with brush or crayon. But superior artistic judgment is one important indicator of aptitude for training in sculpture, etching, painting, decoration, or applied art.

The test is suitable for use with pupils in the seventh grade or higher, and with adults.

Administration.—Seat the examinee at a table on which the test book is placed at a distance making for easy reading. The book should be tilted, so that all portions of the pair of pictures are uniformly lighted and are at the same distance from the eyes. Place the record blank on the table between the test book and the client. This arrangement makes it easy for him to glance at the blank to ascertain in what respect two pictures differ, to examine the pictures, and then to record on the blank his judgment as to which picture is better. Make sure that he understands the instructions given on the form provided for recording his judgments.

Examine the record blank for omissions and, if the examinee feels unable to choose between two pictures, require him to guess.

No time limit is set. Most people complete the test within 45 or 50 minutes.

Scoring.—Score is the number of correct choices out of a possible 125. A scoring key is supplied by the publisher.

Interpretation.—Norms are based on three large groups: junior high school (seventh and eighth grades); intermediate (ninth and tenth grades); and senior high school. Adults' scores are referred to the senior norms.

This test is intended as a first aid in discovering and appraising possible talent. There is no warrant for making inferences from small differences between scores. In general, a Standard Score of 5.5 or better may be considered as a good

TABLE L. NORMS

Raw scores					
Grades 7& 8	*Grades 9 & 10*	*Grades 11 & 12 Adults*	*Standard score*	*Centile rank*	*Letter grade*
105	109	112	7.5	99.4	
					A+
102	107	109	7.0	97.7	
					A−
98	104	106	6.5	93.3	
					B+
94	100	103	6.0	84.1	
					B−
89	95	99	5.5	69.1	
					C+
84	90	95	5.0	50.0	
					C−
78	84	91	4.5	30.9	
					D+
73	77	86	4.0	15.9	
					D−
69	71	81	3.5	6.7	
					E+
63	64	75	3.0	2.3	
					E−
60	62	72	2.5	.6	

The Standard Error of Measurement is ±.45 of a Standard Unit, about 4 points.

indication of artistic aptitude. Further evidence may be secured by means of the Lewerenz Tests of Fundamental Abilities in Visual Art, or the McAdory Art Test. Expert appraisal of samples of work actually done, when this can be secured, generally furnishes the most useful single forecast of future accomplishment.

The ability to judge æsthetic merit varies considerably with the kind of material being appraised. This test uses reproductions of paintings; and so counselors will give less weight to the scores when the field of work under consideration deals with art products quite different from those upon which the test is based.

DISTRIBUTOR:

Bureau of Educational Research and Service, State University of Iowa, Iowa City. Test books, $.90 each; record sheets, $2.00 for 100; Examiner's Manual, $.10.

REFERENCES:

1. N. C. Meier (Preface by C. E. Seashore), *Æsthetic Judgment as a Measure of Art Talent*, University of Iowa Studies, Series on Aims and Progress of Research, 1926: Vol. 1, No. 19.

2. N. C. Meier, "Special Artistic Talent" (a review of this and related work), *Psychological Bulletin*, 1928, 25:265-271.

3. Madaline Kinter, *The Measurement of Artistic Abilities.* New York: Psychological Corporation, 1933.

McAdory Art Test

The materials for Margaret McAdory's Art Test (1) consist of 72 plates, each of which pictures a single subject in four different ways. They deal with common objects of everyday life, including furniture, utensils, and textiles, as well as with architecture, paintings, and graphic arts.

The illustrations on each plate, designated as A, B, C, and D, differ with regard to at least one essential art element. Each set of four illustrations has been ranked in order of merit by judges whose artistic ability is well recognized. Closeness of agreement with these rankings is taken as a measure of artistic judgment. The author states that scores on the test are indicative of aptitude for vocations requiring an understanding of art values, such as designers of furniture, clothing, utensils, vehicles, advertisements, art objects, and interiors, also painters, architects, stylists, and buyers for stores.

Æsthetic appreciation is dependent to a large extent upon the particular objects and qualities being judged (2). This may account for the low correlation which has been found between the McAdory and the Meier-Seashore tests. Since the Meier-Seashore test calls for judgment of paintings only, the McAdory test may be more dependable as an indication of aptitude for the applied arts.

Administration.—As many as thirty people can take the test at one time from one set of plates. Instructions are printed on the Record Sheet on which judgments are recorded. No time limits are prescribed. Most people finish within an hour and a half.

Scoring.—One point is given for each placement which agrees with the consensus of the art experts. Be sure to use the revised scoring key, which omits consideration of plates 12, 36, 66, and 71, and alters the original order of merit of several specimens.

Interpretation.—Estimated average age and grade norms of a New York City population are given. These norms, since they represent only averages, are far from satisfactory. A little additional aid to interpretation of adults' scores is found in the fact that only 1 per cent of men score better than 202, and 1 per cent of women better than 220.

It is not necessary to attach great weight to performance on this test, but a score that is much above average is definitely suggestive of possible talent for occupations such as those mentioned above. (See comments on the Meier-Seashore Art Judgment Test and the discussion in the final section of Chapter XV.)

Distributor:

Bureau of Publications, Teachers College, Columbia University. Portfolio of 72 plates with directions and guide for scoring, $15. Record Sheets, 40 cents for 25.

TABLE LI. AGE AND GRADE NORMS

Age norms Yr.	Mo.	Av. score at each age: Male	Female	Grade norms: Middle of grade	Av. score of pupils in each grade: Male	Female
10	0	99	110	3A	87	90
10	6	103	114	3B	90	93
11	0	107	119	4A	93	96
11	6	110	123	4B	96	99
12	0	113	128	5A	99	102
12	6	116	132	5B	102	106
13	0	119	136	6A	106	110
13	6	122	139	6B	109	114
14	0	125	142	7A	113	119
14	6	127	145	7B	117	126
15	0	130	148	8A	121	133
15	6	132	150	8B	125	141
16	0	135	152	9A	130	151
16	6	137	154	9B	135	157
17	0	138	155	10A	140	162
17	6	140	157	10B	144	166
18	0	142	158	11A	149	169
18	6	144	159	11B	153	173
19 and over		145	160	12A	158	177
				12B	162	181

The Standard Error of Measurement is ±5 points.

REFERENCES:

1. Margaret McAdory, *The Construction and Validation of an Art Test.* Teachers College Contributions to Education, No. 383. New York: 1929.

2. Margaret McAdory Siceloff and Ella Woodyard, *Validity and Standardization of the McAdory Art Test.* New York: Bureau of Publications, Teachers College, 1933.

3. Madaline Kinter, *The Measurement of Artistic Abilities.* New York: Psychological Corporation, 1933.

IX

VOCATIONAL INTEREST INVENTORIES

Strong's Vocational Interest Blank

FORMS A AND B FOR MEN; FORMS WA AND WB FOR WOMEN

The Vocational Interest Blank developed and standardized by E. K. Strong, Jr. makes it possible for a person to indicate his liking, dislike, or indifference with respect to each of 420 separate items, including occupations, amusements, activities, school subjects, and personal characteristics, and then to compare his interests as so ascertained with those of people in various occupations.[1] The blank has been filled out by several thousand persons following occupations chiefly on the professional level—lawyers, engineers, physicians, teachers, life insurance salesmen, farmers, dentists, architects, and the like. Strong has found that most of the people following any one of these occupations have certain similarities of interest, and that their interest patterns, as indicated by the way they check the items on the blank, differ significantly from those of people in general. After a person has checked the blank and the appropriate weightings have been given to his responses, it is possible to see whether or not his interests tend to coincide with those of men successfully engaged in any of the occupations on which the blank has been standardized.

This blank does not measure ability. It does, however, reveal a person's community of interest with members of a given profession. It indicates whether—granted the requisite ability and training—he will probably enjoy that kind of work and find himself among associates with tastes similar to his.

The blank is most useful with persons at least 17 years old. It is suitable for ages 15 and 16 if appropriate allowances are made for immaturity and lack of familiarity with many occupations. The interests of boys younger than 15, as measured by this blank, are seldom stable and mature enough to be very significant vocationally.

There are four forms of the Vocational Interest Blank. Form A (for men) and Form WA (for women) are designed for use with persons no longer in school. Forms B and WB are the same as these, except that the introductory page is adapted for use with students.

Forms A and B can be scored for the occupations listed below; also for *interest maturity*, and for *masculinity-femininity* of interest. The occupations are here grouped according to similarity of interest pattern. The most representative occupation in each group is starred. By scoring the blank for each of these seven occupations, it is possible to ascertain approximately a man's relative interest with respect to these occupational groups.

[1] A fuller description of this blank and its uses is found in Chapter VII.

I

*Physicist
Mathematician
Engineer
Chemist
Physician
Dentist
Psychologist
Architect
Farmer
Artist
Musician

IIa

*Lawyer
Journalist
Advertiser

IIb

*Life Ins. Salesman
Real Estate Salesman

IIIa

*Teacher
Minister

IIIb

*Y.M.C.A. secretary
Y.M.C.A. physical director
Personnel manager
School superintendent

IV

*Office worker
Purchasing agent
Accountant
Vacuum-cleaner salesman

V

*Certified Public Accountant

To give the men's blank to women, even when they are considering men's occupations, is a very questionable procedure. Fortunately, the special blanks for women, WA and WB, are now available with scoring directions and standards for the following occupations:

Artist
Author
Dentist
Housewife
Lawyer
Librarian
Life insurance saleswoman
Nurse
Office worker
Physician
Social worker
Stenographer-secretary
Teacher of English in high school
Teacher of mathematics and physical sciences in high school
Teacher of social sciences in high school
Teacher (in general) in high school
Y.W.C.A. General secretary

Administration.—Full instructions are printed on the blank. When handing it to an examinee the vocational motive should be stressed, as he will seldom falsify the statements of his likes and dislikes if he really wants to know for what kind of occupation he is suited. There is little need for supervision as no time limit is set and there are no right or wrong answers. Best results are obtained, however, by emphasizing the instruction to work rapidly rather than to pause and consider.

The average time taken to fill out the blank is about half an hour; 90 per cent do it in 50 minutes or less, while a very few require two hours.

Scoring.—The entire blank must be scored for each occupation considered, a different scoring scale being used for each. To score a person's responses to more than 400 items is a somewhat tedious clerical task, but with the aid of the appropriate stencils it can readily be done for one occupation in 15 or 20 minutes. A practiced clerk can in one hour score a blank for from five to ten occupations.

When it is desired to ascertain a person's score for a number of occupations, it is economical to send the blank to the nearest center having special Hollerith facilities, where the blank can be scored for twenty-seven occupations for $1; and, in lots of ten or more, for eighty cents each. The corresponding cost for scoring the women's blank for interest in nine occupations is 50 cents, and for eighteen occupations, 75 cents. In quantities, the rates are 35 cents for nine occupations and 60 cents for the larger number. These facilities are available at the following addresses:

Professor E. K. Strong, Jr., 672 Mirada Ave., Stanford University, California.
Statistical Bureau, Columbia University, New York.
Psychological Corporation, 522 Fifth Avenue, New York.
University of Minnesota Testing Bureau, Minneapolis.

Interpretation.—Any counselor, before considering the data from a client's Vocational Interest Blank, will wish to read carefully Strong's Manuals, supplied without charge; and to be familiar with some of the publications cited below, particularly Berman, Darley, and Paterson (5).

Numerical scores may be translated into standard scores, percentile ranks, or, preferably, letter ratings. An **A** rating means that one has the interests characteristic of persons successfully engaged in the occupation specified; **B** carries a similar implication, but with less certainty; **C** means that one does not have such interests. In other words, in answer to the question, "Shall I probably like this sort of a career?" **A** means "Yes," **C** means "No," and **B** means "Perhaps."

A counselor may suggest for serious consideration any occupation in which the rating is **A** or **B** +. Conversely, no occupation in which the interest rating is **C** should be finally selected without very careful scrutiny.

The interests of young people who rate **B** sometimes ripen and take shape later as undoubted interests in that line. This possibility must be taken into consideration. **C** ratings, on the other hand, rarely change to **A** in later years.

The distribution of a person's interest ratings among the different groups of occupations is as revealing as is his highest rating. He may, for example, have no A rating, but have several B's, all clustering in the science group, the language group, the business group, or the social-service occupations. He may have an A rating in two or more quite different professions, such as journalism, architecture, and teaching, in which event he may wish to aim at a career which will bring all of these interests to a focus—as he might do if he were eventually to become a teacher of architecture, at the same time editing an architectural journal published by his university.

Not infrequently a counselor discovers that a young man has no A rating in any of the professions for which interest scales are available, but has some scattered B ratings. His interests may not have matured; or they may closely resemble those of men in an occupation not represented in the list; or they may actually be widely diversified. A young man with this particular interest pattern not infrequently enters the field of business.

Whatever the vocational interest pattern, as shown by the distribution of the several ratings, it furnishes an excellent point of departure in the vocational interview.

An interviewer appreciates the opportunity to note not only the final ratings, but also some of the separate responses on the blank, since they suggest many a good topic of inquiry and give hints regarding significant traits of personality, as well as interests.

Reliability varies with the occupation for which the blank is scored, the scale for Certified Public Accountant being the least reliable. All scales, however, are sufficiently reliable to make it very unlikely that a re-test within a few months will change a person's classification as A, B, or C. The likelihood of changes with maturity are fully treated in Strong's volume on *Change of Interests with Age* (3). The changes after age 25 are relatively small.

This Vocational Interest Blank is one of the most valued aids to counseling which prolonged scientific research has produced.

DISTRIBUTOR:

Stanford University Press, Stanford University, California. Single copy, 10 cents; ten copies, 90 cents; twenty-five, $2.00; fifty, $3.50; 100, $6.00; 500 or more, $5.00 per hundred. Single scale, $1.00; 2 to 8 scales, 80 cents each; 9 or more scales, 70 cents each. *Manual* is supplied on request.

REFERENCES:

1. E. K. Strong, Jr., "Vocational Interest Test," *Educational Record*, April, 1927.

2. E. K. Strong, Jr., "Diagnostic Value of the Vocational Interest Test," *Educational Record*, January, 1929.

3. E. K. Strong, Jr., *Change of Interests with Age*. Stanford University Press, 1931.

4. E. K. Strong, Jr., "Classification of Occupations by Interests," *Personnel Journal*, April, 1934.

5. I. R. Berman, J. G. Darley, and D. G. Paterson, *Vocational Interest Scales.* Minneapolis: University of Minnesota Press, 1934.

6. E. K. Strong, Jr., "Interests and Sales Ability," *Personnel Journal*, 1934, 13:204-216.

7. E. K. Strong, Jr., "The Vocational Interest Test," *Occupations*, April, 1934, 12: No. 8, 49-56.

8. E. K. Strong, Jr., "Predictive Value of the Vocational Interest Test," *Journal of Educational Psychology*, 1935, 26:331-349.

Manson's Occupational Interest Blank for Women

Grace E. Manson's Occupational Interest Blank was, for a few years following its publication in 1931, the best available measure of occupational interests of women. It contains a selected list of 160 occupations. The client indicates whether she likes, is indifferent to, or dislikes each of these. The methods used in developing the scoring system were similar to Strong's; but the blank does not cover such a variety of items, nor are the resulting scores as clear cut and reliable. They do serve to indicate the similarity between a woman's occupational interests and those typical of women in each of ten occupations. They are suggestive as to which of these lines of work she would be more apt to enjoy, and furnish an excellent point of departure when interviewing.

The ten occupations for which scoring scales are available fall into five groups: teaching, higher clerical, lower clerical, sales and nursing. The use of the blank is not, however, limited to those who are considering preparation to enter one of the ten specific occupations. The *Manual* contains also information regarding the interest scores made by women in the occupations of librarian, college instructor, normal-school instructor, educational supervisor, high-school principal, grade-school principal, executive secretary, treasurer, assistant treasurer, secretary-treasurer, assistant cashier, teller, and partner in a retail store. In an appendix are shown the typical attitudes toward each of the 160 occupations listed on the blank, as expressed by women in fourteen occupational groups, namely, clerical, teaching, sales, health, financial, production, food, welfare, library, legal, editorial, purchasing, research, and personnel. With these data at hand, a counselor may review a woman's interests as expressed by her way of checking the blank, and find suggestions of possible concentrations of interest to be explored more fully in the course of the personal interview.

When the blank is used with girls younger than 17 or 18 the significance of the scores is extremely doubtful.

Administration and Scoring.—Instructions for filling out the blank are found on each copy. No time limit is set.

Scoring keys are available for each of the occupations listed below. An experienced clerk can score a blank for one occupation in about 3½ minutes. The numerical scores are then translated into letter ratings, A, B, or C, as shown in Table LII.

Interpretation.—An A rating in an occupation indicates that a woman's occupational interests are similar to those characteristic of women in the occupation;

Table LII. Norms for Translating Scores into Letter Ratings

The dividing line between B and A is placed[1] at a point such that 75 per cent of the women in the occupation rate A on the interest scale for that occupation. Any score between that point and zero rates B; below zero, C.

Occupation	*Letter rating* A	B	C
Group I. Teaching			
1. High-school teacher	40	0	
2. Grade-school teacher	30	0	
Group II. Higher Clerical			
3. Private secretary	50	0	
4. Stenographer	40	0	
5. Office manager	50	0	
Group III. Lower Clerical			
6. Office clerk	20	0	
7. Bookkeeper	30	0	
Group IV. Sales			
8. Retail saleswoman	40	0	
9. Sales proprietor	40	0	
Group V. Nursing			
10. Trained nurse	40	0	

[1] Except for the sales occupations.

a C rating means that her interests are no more like those of women in that occupation than are the interests of business and professional women in general; and a B rating, like A, indicates similarity, but with less certainty. (It should be noted that in some of the occupations, particularly those in the Sales Group and the Teaching Group, from a fifth to a half of those engaged in them have interests not characteristic of the occupation; they have only a C rating.)

The blank does not provide a measure of ability. A woman may rate A, let us say, in interest in nursing, and yet be too dull to complete the course of training. The proper interpretation is this: granted the requisite ability and training, a woman who rates A in an occupation is more likely to find that kind of work congenial than she would an occupation in which her interest score is C.

Distributor:

Bureau of Business Research, University of Michigan, Ann Arbor, Mich. Three cents each, for first hundred; larger quantities, 2½ cents. Scoring stencils, $1 for set of ten. The first reference listed below is used as the *Manual.*

References:

1. G. E. Manson, *Occupational Interests and Personality Requirements of Women in Business and the Professions.* Ann Arbor: Michigan Business Studies, 8:3, 1931, $1.

2. I. R. Berman, J. G. Darley and D. G. Paterson, *Vocational Interest Scales.* Minneapolis: University of Minnesota Press, 1934.

3. D. Fryer, *The Measurement of Interests.* Appendix V., 470-478. New York: Henry Holt and Company, Inc., 1931.

Interest Questionnaire for High-School Students (Boys)

O. K. GARRETSON AND P. M. SYMONDS

Adapted for use in the eighth and ninth grades, this six-page interest inventory helps boys to choose between academic, technical, and commercial curricula. It is somewhat similar in principle to Strong's blank, listing occupations, school subjects, activities, things to own, magazines, and prominent men—243 items in all—toward which the student indicates his interest, indifference, or dislike.

The majority of boys in the academic, technical and commercial high schools in which the blank was standardized have patterns of interest typical of the kind of school they attend; and so it is possible to find, by using three scoring keys, a student's community of interest with each of these three groups. Although there is considerable overlapping between the fundamental interests of boys in different kinds of school, the test predicts fairly well the type of school a boy will choose.

This test aims to answer only the question, "How interested would this boy probably be in each of the three types of curricula?" No significant relationship has been found between scores and actual school grades.

Administration.—No time limit is set. General instructions are given in the *Manual of Directions*, and further directions are printed at the beginning of each of the eight sections. They may be amplified if necessary. Thirty minutes is usually long enough for filling out the inventory.

Scoring.—Three separate scoring keys are provided for finding academic, technical, and commercial interests. Instructions for their use are given in the *Manual*.

Interpretation.—The accompanying table gives percentile distributions of the scores of 800 students classified according to their course of study, the scores being in terms of the corresponding preference scale. Neutral interest in terms of the scales is denoted by a score of 234. Scores higher than this indicate positive interest in the work of a curriculum, whereas lower scores indicate dislike. Examination of the table with this in mind reveals that the scale for technical preference is more effective than either of the others.

Table LIII. Tentative Norms

Academic students scored in academic interest	*Commercial students scored in commercial interest*	*Technical students scored in technical interest*	*Centile rank*
265.2	274.6	267.4	90
254.2	263.7	260.6	80
249.6	255.4	255.1	70
244.2	248.9	250.6	60
240.0	243.1	248.2	50
236.2	238.6	245.3	40
233.6	233.5	241.8	30
228.9	228.7	237.5	20
222.7	220.8	231.7	10

Interpretation should be made only in the light of all three scores, for even if a student scores high in interest in one curriculum he may score even higher in another.

The test is a supplement to measures of general educability and special aptitudes. Its use is indicated when a boy's real interests are in doubt.

DISTRIBUTOR:

Bureau of Publications, Teachers College, Columbia University, New York. $3 for a hundred, including *Manual* and scoring keys.

REFERENCES:

1. O. K. Garretson, *Relationships Between Expressed Preferences and Curricular Abilities of Ninth Grade Boys.* New York: Bureau of Publications, Teachers College, 1930.

2. P. M. Symonds, *Tests and Interest Questionnaires in the Guidance of High School Boys.* New York: Bureau of Publications, Teachers College, 1930.

X

COOPERATIVE TEST SERVICE ACHIEVEMENT TESTS

THE examinations currently made available by the Cooperative Test Service of the American Council on Education are listed below. A *Booklet of Norms and Reliability Coefficients* issued annually (25 cents), gives end-of-the-year norms for the several years of high school and the first two years of college. The prices quoted are basic prices, subject to discount in quantities of 500 or more. Shipping charges are extra. School officials may secure samples at 10 cents each, except that the two college tests mentioned at the end of the list are 15 cents each. The address of the business office of the Cooperative Test Service is 437 West 59th Street, New York.

ENGLISH TESTS FOR HIGH SCHOOL AND COLLEGE

Cooperative English Test, Series 1. Part I, English Usage, 65 minutes; Part II, Spelling, 10 minutes; Part III, Vocabulary, 20 minutes; total, 95 minutes. 5 cents. Five forms.

Cooperative English Test, Series 2. (Less difficult.) Part I, English Usage and Spelling, 55 minutes; Part II, Vocabulary, 20 minutes; total, 75 minutes. 5 cents. Five forms.

Cooperative Literary Acquaintance Test. Two hundred multiple choice items on English literature and general literature of the type included in English courses. Time, 45 minutes. 5 cents. Five forms.

Cooperative Literary Comprehension Test. A test of reading comprehension of literary materials. 45 minutes. 4 cents. Two forms.

FOREIGN-LANGUAGE TESTS FOR HIGH SCHOOL AND COLLEGE

Cooperative French Test. Part I, Reading, 25 minutes; Part II, Vocabulary, 25 minutes; Part III, Grammar, 40 minutes; total, 90 minutes. 5 cents. Five forms.

Cooperative German Test. Part I, Reading, 25 minutes; Part II, Vocabulary, 25 minutes; Part III, Grammar, 40 minutes; total, 90 minutes. 5 cents. Five forms.

Cooperative Spanish Test. Part I, Reading, 25 minutes; Part II, Vocabulary, 25 minutes; Part III, Grammar, 40 minutes; total 90 minutes. 5 cents. Five forms.

Cooperative Latin Test. Part I, Reading, 40 minutes; Part II, Vocabulary, 15 minutes; Part III, Grammar, 35 minutes; total, 90 minutes. 5 cents. Four forms.

FOREIGN-LANGUAGE TESTS FOR JUNIOR HIGH SCHOOL

Cooperative French Test, Junior Form. Part I, Reading, 25 minutes; Part II, Vocabulary, 25 minutes; Part III, Grammar, 40 minutes; total, 90 minutes. 5 cents. Four forms.

Cooperative German Test, Junior Form. Part I, Reading, 25 minutes; Part II, Vocabulary, 25 minutes; Part III, Grammar, 40 minutes; total, 90 minutes. 5 cents. Three forms.

Cooperative Spanish Test, Junior Form. Part I, Reading, 25 minutes; Part II, Vocabulary, 25 minutes; Part III, Grammar, 40 minutes; total, 90 minutes. 5 cents. Three forms.

Cooperative Latin Test, Junior Form. Part I, Reading, 40 minutes; Part II, Vocabulary, 20 minutes; Part III, Grammar, 30 minutes; total, 90 minutes. 5 cents. Four forms.

MATHEMATICS TESTS FOR HIGH SCHOOL AND COLLEGE

Cooperative Algebra Test (Elementary Algebra through Quadratics) Time, 90 minutes. 4 cents. Five forms.

Cooperative Intermediate Algebra Test (Quadratics and Beyond). Time, 90 minutes. 4 cents. Three forms.

Cooperative Plane Geometry Test. Time, 90 minutes. 4 cents. Five forms.

Cooperative Solid Geometry Test. Time, 90 minutes. 4 cents. Four forms.

Cooperative Trigonometry Test. Time, 90 minutes. 4 cents. Five forms.

Cooperative General Mathematics Test for High-school Classes. Time, 90 minutes. 4 cents. Four forms.

Cooperative General Mathematics Test for College Students. Time, 120 minutes. 5 cents. Four forms.

SCIENCE TESTS FOR HIGH SCHOOLS

Cooperative General Science Test. Time, 90 minutes. 5 cents. Four forms.

Cooperative Biology Test. Time, 90 minutes. 4 cents. Four forms.

Cooperative Physics Test. Time, 90 minutes. 5 cents. Five forms.

Cooperative Chemistry Test. Time, 90 minutes. This test may also be used for first year college classes. 4 cents. Four forms.

SCIENCE TESTS FOR COLLEGE

Cooperative General Science Test for College Students. Time, 60 minutes. 5 cents. Four forms.

Cooperative Zoology Tests for College Classes.

Part 1. A test covering four informational objectives of elementary zoology: 1. Information, 2. Terminology, 3. Identification of Structures, 4. Identification of Functions. Time, 120 minutes. 5 cents. Two forms.

Part 2. A test covering two scientific-method objectives of elementary zoology: 1. Interpretation of Experiments, 2. Application of Principles. Time, 90 minutes. 5 cents. Two forms.

Part C. A composite test covering two informational objectives and one scientific-method objective of elementary zoology: 1. Information, 2. Terminology, 3. Application of Principles. Time, 120 minutes. 5 cents. Two forms.

Cooperative Botany Tests for College Classes.

Part 1. A test covering four informational objectives of elementary botany: 1.

Information, 2. Terminology, 3. Identification of Structures, 4. Identification of Functions. Time, 120 minutes. 5 cents. Two forms.

Part 2. A test covering two scientific-method objectives of elementary botany: 1. Interpretation of Experiments, 2. Application of Principles. Time, 90 minutes. 5 cents. Two forms.

Part C. A composite test covering two informational objectives and one scientific-method objective of elementary botany: 1. Information, 2. Terminology, 3. Application of Principles. Time 120 minutes. 5 cents. Two forms.

Cooperative Chemistry Tests for College Classes.

Part 1. A test covering three informational objectives of elementary chemistry: 1. Information, 2. Terminology, 3. Symbols, Formulæ, and Equations. 5 cents. Two forms.

Part 2. A test covering two scientific-method objectives of elementary chemistry: 1. Interpretation of Experiments, 2. Application of Principles. 5 cents. Two forms.

Part C. A composite test covering two informational objectives and one scientific-method objective of elementary chemistry: 1. Information, 2. Terminology, 3. Application of Principles. Time, 120 minutes. 5 cents. Two forms.

Cooperative Physics Tests for College Students.

Mechanics. Time, 60 minutes. 2 cents. Seven forms.
Heat. Time, 30 minutes. 2 cents. Seven forms.
Sound. Time, 20 minutes. 2 cents. Seven forms.
Light. Time, 40 minutes. 2 cents. Six forms.
Electricity. Time, 50 minutes. 2 cents. Six forms.
Modern Physics. Time 25 minutes. 2 cents. Six forms.

Cooperative Geology Tests.

Historical Geology, Part I. Time, 80 minutes. 4 cents. Two forms.
Historical Geology, Part II (Paleontology). Time, 40 minutes. 4 cents. Two forms.
Physical Geology. Time, 90 minutes. 5 cents. Two forms.

SOCIAL STUDIES TESTS

Cooperative American History Test. Time, 90 minutes. 5 cents. Six forms.

Cooperative Modern European History Test. Time, 90 minutes. 5 cents. Six forms.

Cooperative Ancient History Test. Time, 90 minutes. 5 cents. Four forms.

Cooperative Medieval History Test. Time, 90 minutes. 5 cents. Three forms.

Cooperative English History Test. Time, 90 minutes. 5 cents. Three forms.

Cooperative World History Test. Time, 90 minutes. 5 cents. Three forms.

Cooperative Economics Test. Time, 90 minutes. 5 cents. Two forms.

OTHER TESTS FOR COLLEGE

Cooperative Contemporary Affairs Test. Part I, Public Affairs, 60 minutes; Part II, Aesthetic Interests, 60 minutes; total, 120 minutes. 6 cents. Three forms.

Cooperative General Culture Test. Part I, History and Social Studies, 80 minutes; Part II, Foreign Literature, 55 minutes; Part III, Fine Arts, 45 minutes; total, 180 minutes. 10 cents. Four forms.

MINNESOTA OCCUPATIONAL RATING SCALES[1]

Showing representative occupations rated in terms of Abstract Intelligence, Mechanical Ability, Social Intelligence, Artistic Ability and Musical Talent

RATINGS of occupations have at least two uses. Their main value is seen in studies of populations regarding which there are available no test scores, but only occupational data—for example, in studies of the parents of gifted children or feebleminded children; or of fathers of students in a music school, a trade school, or a school of law. In such studies the ratings permit investigators to secure rough quantitative estimates of the status of these parent populations. Another kind of use becomes evident when students of aptitudes take these ratings as points of departure from which to develop classifications showing clusters or families of similar occupations,[2] as well as more precise measures of the traits in question and of their distribution in representative occupational groups.

Several investigators have developed classifications of occupations with respect to intelligence, determining the average intellectual requirements of each occupation through the consensus of opinion of a number of raters. The following classification differs from the Barr-Taussig scale and other previous lists in including a larger number of occupations, and in including several additional types of ability. The occupations selected were classified with respect to abstract intelligence, mechanical ability, social intelligence, artistic ability, and musical talent by twenty industrial and vocational psychologists. In addition, eight musicians and five artists supplied ratings with reference to musical ability and artistic ability, respectively.

As an aid in securing greater agreement among raters, the abilities were arbitrarily defined as follows:

By *abstract intelligence* is meant the ability to understand and manage ideas and symbols.

Mechanical ability includes both the ability to manipulate concrete objects—to work with tools and machinery and the materials of the physical world, and the ability to deal mentally with mechanical movements.

By *social intelligence* is meant the ability to understand and manage people—to act wisely in human relations.

Artistic ability refers both to the capacity to create forms of artistic merit and the capacity to recognize the comparative merits of forms already created.

Musical talent requires the capacity to sense sounds, to image these sounds in reproductive and creative imagination, to be aroused by them emotionally, to be capable of sustained thinking in terms of these experiences, and, ordinarily, the ability to give some form of expression in musical performance or in creative music.

The categories as defined and used as a guide by the raters follow:

[1] Prepared by Eleanor S. Brussell, Harold Cisney, and Minnesota Mechanical Abilities Research Staff under the direction of Donald G. Paterson; 1936 revision by D. G. Paterson, Gwendolen Schneidler and J. Spencer Carlson.

[2] M. R. Trabue, "Functional Classification of Occupations." *Occupations*, 1936, 15: 127-132.

SIX CATEGORIES OF ABSTRACT INTELLIGENCE

I. *High professional and executive occupations:*

Requiring very superior intelligence with training equivalent to a college graduate from a first-class institution.

High standards, with ability for creative and directive work, such as lawyer, college president, president of a large manufacturing concern, etc.

II. *Lower professional and large business occupations:*

Requiring superior intelligence with training *equivalent* to 2 or 3 years of college or to that of executive of moderately large business.

Achievements less creative than in group 1, but also demanding executive and leadership ability, such as executive of a moderately large business, veterinary doctor, high-school teacher, etc.

III. *Technical, clerical, supervisory occupations:*

Requiring high average intelligence with training *equivalent* to high-school graduation.

Minor executives (foremen, department heads) or highly technical work often involving dealing with abstract classifications and details, such as railroad clerks, some retail dealers, photographers, telegraphers, shop foremen, stenographers, etc.

IV. *Skilled tradesmen and low-grade clerical workers:*

Requiring average intelligence with *equivalent* of some training beyond the eighth grade.

Mechanical work demanding specialized skill and knowledge; tasks mostly of a complicated but concrete nature and requiring particular technical training, such as auto mechanic, stationary engineer, file clerk, typist, etc.

V. *Semi-skilled occupations:*

Requiring low average or slightly below average intelligence, with training *equivalent* to seventh or eighth grade.

Work demanding a minimum of technical knowledge or skill but a maximum of special abilities, such as dexterity in the performance of repetitive and routine work, such as packer in factories, operatives in factories (operate machines but do not understand principles and are unable to repair or set up the machine), lowest grades of clerical work also, such as number sorters, delivery men.

VI. *Unskilled occupations:*

Requiring inferior intelligence only, with no formal training necessary.

Routine manual work under supervision and requiring no skill or technical knowledge, such as day laborers, railroad section hands.

SIX CATEGORIES OF MECHANICAL ABILITY

I. Inventive—requires highest degree of mechanical ability and knowledge, usually specialized training of high order, and sufficient mastery of principles involved to utilize them in independent and creative capacities.
   Examples: Inventive mechanical genius, machine designer, mechanical engineer.

II. Higher technological—requires mechanical ability and knowledge of high degree, considerable specialized training, and mastery of principles permitting independent, although not necessarily original, work.
   Examples: Master mechanic, toolmaker, civil and electrical engineers.

III. Skilled tradesmen, *high level*—requires mechanical ability and specialized skill. Must be able to do critical work, check results, etc. Competent to work without immediate supervision.
   Examples: Draftsman, electrotyper, engraver.

IV. Skilled tradesmen, *low level*—requires some mechanical ability and skill, but only a limited knowledge of the processes involved. The work is partly pre-planned and requires some supervision.
   Examples: Bricklayer, metal finisher, tire-repairer, cobbler.

V. Semi-skilled operatives—requires manual dexterity, but little specialized skill or knowledge, except what can be acquired in a short period of training; usually involves adjustment to an externally imposed rhythm.
   Examples: Telephone operator, lathe operator, wrapper, bench assembly worker.

VI. Unskilled—requires no technical knowledge and no minimum limit of mechanical ability, although the degree of the latter may in part determine the efficiency of the worker.
   Examples: Day laborer, street-sweeper, lawyer, writer, public officials in non-mechanical occupations.

SIX CATEGORIES OF SOCIAL INTELLIGENCE

I. Persuasive—*face-to-face*—direct contact with the public in attempting to convince them or in some way directly influence the people in question.
   Examples: Politician, life insurance salesman, bond salesman.

II. Managerial—requires ability to understand and control people, either as workers or as clients; must be able to inspire confidence and cooperation.
   Examples: Executive, factory manager, foreman, lawyer, physician, secretary.

III. Persuasive—*indirect*—seeks to convince or influence the public in other than direct, face-to-face situations; usually through mediums of communication such as the newspaper, radio, etc.
   Examples: Advertising-copy writer, publicity writer, radio speaker, actor.

IV. Business contact and service—direct contact with the public in retail sales-work involving a small degree of salesmanship, or contact with the public for the purpose of giving information or assistance.

Examples: Sales clerk, information clerk, hotel clerk, theatre usher.

V. Rank-and-file workers—require only ability to get along with supervisors and fellow workers.

Examples: Day laborer, factory worker, office clerk.

VI. A-social occupations—no public contact; individual work usually requiring specialized skills and knowledge.

Examples: Watchmaker, bookkeeper, night watchman, mathematician, technical laboratory research worker.

SIX CATEGORIES OF MUSICAL TALENT

I. Creative and interpretative—requires highest degree of musical talent, which may be manifested either in original compositions or in original interpretation of music.

Examples: Composer, concert artist, symphony conductor.

II. Higher professional occupations—require musical talent and knowledge of high degree, also a certain amount of interpretative ability, but not a high degree of originality.

Examples: Soloist in symphony orchestra, director of famous choir, teacher in conservatory or in university.

III. Technical occupations—require somewhat above the average amount of musical talent, but mainly a high degree of technical knowledge and well-developed musical discrimination.

Examples: Arranger of music, music critic.

IV. Lower professional occupations—require an average amount of musical talent and some technical knowledge—the average professional musician.

Examples: Player in dance orchestra, music-teacher (in grade school).

V. General and mechanical occupations—require a small amount of musical talent, but a greater degree of either general musical information or mechanical knowledge and skill.

Examples: Retail dealer in music, clerk in a music store, repairman of musical instruments, instrument-tester in a factory.

VI. Non-musical occupations—presence or absence of musical talent does not influence this type of work.

Examples: Lawyer, day laborer.

SIX CATEGORIES OF ARTISTIC ABILITY

I. Inspired art—requires highest degree of creative ability; highly original and individual work, reflecting the ideas and personality of the artist.
   Examples: Sculptor, artist, etcher (each having high national reputation).

II. Professional—requires high degree of artistic ability and skill, usually applied to practical situations.
   Examples: Architect, teacher in art institute or university.

III. Commercial—average commercial art work, requiring a fair degree of artistic ability and some originality; usually rather specialized work.
   Examples: Magazine illustrator, interior decorator, clothing designer, landscape gardener, advertising layout work.

IV. Crafts and mechanical art work—requires some artistic ability, but mainly mechanical knowledge and motor skill.
   Examples: Potter, draftsman, weaver, sign and poster painter.

V. Routine work—semi-skilled or unskilled work in which artistic ability plays a very minor part.
   Examples: House-painter, paperhanger.

VI. Non-artistic—artistic ability is not involved in these occupations.
   Examples: Lawyer, bookkeeper.

The ratings reported on the following pages represent the *median* category ratings supplied by the twenty or more raters. When a definite consensus of opinion was not apparent, no category rating is given; hence blanks occur here and there throughout the list of occupations.

THE RATING SCALES

Occupation	*Abstr. Intel.*	*Mech. Abil.*	*Soc. Intel.*	*Mus. Tal.*	*Art. Abil.*
Accountant, auditor, abstractor—private or public; 4 yrs. college	2	6	5	6	6
Actor—average; in drama or musical production	3	6	3	4	
Actor—highest type professional actor	2	6	2	5	
Actor—vaudeville or variety; singing, dancing, etc.	4	5	3	4	5
Advertising artist—illustrates advertisements	3		3	6	3
Advertising expert or ad writer—plans and writes copy	2	5	3	6	
Agent—express or freight; in charge of depts.	3	5	4	6	6
Agent—ticket; employed in ticket offices, depots, etc.	4	6	4	6	6
Agent and canvasser—house to house canvassing and demonstrating	4	5	1	6	6
Annealer, temperer—of edge, face, and spring tools; in factory	4	3	6	6	6
Apiarist—keeper of bees	4	5	6	6	6
Appraiser—estimates values for insurance companies, taxation, etc.	3	5	4	6	6
Architect—training equal to college graduate	1	2	4	6	2
Arranger of music—general; band, orch., or choir	3	6	5	3	6
Arranger of music—popular; for dance orchestra	3	6	5	3	6
Arranger of music—symphonic; for symphony orchestra	2	6		2	6
Astronomer—professor of astronomy in univ. or coll.	1	3		6	6
Athlete—professional; depends on this for income	4	4	4	6	6
Auctioneer—general	4	5	1	6	6
Auto assembler—in auto factory	5	4	5	6	6
Auto racer—earns living racing, and testing autos on speedway	4	3	5	6	6
Aviator, aeronaut—flyer; involves technical knowledge of aeronautics	3	2	5	6	6
Baker—not owner; employed in bakery	5	5	5	6	6
Banker and bank official—exec. head of fairly large bank	1	6	2	6	6
Banker and bank official—of small town or small bank	2	6	2	6	6
Bank teller—routine work; cashes checks, takes in deposits, etc.	3	5	4	6	6
Barber—not owner; has charge of chair	5	4	4	6	6
Barber—owner of shop	4	4	4	6	5
Bartender—in hotel, restaurant or night club	5	5	4	6	6
Bell boy, bell hop—in hotel	5	5	4	6	6
Blacksmith, farrier, horseshoer—gen. work in rural comm.	5	4	5	6	6
Boatman—canal hand, lock keeper	5	5	5	6	6
Boilermaker—heavy work; riveting and handling plate metal	5	4	5	6	6
Boiler washer—R. R. engine hostler	5	5	5	6	6
Bookbinder—skilled oprtr. in bindery; runs machine for sewing, trimming, etc.	4	3	5	6	
Bookkeeper—high school or bus. coll. training	3	5	6	6	6
Bootblack—in shoe shine parlor or barber shop	6	5	4	6	6

THE RATING SCALES—*Continued*

Occupation	*Abstr. Intel.*	*Mech. Abil.*	*Soc. Intel.*	*Mus. Tal.*	*Art. Abil.*
Brakeman—on freight or passenger train	5	3	5	6	6
Bricklayer—skilled labor	5	3	5	6	6
Broker—loan broker; or finance company official	2	6	2	6	6
Broker—pawnbroker; owns and operates shop	3	5	2	6	6
Broker and commission man—wholesale dealer in fruit, grain, livestock, etc.	3	6	2	6	6
Broker and promoter—stocks and bonds	2	6	1	6	6
Builder or bldg. contractor—in charge of construction	3	2	2	6	4
Butcher—not shop owner; able to make cuts properly	5	4	5	6	6
Buyer—for dept. store	3	5	2	6	
Buyer—for hardware store	3	4	2	6	
Cabinetmaker—skilled work in furniture factory	4	3	5	6	4
Canvas worker—in tent and awning factory	5	4	5	6	6
Carpenter—knows wood-working tools; can follow directions in processes of wood construction	4	4	5	6	5
Cartoonist—newspaper or magazine	3	4	3	6	3
Cashier—makes change; retail stores, etc.	4	5	4	6	
Caterer—owner; in charge of directing the catering service	3	5	2	6	
Chambermaid—makes beds and cleans rooms in hotel or rooming house	6	5	5	6	6
Chauffeur—incl. taxi and bus driver; some knowledge of auto mechanics	4	3	4	6	6
Chef—employed in first class hotel	4	4	5	6	
Chemist, industrial—thorough knowledge chemistry of manufacturing processes	1	2	6	6	6
Chiropodist—special training required not medical course	4	4	4	6	6
Chiropractor—special training, about 1 yr.; not col. grad.	3	4		6	6
Choir director—in large city church	3	6	2	2	6
Choir singer—in large city church	4	6	5	3	6
Circus roustabout—does heavy work about circus	6	4	5	6	6
Cleaner—scrub woman	6	6	6	6	6
Clerk, express—in charge of desk; receiving or sending	4	5	4	6	6
Clerk, filing—little technical knowledge; routine	4	5	5	6	6
Clerk—in art store	4	5	4	6	4
Clerk—in music store; must be able to play popular music on piano	4	5	4	5	6
Clerk, railroad—railway mail clerk	3	5	5	6	6
Clerk, shipping—in wholesale co.; in charge receiving or sending goods	3	5	5	6	6
Clerk, stock—checks stock	4	5	5	6	6
Cobbler, shoemaker—repairer in shoe shop	5	4	5	6	6
Collector—employed to collect debts, etc.	4	6		6	6
Compiler—of census, bibliographies, etc.	3	6	6	6	6
Composer—of classical and concert music	2	6		1	6
Composer—of popular songs	3	6		3	6
Compositor, typesetter—sets up type; does skilled hand work	4	3	5	6	5

THE RATING SCALES—*Continued*

Occupation	*Abstr. Intel.*	*Mech. Abil.*	*Soc. Intel.*	*Mus. Tal.*	*Art. Abil.*
Concert artist—high class vocalist or instrumentalist	2		3	1	
Concrete worker—concrete construction work	5	4	5	6	6
Conductor—of high class concert band or theatre orchestra	3		2	2	
Conductor—of popular dance orchestra	4	5	2	3	6
Conductor—of symphony orchestra	2	5	2	1	
Conductor—on railroad passenger train	3	5	4	6	6
Conductor—on street car	4	5	4	6	6
Cook—in restaurant or small hotel	5	4	5	6	6
Cooper—makes barrels in factory	5	4	5	6	6
Dairy hand—milking and care of stock; under supervision	5	5	6	6	6
Dancer—high class interpretive dancing	3	5	3		3
Day laborer—on street in shop or factory, or as roustabout	6	6	5	6	6
Decorator—draper, window dresser, etc.	3	4	3	6	3
Deliveryman—delivers groceries, etc, with auto	5	4	4	6	6
Dentist—2–5 years experience in small town	3	2	2	6	6
Dentist—great; in city	2	2	2	6	6
Designer—automobile bodies and accessories	3	1		6	3
Designer—fine jewelry and silverware	3	2	6	6	3
Designer—furniture and house furnishings	3	2		6	3
Designer—high grade millinery	3	4		6	3
Designer—high grade women's clothing	3	3		6	3
Designer—machinery and motors	2	1	6	6	4
Designer—printed textiles	3			6	3
Designer—ready-made clothing for men and women	3	3		6	3
Designer—stage settings for plays, operas, etc.	2	2		5	2
Designer—tapestries, carpets, and rugs	3	3	5	6	3
Designer—wall paper	3		5	6	3
Detective—traces clues; employee of detective bureau	3	4	2	6	6
Ditcher—drains farms	6	5	6	6	6
Draftsman—mechanical	3	3	6	6	4
Drayman, expressman, baggageman, teamster—transports express, merchandise, etc., under supervision	5	5	5	6	6
Dressmaker—at home or in small shop; may employ a few helpers	4	4	4	6	4
Dressmaker's helper—finishing work; routine	5	5	5	6	5
Druggist, pharmacist—coll. grad.	2	4	4	6	6
Dry cleaner—employed in dry-cleaning establishment	5	5	5	6	6
Dry cleaner—owner or manager; average business.	4	4	4	6	6
Dyer—routine work in factory	5	5	5	6	6
Editor, publisher—large city paper, or head of natl. mag.	1	5	2	6	6
Editor—small paper; considerable job work	2	3	3	6	6
Educational administrator—supt. or prin. of school	2	5	2	6	5
Electrician—installs wiring systems; general electrical work	4	3	5	6	6

THE RATING SCALES—*Continued*

Occupation	*Abstr. Intel.*	*Mech. Abil.*	*Soc. Intel.*	*Mus. Tal.*	*Art. Abil.*
Electrotyper—prepares wood-cuts	4	2	5	6	4
Elevator tender—routine work; requires little knowledge or training	6	5	5	6	6
Employment manager, personnel manager—college graduate or equivalent education	2	5	2	6	6
Engineer, architectural—coll. grad.	1	2	3	6	2
Engineer, civil—4–5 yrs. coll. tr.; plans and constructs roads, bridges, etc.	1	2		6	
Engineer, consulting—in charge corps of engineers.	1	2	2	6	5
Engineer, electrical—college training	2	2		6	6
Engineer, locomotive—freight or passenger train	3	2	5	6	6
Engineer, marine—runs engine on large ship	3	2	5	6	6
Engineer, mechanical—designs and constructs machines and machine tools	1	1	5	6	4
Engineer, mining—thorough knowledge mining and extraction of metals	1	2	5	6	6
Engineer, stationary—in coal mines; brakeman, etc.; requires special training as operative	4	3	5	6	6
Engineer, technical—thorough knowledge industrial processes	1	1	5	6	6
Engraver—jewelry and silverware	4	3	6	6	4
Executive—minor; in business or manufacturing	3		2	6	6
Farm laborer—unskilled	6	5	6	6	6
Farm tenant—on small tract of land	5	4	5	6	6
Farmer—owner or mgr. of moderate sized tract of land	4	4	4	6	6
Finisher—of metal; polishes and lacquers metal fixtures, etc.	5	3	5	6	5
Firefighter, fireman—in city; handles fire fighting apparatus	5	3	5	6	6
Fireman—railroad, on freight or passenger train	5	3	5	6	6
Fireman—stationary engines	5	4	5	6	6
Fisherman—employed or engaged in catching fish.	5	5	6	6	6
Floorwalker and foreman—in stores; in charge of depts. and may direct sales clerks	4	6	2	6	6
Floriculturist—grower of ornamental flowering plants	4	4	5	6	4
Foreman—construction	3	3	2	6	6
Foreman, overseer—small factory or shop	3	2	2	6	6
Foreman—large factory	3	3	2	6	6
Foreman—in transportation	3	3	2	6	6
Foreman—in warehouses, stockyards, etc.	4	4	2	6	6
Forest ranger—looks for forest fires, etc.	4	4	6	6	6
Foundry worker—inc. moulders, founders, and casters	5	4	5	6	6
Garbage collector—in city	6	5	5	6	6
Gardener—tends garden and lawn of private home.	5	4	5	6	5
Gardener—truck farming; owns and operates small plots	3	4	5	6	6
Gardener—landscape	4	3			

THE RATING SCALES—*Continued*

Occupation	*Abstr. Intel.*	*Mech. Abil.*	*Soc. Intel.*	*Mus. Tal.*	*Art. Abil.*
Geologist—locates ore deposits, oil fields, etc., employed by mining company	2	3	6	6	6
Glass blower—blows window glass, bottles, etc., in factory	4	3	5	6	6
Guards, watchmen, doorkeepers—routine work	6	6	5	6	6
Gunsmith—makes or repairs small firearms; has small shop	4	3	5	6	6
Hairdresser, manicurist—employed in shop	5	4	4	6	5
Harness maker—makes and repairs harness; does general leather work	4	3	5	6	6
Hobo—vagrant	6	5	5	6	6
Hospital attendant—carries meal trays, etc.	5	5	4	6	6
Hostler—care of horses in livery, feeds; cleans stable	6	4	6	6	6
Hotel keeper—owns or manages average hotel	3	5	2	6	6
Hotel mgr.—manages large hotel in city	2	5	2	6	6
Housekeeper—takes care of private home; cooks, cleans, etc.; general housework	5	5	4	6	6
Huckster, peddler—fruit and vegetables	5	6	4	6	6
Illustrator—books, magazines, newspapers	3	4	3	6	3
Illustrator—greeting cards; Christmas and birthday cards	4	4	3	6	3
Inspector—lumber	4	4	5	6	6
Inspector, sampler—factory, railway, etc.	4	4	5	6	6
Inspector—street railway	4	4	5	6	6
Inspector—telephone and telegraph	3	3	5	6	6
Inspector and tester—in musical instrument factory	4	3	5	5	6
Insurance agent—sells policies for a company	3	6	1	6	6
Interior decorator—requires ability in drawing, knowledge of color harmony, designing, etc.	3	3	3	6	3
Inventive genius—Edison type	1	1	6	6	6
Inventor—of commercial appliances	2	1	6	6	5
Irrigator and ditch tender—routine work on irrigation ditch	6	5	6	6	6
Janitor, sexton—church, office building, apartment, etc.	5	4	5	6	6
Jeweler—maker of watches in factory	4	2	5	6	5
Journalist—high class; writes feature articles for newspapers and magazines	1	6	3	6	6
Judge—municipal, district, and federal courts	1	6	2	6	6
Junkman—collector of junk	6	5	5	6	6
Justice of peace—in small town	3	6	3	6	6
Keeper—of charitable and penal institutions	3	5	2	6	6
Laborer—construction	6	5	5	6	6
Laborer—in factories; such as packers, wrappers, counters, etc.	5	5	5	6	6
Land owner and operator—very large farm or ranch	2	4	2	6	6
Landscape artist—depends on this work for income	3	4	3	6	3
Lathe hand—routine lathe work in factory	5	5	5	6	6
Laundry owner and mgr.—of average laundry	3	4	3	6	6
Laundry worker—various kinds of work; practically unskilled	5	4	5	6	6

THE RATING SCALES—*Continued*

Occupation	*Abstr. Intel.*	*Mech. Abil.*	*Soc. Intel.*	*Mus. Tal.*	*Art. Abil.*
Lawyer—average civil or criminal lawyer	2	6	2	6	6
Lawyer—eminent	1	6	1	6	6
Leather worker—skilled work; makes traveling cases, novelty goods, etc.; mostly hand work	4	3	5	6	4
Lettercarrier—on city mail route	5	6	4	6	6
Librarian—for symphony orchestra; has charge of music scores	3	6	5		6
Librarian—in small institution or public library	3	5	4	6	6
Lifesaver—on municipal beach	5	5	4	6	6
Lighthouse-keeper	4	4	6	6	6
Lineman—tel. and teleg.; installs and repairs systems	4	3	5	6	6
Linotype operator—on average newspaper	4	3	5	6	6
Lithographer—makes prints from designs which he puts on stone	4	2	5	6	4
Livery stable keeper and manager	4	5	4	6	6
Longshoreman—loads and unloads cargoes	6	5	5	6	6
Lumberman—laborer	6	5	5	6	6
Lumberman—owner or mgr. lumber camps or company	3	4	2	6	6
Machinist—in large factory; highly specialized work	4	3	5	6	6
Mailcarrier—on rural route; uses automobile	5	5	4	6	6
Manager or superintendent—average size factory	2		2	6	6
Manufacturer—employs from 10 to 50 men; makes small articles	3	3	2	6	6
Marshal, constable—small town	4	5	4	6	6
Master of ceremonies—in large theatre; plays several instruments and directs orchestra	3	5	2	3	
Mechanic, airplane—requires technical knowledge as well as mechanical skill	4	2	5	6	6
Mechanic, average—auto mechanic; in garage	4	3	5	6	6
Mechanic, average—in foundry	4	4	5	6	6
Mechanic, general—handyman	4	4	5	6	6
Mechanic, master—thorough knowledge of his field	3	2	5	6	6
Merchant, great—owns and operates million-dollar business	1	5	2	6	6
Merchant, great wholesale—business covers one or more states	2	6	2	6	6
Messenger boy—in office or store, incl. teleg. and exp. mess	5	6	4	6	6
Miller—feed mill; grinds grain for farmers	5	4	5	6	6
Miller—flour mill; thoroughly familiar every detail of work	4	3	5	6	6
Milliner—owner; makes hats in small shop; may have few helpers	4	4	4	6	4
Milliner's helper—employed under supervision	5	5	5	6	5
Millwright—keeps machinery in running order; makes repairs	4	3	5	6	6
Miner—digger and shoveller	5	4	5	6	6
Monument maker—carves gravestones	4	4	5	6	4
Motor-cyclist—rapid delivery service	5	4	5	6	6

THE RATING SCALES—*Continued*

Occupation	*Abstr. Intel.*	*Mech. Abil.*	*Soc. Intel.*	*Mus. Tal.*	*Art. Abil.*
Motorman—electric railroad	4	4	5	6	6
Motorman—street railway	5	4	5	6	6
Moving picture operator—operates protection machine	4	3	6	6	6
Munition worker—average	5	4	5	6	6
Music critic—for large newspaper or magazine	2	6	3	3	
Music entertainer—plays or sings in vaudeville	4	5	3	4	6
Music publisher—manager of company	2	6	2	3	6
Notary public—attests or certifies deeds, etc.	4	6	4	6	6
Nurse and masseur—graduate from an accredited hospital	3	4	4	6	6
Nurseryman—owner or manager	3	4	4	6	5
Oculist—treats diseases of the eye	1	3		6	6
Odd job man	5	4	5	6	6
Officer—army	2	4	2	6	6
Officer—ship	2	3	2	6	6
Official or inspector—city or county	3		2	6	6
Official—mfg.; head of large company	1		2	6	6
Official—of insurance company	2	6	2	6	6
Official or inspector—state and federal; cabinet officer, diplomat, etc.	1	6	2	6	6
Official or superintendent—railroad	2	3	2	6	6
Oil well driller	5	3	5	6	6
Operatic director—produces and directs grand operas	2	4	2	1	
Operative—in factory; operates machine; semi-skilled	5	5	5	6	6
Organist—in large city church	3	5		2	6
Organist—in large city theater	3	5		3	6
Ornamental iron worker—manufactures and erects grill work, railings, stairs, fences, etc.	4	3	5	6	4
Osteopath—training equal to college graduate	2	3		6	6
Painter—general; paints houses, etc.	4	4	5	6	5
Painter—glazier or varnisher in factory	5	4	5	6	5
Painter of murals—for public buildings	3		3	6	1
Paperhanger	5	4	5	6	5
Pattern-maker—metal	4	2	5	6	5
Pattern-maker—wood	4	2	5	6	5
Photo-engraver, etcher—makes plates for reproducing pictures or line drawings	3	3	5	6	4
Photographer—requires few months training, experience	3	3	4	6	4
Physician or surgeon—6–8 yrs. post-high school training	1	3	2	6	6
Piano or organ tuner—knows construction of musical instruments	4	3	5	5	6
Plasterer—has necessary knowledge of materials	4	3	5	6	5
Plumber and steamfitter—average training; under supervision	4	3	5	6	6
Policeman—average patrolman	5	6	4	6	6
Policeman—sergeant or chief	4	6	2	6	6
Politician—party worker; holder of political office.	3	6	1	6	6
Porter—personal service on train	5	5	4	6	6

THE RATING SCALES—*Continued*

Occupation	*Abstr. Intel.*	*Mech. Abil.*	*Soc. Intel.*	*Mus. Tal.*	*Art. Abil.*
Portrait painter—high class artist	2	3	3	6	1
Postmaster—in city up to 10,000 pop.; 2nd class P. O.	3	5	2	6	6
Potter—makes jugs, jars, crockery, earthenware, etc.	4	4	6	6	4
Poultry raiser—small poultry farm	5	5	6	6	6
Preacher, clergyman, minister—average; college graduate	2	6	1	5	6
President—college	1	6	2	6	6
Printer—of small shop; job work	3	3	4	6	5
Probation and truant officer	3	6	2	6	6
Professional musician—in high class concert band or theater orchestra	4	3		3	6
Professional musician—player in dance orchestra	4	4	4	4	6
Professor—university; M.A. or Ph.D.; writes, teaches, does research	1	4	2	6	6
Pseudo-scientist—fortune teller, astrologer, spiritualist, etc.	4	6	2	6	6
Radio announcer—average radio station	3	5	3	5	6
Radio artist—plays or sings on national broadcast programs	3	6	3		6
Radio operator—in broadcasting station	3	3	5	5	6
Real estate agent—sells or rents property on commission	3	6	1	6	6
Religious, charity and welfare workers—practically untrained; small salary	4	6	2	6	6
Repairman, electrical—repairs electrical utensils, devices, and machines or motors	4	3	5	6	6
Repairman, general—repairs broken articles; uses woodworking tools	4	3	5	6	5
Repairman, mechanic—in shop or factory; keeps machines in condition	4	3	5	6	6
Repairman, music—repairs musical instruments	4	3	5	5	5
Repairman, radio—technical knowledge and skill required	4	2	5	6	6
Repairman, tire—in general auto repair shop; knowledge of vulcanizing required	4	4	5	6	6
Reporter—on newspaper; general routine work	2	5	3	6	6
Research leader—like Binet, Pasteur, etc.	1	3	6	6	6
Restaurant keeper—small cafe or lunchroom	4	5	4	6	6
Retail dealer[1]—art supplies and pictures	3	5	4	6	4
Retail dealer—automobiles; average size business	3	4		6	6
Retail dealer—baker	4	5	4	6	6
Retail dealer—books and stationery	3	6	4	6	5
Retail dealer—boots and shoes	4	5	4	6	6
Retail dealer—butcher	4	4	4	6	6
Retail dealer—buyer and shipper of livestock, grain and farm produce	4	5	4	6	6
Retail dealer—candy and confectionery	4	5	4	6	6

[1] The title "Retail dealer" includes only the owner or manager of a store or shop, not an employee.

THE RATING SCALES—*Continued*

Occupation	*Abstr. Intel.*	*Mech. Abil.*	*Soc. Intel.*	*Mus. Tal.*	*Art. Abil.*
Retail dealer—cigars, cigarettes, and tobacco	4	6	4	6	6
Retail dealer—coal and wood	4	5	4	6	6
Retail dealer—costumer; clothing for men and women	3	6	4	6	5
Retail dealer—dairyman; small dairy	4	4	4	6	6
Retail dealer—department store	3	5	4	6	5
Retail dealer—druggist or pharmacist	3	4	4	6	6
Retail dealer—drygoods, fancy goods, notions	4	5	4	6	5
Retail dealer—florist	4	5	4	6	4
Retail dealer—flour and feed	4	5	4	6	6
Retail dealer—fishmonger	4	5	4	6	6
Retail dealer—fruitman	4	5	4	6	6
Retail dealer—furniture	4	5	4	6	5
Retail dealer—furrier	3	5	4	6	5
Retail dealer—garage-keeper	4	3	4	6	6
Retail dealer—general store, in country	4	4	4	6	6
Retail dealer—grocer	4	5	4	6	6
Retail dealer—haberdasher	3	6	4	6	5
Retail dealer—hardware	3	4	4	6	6
Retail dealer—harness, saddlery, leather, hides	4	4	4	6	6
Retail dealer—ice	4	5	4	6	6
Retail dealer—jeweler	3	4	4	6	4
Retail dealer—lumber	4	4	4	6	6
Retail dealer—music store; sheet music, scores, etc., including musical instruments	3	5	4	5	6
Retail dealer—newsdealer	5	6	4	6	6
Retail dealer—oil, paint, wallpaper	4	5	4	6	5
Retail dealer—optician	3	3	4	6	6
Retail dealer—pop corn stand	5	6	4	6	6
Retail dealer—produce and provisions	4	5	4	6	6
Retail dealer—tailor	4	4	4	6	5
Riveter—steel construction work	4	4	5	6	6
Roofer and slater—applies roofing materials	5	4	5	6	6
Sailor—deck hand	6	5	5	6	6
Sales clerk—retail selling from counter	4	5	4	6	6
Salesman—automobile	3	4	1	6	6
Salesman—specialty	4	4	1	6	6
Salesman—stocks and bonds	3	6	1	6	6
Salesman—technical; college trained	2	3	1	6	6
Salesman—traveling; retail; sells drugs, groceries, drygoods, etc.	3	5	1	6	6
Salesman—traveling; wholesale; takes orders from stores for clothing, groceries, etc.	3	5	1	6	6
Sawmill-worker—heavy work; little skill required	5	4	5	6	6
Scientist—applied; bacteriology, psychology, etc.	1	3	4	6	6
Sculptor—great; national reputation	1	2	4	6	1
Secretary—private sec. to high government official, business or professional man	2	5	2	6	6
Section hand—railroad; replaces ties, etc.; under supervision	6	5	5	6	6
Servant—personal and domestic; butler, coachman, footman, maid, valet, etc.	5	5	4	6	6

THE RATING SCALES—*Continued*

Occupation	*Abstr. Intel.*	*Mech. Abil.*	*Soc. Intel.*	*Mus. Tal.*	*Art. Abil.*
Sheet-metal-worker—in factory; routine work	5	4	5	6	6
Sheriff—county	4	5	2	6	6
Shiprigger—installs cordage system on sailing vessel; under supervision	5	3	5	6	6
Shop mechanic—railroad	4	3	5	6	6
Show card writer—letter cards for theaters, stores, etc.	4	4	4	6	4
Showman—manager of theatrical production	3	5	3	6	4
Sign painter—paints large outdoor signs	4	4	5	6	4
Singer—in musical production; opera, musical comedy	4	6	3	3	5
Smelter worker—operates blast furnace used in smelting and refining ores	5	4	5	6	6
Social worker—routine work; writes case histories, etc.; special training required	3	6	2	6	6
Social worker—supervisor; head of department; college training required	2	6	2	6	6
Soldier—private in standing army	5	5	5	6	6
Stage hand—manipulates scenery in large theater or opera house	5	4	5	6	6
Station agent—in small town; acts as baggage man, freight agent, etc.	4	4	4	6	6
Statistician—engaged in original research in statistics; college training in math. necessary	1	5	6	6	6
Statistician—clerical worker; manipulates formulas under supervision	3	5	5	6	6
Steeple jack—paints and repairs church spires, flagpoles, etc.	4	3	6	6	5
Stenographer—writes shorthand and uses typewriter	3	5	5	6	6
Stock clerk—checks stock in factory, large department store or warehouse	4	5	5	6	6
Stonecutter—quarry worker	5	4	5	6	6
Stone mason—skilled worker	4	3	5	6	4
Street-sweeper—in city	6	5	5	6	6
Structural steel worker—heavy work demanding some skill	5	3	5	6	6
Surgeon—great; Mayo brothers, etc.	1	2	2	6	6
Surveyor—transit man; city or county	3	3	5	6	6
Switchman and flagman—tends switch in railroad yard	5	3	5	6	6
Tailor—not owner; works in tailor shop	4	4	5	6	5
Teacher, art—in grades	3	4	2	6	3
Teacher, art—in high school; 3 to 4 yrs. of special training	2	3	2	6	3
Teacher, art—in college or art school; trains pupils for careers in art	2	3	2	6	2
Teacher, athletics and dancing—special training required	3	4	2	6	
Teacher, college—has B.A. or M.A.; not the most progressive	2	6		6	6

THE RATING SCALES—*Continued*

Occupation	*Abstr. Intel.*	*Mech. Abil.*	*Soc. Intel.*	*Mus. Tal.*	*Art. Abil.*
Teacher, grammar school—normal graduate; expects to make profession of teaching	3	5	2	6	6
Teacher, high school—college graduate	2	5	2	6	6
Teacher, manual training—special training necessary	3	2	2	6	4
Teacher, music—band instruments	3	3	2	4	6
Teacher, music—in college; practical work; trains for teaching of music or concert career	2		2	2	
Teacher, music—in college; theoretical; history and theory of music	1	5		2	6
Teacher, music—in grade school; teaches simple songs and fundamentals of music	3	5	2	4	6
Teacher, music—in high school; leads group singing; has charge of glee clubs, orchestras, bands, etc.	2	4	2	3	6
Teacher, music—instrumental or vocal teacher in small town	3	4		4	6
Teacher, music—private lessons on piano, violin, or voice; training for concert work	3	4		2	6
Teacher, primary—no college training; two years special training	3	6	2	6	6
Telegraph operator—special training and skill	3	4	5	6	6
Telephone operator—special training	4	5	4	6	6
Textile worker—routine factory work	5	5	5	6	6
Theater usher	5	6	4	6	6
Tinsmith—makes vessels, utensils from plated sheet metal, and does repair work	4	3	5	6	5
Toolmaker—highly skilled work in factory	4	2	5	6	
Track-layer—does heavy work under supervision	6	4	5	6	6
Train dispatcher—must be mentally alert	3	4	4	6	6
Truck driver—heavy work	5	3	5	6	6
Typist—no shorthand; types from copy	4	5	5	6	6
Undertaker—embalmer; 6 months to 1 year of training	4	4	4	6	6
Undertaker—funeral director	3	4	2	6	5
Upholsterer—renovator of furniture, etc.; small shop	4	4	5	6	5
Veterinary doctor; special training; some college work	2	3	4	6	6
Vulcanizer — understands process of hardening rubber	4	3	5	6	6
Waiter, head—in hotel or restaurant; in charge of dining room waiters	4	5	2	6	6
Waiter—in small restaurant or cafe	5	5	4	6	6
Waterworks man—a variety of jobs, all unskilled	5	4	5	6	6
Wheelwright—makes or repairs wheels; small shop	4	3	5	6	6
Wholesale dealer—fairly small; includes exporter and importer	3	5	4	6	6
Wood-carver—highly skilled work in furniture factory	4	3	5	6	4
Writer, author—great; Van Dyke, etc.	1	6	3	6	
Writer, author—magazine articles or books; either fiction or non-fiction	2	6	3	6	6
Yardman—railroad	5	4	5	6	6
Y. M. C. A. official—secretary, etc.	3	6	2	6	6

DIRECTORY OF PUBLISHERS AND DISTRIBUTORS

(Addresses of branch offices, as well as main headquarters of test publishers, are given in Buros' Bibliography. The Psychological Corporation keeps in stock blanks of many other publishers as well as its own. The C. H. Stoelting Company is the largest manufacturer of psychological apparatus.)

American Council on Education, 744 Jackson Place, Washington, D. C. Cooperative Test Service, 437 West 59th Street, New York.
Ann Arbor Press, Ann Arbor, Mich.
Bureau of Educational Measurements, Kansas State Teachers College, Emporia, Kans.
Bureau of Educational Research and Service, State University of Iowa, Iowa City, Iowa.
Bureau of Publications, Teachers College, Columbia University, New York.
Colorado State College of Education, Greeley, Colo.
Cooperative Test Service, 437 West 59th Street, New York.
Courtis Standard Research Tests, 1807 E. Grand Boulevard, Detroit, Mich.
F. A. Davis Company, 1914-16 Cherry St., Philadelphia, Pa.
Department of Educational Research, University of Toronto, Toronto, Canada.
Division of Educational Reference, Purdue University, Lafayette, Ind.
Educational Records Bureau, 437 West 59th Street, New York.
Educational Test Bureau, Inc., 720 Washington Ave., S. E., Minneapolis, Minn.; 3416 Walnut St., Philadelphia, Pa.
Edwards Bros., Inc., 310 S. State St., Ann Arbor, Mich.
English Bureau, University of Oregon, Eugene, Oregon.
Ginn and Co., 15 Ashburton Place, Boston, Mass.
Graybar Electric Co., Graybar Building, New York.
Gregg Publishing Co., 270 Madison Ave., New York.
Harlow Publishing Co., Third and Harvey Sts., Oklahoma City, Okla.
George G. Harrap and Company, Ltd., 182 High Holborn, W. C. 1, London, England.
W. Wilbur Hatfield, 211 W. 68th St., Chicago, Ill.
Hill-Brown Printing Co., Hamilton, Ohio.
Houghton Mifflin Co., 2 Park St., Boston, Mass.
Inor Publishing Company, R. K. O. Building, New York.
Institute of Educational Research, Teachers College, Columbia University, New York.
Johns Hopkins Press, Homewood, Baltimore, Md.
Keystone View Co., Meadville, Pa.
Marietta Apparatus Company, Marietta, Ohio.
Melbourne University Press, Melbourne University, Carlton N 3, Melbourne, Victoria, Australia.

Ohio College Association, Committee on Intelligence Tests for Entrance, Ohio State University, Columbus, Ohio.
Ohio State Department of Education, Columbus, Ohio.
Palmer Co., 120 Boylston St., Boston, Mass.
Psychological Corporation, 522 Fifth Avenue, New York.
Psychological Institute, 3506 Patterson St., N.W., Washington, D. C.
Public School Publishing Co., 509-13 N. East St., Bloomington, Ill.
Publication Press, Inc., 1511 Guilford Ave., Baltimore, Md.
Charles Scribner's Sons, 597 Fifth Ave., New York.
Turner E. Smith and Co., 424 W. Peachtree St., N.W., Atlanta, Ga.
Southern California School Book Depository, Ltd., 3636 Beverly Boulevard, Los Angeles, Calif.
Stanford University Press, Stanford University, Calif.
C. H. Stoelting Co., 424 N. Homan Ave., Chicago, Ill.
University of Chicago Press, 5750 Ellis Ave., Chicago, Ill.
University of London Press, Ltd., 10 Warwick Lane, London, E. C. 4, England.
University of Minnesota Press, Minneapolis, Minn.
Vineland Training School, Vineland, N. J.
Webb-Duncan Publishing Co., 715 N. Hudson St., Oklahoma City, Okla.
Webster Publishing Co., 1800 Washington Ave., St. Louis, Mo.
World Book Co., 333 Park Hill, Yonkers, N. Y.

INDEX